ART AND MASS MEDIA

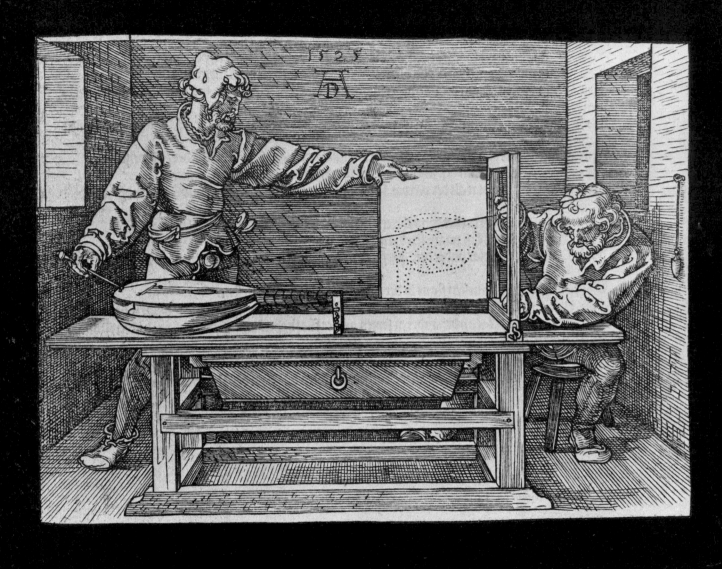

ART
AND MASS
MEDIA

Robert H. Pelfrey *with Mary Hall-Pelfrey*

1817

Harper & Row, Publishers, New York

Cambridge, Hagerstown, Philadelphia, San Francisco
London, Mexico City, São Paulo, Sidney

Cover

Top, from left to right

Apollo, head detail, Alinari/Art Resource, New York; Nam June Paik, *Global Groove* (video), photo by M. Danowski/Courtesy of Electronic Arts Intervix Intermix; Georges Seurat, *Sunday Afternoon on the Island of La Grand Jatte*, 1884–1886, detail, oil on canvas, 81 × 120⅜ inches, Art Institute of Chicago, Helen Birch Bartlett Memorial Collection; Roy Lichtenstein, *Cubist Still Life*, National Gallery of Art, Washington, Lila Acheson Wallace Fund; scene from *Citizen Kane*, Museum of Modern Art, New York, Film Stills Archive/Courtesy of RKO General.

Below

Kenneth Noland, *Ember*, 1960, oil on canvas, 70⅞ × 70⅛ inches, Collection of Dr. and Mrs. Wallace Friedman, San Francisco, California.

The images appearing opposite the title page and the table of contents have been reproduced from figures in chapters 3 and 13, respectively. The images appearing on the first page of each chapter are details from figures in that chapter.

FIRST EDITION

Designed by Design Office Bruce Kortebein

Library of Congress Cataloging-in-Publication Data

Pelfrey, Robert H.
　Art and mass media.

　Bibliography: p.
　Includes index.
　1. Mass media and art.　I. Hall-Pelfrey, Mary.
II. Title.
N72.M28P45　1985　　　　700′.1′05　　　　85-8711
ISBN 0-06-045112-2

85　86　87　88　89　KP　10　9　8　7　6　5　4　3　2　1

To David, Kristen, and Matt—

and to my father.

CONTENTS

PREFACE

Art and Mass Media, as the title indicates, is a different kind of art appreciation book. It approaches art with the premise that the major art forms in students' lives are the popular art forms of the mass media. Its objective is to show how both Western fine art and popular art stem from a common artistic tradition, a tradition that is heavily indebted to non-Western arts from around the world.

Based on these premises, *Art and Mass Media* makes clear to students that the already familiar arts of television, movies, and photography derive from a larger tradition that ranges from ancient Greece to Post-Modernism and encompasses works as diverse as the Parthenon, Rembrandt's paintings, and Judy Chicago's *The Dinner Party.*

The chronological format of *Art and Mass Media* underscores the parallel development of the mass media within the Western artistic tradition. This development is further clarified for the student by grouping the art history periods of Renaissance, Baroque, and so forth, under the larger headings of Perspective Age, Photographic Age, Film Age, and Television Age.

These divisions, summarized by the timeline at the end of the text, emphasize the historical and continuing *interaction* between fine art and the mass media. The final two-thirds of the text, beginning with the Photographic Age, make clear that the interaction between fine art and mass media has continued in both directions. Daumier's lithographs influenced the avant-garde paintings of Manet; avant-garde Surrealist art has had a powerful effect on modern advertising art.

These chapters also show how the interaction between the mass media and contemporary art has created problems as well as opportunities. Many contemporary artists such as Christo and Warhol are so ingenious in their use of mass media publicity that artists and artworks both face the possibility of being reduced to the status of celebrities and mere images.

A final premise of *Art and Mass Media* is that the problem of image-versus-reality extends far beyond the field of art. Our culture mediates an increasing amount of individual and social experience through mass-produced imagery. Seeing a news show on television—unlike the experience of seeing a movie in a theater or a painting in a museum—confronts the viewer with an experience somewhere between a real event and a work of art. A discerning awareness of how our cultural picture of the world is ultimately an artifact shaped by artists as well as by various cultural managers is a valuable by-product of the mutual study of art and mass media.

The overall structure of *Art and Mass Media* thus recognizes the particular complexity of art in our technological culture. Especially for students who will probably take only one course in the visual arts, it encourages a visual literacy that focuses not only on the museum but on the artistic experience encountered in the street and in the living room. Such visual literacy is vitally necessary in order to bring all forms of art closer to life.

Besides those individuals whose writings and art works have contributed to the content of *Art and Mass Media*, many people provided invaluable forms of support and encouragement.

Jim Alford, Barry Frantz, and Barney McGrane—my colleagues at Cuesta College—read portions of the manuscript and added their own insights.

Eileen Wolfe was especially helpful in both typing and editing the original manuscript.

Tom Dorsaneo, Dorian Gossy, Virginia Rich, and Bruce Kortebein were constantly attentive and sympathetic during the production phase of the book.

Mary Hall-Pelfrey collaborated on all phases of the writing, editing, and design processes.

Finally, Mary and I want to personally thank Fred Henry, our editor at Harper & Row, for his trust, his humor, and his professionalism.

INTRODUCTION

FROM GRAFFITI
TO FINE ART

ASSESSMENTS

1. What images do you buy to decorate your room or house? What do you like about having these images? What do you dislike? How do these images contribute to your life? Do most of these images come from mass media sources or from fine art sources?
2. Do you begin your day with mass media—television, radio, newspaper? Is media involved with your pattern of relaxation at the end of the day?
3. Have you ever become so involved in a film, painting, or video that you lost awareness of yourself and, in effect, became lost in the art form? Do you talk to others about films, television shows, or other media and art forms that you experience?
4. Have you had experiences that you wished you could capture or express through some art form like drawing, sculpture, or dance? Do you recall any films, paintings, or videos done by other artists that expressed or captured a feeling or idea that you had once experienced in your own way?
5. What does the word *literacy* mean to you? What would the term *visual literacy* mean?

2

Introduction: From Graffiti to Fine Art— Connections in the Mass Media

A recent article in a Sunday paper described how the work of the New York artist Keith Haring began as subway graffiti and is now shown in fine art galleries in New York and Tokyo (fig. i.1). Haring's work has also been used on the cover of *Vanity Fair* magazine. The article was significant, not because it revealed that major art galleries show graffiti as art, but because it discussed graffiti as art in the Sunday papers—and few people were surprised.

By contrast, when a group of artists in the early 1960s began to produce art based on mass media themes and subjects, the public was both shocked and amused. Andy Warhol's *Marilyn Monroe* (fig. i.2) is an example of the emphasis on mass media subjects and themes, including a direct use of photographs and photographic processes, by this movement, which became known as Pop Art.

Pop Art works were disturbing when they first appeared because they inevitably raised the question, *Is it art?* Pop Art seemed to trivialize the traditional distinction between fine art and mass media popular art. This distinction saw fine art (painting, drawing, sculpture, etc.) as "high art," and popular art (the visual art found in magazines, movies, and on television) as "low art."

The decades succeeding Pop Art, however, have witnessed even stronger links between the mass media and fine art. Judy Chicago's *Dinner Party* (fig. i.3), for instance, used mass media publicity as an integral part of its purpose, celebrating and reclaiming the neglected history of women's social accomplishments. Christo's *Surrounded Islands* proj-

i.1 Keith Haring.
Work shown in installation.
Whitney Biennial Exhibition.
March 15–May 29, 1983

i.2 Andy Warhol.
Marilyn Monroe. 1967.
Silkscreen on paper, 36″ × 36¼″.
Collection of Whitney Museum of American Art, New York.

i.3 Judy Chicago.
The Dinner Party. 1979.
Mixed media, 47′ × 47′ × 47′.
Copyright Judy Chicago, 1979.
Photography by Michael Alexander.

i.4 Roy Lichtenstein.
Cathedral #3. 1969.
Color lithograph, 123.2 × 82.6 cm.
The St. Louis Art Museum, Sidney and Sadie Cohen Print Fund.

i.1

i.2

ect encircled a dozen islands in the Florida Keys with huge floating sheets of pink nylon. Except for a small number of people in airplanes and boats, this work could be seen only on television or in magazine photographs. In this case, the mass media did not just provide publicity *for* the work, the mass media were an integral *part of* the work.

The impact of the mass media on fine art goes beyond widening the range of subject matter or increasing the means of publicity. Even more profound is its effect on our very perception of fine art.

Modern Art and Mass Media: New Ways of Perceiving the Art Object

Roy Lichtenstein's lithograph *Cathedral #3* (fig. i.4) brilliantly suggests the pervasive way the mass media influence our perception of fine art. *Cathedral #3* refers to a famous series of paintings of Rouen cathedral done in the 1890s by the great French Impressionist artist Claude Monet. The dots in Lichtenstein's work are meant to resemble the tiny dots used to print photographs in books, magazines, and newspapers.

The dots in *Cathedral #3* suggest that Monet's painting will be easily recognized, not because so many people have seen Monet's original paintings, but because so many people have seen printed photographs of them. Lichtenstein's work acknowledges that this kind of contact with images instead of real objects is a vital part of our way of seeing art in the modern world.

This is as true for artists as it is for the public; in today's art world even most professional painters, architects, sculp-

i.3

i.4

tors, and others look at mass media images of art more than at unique art objects. For the public, illustrated exhibition catalogues printed by galleries and museums extend the artist's work in time and space far beyond the scope of the actual event. *Vogue, Time,* and other mass circulation magazines carry feature articles on modern art to the public at large on a regular basis. Metropolitan newspapers regularly review exhibitions of contemporary art.

The mass media have made modern art both familiar and popular. Attendance at American art museums exceeds that at professional sporting events. A single statistic summarizes this popularity: over a million people saw the Picasso retrospective exhibit at the Museum of Modern Art in New York in 1981.

Mass Media and Fine Art: What Happens to the Unique Art Object?

The presence of fine art in the mass media has its cost, however. This cost is also dramatized by the dots in Lichtenstein's painting; once in the mass media, the original work of art becomes something else—a mere image. The unique art object made by a unique individual drifts into an environment of swarming images spewed out from our society's innumerable image-making and image-multiplying machines.

This presents an inevitable conflict for fine art. The modern tradition of fine art has stressed three inherent values: the value of the unique art object; the value of the artist's individual personality; and the value of innovative artistic form.

Popular art made for the mass media, by contrast, must make money. It is usually planned from the beginning as a commodity, the visual goal of which is to anticipate and meet the expectations of a large audience rather than to challenge that audience by either personal expression or artistic innovation. A high-quality television show might be canceled or a good movie never made because of audience marketing criteria and the need to make a profit. Many artists are concerned that involvement with the mass media will lead fine art to a similar emphasis on packaging and marketing.

Despite these modern-sounding concerns, the opportunities and dilemmas presented by image-making and image-multiplying machines are not new. They have been a central factor in Western art for the past five hundred years. This text will emphasize the history of painting more than other art forms because the history of Western painting not only summarizes the history of Western images but leads up to and then merges with the early history of the mass media. It is no coincidence that the first person to take out a patent on photography, Louis Daguerre, began his career as a painter.

i.5 *The Comic Art Show.*
Whitney Museum of American Art catalogue cover, 1980.
Courtesy Whitney Museum of American Art, New York. *Dick Tracy,* by Andy Warhol, reproduced by courtesy of Peter M. Brant.

i.6 Jan Vermeer.
A Woman in Blue Reading a Letter. 1662–65.
Oil on canvas, 18¼″ × 15⅜″.
Rijksmuseum, Amsterdam.

Popular Art and Fine Art: Sharing the Space of the Mass Media

Just as the mass media increasingly provide a space for fine art, many major museums today feature exhibitions of such popular art forms as comics (fig. i.5), posters, and industrial design. This recent attention to mass media popular art by museums of fine art is in some ways a return to the artistic richness and balance achieved in earlier periods of Western art.

The paintings that hung on seventeenth-century Dutch walls were not only beautiful, they also pictured the affluence of the Dutch middle-class and symbolized their new political independence in terms that everyone could understand. Jan Vermeer's painting *A Woman in Blue Reading a Letter* (fig. i.6) reveals that maps and other popular forms of printed images hung on the same walls as oil paintings.

The medieval cathedral provided public space for images in stained glass and sculpture. These art forms represented ordinary people alongside saints in symbolic and story form, thus providing a mixture of fine art and popular art that spoke clearly to everyone.

Today's mass media popular art illustrates stories, provides information, and symbolizes public myths. These were once also functions of the fine art now displayed in museums

i.6

i.5

i.7

i.7 Hans Memling.
Portrait of a Man with an Arrow.
c. 1470.
Oil on wood, 9⅛″ × 7⅛″.
National Gallery of Art, Washington,
Andrew W. Mellon Collection, 1937.

i.8 Cover of *Newsweek*, President
Reagan, Feb. 8, 1982.
Courtesy *Newsweek*.

or maintained as historical treasures. The mass media, by presenting both fine art and popular art imagery, provide a space that enables both kinds of art to have their full social impact.

The complementary effects of fine art and popular art in the mass media have far-reaching implications, many of which can be explored by updating a traditional term, *icon*, to apply to the social impact of fine art and popular art in the mass media.

Art as Icon: Images That Reflect Basic Cultural Values

The term *icon* traditionally has referred specifically to a culture's religious images. But since our culture today is not primarily represented by such religious images, popular art and fine art images can be considered as icons insofar as their appearance in the mass media shapes and reflects our culture's basic values.

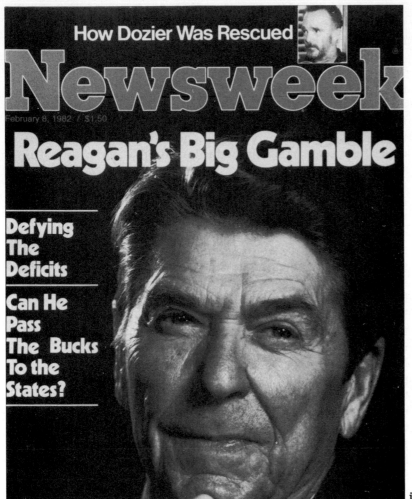

i.8

As icons, for instance, there is a direct connection between the marvelous oil painting by Hans Memling (fig. i.7, plate 1) done over four hundred years ago and the photograph of President Reagan printed on the cover of *Newsweek* (fig. i.8).

The oil painting strongly expresses two enduring values of Western culture, a love of technology and a love of individualism. Technology as a value is expressed by the use of the newly discovered technique of perspective (the technique of creating the illusion of three-dimensional space on a two-dimensional surface). The value of individualism is expressed by the willingness to make realistic portraits of ordinary people.

The image of President Reagan on the *Newsweek* cover shows a continuing stress on the same two values: Technological advances have mechanized perspective into photography. The love of individualism has increased to the point that the president—unlike the kings and rulers of Memling's day—must look as much as possible like the kind of ordinary citizen pictured in the Memling portrait. It is now an essential part of any American president's image.

8

Fine Art and Popular Art: Western Icons for the Global Gallery

The icon effect of our fine art and popular art images is particularly clear in their impact abroad.

Abstract paintings and other forms of contemporary art have been especially associated with the United States since the late 1940s and early fifties, when Jackson Pollock and other New York artists gained international attention with the movement known as Abstract Expressionism. This kind of painting and the styles of modern art that have succeeded it in America are seen abroad not only as art but—like our technology—as symbols of American modernity.

It is America's mass media popular arts, however, that provide America's most powerful icons abroad. American programming makes up as much as forty percent of television time shown in countries ranging from Europe to the Near East to Asia. American popular culture heroes, from Mickey Mouse to the Marlboro Man (fig. i.9) to Rocky, consistently combine a sense of innocence, power, and individualism that has a seemingly universal appeal. The face of Mickey Mouse towers over Tokyo's favorite amusement park—Disneyland. Moviemakers in India have made at least three different versions of *Rocky. Rocky*'s image of a common man dreaming of a better future he could reach through his own efforts became an icon with startling impact in a culture that traditionally views social roles as defined by birth. The Marlboro Man is not just a cowboy who smokes; he is an icon of American independence and self-reliance recognized around the world (fig. i.9).

Television shows like "Dallas" and "Hill Street Blues," despite their radically different settings, each carry a peculiarly American sense of individualism. Shows like these present characters, whether rich or poor, whose actions make a difference. The individual counts.

As icons, however, works of art often take on political connotations unintended by the original artist. Officials in Moscow once ordered an exhibit by Russian painters in a public park bulldozed because it featured abstract paintings like those favored in the West. Soviet authorities apparently feared such paintings would encourage a similar freedom of expression in areas other than art. Since the late 1970s, Americans have often seen Islamic women protesting against American presence in the Middle East. These women are not only expressing political outrage, they are also protesting the intrusion of Western cultural values into their fundamentalist Islamic culture. In this case, magazines such as *Playboy*, sold in the streets of Tehran, became a symbol of Western intrusion in a culture that directs women to veil even their faces in public.

These are a few examples of how people in other countries see our fine art and popular art images as icons, that is, as images that reveal how we live and who we are.

i.9 "Marlboro Man" (Sheriff) advertisement.
Reprinted by permission of Philip Morris Incorporated.

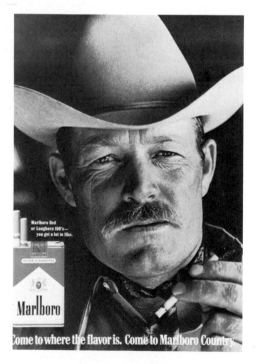

The Individual and the Mass Media: Maintaining the Personal Connection

The range of connections between fine art and mass media popular art we have discussed reflects that our society itself is, in Michael Real's phrase, an increasingly "mass-mediated" culture.[1] It is a culture in which the average American watches over four hours of television each day. It is a culture in which presidential candidates spend tens of millions of dollars on commercials using the same packaging and marketing techniques as those used to sell cars.

In our "mass-mediated" culture, however, advertising itself has strong connections with fine art. Advertising images are made by artists who attended the same art schools as aspiring painters. Courses in advertising teach that a good ad follows the same principles of line, color, and shape as a good painting. Advertising artists study and apply the entire fine art tradition of painting, photography, and film to create images calculated to transform the viewer into a consumer. A sense of visual literacy today requires a knowledge not only of fine art but also of how our fine art tradition has influenced and helped to produce our entire popular art tradition, including advertising.

It is not surprising, then, that one of the crucial dimensions of fine art today is its attempt to define its role within such a mass-mediated culture. The exciting possibilities as well as the hazards involve more than art. By tracing the historical relationship between art and the mass media we will see that this artistic problem mirrors, at each stage of its development, an even larger question: That of the role of art and individual freedom in a mass-mediated culture.

The Greek philosopher Socrates' deceptively simple advice, "Know thyself," has been quoted to Western society for almost twenty-five hundred years. Today, knowing oneself means knowing one's images. The Marlboro Man is an image that invites us to retreat to the nostalgia of the past; *The Dinner Party* (fig. i.3) invites us to escape from the restrictions of the past in order to experience the present in a fuller way.

In the final analysis, it is not the artist who creates the impact of the Marlboro Man or *Rocky* or *The Dinner Party*. It is the public—and each individual—whose approval and love transform these works into icons.

NON-
WESTERN
ART

Villard de Honnecourt
Guido da Siena
Giotto
mappamundi
stained glass
sculpture
Chartres

Polykleitos
Greek
vase painting
sculpture
Parthenon

SUMER
(ANCIENT
NEAR EAST)

CLASSICAL GREECE

MEDIEVAL GOTHIC

image-
producing and
image-
multiplying
techniques

camera obscura

eyeglass lenses

date
discovered

woodcut •--------------------→
(China)

500 B.C.

Plato

St. Francis

Roger Bacon

crusades

CHAPTER ONE

ART CREATES
CULTURE:
CULTURE CREATES
ART

ASSESSMENTS

1. Can you recall your earliest childhood experiences with drawing? Were they positive or negative experiences for you? How did you and others respond to your drawings or paintings?
2. Did you use coloring books? If so, what did you like or dislike about using coloring books? How did coloring books differ from your own drawings?
3. Do you draw, paint, take photographs, or do a craft? If you don't do any of these, would you want to learn?
4. What forms of native art exist or did exist in your geographical area? How does your town or city attempt to connect with its native culture (names of towns or streets, restaurants, logos, festivals)?
5. Do you have any family ethnic or religious customs? What do the objects, foods, clothing, or pictures involved in these customs represent? Do the customs connect you in some way to the past? What beliefs do the customs represent to you today?
6. In what ways do you consider yourself unique, unusual, or "out front"? In what ways do you attempt to change, or create new ideas regarding your inner or outer visual environment?

Perception: Human Sight Is Intelligent

Human sight is the beginning of art, but sight alone is not enough. Sight is one of the human activities that can now be imitated by a variety of machines. Photographic and movie cameras are obvious examples, but mechanized vision today also includes that of robots that can "see" through video-component eyes linked to a computer. Computers themselves can be programmed to produce incredibly realistic images, like the computer-generated image of billiard balls shown in figure 1.1 (plate 2).

Yet despite many apparent similarities, the way in which human beings see is not really like any of the ways imitated by such machines. Human sight is not reducible to what a camera, a robot's sensing device, or a computer can do. The human eye is infinitely more creative and open-ended. In a word, it is intelligent.

Human sight is basically mysterious. Seeing always involves more than what objectively meets the eye. Martha Alf is an artist who draws with a sense of photographic realism that rivals the computer-generated image of the billiard balls in figure 1.1. Her pencil drawings of fruit, however, are more

1.1 Tom Porter.
1984.
Computer-generated image.
Courtesy Lucasfilm Ltd. Copyright 1984,
Lucasfilm Ltd.

1.2 Martha Alf.
Pears Series V, #1 (Four Pears), 1977.
Pencil on bond paper, 12′ × 18″.
Photo: George Hoffman, Glendale, Calif.
Courtesy of the artist.

1.1

than accurate optical images. As she began to draw her recent series of apples and pears she found herself becoming involved in more than the mere facts of shape, shadow, texture, light, and so on that were the basis of her observation and drawing process:

Strictly by chance, one of the pears in Series I was larger and so seemed more dominant than the two smaller ones, who began to seem weaker and submissive. So I deliberately set out to choose pears with those qualities. . . . I would buy at least ten and try them out as if they were actors. . . . [These concerns] kept me interested in the work over the three to six weeks each drawing took.[1]

In *Pear Series V, #1 (Four Pears)*, 1977 (fig. 1.2), for instance, Alf came to think of the pear on the far right, with the leaf that seems to be pointing, as the "accuser."

The complex relationship between these drawings and the eye and mind of Martha Alf reflects the personal and subjective dimension that is always a part of human sight, no matter how technically accurate and objective its operations might be. Human sight is a function of the brain and the mind as well as the eye. This open-ended potential can be summarized by two basic principles that affect both art and human vision: we learn to see, and seeing is a creative, intelligent act.

Learning to See in Three Dimensions: The Eye Follows the Hand

Everyone would agree that we learn to see in the sense that we must learn that a green light hanging over an intersection means "go" and a red light means "stop." But it is also

1.2

14

true that we must learn to see in the most elementary and physical sense of the term: seeing space itself as three-dimensional.

Infants do not see in three dimensions when they are first born; they learn to see three dimensions by touching objects around them. Vision in earliest infancy is evidently experienced as a flat visual field having no spatial depth and continuity. For the infant (up to four months old), an individual object barely exists outside of the act of touching it. The year-old child recognizes (i.e., will search for) and remembers objects that are out of reach. By the age of two, children are distinctly aware of the separateness of the visual world of objects without the personalizing and validating sense of their own touch.

By the time the child reaches the age of two, however, another spontaneous process involving vision and the outside world begins: two year olds, if given the chance, begin to draw. This child-art phase is an indication that making art is not only a natural activity but essential to the full development of thinking and feeling as well as sight. Art is a way of picturing reality, a way of giving to human reality a material,

1.3 Classification system for child art. From *Analyzing Children's Art*, by Rhoda Kellogg. By permission of Mayfield Publishing Company. Copyright 1969, 1970, by Rhoda Kellogg.

1.4 Drawing by Kristen, age 5. *Kristen and her brother.* Crayon on manila paper.

1.5 Drawing by Michaela, age 3½. Black felt-tip pen on bond paper.

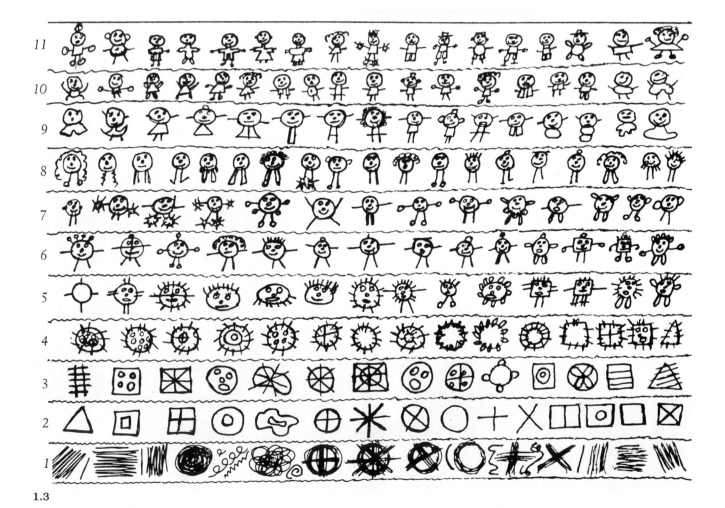

1.3

visible form. All forms of art have a common root in this phase of human development known as child art.

Child Art: The Naturally Creative Eye

The developmental process of child art is universally recognized. In the 1940s, the art educator Viktor Lowenfeld documented a series of artistic stages that corresponded with the psychological development of children from infancy through adolescence. Among the more recent studies of child art development is one by Rhoda Kellogg.[2] She has studied children's art for more than twenty years and has gathered a collection of over a million drawings by children between the ages of two and eight produced in a noninstructional environment of free play. These drawings and Kellogg's observations of children's behavior in producing art have enabled her to describe child art's astonishingly rich and unified sequence of forms.

The development of child art as described by Kellogg follows a sequence, beginning with some twenty kinds of scribbles used by infants and proceeding through the "diagrams," "mandalas," "suns," and "humans" used by the age of four (fig. 1.3). By the age of five or six the child usually begins to combine these basic forms into complex compositions, complete pictures of animals, buildings, people, and other elements drawn from the child's experience (fig. 1.4). Kellogg has documented both a vocabulary of child art and a developmental, integrated sense of form based on this vocabulary.

One of the most remarkable aspects of the child-art phase is that it apparently takes place in children around the world regardless of culture. Child art is an innate process within the human mind and personality that is part of the development of seeing itself.

A second important aspect of child art is that its forms—from "mandalas" to "humans"—are not based on copying reality as it appears to the eye. Children's art can vary from a totally abstract or nonrepresentational image in one drawing to an obviously story-telling or representational one in the next. If one drawing expresses a feeling or idea in abstract shapes, the next drawing might express a similar feeling or idea in story form. It all depends on the inner world of the child, not on the outside world of optical or visual reality.

This interplay of representational and abstract elements is seen most clearly in the first "humans" (fig. 1.5) that the child draws. These look like the familiar "happy faces" ("suns" in Kellogg's terminology) with arms, legs, ears added (or left out) at will. Yet the four- or five-year-old child obviously knows that people's legs do not protrude from their heads! Since the "sun" (or circle) is a naturally occurring form to the child at this stage, he or she simply makes it into a human body. Besides, in a way the child is being very logical: the face is the most defining feature of an individual hu-

1.4

1.5

16

man being. Whatever the particular motivation, every child expresses his or her growing sense of reality by being both an abstract and a representational artist at the same time.

Then comes school.

Even though psychologists like Lowenfeld have documented developmental stages that extend through the adolescent years, interest in art and creativity in our culture show a dramatic decline for most people beginning as early as the primary grade years. This decline, as indicated in studies of creativity cited by the educator Howard Nilis, usually continues into adult life:

Creativity scores inevitably drop about 90% between ages 5 and 7, and by age 40 an individual is only about 2% as creative as he was at 5.[3]

Beyond Child Art: "The Crisis of Realism"

What brings the richly creative interplay of eye and art seen in child art to such a definitive decline? Psychologists do not agree on the precise reason for this seemingly inevitable weakening of artistic creativity, though the emphasis on verbal and mathematical skills in school curricula has received a good deal of blame. The artist and teacher Betty Edwards, however, lays special emphasis on a developmental experience that she calls "the crisis of realism."[4] This phrase describes a common conflict within children, which can begin as early as the age of nine, when children begin to want to make drawings with an increasing degree of visual detail and accuracy. The crisis culminates for most young people around the age of eleven or twelve when their inability to create drawings that "look real" produces so much frustration that they often simply give up drawing—and art—for life.

The example Edwards uses is the frustration of a young person who wants to draw a cube in a realistic way. By "realistic," the child means "as it looks to the eye." Drawings of cubes done in earlier phases of artistic development often included, for instance, various kinds of information about the cube or several different viewpoints (fig. 1.6). Such drawings of cubes are now no longer satisfactory. Realism narrows down to only one kind of cube: those like the ones shown in figure 1.7. This cube, representing the particular kind of artistic realism children admire, is based on the drawing tech-

1.6 Betty Edwards.
"Incorrect" drawings of a cube (from student drawings).
From *Drawing on the Right Side of the Brain*, by Betty Edwards. Copyright 1979. Published by J. P. Tarcher Inc., Los Angeles.

1.7 Betty Edwards.
"Correct" drawings of a cube.
From *Drawing on the Right Side of the Brain*, by Betty Edwards. Copyright 1979. Published by J. P. Tarcher Inc., Los Angeles.

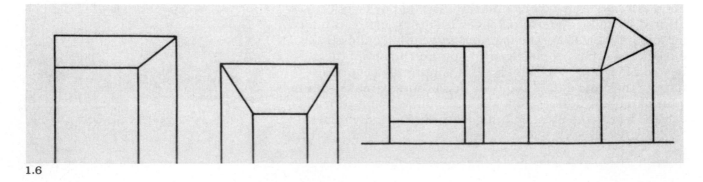

1.6

nique known as perspective. Perspective is the technique for creating the illusion of three-dimensional space on a two-dimensional surface. On a much more basic level, the drawings of the cube in figure 1.7 are exactly the same kind of drawings as the computer-generated image of the billiard balls in figure 1.1. In our culture, realism in art *means* the kind of realism based on perspective. Technically, it means "linear perspective," the kind of perspective that is unique to the Western artistic tradition.

The "Crisis of Realism": A Cultural as well as a Personal Experience

In her book *Drawing on the Right Side of the Brain,* Edwards does make clear that her theory of creativity and her method of drawing are geared to helping people draw realistic images even though—in her own words—"in a sense, realistic drawing is a stage to be passed through, ideally, at around age ten to twelve."[5] In our culture, however, most people never pass through the crisis of realism at all; those who do pass the crisis and continue to make art tend to stay indefinitely in the stage of realism.

Edwards proposes a cure for this problem that uses methods of seeing and drawing based on her studies of the intuitive thinking capacity associated with the right hemisphere of the brain. Though she does not directly speculate on why the crisis occurs in the first place, her analysis strongly supports the suggestion that the "crisis of realism" might be more accurately labeled a "crisis in perspective realism."

"Realism" is a quality that children in all cultures desire in their art as they mature beyond the child-art phase. "Realism," however, is defined in terms that vary according to each particular culture. It is only Western culture that has a standard of artistic reality based so heavily on the rigor—and the limitations—symbolized by linear perspective. It is unfair to blame parents and teachers and friends for conveying the message to the child that his or her drawing is "no good." The message is constantly delivered by the perspective images of the mass media and by an artistic tradition that has been dominated by perspective images for the past five hundred years. Children know, without being told, that their drawings do not "look real."

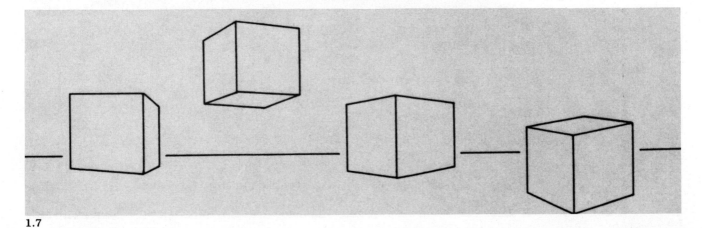

1.7

18

The point of this discussion is not to blame perspective for the general problem of artistic creativity. The point is that the perspective images that are so integral a part of our artistic and cultural tradition are not based on a "natural" way to draw—no culture in history has taken perspective images to the lengths seen in Western art.

In fact, the "crisis of realism" that so many young people in our culture experience has more than a personal significance. A remarkably similar crisis has occurred on a cultural level at least twice during Western history: in the art of ancient Greece and in the art of nineteenth-century France. In the first case (discussed in Chapter 2), Greek art retreated from perspective; in the second case (discussed in Chapter 5 and following chapters), Western art went beyond the limitations of perspective and created the tradition of modern art. In one sense, the discussion of the development of modern art in the later chapters of this book records the ways that modern art has "passed through" the stage of perspective realism. Artists like Grandma Moses (fig. 1.8) have even tapped into the child-art phase of our common experience in order to create works of art that reflect their personal experience better than the realism of perspective does. The discussion should, in addition, help to clarify a remark once made by Pablo Picasso, one of the greatest artists of the twentieth

1.8 Grandma Moses (Anna Mary Robertson).
Hoosick Falls in Winter. 1944.
Oil on canvas, 19¾" × 23¾".
The Phillips Collection, Washington.

1.9 Paintings on a rock face.
Dogon. Mali.
Musée de l'Homme, Paris. Photo: Marcel Griaule.

1.10 Dogon man making ritual drawing in the sand.
Courtesy Wycliffe Bible Translators. Photo: Liz Olson.

1.8

century, that once he could draw like Raphael, but it took him a lifetime to draw like a child.

Besides child art, another artistic source explored by Western artists confronting the "crisis of realism" in the nineteenth century has been the art of native cultures. The different sense of realism in native art has been one of the most important sources of inspiration for the tradition of modern art.

Native Art: Another Kind of Realism

Besides its powerful effect on Western art's modern search for a more complete sense of artistic realism and expression, native art is also important in understanding the basic relationship between art and culture. One reason for this is that native art does not require a radical break with child-art forms in order to achieve its own sense of artistic realism. Children in native cultures do not go through an artistic "crisis of realism" in order to pass through the child-art phase (fig. 1.9). Instead, native art transforms the vocabulary of child art used to express the inner world of the individual child into a language that attempts to encompass many levels of reality in a single whole: nature, human beings, and the spiritual world. Because of this continuity it has with the visual language of child art, native art provides a remarkably clear picture of the direct relationship between art and culture.

Although our culture has a different sense of realism and artistic form, the examples of native art in the rest of this chapter will make it easier to examine the equally vital role of art in our own culture.

1.9

1.10

Native Art: Art That Connects instead of Art That Describes

It is not possible to appreciate native art by simply "looking" at it. Unlike the image of the billiard balls at the beginning of this chapter, a work of native art is not made to be merely seen. Native art does not mirror or reflect life; it is seen by the people who make it as helping to *create* life. Native art is not based on observation; it tries to connect processes. The simplest way to translate this vital aspect of native art into our terms would be to say that art means "power."

Native art expresses the power of nature and the sacred by seeking to invoke, contact, and conform to visible and invisible forces. The sand drawing being made by the man from the Dogon tribe in West Africa (fig. 1.10) will contain bits of food. At night, a fox will come for the food and make new marks over the man's drawing. The next day the completed drawing—made by fox and man—will be interpreted as a sign of future events. Native art often combines sound, touch, smell, and taste with sight and movement. It will often insist that a mask move in dance or be fed blood during a ritual (or even while dormant, between ritual uses). When disorder enters life, art helps restore order.

Our quiet museums, segregated from other aspects of life, simply have no relation to the settings in which native art is used. A striking example of this occurred when an exhibition of the art of the Maori people of New Zealand opened in the Metropolitan Museum of Art in New York City in the fall of 1984. Those who arrived early on the day of the opening saw two Maori warriors in full body painting, brandishing spears, lead a group of ninety other Maoris in a ritual of purification. The Maori elders wanted to soothe the spirits of the ancestors lodged in their "art" who might be disturbed by the unusual journey to the exhibition in the United States.

1.11 *Horned Puffin Eating a Walrus.* Eskimo. 19th century.
Department of Anthropology, Smithsonian Institution, Washington.

The Western sense of realism in art is based on how realistic things look to the eye. The far different sense of realism underlying native art can be understood by discussing the Eskimo mask shown in figure 1.11 (plate 3). This mask depicts a horned puffin eating a walrus. The face on the back of the puffin reflects the Eskimo belief that every living thing has a spirit that at times reveals itself as a fleeting impression of a face. The holes in the two hands extending out from the mask are the hunter's hands permitting the spirit of the animal to escape after the kill. The *inua*, or spirit, of the animal is recognized and appeased even in the process of death. This mask—which we call art—was made to become part of the vital bonding of the human world, the natural world, and the spiritual world into a single whole. A photograph or perspective drawing would present a more accurate picture of a horned puffin, but it would not even attempt to create a connection with the levels of reality that are implied in the Eskimo mask.

This mask represents a tiny fragment of Eskimo art, which is only one of innumerable past and present forms of native art. Native art is best understood in the context of its culture—its whole way of life. The art of the Dogon people of Mali, in western Africa, clearly reveals the vital relationship between art and culture.

Dogon Art: Icons That Humanize the Cosmos

Since native peoples use art as a power for *connecting* reality with human experience, an essential part of appreciating native art is understanding the beliefs that connect art and reality. Dogon art is inseparable from Dogon beliefs, which, like every culture's beliefs, are summarized in myths. A myth is an explanation of events in story form. Dogon myths, again, like every culture's myths, start off this way: "In the beginning. . . ."

Amma, God, created the earth out of clay. It was desirable and beautiful, both male and female at the same time. The anthill represents the female sex, the termite hill, the male. This unity of male and female, and the difficulty of maintaining it, is a central theme of Dogon myth.

When Amma attempted to express his love for the earth in sexual intercourse, the male principle resisted, so Amma destroyed the termite hill—thus leaving the earth only female. Amma then proceeded to express his love without interference. This initial violent and unjust act, though, brought disunity into the world.

Amma again had intercourse with the earth and this time brought forth the original or primordial couple—the first parents of the human race. Also born at this time were the four *nommo* couples. Each of these eight beings were both male and female, with one sex more dominant in each. All Dogon groups trace their descent from these couples.

One nommo was transformed into the serpent Lebe, who led the Dogon people in their migrations into their present territories in the dry, rocky land along the Niger River of sub-Saharan West Africa.

The other nommos re-entered earth through the anthill and then emerged reborn beyond the human condition as spirits. In this state the nommos regularly maintain contact with the ongoing Dogon venture on earth through the religious rites conducted by the village priest, or *hogon*.

The myths also state that in the beginning human beings did not know death. Instead, at an advanced age, each human being was transformed into either a serpent or a spirit. In the new world beyond death, the reborn spoke an unknown language. But one day an old man, amazed at his incipient transformation into this new world, began to speak the secret language of the spirits to the living. This infringement of the divine order caused death, and this old man be-

1.12 Hare mask.
Fiber and wood. Dogon.
Musee de l'Homme, Paris. Photo: José Oster.

1.13 *Togu na* in Dogon village of Anakila.
Drawing by Tito Spini.
From *Togu Na*, by Tito Spini. New York: Rizzoli Publishers, Inc., 1976.

1.14 Front and side views of columns of *togu na* in Dogon village of Anakila.
Drawing by Tito Spini.
From *Togu Na*, by Tito Spini. New York: Rizzoli Publishers, Inc., 1976.

1.12

came the first corpse. Since that time, spirits associated with the souls of the dead rove the country and are regarded as death itself.

To appease the spirits of the dead, the Dogon began to make masks (fig. 1.12) and use them at regular festivals to honor the spirits. Art thus entered the world as a means to heal the breach between life and death itself.

Dogon myth not only reveals the origin of the cosmos and of the Dogon people, it also reveals that art is one of the powers that conquers death. This life-giving role of art is reflected in all forms of Dogon art, from masks to architecture to the shape of the entire village.

Dogon Architecture: Experiencing the Earth in Mythic Form

If the earth is the "Great Mother," the village is a giant human body. At the "head" (north) is the village's most important structure, the *togu na*. Figure 1.13 is a drawing of the togu na in a village called Anakila.

1.13

The togu na is a place of relaxation and conversation for the men of the village. Its most important function is to provide the space where the elders (the eight oldest men, since there were originally eight nommos) carry on important discussions and make decisions that affect the entire village.

Note that the togu na is built close to the ground—in most villages their roofs are barely five feet high. This is to ensure that the "word" of the elder is spoken from a bodily position that ensures calm, centered utterances. The architecture thus embodies the distrust of language reflected in Dogon myth: anyone who rises to speak in anger will hit his head on the ceiling!

The columns of this togu na also reflect Dogon myth (fig. 1.14). From the front, each column resembles a generalized human figure with exaggerated male genitals sculpted in relief. From the side, however, each column has the appearance of a female silhouette showing the face and breasts in profile. Each column sculpturally repeats the mythic belief

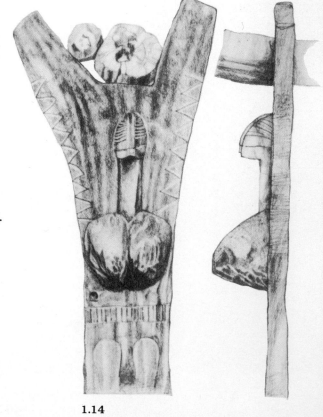

1.14

1.15

that male and female together are needed to create human unity (like the nommos).

The individual houses of the Dogon people are also laid out in the image of the human body (fig. 1.15). The entrance is regarded as the vagina, the living and sleeping area is the chest, and the kitchen is the head. The entire village complex thus becomes a kind of inhabited sculpture through which the Dogon people experience their basic myth as they move through its immobile spaces.

Dogon Masks: Dancing the Experience of Myth

Masks entered Dogon life to heal the breach between life and death. The Dogon point to their village of Yougou-Dogourou as the exact place where the first masks originated. In this sacred village the most ancient masks are kept in caves guarded by the hogon. These caves, closed off and sealed with symbols to protect their sanctuary, keep the power of the original masks under human control.

Some masks can be made only by approval of the hogon. In every Dogon village, however, after proper initiation rites, each male receives the power to make certain other masks for ritual use. The *satimbe* mask, which depicts a female human figure rising from an antelope mask (fig. 1.16) is highly prized among the Dogon. The *kanaga* mask (fig. 1.17) is one of the most common types.

At the proper moment determined by the hogon in each village—at the change of the seasons or on the occasion of an individual death or a marriage, for example—the masks emerge in a burst of energy and the Dogon myths come alive in the ecstatic communal rhythm of dance.

In these ceremonies, the power of the masks and the dance confront, appease, and invoke the power of various animals, reptiles, birds, and spirits—including death itself. The power of the masks can also be invoked for concerns

1.16

of daily life. Figure 1.18 shows a young man in the mask he has fashioned to show a young woman how much he appreciates her beauty. This particular mask embodies the experience of Dogon myth in two ways: it expresses the theme of male-female unity, and it restores the young man to the male-female condition of the nommo ancestors.

By the use of masks in the cycle of ritual and myth the Dogon people, under the direction of the hogon, maintain the world order corresponding to their myths. The sculpture in figure 1.19 sums up the function of Dogon art and myth quite clearly. The primordial couple are seated on a stool consisting of a top disc representing the sky and a bottom disc representing the earth; below them, between the discs of earth and sky, is the tree of life. This tree of life can be seen as the cycle of Dogon myth, a cycle that constantly renews for the Dogon people—through art—their most vital experience of life itself.

1.18

1.17

1.19

1.15 Section of a Dogon village.
Courtesy Wycliffe Bible Translators. Photo: Ed Lauber.

1.16 Satimbe mask.
Fiber and wood.
Musée de l'Homme, Paris. Photo: José Oster.

1.17 Kanaga mask.
Wood and fiber.
Musée de l'Homme, Paris. Photo: José Oster.

1.18 Mask of a young woman (worn by a young man).
Wood and calabash. Dogon.
Musée de l'Homme, Paris. Photo: Marcel Griaule.

1.19 Primordial couple.
Wood sculpture. Dogon.
Photo: Musée de l'Homme, Paris.

Art as Icon: Creating, Affirming, and Sustaining Culture

The study of Dogon culture demonstrates the intimate connections among culture, myth, and art.

Culture can be defined as the shared pattern of customs, ideas, beliefs, images, and language that unite a group. Every culture can be seen as a kind of giant model of what it means to be a human being. Every human being within a given culture conforms in varying degrees to this model. Thus, even though culture is made by human beings, it also makes each individual—to some extent—in its own image. This is just as true of so-called advanced cultures as it is of native cultures.

In our everyday usage the word *myth* tends to mean a lie or a fable—something that is not true, something unscientific. In relation to culture, however, myth does *not* mean a lie. A culture's myth inevitably gives an explanation of how the cosmos (sun, stars, earth) was born. Myth describes who the gods are and how they are to be treated. It tells who men and women are—in their own relationships and in their relationships with the gods, with the spirits of the ancestors, with nature, and with death. Just as every culture embodies a particular model of human nature, so every culture—including our own—has its own myth, its own story of origin and destiny. Every person within a culture lives out a personal version and variation of the culture's myth.

This direct connection between culture and myth means that an icon is more than an image that reflects a culture's basic values. The meaning of the term *icon* must include the crucial role art plays in *forming* the culture's basic picture of what is real. More specifically, art has an icon function insofar as it helps people with a culture experience their basic myth system in a meaningful way. Without this experience of myth, a culture can literally lose its meaning. It then either dies or undergoes radical change based on some new basic myth.

Art as Icon: The Power to Create or Destroy Culture

The disappearance of many native cultures, and the endangered status of many that today survive, is not only due to two centuries of colonization and industrialization. It is also due to the impact of icons from other cultures. Figure 1.20 is an image that leads us back to a consideration of the relationship between native art and our own art and culture.

This advertisement for Polaroid shows one of the photographs from the book *Man as Art*, which features Malcolm Kirk's photographs of Hali tribesmen of New Guinea in the

*The instant image
and man as art.*

The Polaroid SX-70 System

1.20 "The Instant Image and Man as Art."
Polaroid advertisement.
Courtesy Polaroid Corporation.

South Pacific. The advertisement, however, also shows the dilemma currently facing native arts and cultures.

The photograph of the New Guinea tribesman is used here as part of an advertisement. The ad itself can be seen as an icon of Western culture. As an icon, it invites the viewer to experience some of our most basic myths: the Polaroid camera represents the myth of technological progress; the adventurous and talented photographer represents the myth of individualism; the book and its title represent Western belief in the power of technology to transform the cultural and natural resources of the globe into various forms of property or consumer products. The thumb holding the photograph embodies the myth that technology (in this case, photography) is a benignly human element that can intervene in cultural or natural processes without harmful effects.

As noted in the Introduction, however, icons can deceive. This ad also suggests how native cultures are becoming irretrievably linked with technological culture. The thumb visible below the image of the tribesman—like the camera that took the photograph—also symbolizes the presence and the superior power of the same culture whose representative, by taking and printing the picture, intends to show appreciation for the art of the native culture. The problem is that technological art (e.g., the photograph) tends to deprive native art (e.g., the body painting) of its very reason for being— its particular kind of power.

The camera and the photograph symbolize the innumerable elements that now tend to discredit the power of native myths, native art, and therefore, native culture. The tribesman in this photograph, if he follows the pattern repeated in so many native cultures, will tend to admire the culture symbolized by the power of the photograph so much that he will begin to lose his belief in his own culture. He will then change cultures.

If native art has no "crisis of realism" within its own processes of artistic development, it nevertheless does experience a crisis of realism caused by the impact of technological cultures—and their images—on its belief systems.

The Polaroid ad is thus not only a powerful icon representing Western culture. It represents, even though unintentionally, an "anti-icon" to the culture of the New Guinea tribesman.

Having examined the role that art can play in both the making and the possible un-making of a culture, it is now possible to look at the ways that art plays a vital role in our own Western culture.

The Problem of Modern Art and Modern Culture: When Myths Collide

The discussion of Western art, like the discussion of native art, should begin with a brief description of the myth system that underlies its form and its particular sense of realism. A problem immediately occurs, however, that did not arise in the discussion of Dogon art and culture. It is the problem posed by a culture that includes change, innovation, and even revolution as part of its basic myth system. Our culture expects car designs, political campaigns—even the cosmos itself—to constantly change or evolve. Change is also an integral part of our myth of freedom. Individual freedom in our culture is in large part defined as the freedom to change—one's mind, one's job, one's home, and so forth.

Western culture (both in Europe and America) has been based on the myth of change in a special way since at least the late eighteenth and early nineteenth centuries. At that time political and industrial revolutions rocked traditional society to its roots—including the mythic center. During this period artists began to turn to images from past phases of Western culture with a totally new eye. Instead of using past art as a way to enhance the present with the stabilizing glory of the past (which had been the practice in Western art for centuries), artists used past art as part of a search for *alternative,* changing models of thought and action. The late eighteenth-century French painter Jacques Louis David, for instance, painted *The Oath of the Horatii* (fig. 1.21) in 1784 in order to electrify the people of Paris into political awareness. The painting depicts a scene from early Roman history in which three brothers take an oath to oppose the imposition of a king over the Roman people. This painting took on prophetic meaning a few years later when the French king, Louis XVI, was beheaded in the name of the people.

This tension between tradition and change in Western culture persists to this day. Two stories that achieved popularity during the critical late eighteenth- and early

1.21

nineteenth-century period of Western cultural revolution illustrate this tension with remarkable clarity. The first is the true story of Victor, the "wild child" of rural France; the second is the fictional story of Frankenstein.

The Escape to Nature: The Natural Man Myth

The story of Victor is linked to the popularity of the "natural man" myth that had gained prominence in the late eighteenth century. According to this myth, human beings are naturally good; it is society that corrupts. Its clearest formulation was by France's most popular philosopher of the time, Jean Jacques Rousseau, in his *The Social Contract:* "Man is born free, and everywhere he is in chains." The fact that this slogan had been discussed by the learned and the unlearned for many years helps to explain why the capture of a "wild boy" near Aveyron, France, in 1801 aroused such intense interest.

1.21 Jacques Louis David.
The Oath of the Horatii. 1784.
Oil on canvas, 51¼" × 65⅝".
The Toledo Museum of Art, Gift of Edward Drummon Libbey.

The boy had been seen five years earlier, obviously wild, running in a strange, loping gait back into the shelter of the woods near the town. Quite by accident, some farmers caught him. They tired very quickly of viewing "nature's experiment"—as the intellectuals were calling the boy—and willingly let him go to Paris so they could get back to the ordinary routine of farming.

In Paris, Victor was greeted with enthusiasm and great expectations. The French Revolution had swept away the monarchy and the church; Victor—tutored only by nature—might prove that such cultural institutions were indeed useless.

It quickly became obvious to everyone, however, that nature's experiment had produced, not a "new Adam" for the Revolution, but something closer to an idiot. Instead of being open to life, the child's eyes wandered aimlessly, seeming to focus on nothing in particular; he showed no reaction to noises; he seemed to have only four controlling desires: to eat, to sleep, to do nothing, and to run aimlessly around (if given the chance).

Jean-Marc Itard, a young Parisian doctor, disagreed with the general verdict about the boy. He took him under his personal care and worked with him for several years in an effort, through education, to bring him from wilderness to civilization (fig. 1.22). Despite his ingenious methods—which focused on training each of Victor's senses—Itard's efforts were only partially successful. Victor learned rudimentary speech and social behavior but never became a totally integrated member of the society around him. He had been deprived too much of human contact at an early age.

The experience of working with Victor, however, led Itard to a conclusion that was far different from the assumptions behind the natural man myth. He concluded that Victor's condition showed that human beings have almost no instinctual, inherited skills for survival and growth. Human beings are indeed totally open at birth, but also totally unprepared to face life without the human model and training provided by the larger humanity of a culture. A culture is not a luxury, let alone a hindrance to human development; it is a necessity. There is, in other words, no escape back to nature.

The Escape to Technology: The Story of Frankenstein

Mary Shelley's novel *Frankenstein* was published in Paris in 1805, only four years after Victor had arrived there. The story, as we all know from innumerable variations and replays of the original theme, is based on the dream of designing and creating a form of human life superior to ordinary human nature. This new, more powerful form of human nature, as the original version of the story shows, is based on the application of science and technology.

1.22 Francois Truffaut, Director.
The Wild Child. 1970.
Museum of Modern Art, New York, Film Stills Archive.

1.23 Boris Karloff.
Frankenstein. 1931.
Museum of Modern Art, New York, Film Stills Archive.

The stories of Victor and Frankenstein's monster are of special interest because they describe two different paths by which Western artists have explored ways to change the boundaries of culture. They both, however, point to an even more basic myth without which neither the natural man nor Frankenstein's monster could be seriously imagined: this is the basic Western myth of individual freedom, which can be called the myth of the autonomous individual.

This myth presupposes that the individual is, in a sense, capable of more than any culture—any enlarged humanity—can ever completely embody. It is a myth that supports the following observation by the sociologist Clifford Geertz:

One of the most significant facts about us may finally be that we all begin with the natural equipment to live a thousand kinds of life but end up in the end having lived only one.[6]

Our mass media popular art constantly deals with various versions of this myth.

Films like *Greystoke, Splash, The Blue Lagoon* show the continuing appeal of the natural man myth. Several Frankenstein (fig. 1.23) films have been made, along with variations ranging from *Twenty Thousand Leagues Under the Sea* to innumerable Japanese horror movies reflecting the basic appeal of Mary Shelley's original story.

George Lucas's *Star Wars* films brilliantly combine both myths: Darth Vader not only lives within an almost totally artificial body but also extends his power by presiding over a totally artificial world—the Death Star. On the other hand, Obi-Wan Kenobi depends only on natural and spiritual strengths invoked as "the Force."

These films are especially interesting because a third character, Luke Skywalker, embodies the inherent dilemma in our cultural myth of the autonomous individual: Luke must choose between the mythic opposites represented by Darth Vader and Obi-Wan Kenobi. The film does not present Luke's choice as "for" or "against" technology. The rebels (his comrades) use technology, too, and two major characters in the film are robots, Luke's friends See-Threepio and Artoo-Detoo (fig. 1.24). The choice facing Luke is between two different kinds of personal power and—as the fate of Darth Vader shows—two different kinds of personality.

Our fine art is also based firmly on the myth of the autonomous individual and its emphasis on both personality and change. Since the period of political and industrial turmoil in the nineteenth century, Western fine art has undergone a series of revolutions in artistic style and content rooted in the personalities of individual artists. A specific new term, *avant-garde,* came into use in the early nineteenth century to describe this pattern of revolutionary artistic change.

Avant-garde literally means "advance guard," the scouting party in a military campaign that explores the unknown

1.22

1.23

1.24 Artoo-Detoo and See-Threepio (from *Star Wars*).
Copyright Lucasfilm Ltd. Courtesy Lucasfilm Ltd.

territory ahead of the main body of troops. This term accurately describes the experimental, adventurous, and sometimes embattled role of the artists in each generation since that time who have created new ideas of human perception, new political visions, and new approaches to art itself.

The avant-garde tradition of modern art continues today. Modern art sees itself as constantly moving "out front" in the field of visual imagery ranging from painting to film to video. The term *avant-garde* is so historically and conceptually a part of the modern tradition of fine art that it will be used in this book from now on whenever the reference is to the modern tradition of fine art produced since the early nineteenth century.

Avant-garde is particularly appropriate to describe the modern fine art tradition because it accurately reflects the emphasis on both change and individualism that unites the basic myths underlying our technological culture.

The story of how our art, myth, and culture developed this emphasis on the individual is a complex one. The complete story must go back to two especially important sources: the art and culture of classical Greece and that of medieval Europe.

CLASSICAL GREECE AND THE GOTHIC MIDDLE AGES: FOUNDATIONS OF WESTERN ART AND CULTURE

ASSESSMENTS

1. Can you remember seeing your first statue? How did you respond to it?
2. Think about images and statues that you have seen in a cemetery, at Disneyland, McDonald's. What myths are reflected through the monuments and statues (sculptures) in these places?
3. Where in your community do you spend your time? What images are there—what myths do they reflect to you?
4. Think of a building in your community that you like. Does it reflect your personal values?
5. What images are on vases, dishes, or upholstery in your home? In what way do the images on the products you buy reflect beliefs or myths?
6. Can you recall drawing the human figure using the geometric forms of lines, circles, triangles, etc.? Look at one of your photos or magazine pictures in terms of geometry. Could the picture have evolved from geometrical forms?

2.1

The three sculpted faces in figures 2.1, 2.2, and 2.3 are from Sumer, Greece, and the Europe of the Gothic Middle Ages. They are particularly significant because they form a kind of chain that leads to the threshold of the Renaissance, the period in which Western art and culture took a decisive and dramatic step toward modern times. The faces differ very little in technical skill required for their production, despite an interval of over four thousand years. They nevertheless clearly reflect a striking growth in their relative sense of personality; that is, they impress us with their increasingly lifelike and individual presence.

The wide-eyed face of the Sumerian sculpture (fig. 2.1) looks to the skies with a kind of bright fear, revealing the Sumerian attitude toward the gods they believed ruled their cities. Faces like this one stood on rigid bodies locked in an endless ritual of sacred homage. While ordinary people went about their daily tasks, such statues served a vital function: they watched and prayed.

By contrast, the face of the Greek statue (fig. 2.2) observes the world of human affairs. Even though it is the face from a sculpture of the Greek god Apollo, it reflects the Greek confidence in the godlike potential of the individual human being. Its features indicate that the Greeks assumed that the gods allowed human beings at least a negotiable amount of freedom. The uniqueness of Western art, even today, rests firmly on this sense of the uniqueness of the ordinary human being that was the basis of the art and culture of classical Greece.

The face of the medieval sculpture (fig. 2.3) is less rational and heroic than the face of the Greek statue, but something else is there that is entirely new. Even though the

2.2

2.3

face is not more detailed, in the sense of portraiture, it is somehow more personal. The sculpted face reflects not only confidence but also belief in a personal soul. It radiates the confidence of salvation, a salvation medieval culture and art offered to everyone.

Greek art is the decisive point at which Western art turned from its ancient predecessors toward the individualism that becomes apparent in the Gothic art of the Middle Ages and breaks through into definitive form in the Renaissance. In order to understand the unique value of Greek art, it is necessary to have some idea of how it differed from the long tradition of urban art that preceded it. This ancient tradition began in Sumer.

Ancient Sumer (c. 2500 B.C.): The City and the People Serve the King

Ancient Sumer was apparently the first culture to make the leap from village to city. The origins of the Sumerians and the stages of development of the city-state, with its particular myths and heroes, are historical puzzles only partially solved. What is clear is that with the Sumerian city-state a qualitatively new kind of human experience—the urban experience—came into existence.

The ancient cities of Sumer had massive buildings, and the Sumerian social organization was based on specialized bureaucracies. The Sumerians not only invented a form of writing, they also had a rudimentary mass media technology, in the form of written and pictorial messages printed by rolling carved cylindrical seals over clay tablets. These inventions contributed to an orderly and predictable way of life directed toward the gods, whose presence and importance was indicated by the most important structure of the Sumerian city, the massive ziggurat that stood at its center.

The ziggurat was seen as a sacred mountain on top of which was the house of the god of the city, where—on behalf of the people—the Sumerian kings honored and talked with the gods.

The ancient Sumerian city formed an organic unity, an arena in which the mythic life of the king with the gods became—through ritual and art—the experience of the people themselves.

The Victory Stele of Naram-Sin (fig. 2.4) shows the continuation of the Sumerian concept even after their conquest by the Akkadians sometime around 2300 B.C. The Akkadian king, Naram-Sin, ascends a mountain to approach the gods, represented by the sunlike forms in the sky.

The Greek city that emerged some two thousand years later was a radically new kind of arena, an urban space whose art and customs were focused on the mythic importance of the individual human being.

2.1 Head of statue from Abu temple, Tell Asmar. c. 2700 B.C.
Iraq Museum.

2.2 Detail of Apollo from the center of the west pediment of the Temple of Zeus at Olympia.
Alinari/Art Resource.

2.3 Saint Theodore, detail of sculpture from south portal, Chartres Cathedral.
Copyright ARCH. PHOT/SPADEM/VAGA, New York, 1984.

2.4 Victory Stele of Naram-Sin. c. 2300–2200 B.C.
Pink sandstone, approx. 6'6" high.
The Louvre, Paris.

35

2.4

2.5

Classical Greece: From Icons of the King to Icons of the Individual Human Being

The Greek philosopher Plato defined the mythic role of the city quite clearly and simply: "The city is man built large."[1] "Man," to the Greeks, meant the individual human being.

The center of the Greek city, or *polis*, was not a massive building; it was an empty space—the *agora* (fig. 2.5). The agora was the arena where public life took shape. The Spanish writer Ortega y Gassett explained the decisive significance of this new urban space:

The "polis" starts by being an empty space, the agora. . . . The polis is not primarily a collection of habitable dwellings, but a meeting place for citizens . . . a space of the most novel kind, in which man frees himself from the community of the plant and the animal, leaves them outside and creates an enclosure apart which is purely human, a civil space.[2]

The Greek city was set up for human beings to face each other. It was part of the Greek attempt to create a world adjusted to the scale of the individual. In the same way, Greek art attempted to imitate nature and life in vivid and realistic human terms.

Greek Painting: Legends of Lifelike Images

Unfortunately, Greek painting today exists almost exclusively in the form of Roman copies of Greek murals (wall paintings) and mosaics (images composed of colored bits of stone, glass, etc.). Figure 2.6 is a landscape from a house in the Roman city of Pompeii that dates from the first century A.D. This scene is a section of a larger mural sequence that shows the journeys of Odysseus (Ulysses, to the Romans).

The naturalistic sense of space in this painting is achieved by using lighter colors in the background and

2.6

diminishing the size of figures and objects as they recede in space. Though this is a thoroughly ordinary painting done in Roman times, the Greek words hanging above the central figures like words in a modern comic strip confirm its connection to the Greek painting tradition. Like many Roman works of art, it may have been done by a Greek artist.

Another wall painting from Pompeii (fig. 2.7) illustrates other techniques first developed by Greek painters in their quest for realistic images. The upper third of the painting shows open doors, receding columns, and a stairway. Notice, however, that the doors and columns sometimes go up and sometimes go down—they have no consistent sense of common space. One of the fascinating aspects of Greek art is that apparently Greek artists could have explored an art based on consistent, proportional three-dimensional space (linear perspective) but—as a later section of this chapter will discuss—decided not to do so.

2.7

2.5 Plan of Agora, c. 500 B.C.
American School of Classical Studies at Athens: Agora Excavations.

2.6 *Ulysses in the Land of the Lestrigones*.
Fresco.
Vatican Museum. Alinari/Art Resource.

2.7 Wall painting. Pompeii, 1st century A.D.
Alinari/Art Resource.

Another source of our knowledge of Greek painting is descriptions by Roman writers, who make it clear that Greek painting reflected the basic impulses of Greek culture: it was public, competitive, and based on human scale.

Greek culture prized the *agon*, or contest, which proved individual excellence. By the fifth century B.C. the Olympic games (begun in 756 B.C.) included painting as a competition. In fact, famous Greek artists are identified by Roman historians on the basis of the Olympiad in which they achieved their first acclaim. Even outside the Olympic games, competitions between painters became legendary.

In one such event, the artist Zeuxis (fifth century B.C.) painted a mural scene in which some grapes were so real that birds allegedly flew up and pecked at them. Zeuxis then left the area, assured of triumph.

While Zeuxis was absent, his opponent Parrhasius painted—unknown to Zeuxis—a linen curtain covering the grapes. When Zeuxis returned, he ordered the linen curtain covering his work to be pulled back. Thus, by his own action, he conceded victory to Parrhasius.

The Greek love for an art that rivaled nature is reflected also in the legend of Pygmalion, who sculpted a female figure of such beauty that he fell in love with her. The gods themselves were so impressed by the beauty of his statue that they answered his prayers by giving the statue the gift of life.

Despite these legendary feats creating art whose beauty rivaled nature itself, Greek art aspired to more than imitating natural appearances. It was equally commited to a sense of geometry. Indeed, to the Greek mind, nature was insepa-

2.8

rable from geometry, a conviction that came from observations of the stars.

The Greek Cosmos: The Geometry of the Stars

The Greeks looked upon all of nature as possessing some sense of life. Their philosophers believed the stars were composed of a kind of living fire. Nothing that moved of itself lacked life, and perfect movement indicated perfect life.

Figure 2.8 is a photograph made by pointing a camera at the North Star on a clear night and leaving the shutter open for several minutes. Since the only light that hit the film came from each star, the image shows the apparent motion of the stars as seen from earth during the exposure time. The pattern in the photograph shows that an observer on Earth would see the motion of the stars as a series of perfect circular lines (fig. 2.9). The Greeks, like all ancient peoples (and like those who consult horoscopes today), were extremely attentive to the motion of the heavenly bodies. Unlike motion and change observed and experienced on earth, motion in the heavens is both regular and predictable—in a word, geometric.

The sense of realism in Greek art thus had two governing principles: nature has a form and an order invisible to the eye (geometry), and nature has a form and an order visible to the eye (naturalism). The dialogue and the tension between geometry and naturalism can be seen in all forms of Greek art, from vase painting to architecture.

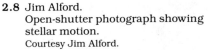

2.8 Jim Alford.
Open-shutter photograph showing stellar motion.
Courtesy Jim Alford.

2.9 Diagram of stellar motion (based on figure 2.8).

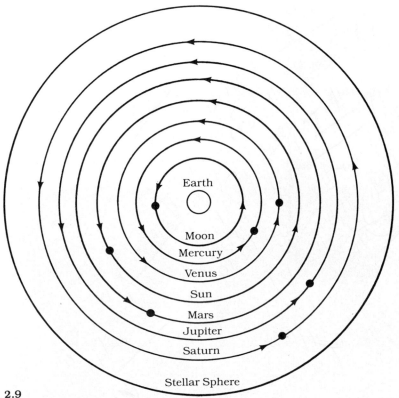

2.9

2.10

Vase Painting: Icons for Private Spaces

Greek vases, like the cartoons and sitcoms transmitted on our television sets today, brought images of fantasy, myth, and everyday life into every home. The television-like impact of these images is even more apparent when we realize that most Greeks were only semiliterate, even during the classical period of their history. The images on the vases had a vital role in making familiar the legendary deeds of Odysseus, Achilles, Theseus, and other heroes as well as the world of the gods themselves.

What is most important in the mythic tradition illustrated in Greek vase painting, however, is not the sequence of familiar myths about the gods, but the gradual emergence of the human figure as the dominant symbol in Greek culture.

In vase painting, this development began about 800 B.C. Vases from this period have designs that are almost purely geometric (fig. 2.10). Recent research indicates that these patterns were probably derived from the textile designs developed by Greek women. The human figure begins to stand out from this geometric web as a peculiar, antlike form by 600 B.C. (fig. 2.11). It then achieves increasingly naturalistic presence within wider spaces of movement until the fully developed human form of the classical period emerges during the fifth century B.C.. (figs. 2.12, 2.13).

Figure 2.13 shows the result of this evolution: the human body, gracefully and with supreme confidence, basks in a space that is now entirely its own. The human figure—like the agora against the background of nature—takes on a spirited, if limited, sense of freedom. These images painted on vases become the appropriate icons for a developing culture whose enlarged humanity was, at least potentially, the ordinary human being.

2.11

2.12

2.13

Greek Sculpture: Icons for Public Spaces

Greek sculpture evolved in a similar way to vase painting, from an emphasis on geometry to an emphasis on naturalism. Figures 2.14, 2.15, 2.16, and 2.17 show this development from about 600 B.C. to the beginning of the classical period, shortly after 500 B.C. Since its evolution took place over a shorter period, Greek figure sculpture makes the revolutionary myth underlying Greek culture even more obvious than it is in the art of vase painting.

These free-standing figure sculptures supported the basic Greek myth of the individual despite their apparent immobility and lack of action. In fact, they displayed the most important action of all: the action of self-contained harmony by which the human being, through reason, achieves a sense of harmony with the surrounding cosmos.

These free-standing sculptures, in other words, were not heroically proportioned individuals with a personal character and a personal history; they were godlike men, or at times, manlike gods. The art historian Christine Havelock has described the impact of these statues this way:

The round sculptures were often very close to life-size and stood on relatively low pedestals. From this we can deduce that they were intended to have a reality and an existence comparable to the spectator's. There is no other way, it seems to me, to understand their materiality, their lifelike qualities (painted lips, eyeball, hair, drapery edges, etc.), and potential movement. When the spectator also observed that men and gods looked very much the same, a feeling of well-being and self-confidence ensued.[3]

This one-to-one relationship between the individual viewer and the sculpted figure was a basic aspect of its icon effect. Even large-scale groups of sculptured figures like those that appeared in the triangular pediments of temples

2.16   2.17

2.14

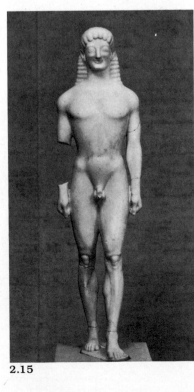

2.15

2.10 Geometric amphora. 8th century B.C.
Staatliche Antikensammlungen, Munich.

2.11 Geometric amphora. 8th century B.C.
National Museum of Athens.

2.12 Geometric krater. 8th century B.C.
4′ 3⅜″ high.
Metropolitan Museum of Art, New York,
Rogers Fund.

2.13 Krater by the Berlin painter. 5th
century B.C.
The Louvre, Paris.

2.14 *Standing Youth* (Kouros). c. 600 B.C.
Marble, 6′ 1½″ high.
Metropolitan Museum of Art, New York,
Fletcher Fund.

2.15 *Kouros from Tenea.* c. 570 B.C.
Marble, approx. 5′ high.
Staatliche Antikensammlungen, Munich.

2.16 *Kouros from Anavysos.*
c. 540–515 B.C.
Marble, approx. 6′ 4″ high.
National Museum, Athens.

2.17 *Kritios Boy,* front and side views.
Acropolis, Athens. c. 480 B.C.
Marble, approx. 34″ high.
Acropolis Museum, Athens.

42

2.18 Olympia, Temple of Zeus, sketch restorations of the east (above) and west (below) pediments. 462–457 B.C. Original length approx. 87'; original height approx. 10' 10".
From *Art and Experience in Classical Greece*, by Jerry Jordan Pollitt. New York: Cambridge University Press, 1972.

2.19 Polyclitus, *Doryphoros*. Original, c. 450–440 B.C.
Roman copy, marble, 6' 6" high.
Museo Nazionale, Naples. Alinari/Art Resource.

2.20 Leonardo da Vinci.
Study of Human Proportions According to Vitruvius. c. 1485–90.
Pen and ink, 13½" × 9¾".
Accademia, Venice.

were given a size and prominence designed to address the perception of the individual viewer below (fig. 2.18). Each figure in the group was always shown in a clear action or pose that carried its message directly to the individual, a message that had already been learned from earlier encounters with vase paintings at home.

It is important to note that these figures of the classical period never lost their basic connection with geometry. The highly naturalistic anatomy of the figure by Polyclitus (fig. 2.19) has a clear impress of geometry in its proportion. Polyclitus wrote a canon, or rule, of proportion (now lost) that became a standard for sculptors throughout antiquity. Since Roman writers referred to it, later, Renaissance artists were inspired to develop a similar canon that would lead to figures with a similar balance of naturalism and geometric proportion. Figure 2.20 shows a famous drawing by Leonardo da Vinci that reflects this search for an artistic formula for human proportion.

2.18

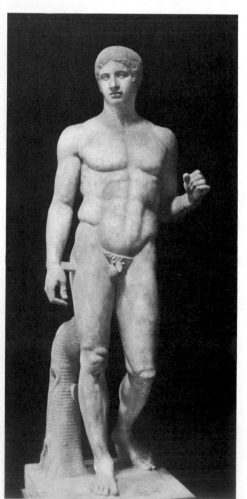

2.19

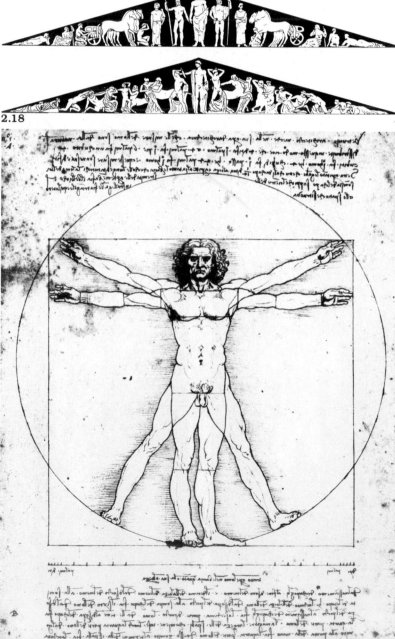

2.20

This dynamic interplay among geometry, naturalism, and adjustment to the perception of the individual viewer are also evident in the architectural masterpiece of ancient Greece, the Parthenon.

2.21 The Parthenon (southeast).
Alinari/Art Resource.

2.22 Section from Panathenaic Procession, Parthenon.
National Museum, Athens.

43

The Parthenon: Cosmic Geometry Adjusted to the Human Eye

The Parthenon (fig. 2.21) was built in the generation following a series of Greek military victories over the Persians that covered a span from c. 490 B.C. to 448 B.C. Like innumerable vase paintings on the same subject, it was a constant reminder of these epic victories.

The Parthenon was built on the Acropolis, the sacred hill above Athens that was believed to be the site on which Athena had successfully contested with Poseidon, the god of the sea. The Parthenon was built on the site of Athena's famous victory and dedicated to her. The sculpted figures that adorned the west pediment section celebrated her victory. Myth again joined daily life, however, in the Parthenon's Panathenaic frieze (fig. 2.22), a 520-foot band of continuous relief sculpture that stretched completely around the outside wall of the Parthenon just below the roof. The frieze begins with ordinary Athenians preparing for the annual procession

2.22

2.21

honoring Athena that went from the agora to the Parthenon. The frieze ends with Athenians meeting the goddess herself.

The core building circled by the Panathenaic frieze had two rooms. The larger room held a colossal 39-foot statue of Athena made by the sculptor Phidias. The smaller room was a treasury that held valuable objects dedicated to the goddess. The Parthenon was not a place for religious services or meetings—it was the house of the goddess.

In another sense, the Parthenon can be called a piece of monumental sculpture. Like Greek figure sculptures, it was constructed in accordance with strict geometric formulas (fig. 2.23), but, again like Greek figure sculpture, its form is also based on many adjustments that make it pleasing to the human eye. Naturalism and geometry are essential elements of its artistic form.

The Parthenon: The Naturalism of the Human Eye

The construction of the Parthenon incorporated a series of minute adjustments, so small that they would have to be called subliminal (below the threshold of conscious perception). Measurement has revealed that there are really very few straight lines in the Parthenon. The columns are not straight. They arc in a subtle curve amounting to one inch for every 522 inches in height. They also tilt slightly toward the center (fig. 2.24); if the columns were extended into the

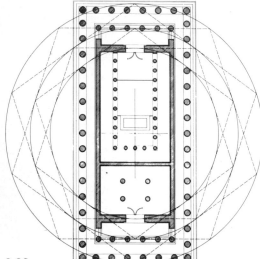

2.23

2.23 Geometric formulas used in construction of the Parthenon.
Design by Dean Snyder.

2.24 Diagram in exaggerated proportion of the horizontal curvature of the Parthenon.
From *Art and Experience in Classical Greece*, by Jerry Jordan Pollitt. New York: Cambridge University Press, 1972.

2.25 Laocoön group, early first century B.C. Marble, (partially restored), 8′ high.
Vatican Museum, Rome.

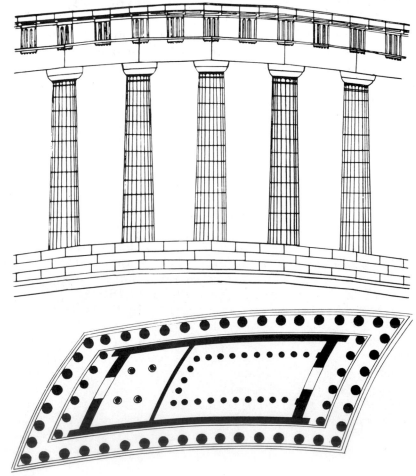

2.24

sky, they would intersect about two and a half miles up. The corner columns are one-fortieth thicker than the others and are placed two feet closer to their adjacent columns.

Without these adjustments, the columns would have appeared distorted, because of the optical illusion created by ordinary vision. The subtle curves, in other words, make the lines of the Parthenon—to ordinary human vision—appear to be straight.

All these adjustments have only one purpose: to give the Parthenon a proper iconic balance between the hidden formulas of geometry and the naturalism of appearances (the human eye). The adjustments in the Parthenon reflect the importance, not of the building, but of the individual viewing it.

The cost of these time-consuming refinements was immense, as the historian Jerry Jordan Pollitt points out:

These delicate variations meant that virtually every architectural member of the Parthenon had to be carved, like a jewel, to separate minute specifications.[4]

The adjustments, Pollitt continues, produced the iconic effect prized by Greek painters, sculptors, and architects. "In the Parthenon things as they 'appear' are harmonized with things as they are 'known.' "[5] Naturalism is in harmony with geometry.

Greek Painting: The Crisis Between the Geometry of the Cosmos and the Geometry of the Eye

Shortly after the completion of the Parthenon (c. 432 B.C.), however, Greek culture went through political and artistic crises. The political crisis grew out of the Peloponnesian War, a series of battles between coalitions of Greek cities headed by Athens and Sparta that lasted from c. 431 B.C. to 404 B.C. Athens and her allies suffered a devastating defeat.

After this catastrophe, Greek art, whose classical flowering had been led by Athens, continued to evolve, but its mood changed from a confidence in human potential as almost godlike to a strong sense of human limitation. In sculpture, the idealism of the classical period developed toward an ever-stronger sense of naturalism, which, for the first time, enabled the display of human emotion. The famous statue of the Trojan priest Laocoön and his sons being killed by a sea serpent (fig. 2.25) is a good example of this more finely detailed naturalism and emphasis on human emotion. How far Greek art had moved in the period from 480 B.C. to the early first century B.C. is seen by comparing the face and figure of *Laocoön* with the *Kritios Boy* (fig. 2.17).

Painting, however, seemed to develop to a point of crisis that did not affect sculpture, a crisis especially important in view of the later development of Western art. Briefly, Greek artists apparently were aware of a technique for creating images in perspective, like those discussed in Chapter 1. Roman writers describe stage designs whose illusionistic effect could only have been obtained by the use of linear perspec-

2.25

tive. In addition, surviving writings of Greek mapmakers also describe the basic mathematical concepts that later inspired the Renaissance discovery of linear perspective.

Apparently, the Greeks reached a kind of cultural "crisis of realism" and turned away.

The evidence that this occurred is contained, not only in the surviving art, but in the writings of the Greek philosopher Plato, who lived in the generation following the disastrous war between Athens and Sparta. Plato's description is highly instructive for an examination of the crisis of Western art in the nineteenth century, when avant-garde artists began to produce nonperspective art. The crisis in Greek painting can be described as the problem of finding the balance between the naturalism of appearances and the geometry that lies, invisible but real, below natural appearances. The question for Greek art became quite clear: Which is more real, nature's appearances or nature's geometry?

2.26 *Battle of Issus* (Alexander mosaic). Mosaic copy from Pompeii of a Hellenistic painting. 1st century B.C. 8′ 11″ × 16′ 9½″.
Museo Nazionale, Naples. Alinari/Art Resource.

2.27 "Plato's couch" drawing (using parallel lines).

2.28 "Plato's couch" drawing (using linear perspective).

2.26

Greek Painting: Images That Deceive

Figure 2.26 shows the Alexander Mosaic, a Roman work based on a famous Greek painting. Even though it is a mosaic copy, it suggests the powerful realism of the original painting. Not only are horses realistically shown from varying angles, but the sense of realism extends to the reflection of a fallen soldier's face in a shield.

The best discussion of this cultural and artistic dilemma is the one in Plato's *Republic.* The extreme nature of Plato's solution for the crisis—he argues that painters (and poets) should be exiled from the ideal state—underscores the importance of the problem. He expressed his concern quite clearly: paintings like this are unrealistic—because they deceive the eye.

Plato backed up his argument by describing the image of a simple couch painted in some kind of linear perspective, as in the drawing in figure 2.27. Imagine Plato's words addressed to that image:

Does a couch differ from itself according to how you view it from the side or the front or any other way? Or does it differ not at all in fact though it appears different?[6]

The key to this passage is the word *appear.* In other words, the image of the couch that shows the back end (the end farthest away from the viewer) as smaller than the front end shows us how it would appear to an individual viewer. But in reference to the real shape of the couch, it is a lie: we know that both ends of the couch are the same size.

Figure 2.28 shows how Plato would apparently prefer it. This drawing of the couch uses the rules of geometry (e.g., parallel lines stay parallel). Which image is really "truer"? If you measure the couch, you would probably have to agree with Plato:

And so scene-painting . . . in its exploitation of this weakness of our nature falls nothing short of witchcraft, and so do jugglery and many other such contrivances.[7]

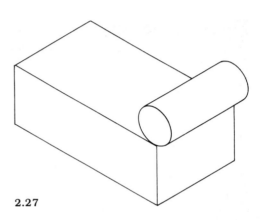

2.27

It is not necessary to agree with Plato's answer and condemn perspective. But to understand Greek art, it is necessary to sense why an art that ignored the kind of geometry that ruled the stars could threaten to produce a highly suspect and basically "unrealistic" form of art. Because of this, Greek painting, despite knowledge and practice of some form of linear perspective, never fully explored its possibilities.

This same attitude also helps to explain why the Greeks, who laid the foundation for Western science, never developed a technological culture. They distrusted technology for the same reasons that they distrusted perspective in art. Technology, to the Greeks, deceived.

One of the foremost Greek scientists and inventors was Archimedes, who designed military and engineering machines that brought him great fame. His biographer, Plutarch, however, specifically comments that Archimedes developed his "machines" as mere accessories of a geometry practiced for amusement. Plutarch further notes that Archimedes, despite his great skill in creating machines, would not consent to leave behind him any treatise on this subject, because the purpose of the machines was to comprehend the

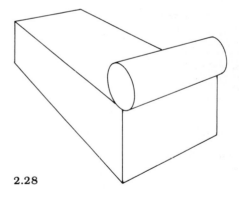

2.28

underlying nature of reality, not to create *control* over reality. The purpose of knowledge, in the Greek sense, was to transform the knower, not the known. The word *machine* itself comes from the Greek word that means "to lie."

Greek culture thus stubbornly insisted on returning all activities back to a focus on the individual. The measure of human beings, in Greek art and culture, was not in how they could extend themselves by developing control over nature, it was in how they could create inner freedom by achieving *harmonia*. This harmony—as Greek art shows—was not something on the outside but, like the geometry of the cosmos, a harmony of soul hidden within the individual.

The Greeks pioneered the basic Western approach to science and art, yet avoided technology and perspective. The medieval period absorbed enough fragments of Greek culture to reconstitute a remarkably similar view of the cosmos, but the medieval view of the individual enabled a qualitatively different attitude toward art and technology to develop. This new attitude was what turned Western culture toward the birth of the modern world.

The Middle Ages: Christianizing the Greek Cosmos

During the fifth century A.D. the Greek and Roman culture that had lasted for over a thousand years was overrun by various nomadic peoples who had for centuries surrounded the urbanized Mediterranean world. After several centuries of almost chaotic flux, a new civilization arose with strong Greek and Roman elements as well as elements derived from the invading peoples themselves. The unifying base was Christianity. The art of this civilization took definitive shape in the second half of the twelfth century in the form known as Gothic. Gothic art is the second clear phase of Western art that significantly contributed to our myth of the autonomous individual and its expression through our present forms of art and technology.

The Gothic Middle Ages, influenced mainly by the writings of Saint Augustine (fifth century A.D.) and a few fragmentary collections of ancient manuscripts, admired and actively absorbed the Greek and Roman tradition. In Paris, Oxford, Bologna, and Chartres schools—the predecessors of today's Western universities—were established that studied this tradition in the light of Christian belief. One of the primary conclusions reached during this medieval absorption of Greek ideas was that geometry was an important part of any true picture or image of reality. The medieval application of this view, however, resulted in a totally different form of art.

Figure 2.29 is an excellent transitional image showing the continuity and also the radical change represented by the Gothic style of the Middle Ages. Although it is a nineteenth-century drawing, it is based on a thirteenth-century manuscript illustration and represents the medieval

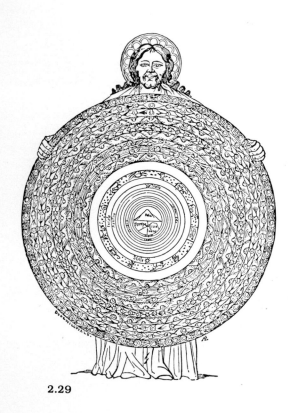

2.29

version of the Greek cosmos. The drawing shows the familiar concentric circles of the Greek cosmos, but with the addition of Christ, whose face and hands appear as the forces holding the cosmos together.

The Middle Ages thus accepted the Greek description of the cosmos, but they saw behind it—as its origin and its destination—the personality of Christ. The genius of medieval art was its ability to create icons that brought the experience of this cosmic personality of Christ down to the level of the individual human being. Medieval art did not try to make the viewer a spectator of the cosmos; it tried to give the viewer the experience of being a participant or pilgrim within it. An important key to understanding the culture-building quality of medieval art is that it is always narrative, or story-telling, in purpose.

The Ebstorf *Mappa Mundi* (fig. 2.30) (plate 4) shows how this attitude affected every aspect of medieval life. This twelve-foot diameter Gothic-period "map of the world," destroyed during World War II, was—like the Christianized Greek cosmos—held in the grasp of Christ. The space inside the circle is far different from modern maps. It consists of illustrations of geography, kinds of people, legends, and other bits of information that the traveler should have about each part of the world as it was known at that time.

2.29 *Christ Holding the Cosmos.*
19th-century drawing based on 13th-century illuminated manuscript.
Bettman Archives, New York.

2.30 Ebstorf *Mappa Mundi (Map of the World).*
13th century (destroyed in World War II).
British Library.

2.30

This medieval map portrays the world as a collection of stories and experiences. It is a visual version of the kind of "map" that we still give verbally when someone asks us about a trip we have taken: our answer usually includes the major scenes and the most important experiences, not the measured distances we traveled.

It is also important to note that both of these images illustrate the medieval idea that all material things, from rocks to animals to human beings, are reflections and images of the presence of God. Since the Bible incorporates the Jewish Scriptures (the Old Testament) and interprets them in terms of the Christian Gospels, medieval culture and art reflect a Judeo-Christian tradition. Based on this tradition, nature was seen as a kind of book filled with sacred stories like the Bible. Everything in nature had a reference to Christ. Each animal reflected the story of Christ in some way. It was believed, for instance, that lion cubs were born dead and then came to life after three days. Within nature, the lion cubs symbolized the Resurrection.

These elements of story and symbol are a basic part of medieval art. Their icon function was to connect the individual—and all of the cosmos—with the life of Christ. The saints who dominate so much of medieval art were seen as "other Christs." All the richness of medieval life and belief are clearly seen in the structure and function of the most important art form of medieval culture: the Gothic cathedral.

The Gothic Cathedral: Model of the Christian Cosmos

The impulse to build cathedrals (churches in towns having a bishop's "chair"—*cathedra* in Latin) was so great in the Gothic period that one estimate counts over ninety cathedrals and some five hundred churches built in France between 1170 and 1280, the heart of the Gothic era.

The cathedral was the central and dominant building in a medieval town. Drama performances and legal procedures were held in front of its portals. Feasts and fairs brought pilgrims—and their money—into the town. Inside the cathedral itself, music, incense, pageantry, and the sacraments of the Church formed a sequence of experiences (Christmas, Easter, Pentecost, and so on) that converted the seasons of nature and ordinary time into the ongoing "story of salvation."

Of the major cathedrals built during the Gothic period, the one that still most perfectly maintains its original sense of place and form in medieval art is the cathedral of Chartres about sixty miles southwest of Paris. Figure 2.31 shows the cathedral and the surrounding city; figure 2.32 shows the cross-shaped form of the cathedral as well as the western front, or facade.

2.31 Chartres Cathedral (view from southeast). Chartres, France. 1145–1513.
Cathedral length, 427′; facade height, 157′; south tower height, 344′; north tower height, 377′.
Giraudon/Art Resources.

2.32 Chartres Cathedral, aerial view of western facade.
© ARCH. PHOT/SPADEM/VAGA, New York, 1984.

2.31

The Cathedral of Chartres: The Sacred Geometry of the Middle Ages

Saint Augustine had defended the Greek geometric view of the cosmos by citing scriptural passages that described God as "making everything by measure and number." Medieval Christian philosophers, like their Greek predecessors, took it as evident that geometry not only described the order hidden behind experience but also *caused* the existence of natural forms. One twelfth-century natural philosopher, Robert Grosseteste of Oxford University, described the place of geometry in nature this way:

Without geometry it is impossible to understand nature, since all forms of natural bodies are in essence geometrical and can be reduced to lines, angles, and regular surfaces.[8]

Within this Christianized Greek mentality of the Gothic period, the cathedral builders became supreme examples of human imitation of God's activity as Creator. Illustrations in stained glass windows and Bibles from this period often show God, like the architect of the cathedral, beginning his work of creation with a geometric compass.

Chartres remains a prime icon for experiencing a sense of medieval culture, in large part because in the twelfth century it maintained the finest cathedral school in Europe. The school of Chartres was particularly devoted to the study of Greek writers, especially Plato, and the sculpture and architecture of Chartres reflect this enthusiasm. Greek philosophers are included among the statues of Christian saints.

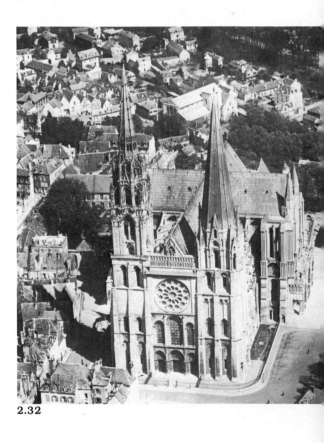

2.32

Special attention was also given to the geometric proportion of Chartres—justified, of course, by its new reference to the creative activity of God.

Chartres was built according to the true measure guaranteed by the use of interrelated rectangles, pentagons, and circles, which marked out its floor plan and walls as definitively as these same shapes delineated the form of the Parthenon.

During the actual building, these dimensions were laid out with pegs in the ground, very much the way one uses the plans in a model airplane kit or the pattern for making a dress. This process of geometric construction resulted in a unity that would be as pleasing to a Greek philosopher as to a Christian theologian. According to the art historian Otto von Simson, the geometric structure of Chartres " 'chains' the individual parts not only to one another, but also to the whole that encompasses them all."[9]

Of course, the ordinary people were thrilled by the building without knowing or caring about either the Greek or the scriptural origins of its hidden geometry. The people were interested in the stories—hundreds of stories—in glass and stone. These stories were the background for the dramatic religious services and sermons that made up the worshipers' conscious experience of the cathedral. The cathedral might be anchored to the cosmos through geometry, but the stone geometry was—for the people—only the scaffolding needed to hold together the stories told in sculpture and stained glass. It was the stories that gave the cathedral life.

The Windows of Chartres: The Mysticism of Light

The effect of the windows of Chartres is impossible to describe with words (fig. 2.33). Just the color blue—an intense purplish blue—of Chartres is a unique visual experience. The light streaming through the glass casts colored beams visible in the air and visible again in dappled patterns of color on the gray walls opposite each set of windows. The light inside the cathedral seems almost alive: it changes with the time of day or with the coming and going of clouds in the sky outside. The color seems to breathe.

The stunning effect of these windows lends support to the words of the twelfth-century churchman Abbot Suger, who defended the use of such windows against the ascetics of his day. Suger invoked one of the basic premises of medieval art: that material things could be shaped into forms that add to the glory of God. Art, according to Suger, could even lead the mind to prayer: "Man may rise to the contemplation of the Divine through the senses."[10]

The stained glass of Chartres provides a powerful experience of the almost mystical possibilities of matter when it is transformed by art. The spell cast by the light of these windows overwhelms the senses, just as it sometimes over-

2.33 Rose window and lancet windows, north transept. Chartres Cathedral. Scala/Art Resource.

whelms the individual stories depicted in the thousands of panels. But that was relatively unimportant; the people knew the stories already. The light that cut through the windows was itself a sermon on the medieval belief that the grace of God penetrated and illuminated all things in history and in the cosmos.

The Sculpture of Chartres: Saints and Heroes Are "Other Christs"

In contrast to what is almost sensory overload by the windows, the sculptures of Chartres are boldly clear and ingeniously laced into the structural form of the cathedral. Figure 2.34 shows the central portal of Chartres's western facade. Around the central figure of Christ are symbols of the four

54

2.34

2.34 Chartres Cathedral, sculpture of central portal, western facade.
© ARCH. PHOT/SPADEM/VAGA, New York, 1984.

2.35 Old Testament figures from the north transept central portal, west side (Melchizedek, Abraham and Isaac, Moses, Saul, David). Chartres Cathedral.
Photo: Robert Pelfrey.

evangelists, a pointed arch peopled with sculpture of angels and elders from the Apocalypse (Last Judgment), and a horizontal band of sculptures of the apostles. Laced into the columns supporting these figures are life-size statues of Christ's ancestors. Architecture and sculpture thus become a symbolic and structural unity. This unity reflected the structure of medieval culture's hero system, which included saints whose role in society ranged from beggars (Saint Francis of Assisi) to kings (Saint Louis VII of France).

Despite the number and diversity of social roles represented in its imagery and sculpture, the sense of history underlying cathedral art is as surprising as the sense of space in the *mappa mundi*. History, in medieval art, is the history of salvation—which means the history of souls, individual souls. Among political leaders, for instance, only Charlemagne manages to secure an important foothold among the windows and sculptures of Chartres. The people, despite the Church's disapproval, insisted on making him a saint of legendary, if fictitious, accomplishments. The meaning of human achievement, like the symbolism of the cathedral, was seen against the background of eternity, not time.

This sense of sacred history produced a complex symbolism, at times as intricate in meaning as the hidden geometry of the architecture. Figure 2.35, for instance, shows a group of five statues from one side of the central entrance in the northern facade of the cathedral.

The five figures represent biblical heroes who came before Christ. Each sculpture, however, not only presents a particular historical person, it simultaneously symbolizes some future aspect of Christ's own role as redeemer. Each figure

2.35

thus assumes a kind of double identity as "another Christ."
All history, according to the cathedral, points to Christ.

The middle figure in this group is Moses—note the
tablets of the Law in his left hand. His right hand is now broken off. The twelfth-century viewer, however, would have
seen a staff holding an image of the "brazen serpent," which
would refer both to the Israelites holding up such images
during their wanderings in the desert and also to the
crucifixion of Christ—who was raised up on the cross.

Similarly, the last figure of this group, King David, wears
a crown and holds a spear, both of which are appropriate to
his life as a warrior-king. But his left hand—now broken
off—once held five nails. These nails turned David into another example of the crucified Christ by referring to Christ's
wounds. David's crown thus symbolizes Christ's crown of
thorns and his spear foretells the spear that pierced Christ's
side.

These statues, however, like Greek figure sculptures discussed earlier, reveal even more about the most fundamental
myth of medieval culture: its view of the spiritual importance
of each human person. In contrast to the way the Greek statues expressed Greek myth through the form of the body as a
whole, medieval sculpture speaks most clearly through the
face. The faces of Chartres, as Kenneth Clark has pointed out,

show a new stage in the ascent of Western man. Indeed, I believe
that this refinement, this look of selfless detachment and spiritual-
ity, is something entirely new in art. Beside them, the gods and
heroes of ancient Greece look arrogant, soulless, even slightly
brutal.[11]

Person over Cosmos: The Base for Technological Expansion

Paradoxically, this new sense of personality on the sculpted faces of Chartres also helps to explain why medieval culture surpassed Greek accomplishments in technology. They present one of the fundamental points of medieval Christianity quite clearly: there were no gods or spirits to appease within nature. Nature was, in the strictest sense of the term, *below* the human being. This attitude did not necessarily mean that nature was to be considered insignificant, evil, or subject to arbitrary exploitation. No greater lover of nature has yet appeared than Saint Francis of Assisi, who preached to the birds and wrote poems to Brother Sun and Sister Moon.

Another saint of the Gothic period, Saint Thomas Aquinas, summarized the medieval attitude in this way: "A single person is more valuable than the entire material universe . . . the person is a kind of spiritual universe."[12]

Besides this expanded notion of human personality, other new attitudes developed with the growth of the medieval monastery.

Medieval Monasteries: The First "Factories" of the West

Monasteries and convents were self-contained communities of religious men (monks) or women (nuns) that developed amidst the collapse of order that followed the disintegration of the Roman Empire. Western monasticism stems largely from the monastic system founded by Saint Benedict in the sixth century A.D.

Monasteries were organized with an almost factory-like regimentation and efficiency. The motto of Saint Benedict's form of monasticism was *Ora et labora* (Work and pray). The monastic sense of order and respect for work led to a revolutionary sense of the dignity of human labor as well as to a radical openness to technology unknown to any ancient culture. During the Middle Ages a flood of technological innovations and improvements were introduced: the stirrup, the yoke for horses in plowing, rotation of crops, the windmill, the wheelbarrow, and so forth. Some twelfth-century monasteries used water power for crushing wheat and sieving flour. The monastery of the twelfth century could, in Jean Gimpel's term, legitimately be called a factory because of its radical increase in the application of technology to practical purposes.

Fortunately, we have an excellent guide to show us the place, both theoretical and practical, of technology in medieval life—the notebooks of a wandering architect of the thirteenth century, Villard de Honnecourt.

Villard de Honnecourt (c. 1250): Geometry That Honors God and Creates Power

Villard's notebooks are a vivid reminder of the fact that geometry was not only used to design cathedrals but was also seen as the underlying form of natural things themselves (fig. 2.36). The geometric habit of seeing and thinking was so strong in Villard that without his notes in the margins, the reader would never sense, for instance, that the image of a lion in figure 2.37 is "drawn from life."

2.36

2.37

2.36 Villard de Honnecourt.
Page from notebooks. 13th century.
Bibliothèque Nationale, Paris.

2.37 Villard de Honnecourt.
Drawing of a lion (from notebooks).
13th century.
Bibliothèque Nationale, Paris.

58

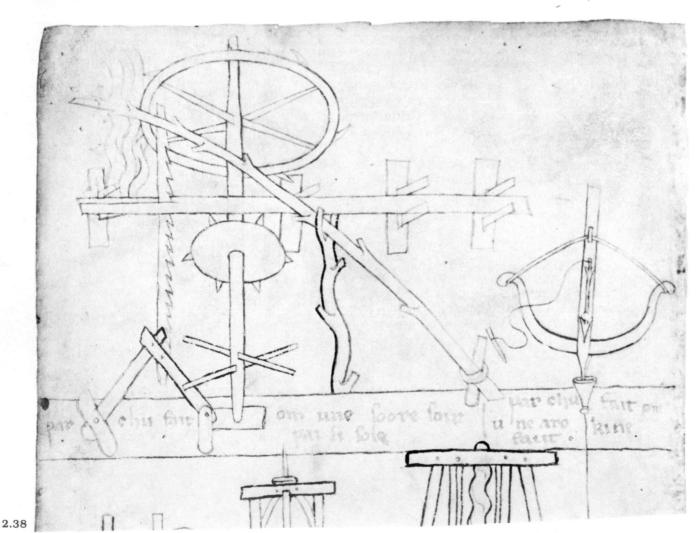

2.39

Two subsequent pages are filled with drawings of devices for building and carpentry. Villard notes: "All these devices were extracted from geometry."[13] He seems to imply that they work *because* they derive from geometry!

Two of Villard's drawings are particularly impressive in showing the new role of technology in the Middle Ages: Figure 2.38 is a detail of a machine shown on another notebook page. Villard has labeled this drawing, with deceptive simplicity: "How to Make a Saw Operate Itself." This drawing is an important illustration of early automation. Archimedes was distressed at having to apply geometry to practical affairs; Villard boasts of it and testifies to its common practice. Greek culture saw technology as a threat to human freedom; the Middle Ages saw it as a source of liberation.

The second drawing (fig. 2.39) is even more significant: it represents the design for a perpetual motion machine—that is, a machine that never stops moving. The importance here is not the machine itself—such a machine cannot be built— but the idea that human beings are free to use the kind of motion that—by the ancient interpretation of the cosmos— was appropriate only to the perfect realm of the heavenly spheres. The Greeks considered it sacrilegious to try to duplicate on earth the perfect motion of the heavens—especially in a machine ("a lie").

The medieval openness to technology is most vividly seen in the writings of a thirteenth-century Franciscan monk, Roger Bacon:

Machines may be made by which the largest ships, with only one man steering them, will move faster than if they were filled with rowers; wagons may be built which will move with unbelievable speed and without the aid of beasts; flying machines can be constructed in which a man may beat the air with mechanical wings like a bird.[14]

Bacon was one of the medieval thinkers who explored the application of Greek and Arabic theories of optics. The eyeglasses on the monk in the illustrated manuscript drawing (fig. 2.40) are one of the practical uses found for these theories during the Middle Ages.

Another practical use was suggested later on in the letter already quoted. Bacon described for the pope a new kind of art based on the application of geometry.

Oh, how the ineffable beauty of the divine wisdom would shine and infinite benefit would overflow, if these matters relating to geometry, which are contained in Scripture, should be placed before our eyes in their physical form! . . . There are three or four men who would be equal to the task, but they are the most expert of the Latins.[15]

There is no evidence that Bacon was referring precisely to linear perspective. Bacon's letter does show the medieval willingness to make pictures based on geometry so that they may be "placed before our eyes in their physical form." This was part of the medieval desire to explore art, science, and technology in new ways. The knowledge needed for perspective was as available as the knowledge for making eyeglasses. The most important ingredient added by the Middle Ages was the desire to see in a new way.

What Bacon could not possibly see was that when the new geometric art of linear perspective appeared a century and a half later it would first transform Western art and science and then transform perception itself. The revolution of perspective is so vast that its effects are still going on today. Western perspective machines, from still cameras to television cameras, computers, and lasers, are creating pictures, not only of what already exists, but of realities that—due to human intervention—will someday come into existence. There are lingering ambiguities surrounding Greek and medieval knowledge of perspective, but the discovery of perspective's revolutionary way of picturing and perceiving the world can be attributed to a specific time, place, and person. Perspective was introduced to the West in 1425 in front of the cathedral of Florence by an artist named Filippo Brunelleschi.

2.38 Villard de Honnecourt.
Detail of page from notebooks. 13th century.
Bibliothèque Nationale, Paris.

2.39 Villard de Honnecourt.
Page from notebooks. 13th century.
Bibliothèque Nationale, Paris.

2.40 Earliest known drawing of eyeglasses. 13th century.
Bibliothèque Nationale, Paris.

2.40

1400

PERSPECTIVE AGE

NON-
WESTERN
ART

Altdorfer
Dürer
Michelangelo   Vermeer   Constable
Leonardo   Teniers   Jones
Memling   Kalf   Delacroix
Bellini   Hals   Turner
Uccello   Rembrandt   Goya
van Eyck   Pozzo   Géricault
Brunelleschi   Caravaggio   Gros
                      Bernini   David

PERSPECTIVE IMAGES

RENAISSANCE   BAROQUE   ROMANTICISM

                                                     ACADEMIC
                                                     PAINTING

image-
producing and   camera obscura
image-   with lens
multiplying
techniques

                        etchings   illustrated newspapers

• woodcut   engravings   wood engraving
(China)
entered into   printing press   steam-powered press
popular use

Galileo

Gutenberg   Newton

CHAPTER THREE

THE

PERSPECTIVE AGE I:

THE RENAISSANCE

ASSESSMENTS

1. Do you equate art with the ability to create realistic images? Do you equate the ability to draw with the ability to draw perspective images?
2. What does the word *renaissance* mean to you? Could it apply to any fine art or popular art today?
3. Think of your room or home as visual space. How does this space compare to the "space" of painting for the artist?
4. Think about how your field of vision changes as you walk around a room. Imagine how your field of vision would change if you looked at the same room through the viewfinder of a camera. Compare this process to the way painters, photographers, or movie directors use their respective framing devices to control the image that you eventually see.
5. Look at the photographs and advertisements in a favorite magazine. What images or experiences are being isolated for your viewing? What thoughts or feelings occur to you?

3.1 Drawing of viewer looking through the hole in Brunelleschi's first painting of the Baptistry of the cathedral of Florence and seeing the painting reflected in a mirror.
From The Renaissance Rediscovery of Linear Perspective, by Samuel Y. Edgerton, Jr. Copyright 1975 by Samuel Y. Edgerton, Jr. Reprinted by permission of Basic Books, Inc., Publishers.

3.2 Jan van Eyck.
Man in a Red Turban. 1433.
Oil, 10¼″ × 7½″.
Reproduced by courtesy of the Trustees of the National Gallery, London.

3.3 Paolo Uccello.
Perspective drawing of a chalice. Early 15th century.
Uffizi Gallery, Florence. Alinari/Art Resource.

3.4 Photographer unknown.
Untitled (Couple Holding Daguerreotype of Family). c. 1850.
One-quarter plate daguerreotype, 3¼″ × 4¼″.
Museum of Modern Art, New York, Gift of Virginia Cuthberg Elliott.

3.1

Filippo Brunelleschi (1377–1446) publicly revealed his discovery of perspective in Florence, Italy, in 1425.

The event was quite simple, almost playful. Brunelleschi brought a little painting based on his new ideas into the square in front of the cathedral. The original painting has disappeared, but accounts of it and how it was used in the demonstration survive. Despite scholarly dispute over details of the event, its main features are clear.[1] Filippo Brunelleschi is the man who personally ushered in the Perspective Age.

Brunelleschi's Experiment: The Duplication of Sight

The scene in front of the cathedral on that August day in 1425 must have been puzzling. People were used to seeing Brunelleschi around the cathedral; its magnificent dome was then being constructed according to his design and under his supervision. But on that day he was not involved with the dome. A crowd of passersby stood in line. He gave each of them, one by one, a small mirror and a small painting. What each one did with the painting and the mirror seemed very strange. Each person put the back of the painting up to one eye and looked through a hole in the painting's center, then held a mirror in the other hand in front of the painting so that the painting itself was seen (through the hole) reflected in the mirror (fig. 3.1).

After looking through the painting at the reflected image of the painting in this way, each person inevitably lowered the mirror and stared at the building beyond—the ancient Baptistry of Florence—then, with obvious eagerness, raised the mirror and looked at the painting reflected in it again at least once more before reluctantly handing both mirror and painting to the next person in line. Everyone was obviously pleased and excited, especially Brunelleschi, who continually shrugged and laughed in enjoyment at the questions and comments surrounding his little experiment.

Brunelleschi wanted to demonstrate that his newly discovered rules of linear perspective could reproduce the exact "look" of things to the eye—the illusion of three-dimensional space on a two-dimensional surface. To show this, he had painted a small picture of the Baptistry on a wooden panel precisely according to his newly developed method.

After painting the building on the panel, he covered the area of the painting above the Baptistry with highly reflective silver leaf to produce a mirrorlike surface. Then he drilled a hole in the painting. A person looking through the hole in the back of the painting at its reflection in the mirror held in front of it could then see more than the precisely painted image of the Baptistry; reflected in the silver-leaf surface surrounding it would be the sky and the moving clouds.

The scene seemed miraculously real! And its reality could be tested: by lowering the mirror while still looking through the hole in the painting, one could see the Baptistry itself—from exactly the same angle that Brunelleschi had drawn and painted it. The real Baptistry looked exactly the same as the painted Baptistry. The moving clouds were a dramatic touch of genius. A miracle, indeed, but a "miracle" of particular importance, because it fused art and science in a common achievement: an image that approximated how the world appears to the human eye.

The Perspective Age Begins: The World Conforms to the Human Eye

The three images in figures 3.2, 3.3, and 3.4 suggest the impact of Brunelleschi's discovery on Western art and culture.

The self-portrait in oils (fig. 3.2) by the Flemish artist Jan van Eyck (1395–1441) was done within a decade of the discovery of perspective. Its incredible detail and sense of three-dimensional form is remarkable even to modern viewers accustomed to perspective imagery. In 1435, such a portrait was revolutionary: its powerful portrayal of an individual human face showed a new emphasis on the subjective dimension of the human personality.

The second image (fig. 3.3) was also completed within ten years of the introduction of perspective. It is a drawing by Paolo Uccello (1397–1475), a Florentine artist who was a friend of Brunelleschi. If van Eyck's painting emphasized the *subjective* individuality of the human face, Uccello's drawing showed how perspective could picture manmade and natural forms with a proportional and measurable sense of *objectivity*.

The third image dates from the end of the Perspective Age, some four hundred years later. It shows an anonymous couple proudly holding a photograph of their friends or relatives in their hands as they pose for a photograph of themselves (fig. 3.4). This photograph grew out of artistic and scientific applications of perspective images begun in the early Renaissance by artists such as van Eyck in northern

3.2

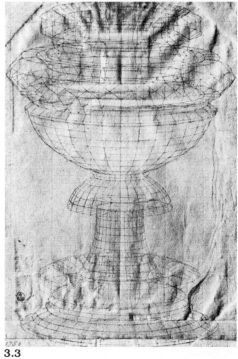

3.3

3.4

Europe and Uccello in Italy. The photograph is the mechanization of perspective.

It is difficult to imagine how anyone could have foreseen the artistic and cultural changes symbolized by these three images. Neither Plato's fear that perspective would produce illusions nor Bacon's conviction that a more "geometric" art would increase religious faith are accurate predictions of what happened. Between 1425 and 1839 perspective replaced the cosmic geometry of the Parthenon and the sacred geometry of Chartres with an art whose basic realism was justified by human perception itself.

The art of the period from 1425 to 1839 falls into the categories Renaissance, Baroque, Rococo, and Romantic. Even though these specific art history terms will be used to describe specific works, the Perspective Age is a useful general term because it focuses on the unifying element that connects the art of this period with the origins of both the mass media art and the avant-garde art of today. Specifically, the term *Perspective Age* brings together three important aspects of this period: it underscores the common thrust of art throughout this period toward the degree of realism eventually achieved in photography; it helps clarify the importance of the "crisis of realism" that occurred simultaneously with the invention of photography; and it suggests the technological enthusiasm that linked art and science throughout this period, an enthusiasm that waned with the invention of photography. Lastly, this term is helpful because it suggests the cultural impact of perspective: perspective changed Western culture by changing human perception itself.

3.5

Perspective's Essential Ingredient: The Vanishing Point

The impact of perspective on perception as well as art can be clearly seen by reviewing how artists from other cultures have created the illusion of three-dimensional space on a two-dimensional surface. Four ways of suggesting space have already been seen at work in the impressive realism of Greek and Roman painting: overlap, size reduction, color variation (atmospheric perspective), and texture gradient (fig. 3.5). Variations of these techniques are present in art from cultures around the world and in different periods of history.

Artists from many cultures have added to these effects by using geometric lines to further organize the sense of space. The parallel line method mentioned in the discussion of Greek and Roman art (fig. 2.7) was also widely used in Oriental and Hindu art, among others.

Figure 3.6 shows a painting based on another method by which Roman artists approximated linear perspective. Figure 3.7 shows how this sense of space is organized by making lines go to a *single line* in the background.

3.6

3.7

Figure 3.8 shows the difference when Brunelleschi's linear perspective is applied to the same painting. Now all the lines—as they appear to the vision of the human eye—are focused on a single point on a line representing the eye level of the artist. A seventeenth-century diagram for a perspective manual (fig. 3.9) shows this effect. This diagram also shows how the perspective image appears to converge on a point in the eye of the viewer. This explains why Brunelleschi put the hole in his painting: it corresponds to the vanishing point in the painted image (and in the eye of the viewer). A viewer looking through this hole while standing at the exact spot where Brunelleschi himself painted the picture would see exactly the same image.

All of these techniques helped to create a sense of three-dimensional space on a two-dimensional surface, but Brunelleschi's linear perspective did more: it not only produced three-dimensional, or realistic images, it produced images that approximate better than any other method how the human eye sees.

It is hard for us to imagine today what an impact seeing the first perspective images must have had. Human sight is a fluid, vanishing experience. Perspective stopped and froze

3.5 Common techniques for creating the illusion of three-dimensional space on a two-dimensional surface. (A) size; (B) surface gradient or texture; (C) overlap; (D) softening of lines and/or colors (atmospheric perspective).

3.6 Wall painting from the cubiculum of the Villa Boscoreale, near Pompeii. 1st century B.C..
Metropolitan Museum of Art, New York.

3.7 Diagram of figure 3.6 showing lack of vanishing point for receding lines.

3.8 Diagram of figure 3.6 showing the effect of taking lines that recede in space to a single vanishing point (linear perspective).

3.9 *On the Principle of Linear Perspective.*
Illustration from *New Principles of Linear Perspective, or the Art of Drawing on a Plane,* by Brook Taylor. London, 1811.
Sterling Memorial Library, Yale University.

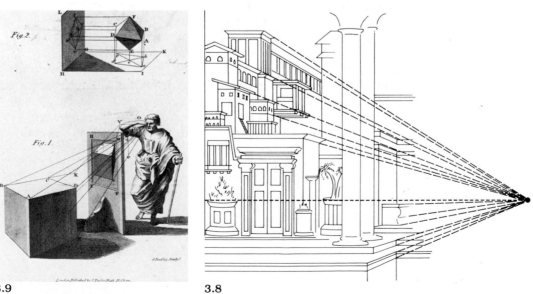

3.9

3.8

66

this experience so perfectly that innumerable people could have the same visual experience as the artist.

The vanishing point concept enabled the artist to begin to grasp, measure, and control the experience of sight itself and then pass on that experience to others.

Perspective's Objectivity: Scale-Model Images of the World

Objectivity is one of the main new features of the perspective image. An objective image is an image that is in some significant and verifiable way exactly like the reality it imitates. Brunelleschi's painting was objective because everyone who saw it agreed that it looked exactly like the Baptistry that was really there.

Objectivity added a new quality of detail to artistic images. However, it produced a revolution in science. Since perspective could stop and isolate forms before the human eye, they could be measured and observed at leisure, like objects. Such objective images detached from the real world by perspective could then eventually be changed and/or controlled. This potential in the objectivity of the perspective image was evident from the very beginning of the Perspective Age. It was especially clear in the work of Brunelleschi's friend who drew the chalice illustrated in figure 3.3, the Florentine artist Paolo Uccello.

Paolo Uccello (1396–1475): Madman for Perspective

Even in a city already renowned for individualistic artistic temperaments, Uccello was a designated eccentric. The Renaissance Florentine biographer Vasari relates in his *Lives of Artists* how Uccello's wife

told people that Paolo used to stay up all night in his study, trying to work out the vanishing points of his perspective, and that when she called him to come to bed he would say, "Oh, what a lovely thing this perspective is!"[2]

The drawing of the chalice shows Uccello's early mastery of the perspective technique. The story confirms all the indications in his art that he was passionately devoted to mapping the new world promised by perspective's objectivity.

Figure 3.10 shows one of Uccello's remarkable series of drawings of a *mazzaccio,* blocking for hats worn by men at that time. Uccello used a series of drawings—like the frames of a movie—to show the *mazzaccio* from different angles, so that it appeared to rotate in space. Uccello's friends were impressed by these drawings, but also amused. What good were they?

3.10 Paolo Uccello.
Drawing of a mazzaccio. Early 15th century.
Uffizi Gallery, Florence. Alinari/Art Resource.

3.11 Computer-generated image of engine.
Courtesy of Ford Motor Company.

3.12 Jan Vermeer.
The Geographer. 1668.
Oil on canvas, 53 × 46.6 cm.
Stadelsches Kunstinstitut, Frankfurt.

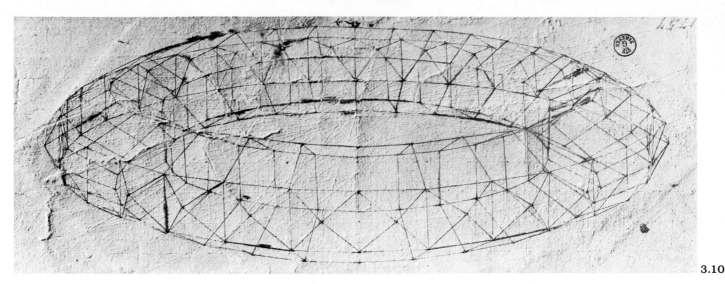

3.10

Today these drawings are no longer merely amusing; we know how useful such drawings are. They look amazingly like the computer images now used to examine visual models of objects, from molecules to planets. Today's computer-generated images are part of the still unfolding possibilities of the perspective image as it will be applied to science, art, and other fields. The resemblance between the chalice and *mazzaccio* drawn by Uccello and the image of the car engine in figure 3.11 is no coincidence. They are both scale images based on perspective. These image-models can be made so exact that they can be manipulated by the computer to show the effects of alterations applied to them. When it does this, the computer is fulfilling the potentiality already contained in Uccello's early fifteenth-century drawings: the use of perspective to create images that are scale models of reality.

This identity between "model of reality" and the perspective image did not have to wait for the twentieth century to have practical application beyond the field of art. The generation after Uccello turned the earth itself into a *mazzaccio* by making scale-model drawings of it called maps. Once maps had been drawn, it was an easy step to the making of the first globes, three-dimensional models of the earth. As one can see in paintings from later in the Perspective Age (fig. 3.12), maps and globes became as typical of the period as oil paintings themselves. The *mappa mundi* (see figure 2.30), with its narrative and symbolic depiction of the world, clearly represented an iconic experience of medieval culture. The drawings of the *mazzaccio,* the maps, and the globe itself are icons of the culture of the Perspective Age. They can be called icons insofar as they gave the individual the experience of being at the center of a world composed of observable, measurable, and controllable objective forms.

3.11

3.12

3.13

3.13 Paolo Uccello.
A Hunt in the Forest. c. 1460.
Oil on panel, 25⁹/₁₆″ × 64¹⁵/₁₆″.

3.14 Paolo Uccello.
A Hunt in the Forest. (Detail of figure
3.13.)

Unforeseen Problems of the Perspective Image: Nature Becomes an Object

Figures 3.13 and 3.14 show the full view and a detail section of Uccello's painting *A Hunt in the Forest.* Notice how the trees, animals, and people look almost like chess pieces carefully moved forward and backward in space to achieve maximum effectiveness in creating the illusion of depth. In fact, the space is almost too perfect, almost too like a world of chess pieces.

3.14

Though Uccello's drawings demonstrate the scientific potential of perspective images, his paintings show that the main artistic use of perspective was to focus on the importance of the human figure. Perspective enabled painters to create a seemingly perfectly ordered space in which the human figure could perform heroic actions, secular or religious, with a new realism and vividness.

Leon Battista Alberti published the first written account of perspective within a decade of Brunelleschi's experimental painting of the Baptistry. Alberti, an architect and artist who knew both Brunelleschi and Uccello, described the appeal of perspective quite simply. He described perspective as a window—a window primarily for viewing the human figure:

First of all, on the surface on which I am going to paint, I draw a rectangle of whatever size I want, which I regard as an open window through which the subject to be painted is seen; and I decide how large I wish the human figures in the painting to be.[3]

Windows and Mirrors: Different Points of View in Northern and Southern Europe

It is important to note that painting in Italy was rooted in the tradition of wall painting. The Italian Renaissance continued an unbroken connection with ancient Greek and Roman mural painting.

Northern European painters, however, enriched Western art by entering the Renaissance from a different background. Their heritage can be traced to the craft art of the nomadic Celtic and Germanic tribes and to the minute detail and rich color of stained glass, windows, and illuminated manuscripts of the Middle Ages.

The human figure was important in northern European art, too, but as part of the scene or story of the painting. The human figure had to share attention, so to speak, with the background details. The manuscript page in figure 3.15 was completed around 1360–65, sixty years before Brunelleschi's experiment in Florence in 1425. The enthusiasm for perspective among northern European artists by the end of the fifteenth century is clear from the illuminated manuscript painting in figure 3.16 dating from about 1492–1504. Notice how the details literally burst into prominence along the margins of the page. The focusing eye of perspective brought these beautiful details of nature into a prominence that in this case overwhelms the figures in the main scene.

Perspective was thus a window for northern artists, too, but their window looked more directly onto nature rather than into a world whose space existed to frame the idealized human form.

3.15 Missal, for Paris use (The Gothic Missal): fols. 63v–64r, *The Crucifixion and Christ in Majesty.* c. 1360–65. Parchment; Latin written in two columns in red, blue, and brown, illuminated with tempera and gold leaf, 7⅝″ × 5⅜″.
Jean Bondo, and his Atelier, Paris.

3.16 *Hours of Ferdinand V and Isabella of Spain*, fols. 72v–73r, "The Crucifixion and Desposition." c. 1492–1504. Parchment: Latin written in red and dark brown, illuminated with tempera and gold, 8⅞″ × 6⅛″.
Flanders, Ghent-Bruges School.

3.15

3.16

3.17 Jan van Eyck.
Giovanni Arnolfini and His Bride.
1434.
Oil on wood panel, approx. 32″ × 22″.
Reproduced by courtesy of the Trustees of the National Gallery, London.

The northern window of perspective is seen in another painting by Jan van Eyck, *Giovanni Arnolfini and His Bride* (fig. 3.17 and plate 5), which was done shortly after Brunelleschi's perspective painting in Florence. Imagine it as a window; through this window the viewer sees an enormous wealth of detail. The painting raises the textures of wood, clothing, and other surfaces to a sensual visual level impossible to achieve in the smaller format of the illuminated manuscript. What made this level of detail possible was a new medium, oil paint, which some historians credit to van Eyck himself. The oil medium allowed layers of color to be applied on top of earlier colors to create a final color that had a jewel-like crispness and transparency.

Without the title, this painting would not seem to have any particular religious meaning. However, in addition to the wedding theme, it is saturated with religious and social meaning. Van Eyck's signature under the mirror suggests that the painting was a kind of legal wedding document. The couple are barefoot because they are on sacred ground (marriage is a sacrament). The dog is a symbol of fidelity ("Fido" comes from the Latin word for faith or faithfulness, *fides*). The oranges symbolize, in the cold of northern Europe, paradise. Miniature figures of Adam and Eve, the first couple, are carved in the bench. Lastly, the mirror itself has been described as a symbol of God—its surface, like the knowledge ascribed to God, encompasses the entire painting in a single glance.

The detail in this mirror reflection is remarkable. Its convex surface not only reflects the entire room but also contains a self-portrait of van Eyck peering into the room through an open door.

The mirror can also serve to illustrate the importance of the vanishing point effect in the perspective image. The position of van Eyck within the mirror in the painting is like the position the viewer occupies in front of any perspective image. The viewer's eye (which began as the position of the artist's eye) appears to coincide with the vanishing point of the image.

The Perspective Age Revolution: A Subjective Self at the Center of an Objective World

The enthusiastic reception of perspective and its immediate adaptation to the artistic traditions of northern Europe and Italy indicates how appealing the new way of picturing the world was. Despite differing applications, its icon effect throughout Europe was the same. Not only did nature (objectivity) and the individual (subjectivity) achieve a new prominence, the entire mentality or attitude toward life made a dramatic shift. Perspective focused attention in a radically new way on the subjective individual while simultaneously emphasizing the objective world of nature instead of the background of eternity symbolized in medieval art.

The art historian Elton Davies called Brunelleschi's painting of the Florence Baptistry a "milestone" in cultural history and compared it "to the Wright Brothers' first flying machine."[4] Psychologically, the little painting did create a change as revolutionary as flight. It began the process of turning attention from God and eternity as the basic reality in art and life to the individual self and human perception as the basic reality. Davies summarizes this impact in the following terms:

Medieval art . . . had its center in the images of God, the saints, and the devil. These were fixed, changeless beings to be viewed by spectators who were moving about. But for Brunelleschi's painting (the first known use of perspective) the human spectator was the motionless center, and so was the spot on the earth's surface where he sat.[5]

The point is not that medieval art failed to generate an experience of the importance of the individual, but its degree and direction. The new direction is clearly seen in the *Madonna and Child* painted by the northern artist, Hans Memling (fig. 3.18).

In this painting, the viewer sees the sacred image through the immediacy provided by the perspective window. A second panel painting, *Portrait of a Donor* (fig. 3.19), accompanied this one and shows the donor who paid to have the pair of paintings done. Note how the donor literally leans on the windowsill of his painting as he gazes into the religious scene so clearly visible in the next one. Even though the Madonna and Child are presented in a remarkably realistic way, it is still clear that the donor—who stood for the ordinary human being in this world—is being elevated to a level of attention that rivals that given to the religious scene.

The shift of mentality reflected by the acceptance of the perspective image is even more clearly seen by examining

3.18 Hans Memling.
Madonna and Child. c. 1485.
Oil on canvas, 14″ × 10½″.
Art Institute of Chicago, Mr. and Mrs. Ryerson Collection.

3.19 Hans Memling.
Portrait of a Donor. c. 1485.
Oil on tempera panel, 13⅞″ × 10¾″.
Art Institute of Chicago, Gift of Arthur Sachs.

3.18

3.19

3.20 Guido da Siena.
Upper quarter of alterpiece (*St. Francis Receiving the Stigmata*).
c. 1225.
Tempera on wood.
Foto Soprintendenza B.A.S.–SIENA.

3.21 Giotto di Bondone.
Vision of St. Francis. c. 1305.
Tempera on wood.
The Louvre, Paris.

three paintings that span the period from the Gothic Middle Ages to the Renaissance. The theme of each painting is the great saint of the Gothic period, Saint Francis of Assisi, as he undergoes a mystical, visionary experience of Christ.

Religious Images in the Perspective Age: From the Space of Eternity to the Space of the Present

In Guido da Siena's painting (c. 1225) the elements of the image are like visual words (fig. 3.20). Each image in the picture exists as a kind of prop for the story. Note the totally flat church on the curiously rounded hill, not to mention the even more curious plant. The two roly-poly bears are hardly more accurate, but they serve quite nicely to remind the viewer that Saint Francis is in the wilderness, where he is loved by all the animals. The gold sky symbolizes the eternal, sacred realm from which the vision of Christ breaks through to transmit the marks of the Crucifixion to Saint Francis.

The painting's narrative/symbolic elements form an icon conveying the experience of a cherished and well-known episode of the medieval story of salvation.

Giotto di Bondone (1266–1337): Intuitive Perspective in the Space of Eternity

Giotto di Bondone's painting of the same subject, done almost a century later (fig. 3.21), is dramatically different. Except for the bears, however, it includes exactly the same elements as the painting by Guido da Siena, including the golden sky symbolizing eternity.

The difference is that each element of the picture has a three-dimensional look to it. Giotto apparently based his style on surviving examples of Roman paintings similar to that shown in figure 2.7. The central image at the bottom of Giotto's painting, for instance, shows a room whose ceiling lines converge toward the back in a way that foreshadows Brunelleschi's discovery of the vanishing point. Yet despite the ingenious *pre*perspective elements, the painting's primary space is still the space of eternity—from which the space and objects of the present world pop out as secondary and temporary phenomena.

Giovanni Bellini (1430–1516): The Sacred Image Seen from the Space of the Present

Lastly, look at Giovanni Bellini's *Saint Francis in Ecstasy* (fig. 3.22). In this painting, perspective totally changes the experience of the viewer, despite the familiarity of theme. Bellini's painting does not present visual words (symbols of

3.20

3.21

3.22

3.22 Giovanni Bellini.
St. Francis in Ecstasy. 1485.
Oil on canvas, 48½″ × 55″.
Copyright The Frick Collection, New York.

3.23 Leonardo da Vinci.
The Annunciation. c. 1472.
Oil, 38½″ × 86″.
The Uffizi Gallery, Florence. Alinari/Art
Resource.

things) through which the viewer puts together a visual story set in eternity. Bellini's painting conveys the experience of the event as if it is occurring in the same world as the viewer and before the viewer's very eyes. The event is now primarily in the world of human perception.

The robust, sculptural figure of Saint Francis presides over a marvelously detailed and cultivated landscape. The sky is blue, not gold, and is streaked with white clouds. The viewer is offered subjective experience of an actual event.

As eyewitness, however, the viewer loses at least one element present in the two earlier paintings: Saint Francis's vision. It is true that Bellini portrays the landscape with such transparent clarity that the viewer senses how nature itself is transformed by the visionary experience of the saint.

But now the viewer experiences the vision of Saint Francis, artistically speaking, from the "other side" of the sacred, from the side visible to ordinary human sight.

Despite the religious subject matter of the painting, it shows how perspective is shifting attention to the objective world of nature and the subjective presence of the viewer. Perception itself, not contemplation, is gradually becoming Western culture's most valued form of experience and knowledge. This shift in emphasis because of the impact of perspective did more than increase interest in the natural world; it also increased interest in *control* of the natural world. This control was itself an increasingly real possibility, due in large part to the objectivity provided by perspective.

Leonardo da Vinci (1452–1519): The Prophet of Objectivity

The artist whose work best reveals the potential for power in the objectivity of perspective is the man whose vision dominates the entire Perspective Age, Leonardo da Vinci.

Leonardo's art continued and in many ways perfected the artistic goals of the Italian Renaissance. He created heroic human figures whose actions were framed in a perfectly controlled perspective space.

Like Bellini's *Saint Francis in Ecstasy,* Leonardo's early painting *The Annunciation* (fig. 3.23) has a sense of natural detail that rivals that of the Northern painters of the Renaissance. The plants in the garden are botanically accurate. The angel's wings are based on observations of birds' wings.

Leonardo's use of perspective as a means to frame the human figure is brilliantly displayed in his mural master-

3.23

piece *The Last Supper* (fig. 3.24). Though damaged by his own ill-fated experiments with media and damaged further by dampness and the accidents of war, the fresco still retains a unique power.

The diagram in figure 3.25 shows how Leonardo, by locating the vanishing point behind the head of Christ, ingeniously framed the entire space of the scene on the central figure of Christ. Despite the agitated movements of the apostles—Christ has just announced that one of them would betray him—the symmetry of the architectural space surrounds Christ like a halo of order and calm. Christ is the controlling center, literally and psychologically, of the entire scene.

Leonardo took his use of perspective even further in order to have a powerful psychological effect on the viewer. *The Last Supper* is located in the dining room of a monastery, and Leonardo painted the life-size scene so that the monks at their meals would appear to be in the same space as the table of Christ and the apostles.

3.24

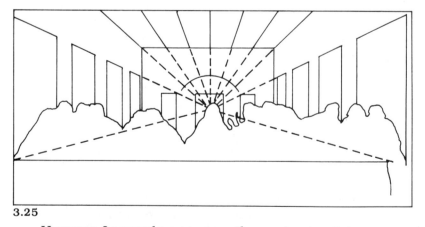

3.25

However, Leonardo was more than a great artist, more than a great scientist and engineer of legendary abilities. He was also a prophet of the modern, technological world we now inhabit. Uccello was fascinated by the transformation of a *mazzaccio* into a perspective image. Leonardo envisioned the transformation of the world itself—a transformation largely made possible, in science and technology as well as

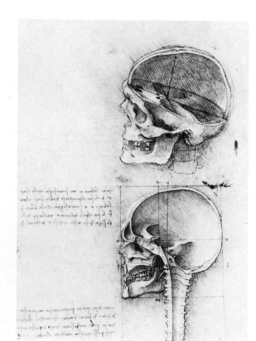

3.26

in art, by the power of the perspective image. Unlike Archimedes, the hero of Greek science, Leonardo not only had knowledge, he also had the desire to use it.

Along with several masterpieces of painting and his legend itself, Leonardo left over two thousand pages of notebook drawings and scribbled ideas that few people saw during his lifetime. It is the notebooks that suggest the full scope of his vision and ambition.

Leonardo's Notebooks: Images of Innocence, Wonder, and Power

His notebooks make abundantly clear that Leonardo was aware of the possibilities implicit in the emerging objective view of the world (fig. 3.26). The depth of his vision is especially clear in his drawings of the human body.

Leonardo describes for the reader his dissection of ten cadavers—five for the muscles and bones and five for the nerves and veins. The resultant drawings are amazing even today.

His method required that the body be "put into perspective." That is, he required himself to draw each part as if it existed in the isolated clarity of three-dimensional space.

Leonardo invented the "exploded drawing," which shows each part separated out slightly from its neighbor. This kind of drawing is familiar today to anyone who has tried to assemble a child's bicycle or a carburetor from a kit. Leonardo wanted to show how the "machine" of the body fit together.

The drawings apply the principle of objectivity like a searchlight exploring a world previously dark. He draws images of the inside of the body: the eye, the inner organs, the womb and the fetus, hypothetically constructed from the womb of a cow (fig. 3.27).

These drawings of the body also show the drawbacks of the perspective image, however. Objectivity requires the observer, at least temporarily, to regard the body as a machine or a mere object in three-dimensional space, an attitude that was unimaginable in Greek or medieval culture.

Leonardo and Technology: From Nature to Artifice

But Leonardo wanted more than a better understanding of nature; he wanted to change nature. The exultant Leonardo wrote not only that he wanted to "know the secrets of things," but also "I want to control rivers."[6] His technological drawings show how this can be done—through the linking of power with knowledge made possible by the perspective image.

After considering the body as a machine, he imagines machines in astonishing variety—an automated filemaker, an "auto-mobile," winged machines for flight (fig. 3.28). The

3.27 Leonardo da Vinci.
Child in the Womb. c. 1510.
Pen and ink.
Royal Collection, Windsor Castle. Copyright reserved. Reproduced by Gracious Permission of Her Majesty the Queen.

3.28 Leonardo da Vinci.
War Machines.
Pen and ink.
Royal Collection, Windsor Castle. Copyright reserved. Reproduced by Gracious Permission of Her Majesty the Queen.

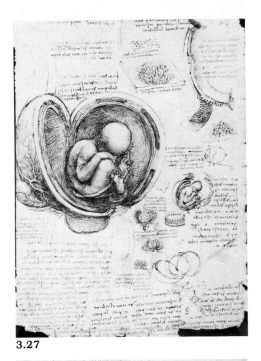

3.27

3.28

78

3.29

3.30

3.29 Leonardo da Vinci.
Mona Lisa. c. 1503–5.
Oil on panel, approx. 30″ × 21″.
The Louvre, Paris.

3.30 Leonardo da Vinci.
Drawing of a lion.
Chalk on paper.
Giraudon/Art Resource.

3.31 Michelangelo Buonarroti.
David. 1501–4.
Marble, height 18′.
Academy Gallery, Florence. (Photo:
Alinari/Art Resources).

power-multiplying devices emerge in a relentless stream of prophetically creative drawings. He sees nature opened up, examined, and then—true to the growing impulses of the age—improved upon. Leonardo is the true hero of the Perspective Age, just as the perspective image is its true icon: he is the hero who changes reality.

Leonardo's notebooks, even more than his painted masterpieces like *Mona Lisa* (fig. 3.29) or *The Last Supper,* show what might be called the "perspective mentality," that is, a way of thinking about reality based on the new viewpoint embodied in perspective:

The eye, which is called the window of the soul, is the chief means whereby the understanding may most fully and abundantly appreciate the infinite works of nature . . . [because] the painter employs the exact images of these forms in order to reproduce them.[7]

This is a perfect definition of objectivity—"the exact images of these forms." With this power, everything is possible. A comparison of Leonardo's drawing of a lion (fig. 3.30) with that of Villard de Honnecourt (fig. 2.37) shows how decisively the new perspective geometry links knowledge with power in a way impossible for the medieval form of geometric drawing. It is the difference between symbolism and objectivity. From this time on, the perspective-trained Western eye will increasingly regard nature as a kind of collection of detachable and movable parts to be rearranged on the chessboard of human purpose. The perspective image, by its very objectivity, encourages this attitude. In Leonardo's notebooks, nature is already beginning to drift out of the geometry of the sacred into the pragmatic geometry of industrial design.

Leonardo's notebooks provide some of the clearest evidence that our current technological society would be impossible to imagine without two powerful effects of the perspective image: first, its practical role as a kind of lever that moves forms away from their natural background toward the objectivity necessary for technological transformation and, second, its psychological effect of encouraging the sense of detachment or distance necessary for a person to effectively intervene in natural processes.

The sense of objectivity extended, in fact, to Leonardo's personality. In the introduction to his edited version of Leonardo's notebooks, Robert Linscott describes him as follows:

Leonardo's thirst was for knowledge of things and forces; never of people and events. In the whole vast manuscript there is virtually no mention of his outward life or the world in which he lived; of friends, of women, of fellow artists, or of the men for and with whom he worked.[8]

Today, this same objective mentality seen so clearly in Leonardo is a stereotype in movies about overspecialized scientists, technicians, and bureaucrats who see only the "objective facts" and not the full human situation.

Michelangelo Buonarroti (1475–1564): The Individual Becomes the Source of Creativity

If Leonardo's notebooks show the new Renaissance sense of objectivity, the art of Michelangelo Buonarroti shows the simultaneous growth of the effects of subjectivity and individualism on the creativity and the social role of the artist.

The early Perspective Age, despite its new emphasis on perception, still retained a sense of connection with the sacred through the underlying geometry of art. As Leonardo wrote in his notebooks, the perspective image made by the artist imitated and rivaled the creativity of God:

In art we may be said to be grandsons to God. . . . Have we not seen pictures which bear so close a resemblance to the actual thing that they have deceived both men and beasts?[9]

Michelangelo's art embodied the theory that the artist could approach the divine creativity, not by imitating the factual details of nature, but by changing the basic rules of art itself. In this way the artist imitates God's originality, since God created the cosmos out of nothing. The cosmos was a unique creation, not a copy. Michelangelo placed the essence of creativity within the artist's self. The artist's personal uniqueness, not fidelity to nature, became a new criterion for art.

Michelangelo explicitly criticized the emphasis on exact copying from nature in the oil paintings of northern European artists:

In Flanders they paint with a view to external exactness. . . . They paint stuffs and masonry, the green grass of the fields, the shadow of trees, and rivers and bridges, which they call landscapes. . . . And all this, though it pleases some persons, is done without reason or art, without symmetry or proportion.[10]

Michelangelo shared Alberti's belief that perspective in painting served primarily to enhance the human figure. To Michelangelo, all that was needed was the human figure itself.

Even though he described himself as a sculptor and resisted the efforts even of powerful popes like Julius II to enlist his talents as a painter, his painted frescoes in the Sistine Chapel are as famous as his sculptures. These unique frescoes can only be understood in terms of his sculpture and in terms of the new subjective concept of creativity that they came to embody.

Michelangelo's early masterpiece *David* (1501–1504) reveals the artist's mastery of proportion and anatomy (fig. 3.31). Behind the statue of David are years of drawing the human body, including knowledge gained from the dissection of several cadavers. *David* is a dramatic artistic realization of this knowledge. Except for the size of the hands, the figure has the classical Greek proportion rooted in accurate detail

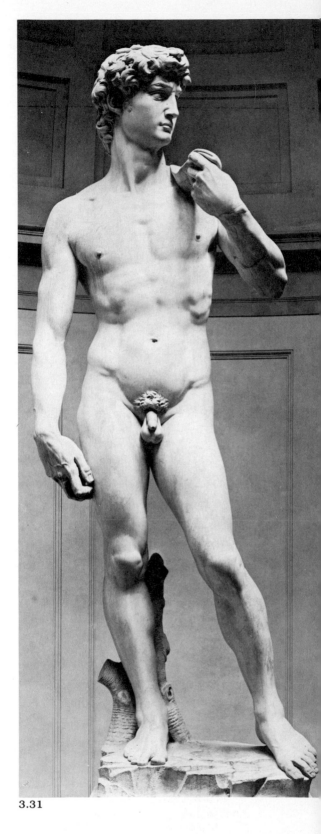

3.31

that characterizes Renaissance art. *David* is Michelangelo's striking embodiment of an individual capable of heroic action in the present world, reflecting the European mood of optimism only a decade after the discovery of America. *David,* in the spirit of the Renaissance flowering of science and art, confidently appraises the horizons of the natural world. In 1504, Europeans looked forward to a dawning golden age of human achievement and prosperity.

Michelangelo's *Moses:* Changing the Rules of Art

Michelangelo's next major project after *David* was his statue *Moses* (fig. 3.32), one of the major sculptures from the tomb of Pope Julius II. The original plans called for the tomb to sit behind the altar in the new Basilica of Saint Peter in Rome, and it was to have over forty figures carved by Michelangelo. The project would have taken a lifetime of work to complete, but it was postponed, and finally canceled, when the more pressing concerns of the Protestant Reformation began to require attention.

In this sculpture Michelangelo discarded the realistic proportion and accurate anatomy he had so clearly mastered. Unlike *David,* with its superb athletic form, *Moses* has no verifiable connection with the world of ordinary experience. *Moses* took on the awesome form of a creature who could never exist, a form put together according to new rules of anatomy derived from the artist's own subjective ideas and feelings. Michelangelo's Titan-like statue provides for the viewer an experience that a more proportional or realistic figure would not: a sense of awesome power that goes beyond the visible and the ordinary.

Most important is that the creativity of the artist is the norm used by Michelangelo to make the art, not the rules of proportion and realistic appearances analogous to perspective. *Moses* is not a scale model; it is Michelangelo's unique creation.

Michelangelo applied the same creative subjectivity to all his subsequent painted and sculpted figures. Whether decorative symbolic figures like *Day* from the Medici tomb in Florence or the famous *Adam* (fig. 3.33) on the ceiling of the Sistine Chapel in Rome, the human figures take their shape and form from the artist's imagination. The response of public and patrons was clear. In his own day, Michelangelo's creativity was given the highest possible praise. He was described by the adjective *divino,* "divine."

Michelangelo's *Last Judgment:* Changing the Meaning of Art

Michelangelo's radically subjective creativity was applied not only to the form of his figures, but also to the content or

3.32

3.32 Michelangelo Buonarroti.
Moses. 1513–15.
Marble, approx. 8′4″ high.
San Pietro in Vincoli, Rome. Photo: Vatican Museums.

3.33 Michelangelo Buonarroti.
Adam (Sistine Chapel ceiling).
1508–12.
Fresco.
Photo: Vatican Museums.

3.34 Michelangelo Buonarroti.
The Last Judgment. 1534–41.
Fresco on the wall of the Sistine Chapel.
Photo: Vatican Museums.

3.35 Michelangelo Buonarroti.
Self-portrait (detail from *The Last Judgment* fresco).
Photo: Vatican Museums.

3.33

themes he used in his art. His *Last Judgment* fresco on the wall behind the altar of the Sistine Chapel (fig. 3.34), for instance, is a bold, startling departure from traditional Last Judgment scenes from the Middle Ages and does not even reflect traditional Catholic theology. The scene reflects, instead, Michelangelo's personal reaction to the troubles that, by the 1530s, had divided Europe into hostile and sometimes warring religious factions. Michelangelo looked upon his earlier enthusiasm for the "pagan" art of antiquity as his personal contribution to the religious strife that racked Western culture.

Instead of Christ the serene, just Judge, Michelangelo presents a vengeful, aggressive Christ who is apparently rising from his seat in order to personally inflict, not only judgment, but punishment. Mary, traditionally an image of hope at the moment of judgment, cannot even bear to look at the impending decree of doom. All this is the more striking when one remembers that the fresco was done in the Sistine Chapel, the pope's private chapel.

Michelangelo has included himself in this judgment by placing a self-portrait in the fresco. Figure 3.35 shows a distorted image of Michelangelo as the skinned face of Saint Bartholomew. Van Eyck's self-portrait in *Giovanni Arnolfini and His Bride* (fig. 3.17) painted a century earlier, is evidence that including such a self-portrait inside a work of art is not unique. What is unique is the highly personal statement made by the position of the self-portrait. Michelangelo places himself among the saved, but he expresses his own sense of guilt and remorse by choosing such a bizarre context for his face.

This somewhat grisly detail only underscores what is already apparent: Michelangelo is freely expressing his feelings and ideas—his own personality—at every level of his art,

3.34

3.35

from its formal structure to its subject matter. He is in this way a forerunner of the modern avant-garde, with its emphasis on the personality of the artist as an integral part of the meaning of the work of art.

In a larger sense, the direction of Michelangelo's work balances the objectivity seen in Leonardo's notebooks. The growing experience and conviction of the Perspective Age was that every individual's approach to the world is highly subjective, even though it begins with the objective world presented to the eye. Giovanni Pico della Mirandola, a theologian and philosopher who lived at the same time as Michelangelo and Leonardo, became well known for expressing the same truth in his paraphrase of the biblical account of the creation:

We have given thee, Adam, no fixed seat, no form of thy very own . . . a limited nature in other creatures is confined within the law written down by Us . . . thou are confined by no bounds; and thou wilt fix limits of nature for thyself. I have placed thee at the center of the world. Thou . . . art the molder and maker of thyself; thou mayest sculpt thyself into whatever shape thou dost prefer.[11]

This description, whether or not it fits Adam, certainly fits—in different ways—the personalities of Leonardo and Michelangelo. But the individualism in these two artists was not isolated or eccentric. The experience of the subjective individual at the center of an objective world was the iconic experience that penetrated all areas of Western culture, from politics to science, from art to religion.

The artistic works of geniuses like Leonardo and Michelangelo give the most enduring and powerful experience of this new cultural image of the human being. Nevertheless, a novel yet equally powerful cultural force carried the same iconic experience far beyond the audience who might see *The Last Supper* or the frescoes in the Sistine Chapel. The same experience of individual subjectivity and visual objectivity was embodied in the emerging Renaissance version of a mass medium: printed pictures.

Printed Pictures: Mass Medium Technology of the Perspective Age

The printing of books from movable type dates from the same period as Brunelleschi's discovery of perspective. Yet the printing of words was only half of the mass media revolution that began in the Renaissance. Printed pictures were the other half.

A printed picture is one that can be multiplied without any change from the original image. During the fifteenth and sixteenth centuries, printed pictures took three forms: woodcuts, etchings, and engravings (see Basic Printmaking Processes in the color section.)

The first printed picture technology used in the West was the woodblock. It probably originated in China, spread to the Near East, and was brought to Europe during the Crusades. At first it was used principally for pictures of the saints and for playing cards.

By the end of the fifteenth century, artists began to use woodcuts, etchings, and engravings for perspective images. The impact of these mass-produced perspective images can be compared to the impact of the mass-produced words of the printed Bible: they gradually but inevitably changed people's expectations and outlook on all aspects of life. The greatest printmaker of the Renaissance was the German artist Albrecht Dürer. His work illustrates the wide range of influence printed images had on the culture of the Perspective Age.

Albrecht Dürer (1471–1528): Printed Images as Fine Art

Albrecht Dürer tried to combine the Italian love of the idealized human figure with his own Northern love for natural detail. Although his earliest works show the flat space of medieval art, Dürer admired the new technique of perspective so much that he became a master of it, and through his etchings, engravings, and woodcuts, he also became its chief advocate throughout Europe. Dürer's woodcut *Man Drawing a Lute* (fig. 3.36) is from a book he wrote on perspective. This woodcut not only illustrates principles of perspective, it also shows an early form of mechanizing the perspective tech-

3.36 Albrecht Dürer.
Man Drawing a Lute. 1525.
Woodcut illustration from *The Artist's Treatise on Geometry.* 1525.
Metropolitan Museum of Art, New York, Harris Brisbane Dick Fund.

3.36

3.37

nique that was developed long before photography. The print documents the eagerness of Western artists to invent and use machines that would help create perspective images.

Dürer made prints for purposes other than information; he became one of the most skilled and versatile printmakers in the history of Western art. His engraving *Saint Jerome in His Study* (fig. 3.37), though not totally accurate in its perspective (the potted plant hanging from the ceiling, for instance, is shown at too steep an angle), is one of his print masterpieces. The space is centered on the heroic figure of the saint. The subtle range of dark and light tones creates a mood of serenity that reflects the saint's contemplative absorption in Scripture. Notice the shadows from the pattern of the bottle-glass windows on the window frames and sills.

This print also illustrates the distinction between fine art and popular art that began to take form at this time. Printed images of scenes from the lives of saints were popular from the time that the woodcut was introduced into Western Europe in the late Middle Ages. Like today's posters and

3.37 Albrecht Dürer.
St. Jerome in His Study.
Engraving, 9¹¹⁄₁₆″ × 7⁵⁄₁₆″.
Cleveland Museum of Art, Purchase,
Leonard C. Hanna, Jr., Bequest.

3.38 Michelangelo Buonarroti.
Studies for the Libyan Sibyl.
Red chalk drawing, 11⅜″ × 8⅜″.
Metropolitan Museum of Art, New York,
Purchase, 1924, Joseph Pulitzer Bequest.

3.38

picture magazines, woodcuts presented images of heroes that almost anyone could afford; they were sold at fairs "one penny plain, two penny colored."

Many artists, like Dürer, made prints that demonstrated the same skill and sense of personal vision as the more valuable oil paintings. In fact, artists often made prints on the same themes as their famous paintings, and these were collected by upper middle class and wealthy buyers. During this period, even drawings and sketches made as preliminary studies became valued in themselves. Figure 3.38 is one of Michelangelo's sketches for a figure on the ceiling of the Sistine Chapel.

As the public art sponsored by the Church began to decline in importance, the division between fine art and popular art became even more significant. Oil paintings and prints by famous artists tended to be displayed in private spaces, like palaces or the homes of the affluent. This distinction between fine art and popular art grew until the mass media of the twentieth century again enabled fine art and popular art to share the same public space.

The main impact of printed images did not stem from art, however. It was the cumulative impact of all the informative, technical, entertaining, and artistic images together that was important. Their wide distribution and their common base in perspective gradually taught all classes of people to expect a new level of factual detail in images, and this expectation applied to all images, whatever their primary purpose.

William Ivins, former curator of prints at the Metropolitan Museum of Art in New York, is the man who drew attention to the impact of printed pictures, an impact that goes far beyond that of the masterpieces that we today honor as fine art in museums.

The printing of pictures, however, unlike the printing of words from movable types, brought a completely new thing into existence. . . . It is hardly too much to say that since the invention of writing there has been no more important invention than that of the exactly repeatable pictorial statement.[12]

Irvins noted that the great Greek philosopher Aristotle took a team of artists on one of Alexander the Great's campaigns so that he could collect and disseminate drawings of plants from countries far away from Greece. His project was abandoned when it turned out that these drawings, when copied from other drawings instead of from the actual plant, quickly lost their accuracy of detail.

The problem was something like the game of Rumor played at parties. The first person whispers something to the next person. That person then whispers what he or she has heard to the next person, and so on around the room. The humor in the game comes when the final person repeats the rumor, which is seldom anything remotely like the original whispered message. The Greek artists' copied drawings became more and more like mere "rumors" of the plants. This lack of a technique for printing pictures might have been itself enough to stall Greek science at this point even if no other factors had blocked its development.

Figure 3.39 is an example of the kind of image that resulted from copying other drawings. Figure 3.40 shows a *printed* image based on an original drawing of a plant. This Renaissance combination of drawing with printmaking technology achieved the goal that had eluded the Greeks: scientifically accurate illustration. This kind of drawing and printing of images was a major factor behind the explosive growth of Western science that took on increased momentum during the sixteenth century.

Figure 3.41 shows how printed pictures affected the kinds of images seen in Leonardo's notebooks. The Flemish artist who cut this image, Stephen of Calcar, had probably seen some examples of Leonardo's anatomical drawings. He worked under the direction of the Flemish anatomist Andreas Vesalius at the University of Padua in Italy in the 1530s. His woodcuts neatly summarize the continuity of the Western artistic tradition at this point in the Perspective Age. The gracefully posed figures take their heroic attitudes from the tradition of Italian painting, which goes back to Greek art. Perspective gives the landscape further artistic value, as it simultaneously gives the peeled-away musculature of the figures the objectivity required by science.

3.39 Anonymous
Plaintain.
Woodcut illustration from *Gart der Gesuntheyt.* Mainz. 1485.
Metropolitan Museum of Art, New York, The Elisha Whittelsey Collection.

3.40 Hans Weiditz.
Woodcut illustration. Brunfels *Herbarium Vivae.* 1530.
Metropolitan Museum of Art, New York, Gift of Mortimer L. Schiff.

3.41 Vesalius.
Muscle Men. From *De Humani Corporis Fabrica.* 1543.
Metropolitan Museum of Art, New York, Gift of New York Academy of Medicine, 1947.

3.42 Michael Wolgemut.
Mantua. Woodcut from *Nuremberg Chronicle.* 1493.
Metropolitan Museum of Art, New York, Rogers Fund, 1921.

3.39

3.40

Printed pictures also began to circulate to a wide public images of general information and entertainment, forming, during the Renaissance, the base of our modern system of mass media information, entertainment, and popular art images. One example of the growing demand for fact in pictures in general during the Renaissance is the illustrations for travel books, which, like printed maps, became immensely popular during the Perspective Age.

The woodcut images of distant cities in these early books were as vague as the woodcuts of plants in the first herbals. Like the medieval *mappa mundi,* they were the result of hearsay. The *Nuremberg Chronicle* of 1493, for instance, had hundreds of woodcut illustrations, but one particular woodcut was used for at least eleven cities. The same woodcut (fig. 3.42) was used for *Mantua* and *Damascus.* Similarly today, in the Saturday-morning cartoons on television, only the faces and arms change, the background stays the same. And like today's cartoon fans, few people at the end of the fifteenth century minded—or even noticed.

But times were already changing. Breydenbach's *Peregrinationes (Travels),* which was published in 1486, shows the changing expectations resulting from perspective images: its woodcuts of cities were so accurate that Venice required a foldout that extended over six feet in length (fig. 3.43).

The landscape paintings of the Greek and Roman tradition have the beautiful but ephemeral qualities of a dream.

3.42

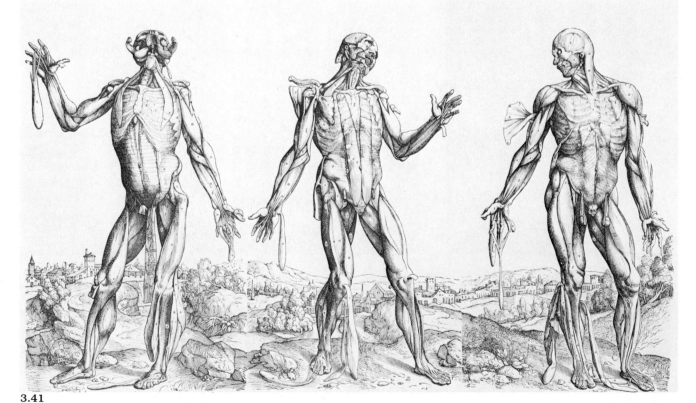

3.41

3.43

3.44a

Medieval scenes are symbolic accessories to the main story. The woodcut scene of Venice, reflecting the main direction of all fine art and popular art images of the Renaissance, is anchored in fact. *The Fall and Redemption of Man* (fig. 3.44), by Albrecht Altdorfer (1480–1538), shows the same sense of factual detail applied to a popular religious woodcut (Altdorfer's print also provides an early example of the serial narrative format that is basic to both modern comic books and movies). The emerging mass media was spreading this new level of perception and this new expectation that perspective images could be not only art but also science—or news.

Thus, centuries before newspaper and magazine photography would dramatically magnify the same process, people during the Renaissance were being taught to see the perspective image as the most real kind of picture in the world. The picture it gave was of an objective world.

3.44b

3.44c

3.44d

3.43 Erhardt Reuwich.
View of Venice. Woodcut illustration from Breydenbach's *Peregrinationes* (Travels). 1486.
Metropolitan Museum of Art, New York, Rogers Fund.

3.44 Albrecht Altdorfer.
The Fall and Redemption of Man, Nos. 16, 18, 21, 22 (scenes from the Passion). c. 1515.
Woodcut.
Cleveland Museum of Art, Purchase, John L. Severance Fund.

ASSESSMENTS

1. Are you familiar with a "pinhole" camera? Have you made one, or looked through one?
2. How do eyeglasses, telescopes, binoculars, microscopes, and cameras become "extensions" of the person who uses them? In what sense can a machine be considered an extension of a person—when does a person become an extension of a machine?
3. Can you recall any commercials, movies, or television shows that invite the viewer to experience a machine or other technology as a personal experience?
4. Think of a building as a form of enclosed space. What buildings have you enjoyed being in? What personal feelings were evoked by this sense of space?
5. What does the word *romanticism* mean to you? How do you relate this word to art?

A meaningful date for the beginning of the second half of the Perspective Age is the year 1610. The drawing of the moon shown in figure 4.1 was done in that year by the Italian scientist Galileo Galilei. Like Brunelleschi's painting, this image was startlingly new. It is a drawing of the moon as seen, for the first time, through a telescope.

4.1

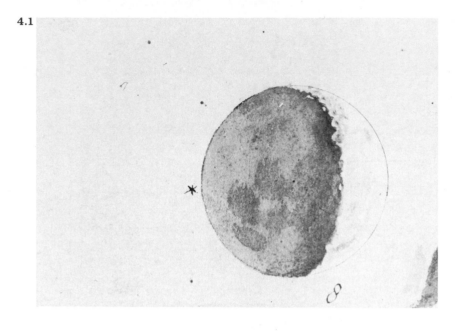

4.1 Galileo Galilei.
Drawing of the Moon. c. 1610.
Biblioteca Nazionale Centrale, Florence.

4.2 Michelangelo da Caravaggio.
The Deposition.
Oil on canvas.
Photo: Vatican Museums.

The Telescope and Western Art: The Artist Confronts the New Cosmos

Galileo's little drawing had as powerful an effect on perception and art as Brunelleschi's first perspective painting. The Greek/medieval/Renaissance picture of the cosmos had posited perfectly round planets—including the moon. Galileo's drawing presented the rude shock of mountains wrinkling the lunar surface. The position of the earth in this new picture of the cosmos was even more shocking: instead of being the motionless center of the cosmos, it moved.

The space of the cosmos also affected the space of art. The stable perspective space that framed the human figures in the paintings of Bellini, Leonardo, van Eyck, and other Renaissance artists had also symbolized the central importance of the individual human being. Like the sacred geometry of Greek and medieval art, Renaissance perspective confirmed the importance of the earth and of human perception itself within the cosmic order.

Artists in the second half of the Perspective Age continued to keep the human being at the center of art. They did this by creating a new sense of artistic space—they made perspective, like the earth, begin to move and take on a dynamic new relationship to the viewer.

The new vision of the cosmos came just as Europe was recovering from the turmoil of religious wars that had divided the continent into Catholic and Protestant regions.

In Catholic countries the new space of art was applied to churches in a way that continued and culminated the tradition of the medieval cathedral. In northern Europe the new dynamic perspective created new kinds of art that reflected the early phases of democracy, capitalism, and the rise of the middle class.

In Catholic Europe, the most influential painter of the seventeenth century was Michelangelo da Caravaggio.

Michelangelo da Caravaggio (1573–1610): The Infinite Cosmos Becomes a Subjective Vision

Seventeenth-century art was originally called Baroque—ornate, extravagant, grandiose—in contrast to the stable, balanced art of the fifteenth and sixteenth centuries. The term *baroque* is now used in a positive sense; it accepts the dramatic exploration of light, space, composition, and human emotion of seventeenth-century art as a major achievement. The work of Michelangelo da Caravaggio introduced the Baroque spirit into painting. His art inspired Baroque painters in northern and southern Europe by dramatically shifting the vanishing point toward the spectator. Renaissance artists like Leonardo, Bellini, and van Eyck used the central vanishing point to create a stable, balanced image. Caravaggio shifted the vanishing point, the light source, and the main character in the action away from the center of the painting. His paintings brought the viewer into the scene with some of the boldness that we now experience with the moving angle shots used by cameras in movie and television productions.

The Deposition (Christ taken down from the cross) shows how Caravaggio's use of a below-center vanishing point produced a dramatic encounter between the viewer and Christ (fig. 4.2). Instead of being placed in an idealized central position, the viewer is placed below the scene and watches the awkward attempt to remove the body of Christ for burial. The rough, homely features of the peasant holding Christ's legs and the plain, ordinary clothing of the grief-stricken women add to the immediacy of the scene. The less stable point of view forces the viewer's eye to move continuously within the scene and gives the painting its momentary, almost journalistic quality. Compared with the static idealized figures and central space of Renaissance paintings, *The Deposition* seems like a still photograph from a documentary.

Caravaggio's use of ordinary people in ordinary dress also decreased the psychological distance between the special space of the painting and the private space of the individual believer.

4.2

92

The iconic impact of his work was especially important at the beginning of the seventeenth century. Catholic art at this time sought to provide a greater sense of personal involvement for believers, similar to that offered by the Protestant approach of individual interpretation of the Bible. Catholic art sought ways to combine the long tradition of communal art in churches with the new need for a greater sense of the personal.

A dynamic new use of space is clearly seen in the architecture of the Basilica of Saint Peter in Rome.

The Basilica of Saint Peter (1506–1667): Connecting Renaissance and Baroque

The Basilica of Saint Peter is one of the architectural masterpieces of the Perspective Age. It is especially important because its construction spanned the Renaissance and Baroque periods and absorbed their different outlooks. Though many important artists were involved in completing the structure, two artists gave Saint Peter's its definitive form: Michelangelo designed the dome and central church, and Giovanni Lorenzo Bernini (1598–1680), the greatest sculptor and architect of the Baroque, designed the piazza and colonnade.

The photograph in figure 4.3 is a view of Saint Peter's

4.3 Aerial view of Basilica of Saint Peter, colonnade and piazza.

4.4 Diagram of the development of St. Peter's basilica. (a) Bramante's circular design; (b) Michelangelo's cruciform revision of Bramante's design; (c) Maderna's extension of Michelangelo's design by lengthening the central aisle (nave); (d) Bernini's colonnade and piazza; (e) Bernini's adjustment of colonnade; (f) Sistine Chapel.

4.3

from Bernini's piazza. The diagram in figure 4.4 shows the floor plan. The first phase of Saint Peter's (*a*) reflects the stable, central perspective of the Renaissance. Plans for the church were originally drawn up by the Renaissance architect Donato Bramante (1444–1514). Michelangelo later changed Bramante's design to a more traditional cathedral (cross-shaped) form (*b*) in order to quiet criticism that the circular design was too much like certain ancient Greek and Roman temples.

Another architect, Carlo Maderna (1556–1629) added the extension (*c*), which gave a more traditional emphasis to the length of the central aisle, or nave.

Bernini designed the final section of Saint Peter's—the piazza and enormous colonnade (*d*) that opened the basilica up in a sweeping movement toward the world outside the church. The massive new space of this addition shattered the architectural similarity of Saint Peter's to Renaissance central perspective and brought its architectural form into the dynamic space of the Baroque.

To keep the immensity of the architectural space from overwhelming the viewer, Bernini designed the wings of the colonnade, which connect the front of Saint Peter's with the oval piazza, to converge toward the viewer (*e*). This adjustment makes the front of the church appear closer to the approaching individual. This is only one of several details of Saint Peter's in which Bernini used his knowledge of perspective to adjust the building to the moving position of the spectator.

The final result of more than a century of building was a spectacular architectural statement that anchored Catholicism in its ancient and medieval traditions (the basilica is built on the presumed burial site of Saint Peter). At the same time, its innovative form looked toward the horizons of the new age with a triumphant, if grandiose, embrace.

Andrea dal Pozzo (1642–1709): Fusing the Space of Architecture with the Space of Painting

The ultimate example of Catholic Baroque art adjusting architecture to the eye of the individual is seen in the work of Fra Andrea dal Pozzo.

Figure 4.5 shows the ceiling of the church of Sant' Ignazio in Rome; its fresco, *The Glorification of Saint Ignatius,* is an amazing feat of perspective. Pozzo, who wrote a treatise on perspective applied to ceilings, created the illusion that the architecture of the church continues up into the unbounded space of the heavens.

This space, however, is occupied. Saint Ignatius is seen being carried into the presence of Christ. The illusionistic effect includes figures whose top halves are painted on the ceiling and whose bottom halves, sculpted in three dimension, reach down from the ceiling onto the walls of the church.

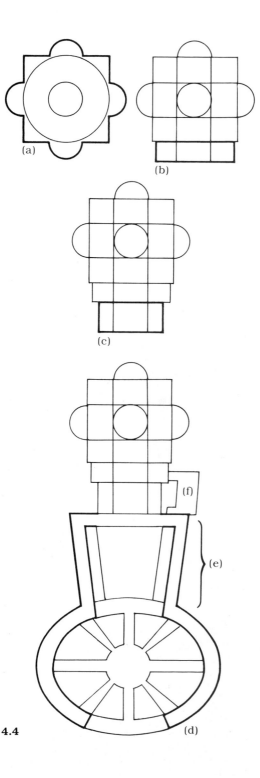

4.4

4.5

4.5 Fra Andrea Pozzo.
The Glorification of Saint Ignatius.
1691–94.
Ceiling fresco in the nave of Sant'
Ignazio, Rome.
Alinari/Art Resource.

4.6 Rembrandt van Rijn.
Hundred-Guilder Print.
Etching, 27.8 × 38.9 cm.
Metropolitan Museum of Art, New York,
Bequest of Mrs. H. O. Havemeyer, 1929. The
H. O. Havemeyer Collection.

4.7 Rembrandt van Rijn.
Christ Preaching to the Poor. c. 1652.
Etching, drypoint.
Cleveland Museum of Art, Gift of the Print
Club of Cleveland in honor of William
Mathewson Milliken.

Pozzo used his virtuoso technique for the specific purpose of transforming an image of infinite space into a personal vision for the viewer: A marker on the floor locates the spot precisely below the vanishing point of the painted image on the ceiling; by standing on this spot the viewer becomes the subjective focus of the vision of Paradise.

It is quite appropriate that this highly illusionistic vision focuses on Saint Ignatius, who was not only a hero of the Catholic Counter-Reformation (he died in 1556) but also devised a new technique of meditation based on visualizing mental pictures of Gospel scenes that were, in effect, perspective images. Bernini himself used this same form of meditation. This form of meditation and this form of art had the same purpose: to place the individual "in the scene" with Christ.

Sant' Ignazio is only one example among similar churches built in Catholic countries of Europe well into the eighteenth century. The visionary ensembles of architecture, painting, and sculpture created by Pozzo and other Baroque artists brilliantly culminated the icon tradition of the medieval cathedral. While continuing to combine all the arts into a public and communal form, they also met the more individualistic needs of seventeenth-century Western culture—they turned the cathedral itself into a gigantic oil painting focused on the subjective individual.

The art of northern Europe during the seventeenth century took on qualities that reflected the changes brought about by the Reformation. Art in Protestant areas, for instance, broke with the tradition of public church art and explored ways to express a new religious outlook. Northern art did not deal with visionary experiences; it found the sacred reflected in everyday life. This approach continued and expanded the tradition of detailed attention to daily life seen in van Eyck's *Giovanni Arnolfini and His Bride* (see fig. 3.17).

The art of Holland is the Baroque art that points most clearly toward modern times. The Dutch masters of the seventeenth century painted pictures that illuminate the emerging forces of capitalism, technology, and middle class political democracy and reveal with special clarity the modern sense of individualism that underlies these cultural changes. This new sense of individualism is especially evident in the art of Rembrandt van Rijn.

Rembrandt van Rijn (1606–1669): The Subjective Cosmos of the Human Personality

Rembrandt's work represents the new Protestant emphasis on the individual as clearly as the art of Caravaggio and Pozzo represents seventeenth-century Catholicism. Specifically, Rembrandt's art is a unique visual interpretation of the Bible in terms of his own personal experience. His art documents how his reading of the Bible transformed his experience of life.

Rembrandt's paintings are of relatives and friends as biblical figures. His etchings were equally rooted in his everyday life; he filled his scenes from the Gospels with the figures he was constantly sketching on his walks through the streets of Amsterdam.

In one of Rembrandt's best known etchings, the "Hundred-Guilder Print" (fig. 4.6), he shows the sick emerging from the darkness toward the luminous figure of Christ. Though the dramatic space and light are derived from Caravaggio, Rembrandt transforms them to produce a sense of intimacy instead of grandeur. A later etching of the same theme is even simpler. In this print, *Christ Preaching to the Poor* (fig. 4.7), Rembrandt emphasizes the power of Christ's words—most of the listeners, rapt in what they are hearing, do not even look at Christ's face.

If Saint Ignatius and Fra Pozzo used perspective to create personal visions, Rembrandt's etchings brought his private and highly personal meditations to the new middle-class public made possible by the revolution of printed pictures. His etchings, like private sermons, hung on domestic walls.

The unparalleled sense of intimacy in Rembrandt's work can be seen even more vividly in his lifelong series of self-portraits

Rembrandt's self-portraits disclose the subjective dimen-

4.6

4.7

4.8

sion of the human personality to a degree never before achieved in Western art. In a way that approaches the revelatory boldness of Galileo's first drawing of the moon, they open up a correspondingly unique sense of the space occupied by the individual self.

Rembrandt used his own face, in Leonardo's phrase, as the "mirror of the soul." He painted over fifty self-portraits, from adolescence to old age. These faces explore and chart his initial joy and success, and then his eventual tragic impoverishment. In his self-portraits, he records each phase with an equally searching and sensitive eye.

The succession of portraits, like a succession of stills from a movie, reveals his life in a few glances: the self-conscious romanticism of youth (fig. 4.8) becomes the smug pride of his successful early artistic career (fig. 4.9) and his happy marriage to Saskia van Uijlenburgh, a beautiful woman of substantial wealth.

Saskia's tragic early death, however, brought more than grief into Rembrandt's life. A codicil to her will specified that he could not remarry without forfeiting his inheritance. Because of economic crisis in Holland and Rembrandt's own refusal to comply with popular taste in painting, he was earning only a low income from his art and desperately needed Saskia's wealth for survival. Rembrandt's sternly

4.9

4.11

4.10

quizzical eye in a mid-forties self-portrait (fig. 4.10) reflects the impact of Saskia's untimely death and the subsequent social condemnation of his decision to live with his unmarried housekeeper, Hendrickje Stoffels.

Rembrandt's self-portrait at 46 (fig. 4.11) is a study in open-eyed suffering: he is bankrupt. Yet his face almost seems to glare defiance at the poverty that he carefully illustrates by the tear in the shoulder of his cloak. By the age of 53 (fig. 4.12), Rembrandt had endured the auctioning of his property and possessions, including his Bible. Within two years, his poverty and debts forced him to form a partnership with Hendrickje and his son, Titus, that gave them legal control over any income from his work. The final tragedies were the death of Hendrickje in 1662 and Titus in 1668. Yet Rembrandt's final searching images of his own face show a mood of serenity, a mood totally lacking in bitterness or self-pity (fig. 4.13 and plate 6). One of his final portraits shows how he lived out his life anchored in his role as painter (fig. 4.14). He is seated like a king; his left hand holds his painter's stick like a royal scepter.

Rembrandt's self-portraits revealing the stages of his journey through life are in one sense, his finest religious images—his art and conviction transform his face into the face of Everyman.

4.8 Rembrandt van Rijn.
Self-portrait in a Cap, Staring. 1630.
Etching, 2″ × 1⅞″.
Rijksmuseum, Amsterdam.

4.9 Rembrandt van Rijn.
Portrait of the Artist as a Young Man. 1629.
Oil on canvas, 14⅞″ × 11⅜″.
Mauritshuis, The Hague.

4.10 Rembrandt van Rijn.
Self-portrait. 1650.
Oil on canvas, 36¼″ × 29¾″.
National Gallery of Art, Washington, Widener Collection, 1942.

4.12

4.13

4.14

4.11 Rembrandt van Rijn.
Self-portrait. 1652.
Oil on canvas, 45″ × 32″.
Kunsthistorisches Museum, Vienna.

4.12 Rembrandt van Rijn.
Self-portrait. 1659.
Oil on canvas, 33¼″ × 26″.
National Gallery of Art, Washington, Andrew W. Mellon Collection, 1937.

4.13 Rembrandt van Rijn.
Self-portrait. c. 1660.
Oil on canvas, 45″ × 37″.
The Greater London Council as Trustees of the Iveagh Bequest, Kenwood.

4.14 Rembrandt van Rijn.
Self-portrait. 1658.
Oil on canvas.
Copyright The Frick Collection, New York.

Seventeenth-Century Dutch Art: The New Social Portrait of Democracy

The art of seventeenth-century Holland not only brought a more private and individual touch to religious themes, it also brought portraits, still lifes, landscapes, and genre scenes (scenes of everyday life) into new prominence. These paintings were sold in a modern capitalist system: most artists specialized in one kind of painting and then sold to individuals on an open market at shops, studios, and fairs. Individual buyers took paintings home for private enjoyment. Paintings were hung on walls beside etchings, maps, and other kinds of printed images.

Portraiture was an especially popular form of painting. Frans Hals (c. 1581–1666) was a master of the highly lucrative trade of group portraiture. In *Archers of Saint Adrian* (fig. 4.15), Hals shows the pride and power of the new middle class. Many of the group portraits of the seventeenth century feature veterans of the Dutch wars of independence from Spain. The *Archers of Saint Adrian* can be compared to a picture of a convivial modern veterans' group enjoying their middle-aged prosperity. In Hals's picture, each face is painted with a sensitive and animated presence. Other artists who specialized in the profitable group portraits like this one produced works with a flattering smoothness that resembles today's airbrushed high-school yearbook photographs—understandable when one remembers that each sitter paid part of the artist's fee.

Hals's single portraits, however, give an individuality to the sitter that rivals the artist's own expressive touch with the brush. In contrast to the uniquely searching and intimate quality of Rembrandt's self-portraits, the portrait of Willem Coymans (fig. 4.16) exemplifies Hals's delight in revealing an individual's "public" face. The self-satisfied expression on that of Coyman is emphasized by the jaunty angle of his hat and the deliberately casual position of his elbow. Hals's own quick brush strokes on the sleeve and hand give the portrait a remarkable spontaneity despite the subject's fashionable clothing and sense of social rank.

4.16

4.15 Frans Hals.
Archers of Saint Adrian. 1627.
Oil on canvas, 103 × 266 cm.
Frans Halsmuseum, Haarlem.

4.16 Frans Hals.
Willem Coymans. 1645.
Oil on canvas, 30¼″ × 25″.
National Gallery of Art, Washington,
Andrew W. Mellon Collection.

4.15

Dutch artists also explored "genre" scenes of everyday life. David Teniers was a Flemish painter influenced by Dutch art. His *Peasants Celebrating Twelfth Night* (fig. 4.17) shows the unruly earthiness of peasants enjoying a holiday. The themes of these popular paintings bought by seventeenth-century middle-class patrons resemble those of sitcoms and other fictional portrayals of the poor in our popular arts today. They usually presented highly animated scenes populated by a picturesque, happy-go-lucky cast of characters. However, such paintings did bring the lower classes into art with a prominence that reflected the growing democratic impulse in Western culture.

Dutch artists also raised still lifes to a new level of significance. Despite the religious symbolism that often made each object in a still life a section of a sermon, Dutch still lifes brought an almost luxurious attention to the detailed material surfaces and textures of ordinary objects.

Willem Kalf (1619–1693) was one of Holland's masters of

4.17 David Teniers.
Peasants Celebrating Twelfth Night.
1635.
Oil on canvas, 18⅝″ × 27½″.
National Gallery of Art, Washington, Ailsa Mellon Bruce Fund.

4.18 Willem Kalf.
Still Life. c. 1665.
Oil on canvas, 25⅜″ × 21¼″.
National Gallery of Art, Washington. Gift of Chester Dale, 1943.

4.17

4.18

still life painting (fig. 4.18 and plate 7). Kalf reveals the effect of light as it is absorbed, relected, or partly trapped by the material surfaces it touches. Kalf's rendering of the textures of the cloth becomes a visual landscape that seems to defy the limits of ordinary observation. Note the light on the semiopaque glass of the knife handle and compare its translucency as it passes through the wine in the glass and the drops of water on the serving tray. Dutch still life painting distilled a richness and mystery like that of medieval stained glass windows. They became windows that captured the light of everyday objects.

The palpable materiality of these paintings also suggests the exuberance of Dutch capitalism, the growing sense of nature as a private possession of the individual, a commodity increasingly accessible to technology and marketing.

In many ways, these small paintings form a direct link with the new cosmos as the exploding ceilings of the Catholic Baroque. Their minute scale of observation comes out of increasing involvement with the scientific measurement of nature. The use of the microscope was pioneered by the Dutch, who were the best lens makers in Europe. Their fascination with observing nature through lenses extended to art as well. By using a device known as the camera obscura, Dutch artists took one more step toward uniting Western art and technology.

The Camera Obscura: A Mechanical Eye for the Artist

The camera obscura ("dark room") is a device based on a method of producing a natural image that was known in Roman times. A small hole in a box acts as a kind of natural lens by producing an upside-down image on the side of the box opposite the hole. Figure 4.19 shows a camera obscura large enough to hold a human being. This kind had been used both for amusement and for the study of optics since the Renaissance; by the sixteenth century, a lens was substituted for the pinhole. The image produced in this kind of camera obscura was used as an aid for artists.

The camera obscura available to Dutch artists of the seventeenth century not only had far better lenses, it also had mirrors inside the box that reinverted the image to right side up so that the viewer could see the subject in a viewfinder on top of the box. It was like a modern photographic camera in every major respect except that it did not use film.

This device was immensely superior to Dürer's device for making perspective images. It performed two important tasks for the artist: first, it reduced the size of the image to a convenient scale; second, it framed a two-dimensional image on the glass viewing plate, making it easy for the artist to study or trace images for his or her own artistic purposes.

A high degree of perfection and artistry in using the camera obscura as an aid in making perspective images is seen in the work of one of the greatest artists of the Perspective Age, Jan Vermeer.

Jan Vermeer (1632–1675): Painting the World Seen through the Lens

Though innumerable artists used the camera obscura to enhance their perception and/or to record their images for painting, Vermeer's work shows the most complete involvement with it as part of the artistic process. His paintings fuse the objective perspective of the lens with the creative perspective of the human eye.

Despite the unique quality of his work, little is known

4.19 *Camera Obscura.*
Engraving, illustration from Kircher's
"*Ars Magna.*" 1630.
Science Museum, London.

4.20 Jan Vermeer.
View of Delft. c. 1661.
Oil on canvas, 98 × 117.5 cm.
Mauritshuis, The Hague.

4.21 Jan Vermeer.
Officer and a Laughing Girl.
1658–60.
Oil on canvas, 19¾″ × 17½″.
Copyright The Frick Collection, New York.

4.19

4.20

about Vermeer himself. He did leave a detailed painting of the section of Delft where he lived (fig. 4.20), and many of his paintings show details of the interior of the house he lived in.

He was obviously known locally as an outstanding artist, and even had a reputation beyond Delft sufficient to attract a visit from a royal picture buyer. Vermeer's alleged reply to the buyer's request to purchase one of his paintings tells as much as is known about his character: he told the gentleman that he had no paintings to sell but recommended a man in town who might have something to offer—decidedly unambitious for a man who later had to declare bankruptcy!

To this anecdote add that fewer than forty Vermeers have survived, and it would seem that Vermeer painted perhaps two or three paintings a year throughout his career. Despite their obvious perfection of execution, this is hardly an output to parallel the kind of total dedication to art that their perfection of execution suggests. Such a rate of production seems hardly sufficient to keep his skills intact.

4.21

The style and thematic development of Vermeer's work over his lifetime, however, suggest that he may have made an early, unsuccessful bid for fame. His earliest works imitate the popular style of the day based on Caravaggio and earlier Dutch masters, but they also show distinct traces of the use of the camera obscura. The enlarged size of the soldier in *Officer and a Laughing Girl* (fig. 4.21), for instance, is a distortion typical of a camera lens, not the human eye.

By the early 1660s, however, a new pnase began that focused on two enduring and highly personal themes for Vermeer: the portrayal of light, and of women (or a woman) in an almost meditatively quiet interior. His style is at once the height of personal sensitivity and privacy and the height of a strangely distant objectivity. The camera obscura helped him combine these two themes into a painting style that is unique in the history of Western art.

The Lacemaker (fig. 4.22) is a masterpiece from this second phase of Vermeer's work. A close examination shows the unmistakable trace of the camera obscura lens: sprinkled around the surface of this small painting are numerous pearl-like dots. These are the so-called circles of confusion—little unfocused beads of light produced by the imperfectly ground lenses of Vermeer's day. They are not an aspect of normal vision. Another painting from this period, *The Girl with the Red Hat* (plate 8), reveals an even more splendid exploration of light.

The interesting thing about these "circles of confusion" in Vermeer's paintings is that there are more of them than would be caused by the lens itself. Vermeer, in other words, not only painted an effect that is not part of normal human vision, he liked it so much that he chose to manipulate it in his paintings as an extension of his personal perception.

Vermeer's involvement with the camera obscura shows how sight itself was coming under increasing human control. The extreme, almost photographic, objectivity of his paintings might also explain why they did not achieve popularity in his own lifetime. Vermeer's painting apparently struck the people of his day as *too* objective. The emotion, unlike that in more popular Dutch art, was too far below the surface. The art historian Lawrence Gowing has theorized:

The rediscovery of Vermeer was hardly possible until photography had demonstrated and popularized the artistic value of the optical image and painting had turned again, with a different view and purpose, towards light as a medium of reporting.[1]

Vermeer would be rediscovered after photography had given "objective" images a dramatically new importance and meaning.

The impending mechanization of art suggested by the use of the camera obscura in seventeenth-century art was not an isolated or accidental development. It paralleled the broad impact of technology in all areas of Western culture. A decisive phase of acceleration began in the eighteenth century. If the seventeenth century was dominated by the sense of the *space* of the new cosmos, the eighteenth century came to be dominated by the new sense of the cosmos as a *machine*.

The Eighteenth Century: The Transition to a Machine Cosmos

The cosmos revealed by the telescope was not just a larger space filled with more stars; it also obeyed different laws. As formulated by Sir Isaac Newton (1642–1727), the cosmos

4.22

was a kind of divinely wound clock. Once started, it moved relentlessly and inexorably according to mathematical laws governing it in its whole and in its parts.

4.22 Jan Vermeer.
The Lacemaker. 1670–71.
Oil on canvas, 9⅞" × 8¼".
The Louvre, Paris.

The objective cosmos that runs like a machine became an increasingly powerful image during the eighteenth century. Figure 4.23 reveals this changing view quite clearly. The human being peers through the outmoded sphere of stars into the wide space of the new cosmos—which, as the image shows with equal clarity, moves itself by mechanical gears.

4.23 Anonymous.
Sun, Stars, Rainbow. 19th century.
Woodcut.
The Bettmann Archive, Inc., New York.

4.24 Fourbisseur.
Swordmaking. 1765.
Engraving from Diderot's
Encyclopedia.
Metropolitan Museum of Art, New York,
Harris Brisbane Dick Fund.

4.23

The cosmos-as-machine was a stunning departure from Greek and medieval ideas. One of its most appealing advantages was that it could be converted into an indefinite, if not infinite, amount of power—through machines based on its own physical laws.

Human reason and the human person, of course, still had an important position in this cosmic machine. But human purpose was now increasingly directed toward using knowledge to crank down power (technology) useful to humanity from the gears that powered the machine of nature.

Thus the machine, far from being the intrusion and distraction seen by the Greeks, now literally connected human beings with the "big machine" of the cosmos; it proved, in fact, that human beings were actually in touch with the big machine of the cosmos. If a machine worked—and produced—its users were connecting with the objective facts composing the objective cosmic machine. To be in harmony with the machine was to be in harmony with the cosmos.

One particular set of printed images that appeared in the eighteenth century shows how the mechanical cosmos was beginning to transform Western society—the engravings from Denis Diderot's *Encyclopedia.* They are also the first

Western icons connecting the machine with the myth of the autonomous individual.

Printed Images from the *Encyclopedia*: Icons of Freedom through the Machine

Denis Diderot (1713–1784) directed the production of seventeen written volumes and eleven volumes of engraved illustrations for his *Encyclopedia* over a span of twenty years despite government harassment and delays (including three months of prison). The *Encyclopedia* was a revolutionary attempt to make knowledge of all the sciences and arts democratically available through printed words and printed images. It was the secular equivalent of the earlier printing of the Bible for the common people.

4.24

The eleven volumes of engravings were absolutely essential to Diderot's purpose. If accurate drawings of flowers are required for scientific understanding and communication, accurate drawings of machines are even more necessary. Imagine trying to fix a carburetor or even assemble a child's toy without accurate pictures along with the instructions. Diderot's engravings are the industrial and craft equivalent of Leonardo's visualizations of the body.

Looking back from our time, however, the *Encyclopedia* images look somewhat different, rather naive, in fact. The mood of these images now reads, in Roland Barthes's term, as a kind of "preindustrial folklore" picturing the worker happily fulfilled through technology:

The engraver represents him for the most part dressed neatly as a gentleman; this is not a worker but a little lord who plays on a kind of technological organ, all of whose gears are exposed; what is striking about the Encyclopedic machine is its absence of secrecy . . . the Encyclopedic machine is never anything but an enormous relay; man is at one term, the object at the other . . . *there is no sense of social distress.*[2] [italics mine]

These pictures were constructed to celebrate the spectacle of workers enjoying access to wonderfully increased power. They are nevertheless equally spectacular as pictures of workers who are literally strapped into the numbing embrace of the machines that have already begun to organize and reshape the human environment. These images, despite the intended optimism, are of machines that obviously use human beings as "extensions of themselves"—note how the little gentlemen in the engraving *Swordmaking* (fig. 4.24) are literally fastened to the machine and must adjust to its demands.

This, however, is only a "preindustrial" image; human beings help power these machines. In the late eighteenth century, technology had begun to harness the power of steam and electricity to the machine, and in the nineteenth century these enlarged machines would begin to absorb whole towns around them, instead of individual human beings. The sense of social distress would then begin to take on revolutionary proportions.

The image of the machine began to work its way into the organization of the state as well as industry. As industry geared up to organize nature and society around its clockwork needs for order and predictability, the state also began to use the growing forms of technology to increase its potential to either serve or manipulate the individual.

The final phase of the Perspective Age, from the late eighteenth century up to 1839, is marked by the unfolding possibilities and dilemmas offered by the varied applications of technology to government and industry. Western art reflects this transitional period in two movements. One movement, Romanticism, reacted against the growth of various forms of mechanization by exalting the subjective feelings of the individual; the artists of the other movement pushed images to the objective limits of perspective—to the borders of photography.

Propaganda and Art: Art Provides Icons for the Modern State

Despite the sometimes crushing impact of the early stages of industrialization, the eighteenth century also saw tremendous changes that enhanced the position of the individual. In the French Revolution (1789) the state itself followed the path that painting had already taken: it broke entirely from the background of the sacred symbolized by the "divine right of kings" and the sanction of an official church. The state, like art, became a purely human creation. And like art, it was based on human perception. It could therefore be observed, measured, and changed.

The French Revolution marks the point when art as propaganda for the state became one of its major cultural roles. *Propaganda* is a term that comes from religion, as in propagating, or spreading, the faith. Since the mythic base of the modern state was no longer the sacred order of king and church, it had to propagandize its own kind of faith, or at least its own justification. Propaganda for the modern

4.25

state, beginning with the French Revolution, attempts to link the personality of the individual citizen with the personality of some heroic figure who personifies the state. Successful propaganda art produces icons that give the individual the experience of being at the center of the world of the state. A forerunner of the forms of propaganda used so extensively in our own day is the propaganda machine of Napoleon Bonaparte.

Making the Technological State More Human: Propaganda and the Cult of Personality

The artist who directed the French Revolution's search for new icons for the state was Jacques Louis David (1748–1825). David became famous just before the Revolution in France with classically inspired paintings that literally glowed with revolutionary fervor. *The Oath of the Horatii* (fig. 1.20) celebrated the heroism of three brothers who defied the restoration of a king in early Rome. *The Death of Socrates* (fig. 4.25) pictured the famous Greek philosopher choosing death rather than accept the unjust verdict rendered by the Athenian political process.

Paintings like these caused intense discussion when they were shown at the semiannual Paris salons. They clearly supported the antiking and antichurch sentiments that were growing in France at this time. David hoped that his paintings would "electrify" the public and make them more open to political change.

David continued to manage the image of the new cult of reason when the Revolution struck with its furious and almost uncontrollable energy. He was a member of the most radical group, the Jacobins, whose leader, Robespierre—the Incorruptible—initiated the infamous Reign of Terror (1793). David himself was called the Robespierre of the brush. During this period, as Pageant Master of the Republic, he initiated great national festivals whose aim was to give the people of France a new sense of mythic unity under the banner of human reason.

A prime icon of the heroic cult of the "Revolution of Reason" is David's portrait of the journalist and leader of the Paris proletariat (working class), Jean Paul Marat (fig. 4.26). Marat is shown after his murder by the Republican patriot Charlotte Corday in 1793. Corday murdered Marat because she felt that he had led the Revolution beyond the original republican goals to something approaching anarchy. Marat became a martyr of the Revolution, and his death inspired a cult that venerated his memory much like that of a saint. David's *Death of Marat* is the first of the modern images of heroes that, like earlier paintings of the saints, reinforce the myth of the modern state as defender of the common man.

The Revolution eventually turned on Robespierre and required his death on the guillotine. David was also arrested

4.26

4.25 Jacques Louis David. *The Death of Socrates.* 1787. Oil on canvas, 51 ″ × 77¼ ″. Metropolitan Museum of Art, New York, Catharine Lorillard Wolfe Collection.

4.26 Jacques Louis David. *The Death of Marat.* 1793. Oil on canvas, 5′3″ × 4′1″. Musées Royaux des Beaux-Arts de Belgique, Brussels.

and expected to be executed. Instead, there was a general amnesty, and the need of the new leader of the Revolution, Napoleon Bonaparte, for a master propagandist brought David back into artistic power.

Jacques Louis David: First Painter to the Emperor

David served Napoleon well. He painted his coronation; he painted the emperor crossing the Alps, as a successor to Hannibal and Charlemagne (fig. 4.27). He also painted private but equally heroic and idealized portraits.

4.27

4.28

Under David's direction, lesser lights like Baron Gros painted nearly religious paintings of the emperor. His *The Pest House at Jaffa* (fig. 4.28) shows Napoleon visiting the dead and dying "citizen heroes" of his ill-fated Egyptian campaign. He seems about to heal their torments, like Christ in Rembrandt's *Hundred-Guilder Print* (fig. 4.6).

The paintings of David and his followers reached a large public by being reproduced as engravings. Even more people were brought into touch with icons of the Napoleonic cult through woodcuts like those that had for centuries featured images of the saints.

Figure 4.29 shows an engraving from 1802, at the beginning of Napoleon's reign as emperor. The children are shown playing and cutting out pictures. Omer picks up a picture of Napoleon and says, "You will not find his equal." Elisa displays proper patriotic fervor by wearing a dress in the Neoclassic style that Napoleon adopted to connect his reign with that of imperial Rome. Urbain, though so young that he has to sit on two stools to participate, is politically precocious enough to applaud Omer's sentiments. Propaganda, then and now, is seldom subtle.

A woodcut made in 1834, almost twenty years after Napoleon's fall (fig. 4.30), demonstrates the effectiveness of his use of popular images that swept all ages into a connection with their emperor. This image is evidence of how enthralled "Omer's" generation still was, at middle age, with the memory of Napoleon. Napoleon is presented here as transformed into a deity in a kind of Valhalla surrounded by his generals.

This image is particularly important because it is an image d'Epinal. Epinal is a town in eastern France that estab-

4.30

lished a small industry producing crude, brightly colored woodcuts like this. *Images d'Epinal* had an importance comparable to that of the *Encyclopedia.* Their bold outlining and bright, flat colors are the forerunners of today's comic strips and newspaper cartoons. They were cheap, easy to distribute, and clear in their propaganda messages to those who could not read. The images of the *Encyclopedia* and the images d'Epinal are examples of how printed pictures, forerunners of the mass media, were involved in the same complex relationship with new forms of power as the fine art of David, Gros, and other artists of the day.

The Subjectivity of Romanticism: The Artist Becomes a Projector

The Napoleonic state lasted only until 1815. The French, exhausted by war and change, then restored a king to the throne. But the idea and the myth of individual freedom had achieved unstoppable popularity. Though temporarily blocked in its political expression, the belief in individual freedom was another major impulse that inspired the artistic movement known as Romanticism.

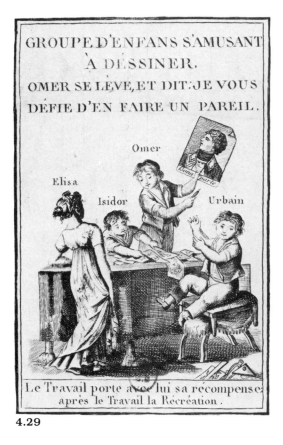

4.29

4.27 Jacques Louis David.
Napoleon at the Great St. Bernard Pass. 1800.
Oil on canvas, 8′11″ × 7′11″.
Kunsthistorisches Museum, Vienna.

4.28 Antoine Jean Gros.
The Pest House at Jaffa. 1804.
Oil on canvas, 17′5″ × 23′7″.
The Louvre, Paris.

4.29 Engraving. 1802.
Bibliothèque Nationale, Paris.

4.30 *Apotheosis of Napoleon.* 1834.
Epinal woodcut.
Bibliothèque Nationale, Paris.

4.31

4.31 Joseph Mallord William Turner.
The Harbor at Dieppe. 1826.
Copyright The Frick Collection, New York.

4.32 Francisco de Goya.
The Family of Charles IV. 1800.
Oil on canvas, 9′2″ × 11′.
Museo del Prado, Madrid.

4.33 Francisco de Goya.
The Naked Maja. c. 1798–1805.
Oil on canvas, 97 × 100 cm.
Museo del Prado, Madrid.

4.34 Francisco de Goya.
The Third of May, 1808. 1814.
Oil on canvas, 8′8″ × 11′3″.
Museo del Prado, Madrid.

Romantic painting dealt with a wide range of subjects and spanned an emotional range from despair to religious exaltation.

In England, for instance, J. M. W. Turner (fig. 4.31) painted nature as the source of both serenity and awe. William Blake created highly subjective religious images that protested both the Industrial Revolution and the new mechanized picture of the cosmos.

The most significant changes in art, however, followed in the wake of Napoleon's impact on continental Europe. Many artists despaired for the possibility of individual freedom through politics. This reaction included disillusionment with David's use of art as a form of propaganda for the state. Such artists began to look increasingly inward for private visions to replace abandoned public expectations. The Spanish painter Francisco de Goya is one of the first to show this transformation of the Romantic artist into a "projector" of his own subjectivity.

Francisco de Goya (1746–1828): The Subjective Vision of Hell

Goya, like Rembrandt, was a remarkable success early in his career. Before he was forty, he was chief painter to the king of Spain. He led a life of unusually ostentatious independence at court, as evidenced by his highly unflattering portrait of the royal family (fig. 4.32) and his risqué portrait of the duchess of Alba, his alleged mistress (fig. 4.33).

The entry of Napoleon's army into Spain in 1808, however, overwhelmed even a nature as cynical and robust as Goya's. His painting *The Third of May, 1808* (fig. 4.34) shows

4.32

4.33

4.34

the mass execution of civilians that continued, as the gas lamps indicate, far into the night. The people of Madrid, on the second of May, had resisted the French army's entry into the city.

Like Rembrandt, Goya also used etchings to explore his personal reaction to the social world. His series entitled *The Disasters of War* portrays the results of the Napoleonic war machine: bodies are shown chewed-up or dismembered and hung from trees. In *The Horrors of War: One Can't Look at It* (fig. 4.35), Goya depicts a scene similar to his painting *The Third of May, 1808,* except that women and children are also included among the victims. If David's paintings and the mass-produced images d'Epinal pictured the appeal of the modern technological state, Goya's etchings became an early witness to the destructive potential of its increasingly effective reach. They have the caustic bite of today's front-page newsphotos from scenes of war and terror. In addition, Goya's etchings are among the earliest examples of the poor pictured as victims instead of being romanticized in picturesque scenarios.

After Napoleon's invasion, Goya shut himself up increasingly in his villa. There, intensified by the burden of progressive deafness, his eye turned inward. Inside himself, however, he saw only nightmares (fig. 4.36). Smeared in blackened colors on the villa's walls were images that mark Goya's mind as one of the first to confront, as a personal inner reality, the experience of nothingness, the experience of social reality as a lie. Goya's "black paintings" are icons of the void. They present a sense of individual subjectivity with nothing sacred or human to connect with outside the self. "For Goya," as Aldous Huxley described it, "the transcendent did not exist."[3]

Théodore Géricault (1794–1824): Society as Madness

Another Romantic whose view of the world was powerfully influenced by the career of Napoleon was Théodore Géricault, who was a young man during the height of Napoleon's career. Like so many other artists, he was swept up in trying to capture the heroism of the time on canvas. His painting *An Officer of the Chausseurs Charging* won him a gold medal at the Salon of 1812.

Napoleon's fall, however, left Géricault disillusioned with the new social order that followed. When the French ship *Medusa* sank off the west coast of Africa, Géricault found the perfect subject to project his views and feelings. He called his painting *The Raft of the Medusa* (fig. 4.37).

The *Medusa* incident became a scandal that involved both heroism and depravity. When the ship was sinking, the captain and the wealthier passengers took the lifeboat and towed the lower-class passengers on a raft hastily con-

4.35

4.36

structed by the ship's carpenter. At sea, the rope connecting the lifeboat and the raft was cut and the raft left to drift out into the Atlantic.

Miraculously, after terrible trials (including cannibalism of the dead in order to survive), the wretched survivors on the raft were rescued. Their story caused a scandal in France because of the class prejudice that contributed to the horrible event.

Géricault approached his painting like the director of a documentary film. He made contact with many of the survivors, including the ship's carpenter (who built Géricault a replica of the original raft). He also went to the morgue and sketched corpses of drowning victims.

The resultant painting was so successful with the public that, after the Salon of 1819 in Paris, he took it to England,

4.35 Francisco de Goya.
The Horrors of War: One Can't Look at It.
Etching and aquatint.
Cleveland Museum of Art, Dudley P. Allen Fund.

4.36 Francisco de Goya.
Saturn Devouring His Children.
1819–23.
Detail of a detached fresco on canvas, full size approx. 4'9" × 2'8".
Museo del Prado, Madrid.

4.37 Théodore Géricault.
The Raft of the Medusa. 1818–19.
Oil on canvas, 16' × 23'.
The Louvre, Paris.

4.37

where he charged admission to see it and earned a considerable amount of money.

But Géricault did not follow up his success with a *"Raft II."* He instead stayed on in England for two years, observing and drawing conditions in London's industrial slums (fig. 4.38). His lithographs on the subject show Géricault's view that it was not only the passengers on the raft of the *Medusa*

4.38

who were in desperate straits, but the growing number of urban workers who were trapped in an increasingly mechanized form of life.

For Géricault, as for Goya, the irrational was already there, within the subjective individual, and also out there, within society itself.

Despite its pessimism, the work of Goya and Géricault strongly affirmed the creative reality of the subjective world of the individual. They not only gave this subjective world form and meaning, they also asserted the right of the individual to comment—to project a judgment—on the external social order. If the new social order was a human creation it could be criticized and changed. The art of Goya and Géricault confirmed the role of artists in calling society to face its own potential for human evil.

The Subjective Center of Romanticism: "Imagination Created the World"

The term that probably best describes the new kind of artistic freedom in the various forms of Romantic art is *imagination*. It was coined in the early nineteenth century by the French poet and critic Charles Baudelaire, who used it to describe the Romantic artist at the "center of the world" in a different sense from that earlier explored by Michelangelo and described by Pico della Mirandola. With this concept, the subjectivity of the artist takes on an almost sacred character of its own. The Romantic artist rises above the objectivity of facts to produce—or project—a new reality. Imagination, says Baudelaire,

decomposes all creation and with the raw materials accumulated and disposed in accordance with the rules whose origins one cannot find save in the furthest reaches of the soul, it creates a new world, it produces the sensation of newness.[4]

To Baudelaire, at the end of the Perspective Age, the artist could proclaim the power of the individual to stand apart from the emerging power of industrialism and the powerful bureaucracies of the state. Romanticism is the first form of Western art that defines individual freedom as distinct from—and sometimes in opposition to—the prevailing institutions of society. For Baudelaire, the artist whose work best embodied this precious quality of imagination was Eugène Delacroix.

Eugène Delacroix (1798–1863): The Sensation of Newness

Like *The Raft of the Medusa* and *The Third of May, 1808* Eugène Delacroix's painting *Liberty Leading the People* (fig. 4.39) provides a brilliant example of the Romantic drive to use the world of external fact to create an art that expresses the subjectivity of the individual. Liberty is presented in the symbolic or allegorical form of a beautiful, partially nude figure of a young woman carrying a musket and waving the tricolor flag of France. The barricades shown in the painting are today still a familiar sight at street demonstrations in Paris. The painting shows Delacroix's admiration for the "people's revolution" of 1830 that brought down the king who replaced Napoleon. The group of figures includes an intellectual with a top hat and a street urchin, along with the workers who charge behind Liberty.

The Romantic artist did not just record facts but took them in and projected them as a reflection of private experience.

Romanticism mirrored the artistic reaction to the mechanization of nature and society by emphasizing the interior space of the individual, but other late eighteenth century artists displayed an equally powerful tendency toward an ever more objective form of art. Romanticism, in a sense, turned the artist into a projector. Other artists took art to the border of photography, with a sense of objectivity that made the artist a camera.

Before Photography: Painting Helps Invent the Language of Photography

In view of Vermeer's achievement discussed earlier, it is surprising that photography was not discovered long before the nineteenth century. The camera obscura of Vermeer's day lacked only film to become a photographic camera. It was discovered early in the eighteenth century that silver nitrate darkened when exposed to sunlight, but applying this knowledge to the making of film for the camera obscura took more than a hundred years longer.

Peter Galassi, curator of photography at the Museum of Modern Art in New York, has put forth a convincing argument to explain this delay. Photography, according to Galassi, could not be invented until Western artists had already begun to paint in the language of photography. Only then could the precise kind of images produced by photography be considered meaningful and valuable.

What precisely is the language of photography? It is a point of view that even Vermeer did not fully explore: it is a visually uncomposed, accidental (untampered-with) view of reality. The camera does not (by itself) tamper with reality; it takes a picture of what is already there. Up until the late eighteenth century, even the most objective artist—like Vermeer—composed or manipulated the elements of the view he or she was recording. Vermeer not only moved furniture and placed figures into balanced compositions, he added visual data—like the "circles of confusion"—that were not really there. The purpose of art was precisely to improve

4.39

4.38 Théodore Géricault.
Pity the Sorrows of a Poor Old Man.
1821.
Lithograph.
Fine Arts Museums of San Francisco,
Achenbach Foundation for Graphic Arts,
Gift of the Bay Area Graphic Arts Council.
1972.

4.39 Eugène Delacroix.
Liberty Leading the People. 1830.
Oil on canvas, 10'8" × 8'6".
The Louvre, Paris.

upon nature. Art "humanized" nature; it did not passively record it. The totally objective images produced by the photographic camera do not have this sense of composition that was considered to be an essential element of art.

In the late eighteenth century, however, a number of artists began to see and paint in a different way.

Galassi has collected a large number of late eighteenth- and early nineteenth-century paintings that are remarkable in their totally uncomposed and objective point of view: the point of view of photography. Thomas Jones's *A Wall in Naples* (fig. 4.40) is a tiny painting that has no hint of the traditional concern for composition. What it does have is a remarkable and almost photographic concern for detail— note the stain left from water running down the wall from the porch. Even in color, this painting (plate 9) carries an incredibly photographic quality. It is so much like a snapshot that it is difficult for us to imagine how totally new it was in the 1780s.

Other painters at this time were producing similarly uncomposed images; another fitting example is John Constable's *Study of Clouds and Trees* (fig. 4.41). Brunelleschi had used silver foil above his painting of the Baptistry of Florence that began the Perspective Age. Constable's painting of clouds symbolizes not only the threshold of a new stage in the mechanization of art but also the completion of a new objective mentality:

Painting is a science, and should be pursued as an inquiry into the laws of nature. Why, then should not landscape painting be consid-

4.40 Thomas Jones.
A Wall in Naples. c. 1782.
Oil on paper, 4⅜″ × 6¼″.
Courtesy Mrs. Jane Evan-Thomas.

4.41 John Constable.
Study of Clouds and Trees. 1821.
Oil on paper, 9½″ × 11¾″.
Royal Academy of Arts, London.

4.42 Joseph Nicéphore Niepce.
View from a Window at Gras. 1826.
Photograph ("heliograph" process).
Humanities Research Center, University
of Texas, Austin.

4.40

ered as a branch of natural philosophy, of which pictures are but the experiments?[5]

Art at the beginning of the Perspective Age, even for a scientist like Leonardo, was seen as a sharing in divine creativity. Constable—unlike his contemporary Baudelaire—saw art as a branch of physics. Art, in both its technological form and its philosophy, was ready to join the objectivity of the clockwork cosmos.

The Invention of Photography: The Clockwork Cosmos Takes a Picture of Itself

Even though photographic processes were patented by the Frenchman Louis Daguerre (1839) and the Englishman William Henry Fox Talbot, the first photograph was taken by Joseph Nicéphore Niepce (1765–1833) in 1826. Unlike Brunelleschi's painting dramatically demonstrating perspective, the first photograph was a private affair and artistically unheralded (fig. 4.42). This blurred image nevertheless was another step in the interaction of art and artist with mechanization.

The photograph has developed such a complex history that it is difficult to appreciate that it arrived in perfect timing with the emergence of the machinelike social order of the Industrial Revolution. Like the new coal- and steam-powered machines of the day, the camera seemed to tap directly into the energies of the machine cosmos and produce a perspective image. This image—as Daguerre said in his speech to the French Assembly upon receiving the patent for the daguerreotype process— "was produced by nature herself."[6]

In photography, the machine cosmos sees itself and creates by its own processes its own perfectly objective image. It was an image, in the words of a disgruntled art critic of the day, produced "as if the human being were not there."[7] To some, it seemed to make human artists obsolete.

Yet we know that photography did not make art or artists obsolete. The creative eye of the artist had helped devise both the machines and the perspective language that ultimately produced photography. The photograph, instead of definitively solving the problem of art by creating "nature's own images," instead provoked a profound crisis—a crisis of realism.

Artists, in fact, very quickly began to explore ways to create an alternative language to that of the new photographic perspective. The search for a new artistic language during the Photographic Age gradually created not only a new art but a new role for artists, the avant-garde.

4.41

4.42

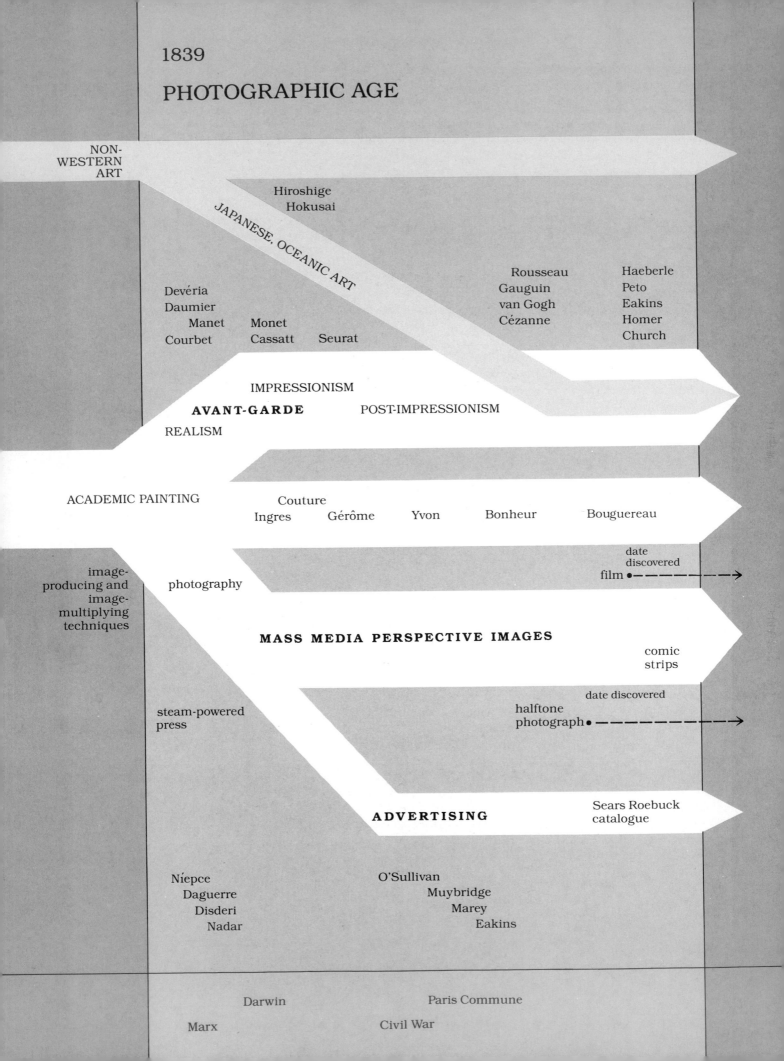

1839

PHOTOGRAPHIC AGE

NON-WESTERN ART

JAPANESE, OCEANIC ART

Hiroshige
Hokusai

Devéria
Daumier
Manet   Monet
Courbet   Cassatt   Seurat

Rousseau   Haeberle
Gauguin   Peto
van Gogh   Eakins
Cézanne   Homer
Church

IMPRESSIONISM

AVANT-GARDE   POST-IMPRESSIONISM

REALISM

ACADEMIC PAINTING

Couture
Ingres   Gérôme   Yvon   Bonheur   Bouguereau

image-producing and image-multiplying techniques

photography

date discovered
film •–––––––––→

MASS MEDIA PERSPECTIVE IMAGES

comic strips

steam-powered press

date discovered
halftone photograph •––––––––––→

ADVERTISING

Sears Roebuck catalogue

Níepce
Daguerre
Disderi
Nadar

O'Sullivan
Muybridge
Marey
Eakins

Darwin   Paris Commune

Marx   Civil War

1 Hans Memling.
Portrait of a Man with an Arrow.
c. 1470.
Oil on wood, 9⅛″ × 7⅛″.
National Gallery of Art, Washington, Andrew W. Mellon Collection, 1937.

2 Tom Porter.
1984.
Computer-generated image.
Courtesy Lucasfilm Ltd. Copyright 1984, Lucasfilm Ltd.

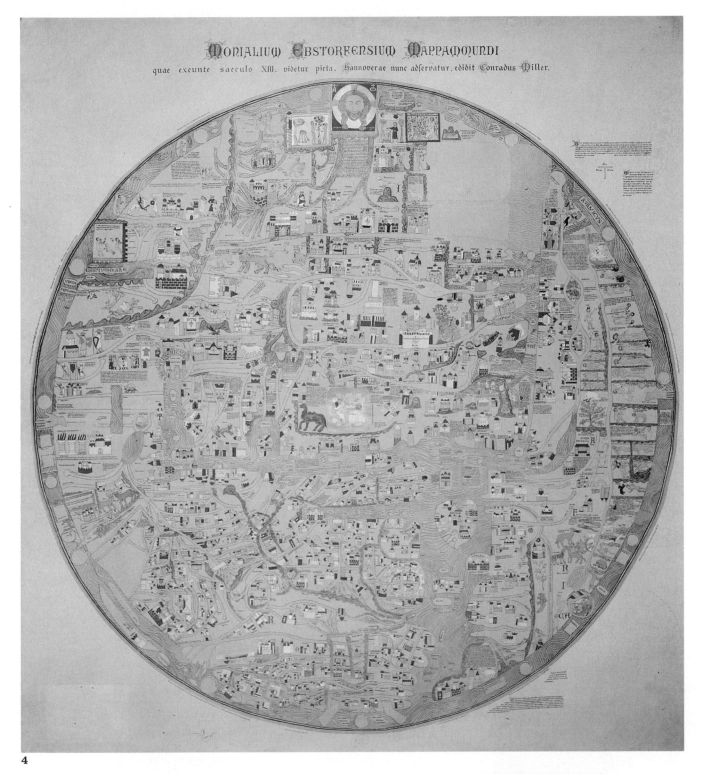

MONIALIUM EBSTORFENSIUM MAPPAMUNDI

quae exeunte saeculo XIII. videtur picta. Hannoverae nunc adservatur. edidit Conradus Miller.

4

3 *Horned Puffin Eating a Walrus.*
Eskimo. 19th century.
Department of Anthropology, Smithsonian
Institution.

4 Ebstorf *Mappamundi* (*Map of the
World*).
13th century (destroyed in World War II).
British Library.

9

6

8

5

7

13

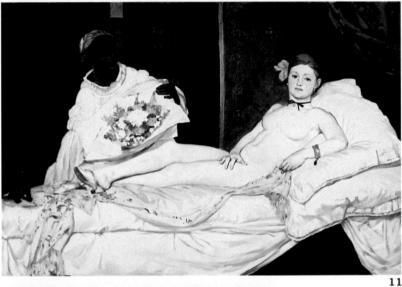

11

10

12

5 Jan Van Eyck.
Giovanni Arnolfini and His Bride.
1434.
Oil on wood panel, approx. 32" × 22".
Reproduced by courtesy of the Trustees of the
National Gallery, London.

6 Rembrandt van Rijn.
Self-Portrait. c. 1660.
Oil on canvas, 45" × 37".
The Greater London Council as Trustees of
the Iveagh Bequest, Kenwood.

7 Willem Kalf.
Still Life. c. 1665.
Oil on canvas, 25⅜" × 21¼".
National Gallery of Art, Washington. Gift of
Chester Dale, 1943.

8 Jan Vermeer.
The Girl with a Red Hat. c. 1660.
Oil on wood, 9⅛" × 7⅛".
The National Gallery of Art, Washington.
Andrew W. Mellon Collection, 1937.

9 Thomas Jones.
A Wall in Naples. c. 1782.
Oil on paper, 4⅜" × 6¼".
Courtesy Mrs. Jane Evan-Thomas.

10 Jean Auguste Dominique Ingres.
Madame Moitessier. 1851.
Oil on canvas, 57¾" × 39½".
National Gallery of Art, Washington, Samuel
H. Kress Collection.

11 Édouard Manet.
Olympia. 1863.
Oil on canvas, 51¼" × 74¾".
The Louvre, Paris.

12 Jean Léon Gérôme.
The Slave Market. c. 1867.
Oil on canvas, 33⁹⁄₁₆" × 24¹³⁄₁₆".
Sterling and Francine Clark Art Institute,
Williamstown, Massachusetts.

13 Édouard Manet.
A Bar at the Folies-Bergère. 1881.
Oil on canvas. 3' 1¾" × 4' 2".
Courtauld Institute Galleries, London.

14 Claude Monet.
Rouen Cathedral, West Facade, Sunlight. 1894.
Oil on canvas, 39½″ × 26″.
The National Gallery of Art, Washington, Chester Dale Collection.

15 Claude Monet.
Rouen Cathedral, West Facade. 1894.
Oil on canvas, 39½″ × 26″.
The National Gallery of Art, Washington, Chester Dale Collection.

16 Georges Seurat.
Sunday Afternoon on the Island of La Grande Jatte. 1884–86.
Oil on canvas, 6′ 9″ × 10′ ⅜″.
Art Institute of Chicago, Helen Birch Bartlett Memorial Collection.

17 Paul Cézanne.
Houses in Provence. c. 1880.
Oil on canvas, 25⅝″ × 32″.
The National Gallery of Art, Washington, Collection of Mr. and Mrs. Paul Mellon.

18 Vincent van Gogh.
The Bedroom at Arles. 1888–89.
Oil on canvas, 29″ × 36″.
Courtesy of the Art Institute of Chicago.

19 Paul Gauguin.
Self-Portrait. 1889.
Oil on canvas, 30¼″ × 20¼″.
The National Gallery of Art, Washington.

16

19

17

18

20

20 Paul Gauguin.
Fatata te Miti (*By the Sea*). 1892.
Oil on canvas, 26¾″ × 36″.
The National Gallery of Art, Washington,
Chester Dale Collection.

21 Frederic Edwin Church.
Twilight in the Wilderness. 1864.
Oil on canvas, 40″ × 64″.
The Cleveland Museum of Art, Mr. and Mrs.
William H. Marlatt Fund.

21

22 Walt Disney.
Pinocchio. 1940.
Copyright 1940 Walt Disney Productions.

23 Pablo Picasso.
Les Demoiselles d'Avignon. 1907.
Oil on canvas, 8′ × 7′ 8″.
The Museum of Modern Art, New York.
Acquired through the Lillie P. Bliss Bequest.

24 Salvador Dali.
The Sacrament of the Last Supper.
1955.
Oil on canvas, 65⅝″ × 105⅛″.
The National Gallery of Art, Washington,
Chester Dale Collection.

25 Jackson Pollock.
Number 1, 1950 (Lavender Mist).
Oil, enamel, and aluminum on canvas,
87″ × 118″.
The National Gallery of Art, Washington,
Ailsa Mellon Bruce Fund.

23

22

24

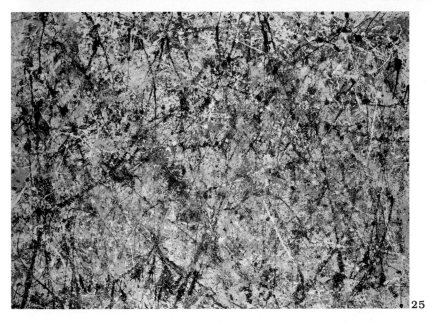

25

27

26

26 Roy Lichtenstein.
Cubist Still Life. 1974.
Oil and magna on canvas, 90″ × 68⅛″.
The National Gallery of Art, Washington, Lila
Acheson Wallace Fund.

27 Frank Stella.
Agbatana I. 1968.
Synthetic polymer on canvas,
120″ × 180″.
Collection of Whitney Museum of American
Art, Gift of Mr. and Mrs. Oscar Kolin.

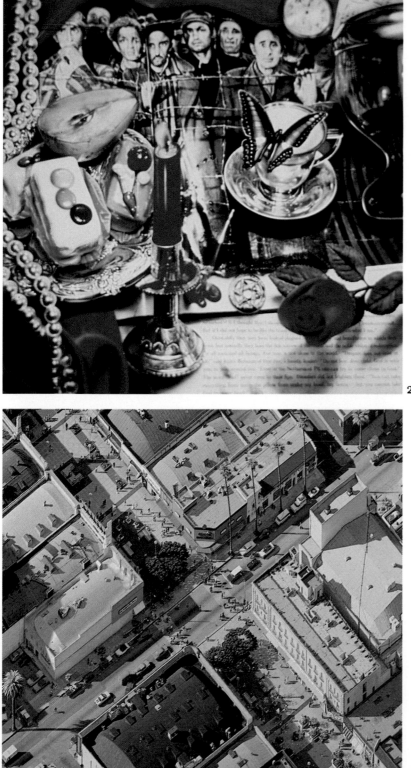

28

29

28 Audrey Flack.
World War II. 1976–77.
Oil on canvas, 96″ × 96″.
Photo courtesy Louis K. Meisel Gallery. *WWII*
by Audrey Flack incorporating a portion of the
Margaret Bourke-White photograph
Buchenwald, 1945. © Time, Inc.

29 James Doolin.
Shopping Mall. 1973–77.
Oil on canvas, 90″ × 90″.
Courtesy of the artist.

30 Billy Al Bengston.
Mahana Draculas (as used in advertisement for First Los Angeles Bank). 1981.
Acrylic on canvas, 76″ × 80″.
Courtesy of the James Corcoran Gallery, Billy Al Bengston, artist.

31 *Placesetting for Judith.* 1979.
Mixed media, approx. 30″ wide.
Copyright Judy Chicago. Executed by Judy Chicago, Juliet Myers, Terry Belcher. Photo: Beth Theilen.

32 Joyce Treiman.
Degas, Cassatt, and Me. 1979.
Oil on canvas, 70″ × 70″.
Courtesy Tortue Gallery.

33 Lita Albuquerque.
Inconceivable Mansions. 1981.
Environmental process piece, Arroyo Grande, California, 1981.
Photos courtesy Lita Albuquerque.

31

30

32

33

34

35

34 Masami Teraoka.
Hanauma Bay series/Video Rental II.
1982.
Watercolor, 28¾″ × 40⅝″.
Courtesy Space Gallery, Los Angeles.

35 Carlos Almaraz.
The Bridge. 1984.
Oil on canvas, 54″ × 96″.
Courtesy Janus Gallery.

36 Leon Golub.
White Squad IV (El Salvador). 1983.
Oil on canvas, 120″ × 152″.

37 Nam June Paik. "Global Groove." 1973.
Color video. 30:00.
Photo courtesy Electronic Arts Intermix, Inc.,
New York.

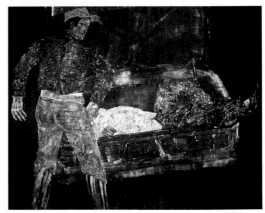

36

37

38 Carol Ann Klonarides and Michael
Owens.
Laurie Simmons—A Teaser. 1980.
Color video. 5:00.
Photo courtesy Electronic Arts Intermix, Inc.,
New York.

39 "Futureworld."
Pentel commercial. 1982.
Courtesy Triton Advertising, Inc.

40 Walt Disney Productions.
Tron. 1982.
Copyright 1982 Walt Disney Productions.

38

40

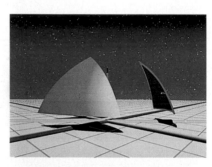

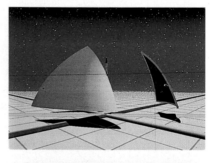

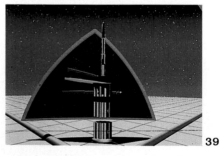

39

BASIC PRINTMAKING PROCESSES

1. Relief Printing. Relief prints are printed images resulting from inking and printing a *surface* whose design has been produced by cutting away areas of the surface so that they will not print.

The *woodcut* relief print process is illustrated on the right. A is a wood block, B is a woodcutting knife, and C is a tool for applying even pressure on the back of the paper to transfer ink from the block to the front of the paper.

Another important kind of relief print is the wood engraving discussed in Chapter Eight.

See illustrations 3.36, 4.30, 6.8, 7.7.

2. Intaglio Printing. *Intaglio* prints are printed images resulting from wiping ink into a design of lines and shapes *below the surface* ("intaglio") of the plate. The plate is prepared for printing by daubing ink into the shapes and lines and then cleaning ink from the surface of the plate. After placing dampened paper on the surface of the plate, it is run through the rollers of a press, which exert enough pressure to force the softened paper into the inked areas below the surface of the plate.

Three common intaglio processes are illustrated on the right. *Engraved* lines are produced in a metal plate (usually zinc or copper) by an engraving tool (B) which pushes a metal furrow in front of it. *Drypoint* lines are produced by dragging or drawing an etching needle across the plate in the same way one draws with a pencil. The sharp point of the etching needle creates a tiny furrow of metal which catches ink and, when printed, produces a line that is slightly blurred compared to the clean line produced by the engraving tool. An *etched line* is produced by covering the metal plate with an acid-resistant material and then scratching lines through this material to the surface of the plate. When the plate is then placed in acid (D), the acid "etches" the lines into the surface of the metal.

Other forms of intaglio printing include aquatint and mezzotint (see Glossary).

See 4.6, 5.21, 8.13 for etchings; 3.37, 4.24, 6.10 for engravings.

3. Planographic Printing. Planographic prints are images printed from a surface that has been treated chemically to make the non-image (non-inked) area resistant to ink and attractive to water. Once the non-image area of the surface has been made resistant to ink, a roller charged with ink can be rolled over it and the ink from the roller will transfer only to the image area of the surface. After each inking with the roller, the surface is covered with paper and rolled through a press under great pressure.

Since limestone was the first material used for the planographic process of ink and water chemical treat-ment, the name *lithography* ("litho"–stone, "graphy"–drawing) is still used to describe the process even when metal plates are used.

The lithographic process illustrated on the right shows a traditional lithographic stone (A), on which an image is being drawn by a brush (B) and a greasy crayon (C). After the non-image areas of the stone are made attractive to water, the inked image is run through a press (D) and printed.

See 6.12, 8.6, 9.20, 11.4.

4. Stencil Printing. Stencil prints are printed images made by passing ink through the openings of a stencil or cut-out pattern. *Silkscreening* (or serigraphy) is a common stencil technique used in art and industry today. A silkscreen consists of a fiber mesh or screen stretched over a wood or metal frame (A). A stencil (B) is attached to the bottom of the screen. A squeegee (C) then draws ink over the top of the screen so that the ink passes through the openings of the stencil and prints an image on the paper beneath the screen.

See i.2, 11.13, 11.19.

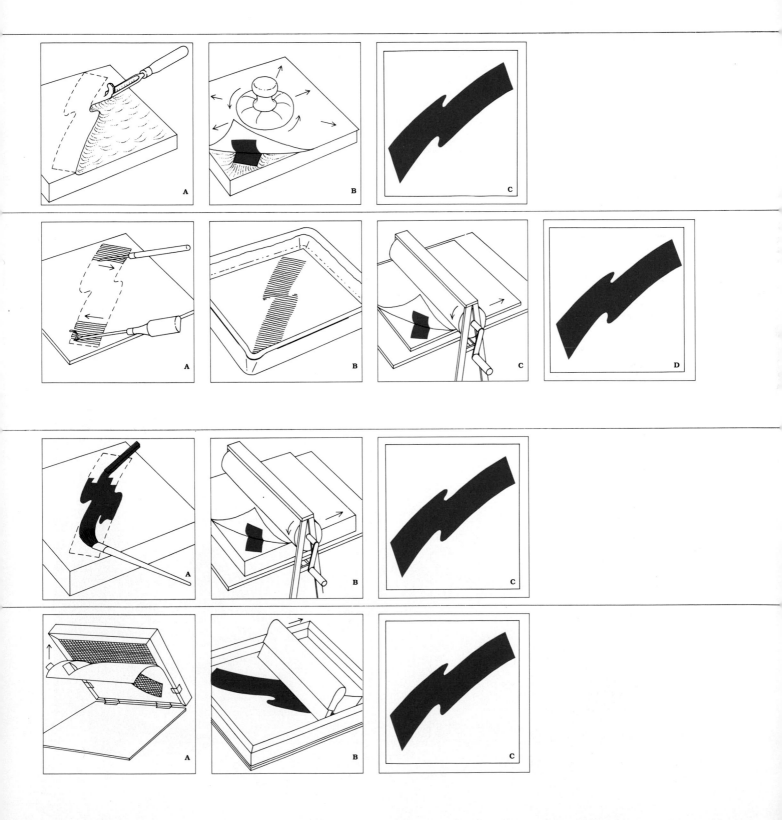

SILKSCREEN COLOR PRINTING

The panels on the right show the separate color runs that were involved in the printing of Walter Askin's silkscreen "Rainbow Score" reproduced below. Superimposing separate blocks, plates, or runs of color in a similar way has traditionally been used in all the printing methods illustrated in Basic Printmaking Processes. Another traditional method of achieving color in printed pictures has been by hand coloring a finished black-and-white print. Woodcuts of saints at late medieval fairs were sold "a penny plain" and "two penny colored."

Walter Askin.
Rainbow Score. 1973.
Silkscreen print, 40″ × 28″.
Courtesy of the artist.

FOUR-COLOR PROCESS PRINTING

Printing of photographs in color, including color photographs of works of art, is a twentieth-century development that has revolutionized both fine art and mass media. The panels on the right show the four separate plates which, when printed in combination, reproduced the image of Jim Alford's photograph, "Rhyolite Series (1984)." The same four colors in combination are used in any four-color printing, for together they can produce the entire spectrum of colors. The image produced by each of these photographic plates has a unique feature that contributes to the photographic image. Each is broken down in patterns of halftone dots whose position and quantity on each plate not only determine structure (as they do in a black-and-white halftone photograph), but also show the specific proportion of color (yellow, magenta, cyan, or black) that is reflected in each section of the photograph. Each plate, in other words, contributes a proportional amount of both color and structure to the full-color printed photograph.

yellow

magenta

yellow and magenta

cyan

yellow, magenta, and cyan

black

yellow, magenta, cyan, and black

Jim Alford.
Rhyolite Series. 1984.
Color photograph.
Courtesy of the photographer.

COLOR WHEEL

Hues (Showing Complementary and Analogous Relationships)

Complementary Relationships

Analagous Relationships

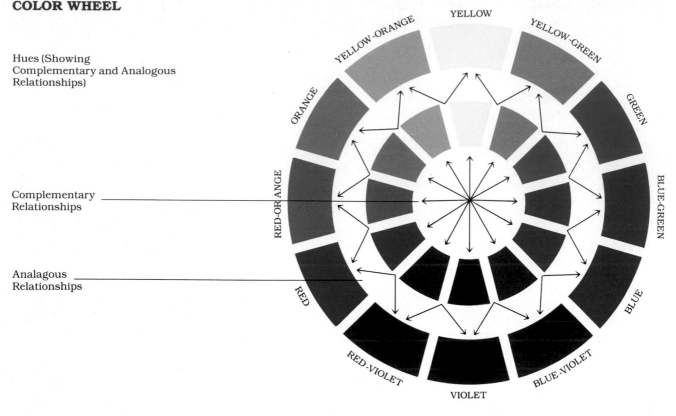

Cool and Warm Colors   Two important conversational terms for color are *cool* for the colors that extend from blue-violet to yellow-green and *warm* for the colors that extend from yellow to red-violet.

Successive Contrast   This term refers to the experience of retaining the complementary afterimage of a given color. After looking for about a minute at the yellow/violet figure, focus on the black dot in the middle of the white square on the right. You will see a slight impression of a violet square with traces of yellow. Simultaneous contrast, a less common phenomenon, is the tendency to see, within a given color, glimpses of the complementary hue of the adjacent color.

Hue and Value   The term *hue* refers to basic color—red, blue, and so forth. The term *value* refers to dark and light variations of hue. The figures below are composed of two hues, red-orange and blue-green. Note that the values of the red-orange circles are constant, but the changing values of the blue-green background make the values of the red-orange circles appear also to change.

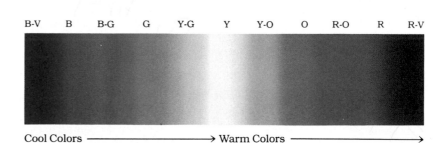

Cool Colors ⟶ Warm Colors ⟶

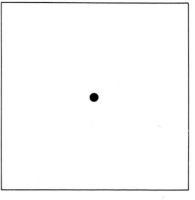

Successive Contrast

Hue: Red-orange and blue-green.
Value: Red-orange is constant in value; blue-green varies in value.

CHAPTER FIVE

THE
PHOTOGRAPHIC AGE I:
PHOTOGRAPHY,
ACADEMIC PAINTING,
AND THE CRISIS
OF REALISM

ASSESSMENTS

1. Can you recall when you first saw a photograph of yourself? What was your reaction?
2. Recall the experience of having your high school yearbook picture taken. Did the photograph meet your expectations? If it did—why? If not—why not? What visual aspects of how you see yourself were or were not recorded by the photograph? Why not?
3. What does the word *academic* imply?
4. In your opinion, does photography compete with drawing or painting in any way? In what ways are photographs and perspective paintings similar/dissimilar? In what ways are a painter and a photographer similar/dissimilar?
5. Have photographs contributed in any way to the formulation of your personal, sexual, social, or political viewpoints? Can you recall specific photographs that changed your views?
6. What art form do you think most clearly reflects the values of American middle-class life today? How do you personally respond to this art form?

120

The photograph of a leaf in figure 5.1 provides a good example of why photography confronted art with a "crisis of realism." In this photograph dating from the first decade of photography, the image is quite simple, yet the delicately outlined network of veins reveals detail unreachable by human art. For modern viewers, even after a century and a half of photography, this leaf still seems to have an almost miraculous presence in the photograph. The leaf is somehow made visible, as Daguerre said, "by nature herself."

5.1 Anonymous.
A Single Leaf.
Early photograph on paper.
Photo: Science Museum, London.

This photograph fulfills the dream, first implied by Brunelleschi's painting of the Baptistry of Florence, of creating an optically exact picture of reality. It also echoes Roger Bacon's medieval vision of pictures based on the "true geometry" of nature. Nevertheless, the image of the leaf presented a dilemma undreamed of by Brunelleschi: What is the role of art if a machine can produce such a realistic image? During the period between 1839 and 1905, Western artists struggled with this question, directly and indirectly. Their struggle generated two opposing kinds of response. One, that of Academic painting, used perspective to create an art that imitated the optical realism of photography. The other, avant-garde art, broke with the perspective tradition and began to create new artistic languages that ultimately opened up new views of reality as well as new forms of art.

This chapter will emphasize the relationship between photography and Academic art. Chapter 6 will discuss the pivotal avant-garde artist, Édouard Manet. Chapter 7 will discuss the evolution of avant-garde art after Manet up to the beginning of the twentieth century.

The Arrival of Photography: Academic Painting Imitates Photography

Niepce's invention of photography in 1826 went almost un-noticed, but its public patent by Louis Daguerre in 1839 dramatically projected it before both artists and the public. The public, as this chapter will show, welcomed photography with enthusiasm. Most artists, however—despite their histor-ical role in the development of photography—tended to see the photograph as a threat. Photography quickly began to take away many of the functions that had provided the basic livelihood of artists, like portraiture and various kinds of illustration. One of the most prominent artists in France at the time, Paul Delaroche, expressed the prevailing artistic sentiment quite simply. "Painting," he said, "is dead."[1]

Delaroche, however, was wrong. Even though twentieth-century mass media photography and film imagery eventu-ally displaced the tradition of Academic painting, during the nineteenth century the challenge of photography inspired Academic painters to achieve remarkable feats of photo-graphic realism in their art. These paintings were not only the most popular paintings of the period, they clearly reflected the values and ideals of the society that regarded them so highly: nineteenth-century middle-class industrial democracy.

Jean Auguste Dominique Ingres (1780–1867): Academic Painting before Photography

Academic painting is a term that can refer to any painting sponsored by the French Academy of Art from the time it was established by Louis XIV in the seventeenth century as part of his attempt to bring all aspects of French culture under royal control.

From that time, the Academy controlled French art in three ways: it set training and admissions standards for its own art school in Paris (École des Beaux-Arts); it sponsored annual or semiannual Salons, or public exhibitions, in Paris; and it controlled membership in the Academy itself.

David had given the Academy a more democratic form during the Revolution. He also opened up the Salons, so that the number of exhibited works during the Revolution swelled from several hundred to several thousand. David further revised the Academy and Salon under Napoleon, continuing the progress toward openness initiated earlier. The demo-cratic tenor of the Academy is reflected in the fact that, of the 410 artists represented in the Salon of 1808, 50 were women.

After Napoleon's fall, David's star pupil, Jean Auguste Dominique Ingres, took over as director of the Academy. Following the example of David under Napoleon, Ingres produced paintings that glorified the center of power in the new social order: the middle class (*bourgeoisie*). The Academy and its Salon system thus had had a long history as the main force in French art by the time photography became an artistic concern in 1839. The paintings of Ingres also reveal how the photograph, when it publicly appeared in 1839, could fit right into the Academic style of painting and ultimately become its chief rival.

Ingres and Academic Painting: "Classicizing the Middle Class"

Academic painting in the early decades of the Photographic Age provides a particularly significant picture of how the bourgeoisie saw the world, and themselves. One of the most important needs of the politically dominant middle class of the nineteenth century was for validation of its new position of power. The newly arrived businessmen and industrialists wanted to appear as a direct extension of the traditional society they had overturned and replaced. Since scenes from classical mythology and history had been the main themes of traditional aristocratic painting, Ingres used similar themes to "classicize," so to speak, the bourgeoisie. Academic paintings thus had the icon function of portraying the middle class as the heroic element maintaining the new social order.

The use of classical and mythological themes by Ingres, however, lacked the political fervor—let alone the revolutionary impact and message—of David's early historical and mythological works. David intended his paintings to electrify the public with enthusiasm for new political possibilities. The retellings of classical myth by Ingres functioned more like comfortable, dreamy props or set decorations for the stage now securely occupied by the middle class.

In a painting like *Jupiter and Thetis* by Ingres (fig. 5.2), for instance, the refined technique failed to cover up the cardboard mythological decoration underneath. Only the photographically factual appearance and the polished, neat surface related to the unrelenting pragmatism that was the true strength of his middle-class sponsors.

Portraits by Ingres: The Faces of the Middle Class

The most impressive paintings by Ingres were not the classical "Salon machines" (paintings done for Salon competition) but his brilliant portraits of upper middle class society.

His portrait of Madame Moitessier (fig. 5.3 and plate 10) presents a person whose eminently self-satisfied expression was highly representative of the successful middle class and its values. The painter's style brilliantly expresses the middle-class quest for propriety and order. His style is a study in the restraint prized by the middle class: every form

5.2

5.3

has its clear outline; nothing is left to chance; emotion, when it appears, is sheltered below a surface as controlled and polished as a mirror. The factual clarity of his style also stresses the middle class love for fact, a love that was to find even more fulfillment in the photograph.

The portrait of Madame Moitessier shows the painter's skill at rendering an almost photographic likeness. Like an airbrushed yearbook photograph, however, the features gave little hint of personal character or feeling. Ingres framed the smoothed-out face and plump but dainty hands with a properly sober background and color scheme tastefully relieved by hints of wealth in the jewelry and the clothing.

The iconic experience of the painting is further clarified by a comparison with another painting by Ingres, *Comtesse d'Haussonville* (fig. 5.4). One has no way of knowing that this beautiful lady was an aristocrat—in contrast to the middle-class Madame Moitessier—unless one reads the title of the painting. Academic painting illustrated and enforced the new social reality: the dethroned aristocracy imitated the fashionable dress of the upper middle class, the new aristocracy of industrial capitalism.

The brilliant portrait of the newspaper editor Louis François Bertin by Ingres (fig. 5.5) added a different dimension to his portrait of the middle class. Bertin was not shown enjoying the role and the rewards of the new culture; instead, he looks at us with a face and posture that express that rest-

5.2 Jean Auguste Dominique Ingres. *Jupiter and Thetis.* 1811. Oil on canvas, 10'10" × 8'5". Musée Granet, Aix-en-Provence.

5.3 Jean Auguste Dominique Ingres. *Madame Moitessier.* 1851. Oil on canvas, 57¾" × 39½". National Gallery of Art, Washington, Samuel H. Kress Collection.

5.4 Jean Auguste Dominique Ingres. *Comtesse d'Haussonville.* 1845. Oil on canvas, 4'5½" × 3'¼". Copyright The Frick Collection, New York.

5.5 Jean Auguste Dominique Ingres. *Louis François Bertin.* 1832. Oil on canvas, 46" × 35½". The Louvre, Paris.

5.4

5.5

lessness to do, to accomplish, that is the mark of the techno-logical mentality at the center of the middle class outlook on life. It is easy to sense his impatience to get the sitting over with so he can move on to something more useful.

Thus Ingres presented a kind of double portrait of the middle class: the mythic paintings, heroic but sentimental-ized, show their pretensions and aspirations; the portraits show their proudly practical, energetic side, the real strength of the new middle-class social order.

Photography: Icons that Challenged the Academy

Unlike the Romantic artists who implicitly, and sometimes explicitly, championed the subjectivity of the individual over the power of the state, Academic painters reinforced the out-look of the politically dominant middle class. The only major challenge to the social message and artistic style of Ingres and his followers came from the maverick Delacroix; public sentiment—especially from the upper middle class public—sided with Ingres and the Academy.

The arrival of photography in 1839, however, had an immediate and profound impact on middle-class society—and on Academic painting.

Within a decade of its public patent, photography became a major enthusiasm—and business—in Paris. One contem-porary cartoonist saw Paris swept away by "Daguerreo-typomania" (fig. 5.6) as early as 1840. By 1855 photography was included in the Paris World's Fair exhibition. In 1859 the Academy admitted photographs into the Salon, and by 1862 the French government officially declared, over the protests of the League of Artists Against Photography (led by Ingres), that photography was legally an art.

Photography, the ultimate icon of fact, triumphed with remarkable speed. The challenge to artists was equally profound.

Ingres, for instance, saw the arrival of the photograph as a threat to his fact-centered paintings and to the entire Aca-demic tradition he led. He called the new machine-produced images faultographs. Nevertheless, Ingres and other Aca-demic painters set a course of determined imitation of photo-graphic illusion and detail. They even admitted that they used photographs as "sketches" of nature to aid them in their painting. Academic painters still had three advantages over photography: color, size, and composition. By manipu-lating these elements, they kept their paintings "one step ahead" of the photograph throughout the nineteenth century.

The challenge of the photograph, however, came from more than its power of illusion and detail. The photograph produced a new experience of the world. The richness and complexity of this photographic experience, not just the technical perfection of photographic images, is what ulti-mately undermined the appeal of Academic art.

5.6 Maurisset.
La Daguerréotypomanie. 1840.
Lithograph.
Photo: Science Museum, London.

5.7 Paul Nadar.
Aerial Photograph Taken from a Balloon. 1858.
Bibliothèque Nationale, Paris.

5.8 Anonymous.
A Hand.
Early photograph on paper.
Photo: Science Museum, London.

5.6

The Photograph: Icon of the Expanding World of Fact

Some of the complex experiences presented by the photograph became evident in the work and attitude of one of the earliest and most influential photographers of the nineteenth century, Paul Nadar (1820–1910).

In the 1840s Nadar took to photography with the exuberance of a pioneer. After several failures, he succeeded in taking the first photographs of Paris from a balloon (fig. 5.7). To a generation that witnessed (or at least saw the re-runs of) live broadcasts of astronauts landing on the moon, this might not seem terribly impressive. In 1856, however, this photograph epitomized the marvelous sense of freedom photography provided.

Since Nadar's photograph enabled the ordinary person to gaze at Paris "from the sky" by merely looking at a photograph, why couldn't the entire cosmos—eventually—yield equally informative and gratifying results? Nature was the Great Fact; the photograph made fact accessible to the human eye. All one need do was position the camera, focus the lens, and shoot.

Nadar's aerial photograph of Paris showed how, through the photograph, the autonomous individual was now free to explore the universe wherever the camera might go.

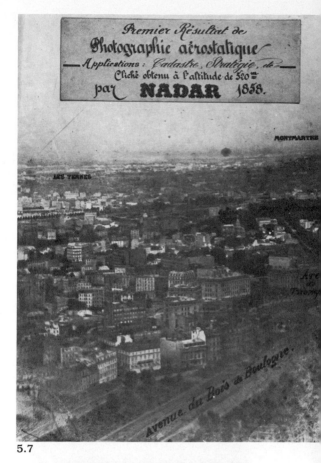

5.7

Photography as Icon I: Enlarging Nature's Self-Image

In many ways, however, the initial power of photography was easier to see in far simpler images than Nadar's triumphant aerial view of Paris. The leaf in figure 5.1 still projects the feeling of mystery in the idea of nature literally impressing its image onto photographic plates.

There is an inescapable poignancy in the equally early photograph of a human hand in figure 5.8. This image, like similar images of the human hand traced onto the walls of prehistoric caves, shows the photograph continuing perhaps the oldest continual role of art in every form of culture: insistence on the presence and the importance of the human story within nature.

Photography moved on and increased its scope and its ability to record detail decade by decade throughout the nineteenth century. Everyone, through photography, could see the Alps, the Nile, and the Amazon. Wealthier individuals found themselves in a whole new kind of picture—the tourist snapshot (fig. 5.9)—in which nature and history posed as the background for the proud individual featured as the central attraction.

Photography not only yielded up enlargements of nature previously unseen by most human beings, it also presented enlargement of nature *unseeable* by the human eye. At first

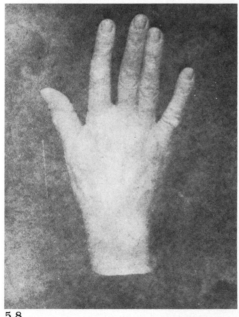

5.8

5.9

it presented close-ups of ordinary forms, like Fox Talbot's photograph of butterfly wings (fig. 5.10). Even Leonardo's incredibly detailed drawings of natural forms, like the oak leaves and acorns in figure 5.11, seem vague by comparison. Later in the century, Eadweard Muybridge photographed animals in motion (fig. 5.12), and beautiful photographs by Étienne-Jules Marey revealed the flight of birds in a single, fused sequence. Photography began to provide not only a better, but an entirely new, vision of nature.

Photography as Icon II: Pictures of the Enlarged Humanity of Culture

Nadar's view of Paris from the air also prefigured photography's power to provide new ways of seeing the reality of human cultures, both familiar and foreign.

Exotic glimpses of China, Africa, and the Near East both startled and amused European eyes. The photograph also

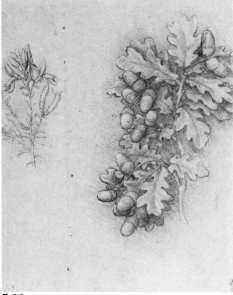

5.11

5.10

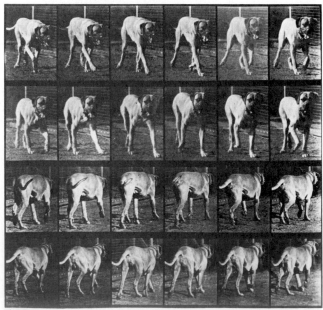

5.12

5.9 Rev. C. R. Jones.
Rome, the Coliseum, outer view.
Calotype process.
Photo: Science Museum, London.

5.10 William Henry Fox Talbot.
Wing of a Lantern Fly.
Calotype photo micrograph.
Photo: Science Museum, London.

5.11 Leonardo da Vinci.
Drawing of oak leaves with acorn, and dyer's greenwood. c. 1505.
Pen and ink.
Copyright reserved. Reproduced by Gracious Permission of Her Majesty the Queen.

5.12 Eadweard Muybridge.
Dog (from *Animals in Motion*, plate #705). 1899.
Cleveland Museum of Art, Gift of Phyllis Seltzer in memory of John Cook.

quickly brought home the horrors of domestic and foreign wars. Photographs of the Paris Communards, the socialist revolutionaries who seized the city in 1871, were later used by the government when it regained control to identify individuals to be executed. Photographs of the Crimean War brought home the enlarged and vacant image of death with none of the glory of the earlier portrayals of Napoleonic legend (fig. 5.13).

Nadar was also the proper introduction to another important iconic experience that was enlarged by the photograph: objective pictures of the human face.

Photography as Icon III: The Experience of the Individual Human Face

Nadar's adventuresome approach to photography made him the wealthiest and most sought-after portrait photographer of businessmen, industrialists, and politicians in Paris. It was

5.13 Roger Fenton.
Crimea: Valley of the Shadow of Death.
Photo: The Science Museum, London.

5.14 Paul Nadar.
Sarah Bernhardt.
Daguerreotype.
Giraudon/Art Resource.

5.13

5.14

his sensitive portraits of important figures in the Paris art world, however, that earned him a reputation as the century's first great photographer.

Nadar's portraits show an uncanny ability to suggest the sitter's unique qualities of personality. Among his portraits are photographs of Baudelaire, Delacroix, and Ingres. The great actress Sarah Bernhardt posed as Manon (fig. 5.14), a role in which she captivated Parisian audiences. The photograph captures the controlled and passionate intensity that made Bernhardt's private life as dramatic as the roles she played on stage.

The public responded enthusiastically to such portraits of famous people. In 1855, at Paris's Great Industrial Exposition there were scores of such photographs of the rich and famous. Such a response is easily recognizable today: the photograph had created the "celebrity."

At the Exposition, the public gathered around the numerous photographs of important and famous people. Today it is hard to comprehend the impact of seeing for the first time, before one's very eyes, the personalities one had only known and admired from afar.[2]

This experience quickly became more democratic. In the 1850s, the Paris photographer André Disdéri patented a process for producing small two-and-a-half-by-four-inch photographs (like passport photographs today), an inexpensive, standardized format that enabled lower middle class people to have their pictures taken. This was perhaps the most important impact of photography: everyone got into the picture.

Now, for a reasonable sum of money, a member of the economy-minded petite bourgeoisie could satisfy his desires both to emulate the rich and preserve his image for posterity.[3]

Photography not only put every man and woman (at least potentially) "into the picture," it also gave the individual control over his or her presence in pictures for the first time. Presence in pictures had always been a sacred, royal, or aristocratic privilege, or a privilege of the wealthy, that in each case implied (or asserted) a correspondingly important role in the social and/or cosmic hierarchy. With photography, everyone assumed a presence of potentially equal importance.

Napoleon III, the emperor of France between 1850 and 1870, used the new popular art of photography in a similar way to the earlier Napoleon's use of woodcuts and engravings. In order to create a bond between himself and his fellow citizens, in 1859 Napoleon III had his picture taken in this small format at Disdéri's studio. By allowing himself to be "reduced" to the dimensions of middle-class photography, the emperor shrewdly transformed the small photograph into a symbol of one of the most popular slogans of the nineteenth century: "Every man an emperor!"

Photography as Icon IV: The Machine as Symbol of Progress and Civilization

Photography made everyone an artist. Or, more precisely, it automated the making of perspective images, so that, not only could everyone be "in" pictures, everyone could also "take" pictures (fig. 5.15). This aspect of photography as machine-made image is also part of its iconic experience: the experience of a world brought increasingly subject to human control and manipulation through technology.

By the mid-nineteenth century, many people saw Western culture at the beginning of a golden age brought by the benefits of science and the machine. The photograph was an icon of the new age, not only because it came from a ma-

5.15 Advertisement for original Kodak roll
film camera. 1889.
Photo: Science Museum, London.

chine, but also because it seemed to prove that the view of
the cosmos as a machine was true.

Academic Painting I: Keeping a Step Ahead of the Photograph

The paintings of David and Ingres show the high level of
optical realism achieved by Academic painting before the
invention of photography. After 1839, Academic painters
redoubled their determination to create detail in their paintings realistic enough to rival that of the small photographs of
the mid-nineteenth century.

The attention to "photographic" detail in Academic
painting after 1839 at times became obsessive. The Salon of
1861, for instance, exhibited a large number of battle scenes
that provoked public criticism because of their close resemblance to photography. Nadar published a cartoon that
summed up the concern. Several elegantly framed battle
scenes hung together on a wall. Curling up from each canvas
was a plume of smoke that floated out beyond the border of
the frame.

Figure 5.16 shows one of the most popular battle scenes
from that Salon, Adolphe Yvon's *The Battle of Solferino*.
Paintings like this prompted the following comment from the
contemporary art critic Théophile Gautier:

One can guess from the crispness of the details, from the mathematically correct placing of the shadows, that he has taken the daguerreotype as a collaborator. The daguerreotype, which has not
been named and which hasn't received any medal, has nonetheless
done much work at the exhibition.[4]

This painting eventually took the art and photography
controversy into the courtroom. Yvon had used a photograph

of Napoleon III on horseback as the source for the central figure in the painting; the emperor had agreed to the photograph in order to avoid long hours of posing. Yvon was infuriated, however, when the photographer began to sell copies of it and sued the photographer. Yvon claimed that the photograph was his alone because he had arranged for the sitting and had decided the pose. Yvon won the case.

5.16

5.16 Adolphe Yvon.
The Battle of Solferino. 1861.
Oil on canvas.
The Louvre, Paris.

5.17 Thomas Couture.
The Romans of the Decadence. 1847.
Oil on canvas, 15′1″ × 25′4″.
The Louvre, Paris.

5.18 Adolphe William Bouguereau.
Nymphs and Satyr. 1873.
Oil on canvas, 102⅜″ × 70⅞″.
Sterling and Francine Clark Art Institute,
Williamstown, Massachusetts.

Academic Painting II: Adding Feeling to the Photographic Facts

Academic painters not only stayed ahead of photography by imitating its detail and adding color, size, and composition; they also tried to improve on photography by adding feeling to the facts.

Besides scenes of military glory, Academic painting portrayed eroticism. Academic painters explored and exploited sex for its emotional appeal long before Hollywood films or advertising retraced many of the same steps. A painting by Thomas Couture (1815–1879), *The Romans of the Decadence* (fig. 5.17) was one of the most popular Salon paintings of the entire nineteenth century. He filled its carefully researched Roman architectural setting with life-size figures of, as the title makes clear, "decadent Romans." Couture gave just enough photographic accuracy to enable the viewer's own imagination to easily transform the picture into an entire drama. The title not only serves to suggest the plot, it also allows the viewer a sense of moral righteousness. Even though Couture opposed the rigidity of the Academy and considered his painting a challenge to the decadence of contemporary French Society, *The Romans of the Decadence* has become a symbol of the artificiality of the Academic approach to art.

5.17

Later in the century, Adolphe Bouguereau (1825–1905) became famous for erotic scenes that anticipate the slick, soft-focus fantasy of modern magazine photography. *Nymphs and Satyr* (fig. 5.18) is one of Bouguereau's more restrained works of this type.

The frivolity of these examples, however, does not do justice to the overall scope and impact of Academic painting, which sometimes combined a high degree of technical perfection with genuine feeling for a subject. The paintings of historical scenes by Jean Léon Gérôme (1824–1904) show a bold sense of color, a flair for historical detail, and a movie director's sense of staging. The results were often impressive. Gérôme's painting *The Grey Eminence* (fig. 5.19) uses a far more dramatic sense of space than the long horizontal display of the figures in *The Romans of the Decadence*. Gérôme's painting resembles a still from a Hollywood movie: Couture's painting suggests a curtain call for a stage play.

The studied yet passionate paintings of horses by Rosa Bonheur (1822–1899) were praised by both Napoleon III and Delacroix. Her immense canvas *The Horse Fair* (fig. 5.20) was a sensation at the 1853 Salon. It later toured England and the United States for three years. Its gigantic size and dramatic appeal made it a pre-movie "spectacular."

The Horse Fair illustrates the connection between Academic painting and popular art during the Photographic Age. When Bonheur sold the painting for forty thousand

5.18

5.19

5.20

5.19 Jean Léon Gérôme.
The Grey Eminence. 1874.
Oil on canvas, 25¾″ × 38¾″.
Courtesy of Museum of Fine Arts, Boston,
Bequest of Susan Cornelia Warren.

5.20 Rosa Bonheur.
The Horse Fair. 1853.
Oil on canvas, 8¼″ × 16′7½″.
Metropolitan Museum of Art, New York,
Gift of Cornelius Vanderbilt, 1887.

pounds, the price included reproduction rights (copyright).
Sales of the subsequent engraving of *The Horse Fair* in
Europe and America brought the owner of the painting a fortune. The demand for publication rights is evidence that
inexpensive engravings and lithographs took Academic
painting to a far broader audience for a far greater range of
impact than the Salon exhibition by itself would suggest. As
Robert Hughes has pointed out:

The ownership of these rights was of vast importance. . . . It affected
the price of popular pictures in exactly the same way that the market for film and TV rights affects the price of popular novels today.[5]

These paintings show the basic importance of Academic paintings: Socially, they were important precisely because they reflected the popular ideals and tastes of their upper middle class sponsors; artistically, they showed (and still show) an impressive power to forcefully place the viewer within a scene or an event. This ability, according to the art historian Leo Rosenthal, was the main intention of the Academic painter's style:

Painting for them [the Academics] is only a medium; the interest of the picture does not depend on its aesthetic merit, but on the scene represented: the painter must be a clever dramatist, a good costume designer, an adroit stage director.[6]

Academic painting was popular because it had the content of mass media art—dramatic stories, sex, violence, travelogues, soap operas, fantasy, and so forth. It presented this content in photographically realistic imagery that anyone could understand. But oil painting would not be able to compete against the narrative illusion of color photography and motion pictures in the twentieth century.

The photographically detailed scenes that Academic painters made real enough for the entire public to enjoy did not include, however, facts Salon visitors preferred not to see. If Academic paintings were the only visual record of the nineteenth century, it would appear to have indeed achieved the golden age to which it aspired. The real social and artistic world of the nineteenth century, however, was far broader than the world glimpsed in the lustrous canvases of Gérôme, Bouguereau, and Ingres. Their realism not only was not enough, it was ultimately deceptive. It disguised the crisis of realism that affected both society and art at the time.

In social terms, there were no Academic paintings of the Europe-wide workers' revolt of 1848—at least from the workers' point of view. The artistic dimension of the crisis became visible, however, in the public reaction to the Great Exhibition of 1851 in London.

The Great Exhibition of 1851: Celebration of the Myth of Progress through the Machine

The Great Exhibition was a world's fair that brought together machines and crafts from all over the world. Its main purpose was to show that the age of capitalism, of science, and of machinery was ushering in the kind of golden age that shimmered on the surface of Academic painting.

The art historian Nikolas Pevsner describes England on the eve of the Great Exhibition as the "workshop of the world and the paradise of a successful bourgeoisie, governed by a bourgeois and efficient prince consort."[7]

The prince consort was Prince Albert, who helped open the Exhibition. The following words are from his public address:

134

Nobody who has paid any attention to the particular features of the present era will doubt for a moment that we are living in a period of most wonderful transition, which tends rapidly to the accomplishment of that great end to which indeed all history points, the realization of the unity of all mankind.[8]

The Machine Cathedral: The Crystal Palace

Framing the prince's address was the marvelous structure that was built to both contain and symbolize the event, the Crystal Palace (fig. 5.21).

Designed as a prefabricated structure made entirely of iron and glass, it was 1,851 feet long and spacious enough to hold nine cathedrals the size of Chartres. Like the cathedrals, the Crystal Palace had an almost visionary impact appropriate to its time. The architectural space of the Crystal Palace needed no stained glass or ceiling painting to convey its iconic message; the blue-colored iron structure was so high that viewers commented on how it seemed to merge with the sky seen through the clear windows. The new industrial material, iron, reached so high that it visually joined the earth with the sky.

The enormous process of building the Crystal Palace was as remarkable as its visionary effect. Joseph Paxton, the architect, designed the iron beams in modular lengths of twenty-four feet. This standardized, mass-produced building

5.21 Joseph Paxton.
Crystal Palace, London. 1850–51.
Cast iron and glass. Width 408',
length 1,851'. (Etching)
Victoria and Albert Museum, London.

5.22 Joseph Paxton. Crystal Palace.
Interior view.
(Etching by Lothar Buchar).
Victoria and Albert Museum, London.

5.21

material made it possible for construction to be completed in less than a year; it and the efficient building process were acknowledged as symbols of the point in time—1851—at which the technological spirit had definitively established itself as proof of the inevitable progress of Western culture.

Proof of the superiority of Western culture was part of the plan of the Crystal Palace and the Great Exhibition. This superiority was to be seen not only in the technological form of the Crystal Palce but also in the industrial machinery—from dynamos to train engines—displayed inside (fig. 5.22). Other galleries showed Western machine-produced crafts—rugs, tapestries, furniture, and so on—alongside handmade crafts from the "less advanced" countries of the world.

But this display of machine-produced crafts next to handmade crafts did not turn out as planned. Even to those who sponsored the exhibition, the machine-produced crafts were embarrassingly inferior, an unqualified disaster. This inferior quality of machine-produced crafts was a major shock to European visitors. Pevsner comments on the disappointment of thousands of viewers who

had grown up amid unprecedented discoveries in science and technique. There were the new railways and powerlooms, there were the most cunning inventions to facilitate the production of almost any object formerly made so laboriously by craftsmen—why should these wonderful improvements not help to improve art as well?[9]

However, the crafts and designs executed by machines were shockingly inferior to those produced by hand in the "less developed" cultures. Even realistic images failed: visitors complained about having "to step over bulging scrolls and into large, unpleasantly realistic flowers" that were part of the design of machine-produced carpets.[10]

5.22

The shock of the machine-produced crafts revealed the human and artistic dilemma at the heart of the Photographic Age: how can art built on optically realistic images of objective facts adequately express the inner world of human feeling and subjectivity?

The artistic crisis inside the Crystal Palace was paralleled by a social crisis outside the Crystal Palace. The social crisis was produced by the organization of society itself around the machine.

The Industrial Revolution: Organizing Society around the Machine

The engravings from the *Encyclopedia* had pictured the effects of the machine in almost as optimistic a way as that suggested by the displays of machinery in the Great Exhibition. These engravings form the "pre-industrial" vision of technology. The vastly larger steam- and coal-powered machines that tapped into the clockwork cosmos during the nineteenth century made them look like toys. In many European towns the factory had taken over the cathedral, not only as the town's most prominent building, but also as its true organizing principle. What such a factory town was like emerges in the vivid description of Charles Dickens's "Coketown":

It was a town of unnatural red and black, like the painted face of a savage. It was a town of machinery and tall chimneys, out of which interminable serpents of smoke trailed themselves forever and ever, and never got uncoiled. It had a black canal in it, and a river that ran purple with ill-smelling dye. . . .

It contained several large streets all very like one another, and many small streets still more like one another, inhabited by people equally like one another, who all went in and out at the same hour, with the same sound upon the same pavements, to do the same work, and to whom every day was the same as yesterday and tomorrow, and every year the counterpart of the last and the next. . . .

Fact, fact, fact, everywhere . . . and what you couldn't state in figures, or show to be purchasable in the cheapest market and salable in the dearest, was not and never should be, world without end. Amen.[11]

By the mid-nineteenth century, the autonomous and reasonable being in Diderot's engravings had too often become a laborer who led a squalid life centered around a factory that produced woolens or shoes. More precisely, the machines served woolens or shoes and people served the machines. Géricault's lithograph of the derelict old man on the London streets (fig. 4.38) is a portrait of this large group of nineteenth-century working-class people who became known as "the proletariat."

The Industrial Revolution accomplished with astonishing rapidity two changes unknown to previous centuries: it replaced the work of the craftsman, and it began the transformation of the physical and social environment into one congenial to business and industry.

The Great Exhibition proved that machines could produce realistic imagery. It proved that machines could produce many products more cheaply. It proved that technology could tap into the energies of the cosmos. But it also proved that machines could not replace human sensitivity.

Baudelaire: An Appeal to the Bourgeoisie

Baudelaire had addressed these issues before the invention of photography, when he defended the subjectivity and feeling in the art of Romantics like Delacroix. Like Dickens, with his description of "Coketown," Baudelaire saw a compulsive attachment to facts and utility as the major flaw permeating the new industry-based society, despite the many benefits such a society offered. He addressed this issue, and the bourgeoisie, directly in his review of the Salon of 1847:

To the Bourgeoisie:
You need art . . . because public business and trade take up three-quarters of your day . . . and yet it is just that if two-thirds of your time are devoted to knowledge, then the remaining third should be occupied by feeling—it is by feeling alone that art is to be understood; and it is in this way that the equilibrium of your soul's forces will be established.[12]

Baudelaire's views are strikingly similar to those of the great contemporary scientist Charles Darwin. At the end of his life, Darwin described how his mind had come to dominate his ability to feel:

My mind seems to have become a kind of machine for grinding general laws out of large collections of facts. . . . If I had to live my life again, I would have made a rule to read some poetry and listen to some music at least once a week. . . . The loss of these tastes is a loss of happiness . . . by enfeebling the emotional part of our nature.[13]

The dilemma facing art was similar to the crisis of realism affecting Western culture as a whole: How do machines serve society and the individual without society and individuals becoming enslaved to machines? How does an art based on objectivity and photographic realism deal with the inner world of human feeling?

Those who opposed either the artistic or the social dominance represented by Academic painting became known as the avant-garde. The long and bitter battle between Academic painting and the avant-garde emerged with special clarity (at about the same time as the Crystal Palace) in the work and art of the artist, Gustave Courbet.

Gustave Courbet (1819–1877): "Bohemian" Painter of Unwanted Facts

In one sense, Courbet's approach reflected the objective viewpoint of the middle class. Courbet saw art as a kind of scientific instrument for portraying observable facts:

The art of painting can consist only in the representation of objects visible and tangible to the painter. . . . I also hold that painting is an essentially concrete art, and can consist only of the representation of things both real and existing. . . . Show me an angel and I will paint one.[14]

It is hard to imagine a more bluntly factual approach. Courbet's troubles with Academic painting arose primarily because he chose to present "unwanted" facts—without the comforting gloss of sentiment mastered by Academic painting. The middle class did not appreciate Courbet's facts at all.

By the standards of the Academy, Courbet's *Burial at Ornans* (fig. 5.23) presents the world far too rudely. The faces of the people—portraits of Courbet's friends in Ornans, his hometown—are weary and downright homely. Courbet presented the people and the landscape with the crudity and coarse surface of peasant life itself; he even allowed a dog to wander into the center of the painting. His thick brushwork literally thrust the world of fact at the spectator, unmitigated by any reassuring charm. Ornans was a peasant town; noth-

5.23 Gustave Courbet.
Burial at Ornans. 1849.
Oil on canvas, 10'3" × 20'10".
The Louvre, Paris.

5.24 Gustave Courbet.
The Stonebreakers. 1849.
Oil on canvas, 63" × 102". (Destroyed in World War II).
Photo: Staatliche Kunstsammlungen, Dresden.

5.23

5.24

ing in the painting appealed to the middle-class image of the world or of themselves.

Peasants had been acceptable as sentimental subjects of small paintings since the genre scenes introduced by Dutch painters in the seventeenth century. But not only were Courbet's peasants rudely unsentimental, their insignificant lives were blown up to the same scale as the mythological and historical paintings of the Salon. It was one thing for the emperor to condescend to fit his image to the scale of popular photographs; it was a revolutionary act for a painter to elevate peasants to the heroic scale of the emperor.

Even more than this rudeness, Courbet's painted world was a mote in the eye: it accused. Precisely by its photographic objectivity it became a far too realistic mirror of facts about the new social order that the middle class hoped, through the sentimental consolations and distractions of most Academic art, to ignore.

Courbet's painting *The Stonebreakers* (fig. 5.24) was equally unacceptable. It shows a boy assisting an older man in unskilled and repetitious manual labor. Courbet's brush merely observes the scene with complete objectivity. The lack of emotion in the painting underscores the emptiness of the activity itself.

The people in *The Stonebreakers* are not heroic embodiments of the new age; they are the passive victims of its forces. Courbet's friend, the socialist Pierre Proudhon, described the old man in the painting this way:

His motionless face is heartbreakingly melancholy. His stiff arms rise and fall with the regularity of a lever. Here indeed is the mechanical or mechanized man, in the state of ruin to which our splendid civilization and our incomparable industry have reduced him.

Proudhon went on to describe the boy:

This modern servitude devours the generations in their growth: here is the proletariat.[15]

The embarrassment of these paintings was not like that in Dickens's description of "Coketown," with its brutal picture of a mechanized labor force and social order. Courbet's proletariat subjects—the rural poor—are luckier. But it is the dullness, the emptiness, of their existence that Courbet reveals in its stark reality. The civilization of pragmatism and fact—the civilization of the nineteenth-century bourgeoisie—even when it is not cruel, is excruciatingly dull. It kills with utility.

Courbet welcomed the hostility his paintings provoked in polite middle-class society. When his paintings were rejected from the Paris Worlds' Fair of 1855, he set up his own "one-man show" nearby and entitled it, "The Pavilion of Realism." The title was appropriate. His paintings underscored the crisis of realism that Academic painting, seen by itself, disguised. His paintings showed the split in the new

140

industrial society that kept the poor from sharing in the increasing prosperity of the middle and upper classes.

The centerpiece of this rebellious and defiant street exhibition was Courbet's only major symbolic work. Since it summed up his views of the true calling of the artist, he titled the painting *The Studio: A Real Allegory of the Last Seven Years of My Life* (fig. 5.25).

The left side of the painting is occupied by characters who gravitate from the shadow toward the light of the artist at work before his easel—Courbet himself. This flattering arrangement is similar in composition to Rembrandt's *Hundred-Guilder Print* (fig. 4.6), which Courbet had seen and admired during a trip to Amsterdam. The plumed hat and guitar symbolize Courbet's rejection of Romanticism. The mannequin of Academic drawing studios, hanging like a crucifixion scene, is also discarded.

On the right are writers and colleagues whom Courbet sees as contributing to a more enlightened social vision. This group includes portraits of Baudelaire and Proudhon.

At the center of the painting, a nude female figure gazes over Courbet's shoulder. In Academic and traditional art, she would represent the inspiration of the Muses. In Courbet's painting, she is an ordinary woman; her feet are firmly on the ground, firmly in reality. The two children near the artist's easel are especially interesting. One child gazes at the artist at work. The other draws a figure on a piece of paper

5.25 Gustave Courbet.
The Studio: A Real Allegory of the Last Seven Years of My Life. 1855. Oil on canvas, 11′9¾″ × 19′6⅝″. The Louvre, Paris.

5.25

that resembles the drawings made by cartoonists to satirize the figures in Courbet's paintings. If children represent the future, the future clearly belongs to Courbet.

The precise meaning of the painting in all its detail has never been worked out. Its general message, though, is quite clear. The painting fits its title: it is an allegory, a symbolic representation of Courbet's life as an artist, including its meaning as a social and moral force. Courbet appoints himself, not to reflect the reigning social and artistic values, but to be "out front"—"avant-garde"—in changing those values.

Courbet served notice with this painting, appropriately exhibited as a rebel exhibition, that he took his role as an artist with a radically new seriousness. The artist must no longer paint pictures to match the vision of others. The artist must take the initiative in provoking social change. David had also hoped to change society through art, but his art had ultimately become propaganda for the state; most of all, it was based on the ideas of others. Courbet, alone before his easel, places the artist as the originator—the seer—not the mere translator of approved visions.

Regardless of the validity of his particular social ideals, Courbet's self-proclaimed Realism unmasked the "realism" of the Academic painters by revealing the inherent social and artistic instability underlying the culture of the Photographic Age. As Courbet's work showed, this instability stemmed from the existence of two segments that were outside middle-class culture and that represented potential social and cultural revolution and change: the proletariat, or working class, and the artistic avant-garde.

Courbet relished his avant-garde role in middle-class society. He called himself a "bohemian." In 1871 he joined the "Communards," the socialists who attempted to take Paris and secede from France in order to form a socialist state. Courbet escaped execution when the Commune fell, though he did have to serve a term in jail and then go into exile.

Yet despite the political and artistic integrity of Courbet in his role as an avant-garde artist, his very dependence on a basically photographic style of painting compromised his protest against the mechanical coldness that threatened to cancel genuine progress. If Academic paintings resemble Hollywood melodrama and sentimentality, Courbet's paintings resemble today's filmed documentaries. Facts are still the heroes in Courbet's paintings, even though they are socialist facts instead of bourgeois facts. Courbet's art carried a revolutionary social message, but its artistic form was still rooted in the photograph.

Baudelaire: "The Universe without Man"

In 1859, even after Courbet's defiant one-man street exhibition, Baudelaire saw the preoccupation with fact as still threatening to overwhelm the quality of both art and society.

He even chided the newer, more ruggedly honest painters who followed Courbet's example. He did not call them Realists, he called them "positivists":

They say, "I want to represent things as they are, or rather as they would be, supposing that I did not exist." In other words, the universe without man.[16]

Baudelaire thus concluded, after reviewing the Salon of 1859 (which included a show of photography), that the invention of photography had been a disaster. He saw photography as the perfect art form for the middle class, who approached technology and utility with an almost religious faith:

And now the faithful says to himself: "Since photography gives us every guarantee of exactitude that we could desire (they really believe that, the mad fools), then photography and art are the same thing." From that moment our squalid society rushed, Narcissus to a man, to gaze at its trivial image on a scrap of metal. . . .

Each day Art further diminishes its self-respect by bowing down before external reality; each day the painter becomes more and more given to painting not what he dreams but what he sees. . . . Could you find an honest observer to declare that the invasion of photography and the great industrial madness of our times have no part at all in this deplorable result?[17]

In 1859, in Baudelaire's view, Academic painting, photography, and even the defiant avant-garde art of Courbet were part of the enclosed circle of mechanization and the cult of Fact. To Baudelaire, Courbet had not solved the artistic crisis of realism, though he had clarified its existence and shown its social dimensions.

What Baudelaire did not see yet appearing was a kind of painting that truly depicted, in his phrase, the "heroism of modern times"—a heroism that did not exclude the bourgeoisie but included their achievements and added to them the values that, in the realm of art, come under the term *imagination*—feeling added to fact.

This kind of painting was about to appear under the hand of one of Baudelaire's own artist friends, a man who was, paradoxically, a follower of Courbet and a student of Couture: Édouard Manet.

Manet proceeded to again illustrate the point that artists themselves had invented—beginning with perspective—the language that was eventually built into photography. It was therefore one of the obligations of artists themselves to invent a language that went beyond perspective and beyond photography. Manet began to invent such a language; even more than Courbet, he is the founder of the modern tradition of the avant-garde.

ASSESSMENTS

1. Have you ever wanted to photograph, draw, or paint something you thought valuable or interesting, but didn't follow through because it had not been done before? Or because it was against some social convention?
2. How important are conventions and fads in determining your style of dress?
3. In your opinion, does a painting have value in itself, or must it represent something else beyond it?
4. Are you aware of what you first see when you notice a painting—the overall picture, content, color? Something else?
5. Many artists use art to express and create personal meanings. Do you think you could use art the same way, even if you don't consider yourself an artist?

Courbet's art illustrated the social and artistic limitations that were helping to produce a crisis of realism within Western culture. His paintings criticized a social organization, based on the priority of profit and utility, that had produced a large mass of rural and urban poor—the proletariat. His paintings also challenged the Academy's narrow interpretation of traditional themes and tendency to either sentimentalize or ignore many aspects of modern life.

The art of Édouard Manet (1832–1883) struck even closer to the center of the nineteenth century's social and artistic crisis. Manet painted unwelcome scenes of modern Paris, and he challenged the limitations of the Academic style of photographic realism.

Manet, however, was much different from Courbet in both personality and art. Courbet's rebellious role was self-chosen: he bragged about being a "bohemian" (that is, a wanderer, an outsider). As the portrait of him by his young friend Henri Fantin-Latour (fig. 6.1) clearly implies, Édouard Manet was not a likely candidate for the role of challenger of the status quo, either socially or artistically. Manet was a most reluctant rebel.

A social "insider" as much as he was an outsider, he had an independent income and moved comfortably among the rich; Courbet relished the discomfort he caused the upper class. Manet kept his social passport valid in upper-class Paris as well as in bohemian Paris. In his studio, he dressed as impeccably as he did for his strolls and visits to the social world of the most fashionable cafes. When his art brought scorn from the Establishment, Manet—unlike the defiant Courbet—felt great personal pain. But in fact, it was just this desire to keep one foot in the museums and the other in the modernity of the streets that enabled him to become the pivotal figure of the avant-garde. The nineteenth-century crisis of realism was part of Manet's own experience and personality.

Manet's art addressed the social and artistic crisis of realism in several ways. He painted scenes of modern Paris in order to close the gap between the stuffy traditionalism of Academic painting and the actual way of life of modern Parisians. He attempted to address the challenge of photography, not by imitating its factual detail, but by incorporating aspects of its new way of seeing into painting. Perhaps most important, Manet's style of painting began to move away from perspective itself, which Academic painters had perfected to the limits of photographic realism. His art changed the basic visual language that had ruled Western art since Brunelleschi's perspective experiment in the early fifteenth century. In summary, Manet helped resolve the nineteenth-century crisis of realism by reorienting the subject matter and form of painting toward a more direct and flexible contact with modern life.

If Brunelleschi's little painting of the Baptistry of Florence began the Perspective Age, honor for the definitive avant-garde break with the dominance of Academic subject

6.1

matter and photographic realism can be divided between two early paintings by Manet: *Luncheon on the Grass* (fig. 6.2) and *Olympia* (fig. 6.3) and (plate 11). Unlike Brunelleschi's perspective, however, the new visual language of Manet's paintings provoked fierce and almost universal scorn.

The Salon of 1863: The Shock of the New

Manet did not intend to shock anyone when he submitted *Luncheon on the Grass* to the Salon of 1863. He had looked forward to the Salon with high hopes; one of his earlier paintings, *Spanish Guitar Player*, had earned him critical praise and an honorable mention in the same Salon (1861) that had honored Yvon's *The Battle of Solferino* (fig. 5.16). Manet hoped to follow his early success with a painting that would be strikingly original—original enough to stand out in a crowd of almost a thousand accepted works. He also wanted it to be sufficiently rooted in tradition to appeal to Academic and middle-class taste.

  Luncheon on the Grass, however, was a complete fiasco. The official Salon of 1863 rejected it. It then became the derided and notorious centerpiece of the Salon of the

6.1 Henri Fantin-Latour.
Portrait of Édouard Manet. 1867.
Oil on canvas, 46″ × 35½″.
Art Institute of Chicago, Stickney Fund.

6.2 Édouard Manet.
Luncheon on the Grass. 1863.
Oil on canvas, 7′3¾″ × 8′10¾″.
The Louvre, Paris.

6.2

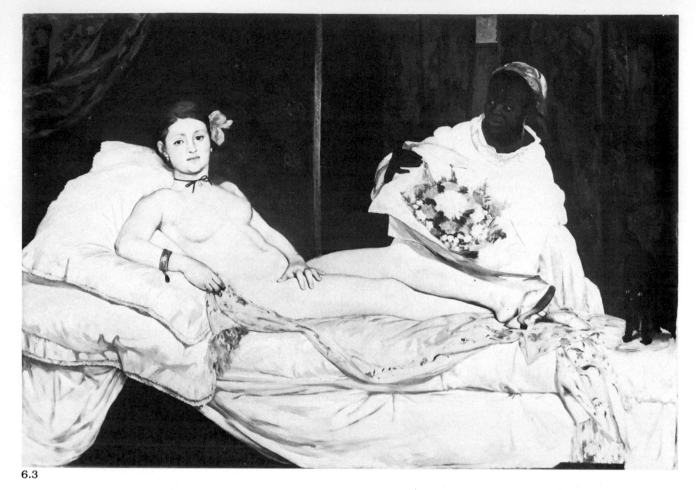

6.3

Rejected (*Salon des Refuses*), an exhibition hastily put together by the government after a public outcry by artists, like Manet, whose work had been rejected by the official Salon. Over four thousand works were rejected by the jury in 1863.

The second painting, *Olympia*, although painted in 1863, was submitted and accepted in the official Salon of 1865. Unfortunately for Manet, *Olympia* became the derided and notorious centerpiece of the *official* Salon!

What caused such a remarkably hostile public reaction? Despite his drive for acceptance, Manet's works provoked an even more hostile response than Courbet's earlier socialist-inspired paintings of rural peasants and workers. The reasons for the strength of this public and critical reaction are very complex; the depth of this reaction helps to indicate the dimensions of the crisis of realism that underlay nineteenth-century art and society.

Manet's Strategy: Modernizing "High Art" Subject Matter

Ironically, Manet calculated his potential for success with both paintings by basing them on the firmest possible grounds. The theme and composition of *Luncheon on the Grass* were derived from an Italian Renaissance masterpiece painted in 1510 by Giorgione da Castelfranco (c. 1476/8–1510) (fig. 6.4) that hung in the Louvre. Giorgione's painting was well known to the same public and critics who would see *Luncheon on the Grass*.

Olympia was based on an equally traditional and secure source: the *Venus of Urbino* by Titian (c. 1487–1576) (fig. 6.5), painted in 1538.

6.4

6.5

6.3 Édouard Manet.
Olympia. 1863.
Oil on canvas, 51¼″ × 74¾″.
The Louvre, Paris.

6.4 Giorgione da Castelfranco.
Pastoral Concert. c. 1510.
Oil on canvas, 3′7¼″ × 4′6⅜″.
The Louvre, Paris.

6.5 Titian.
Venus of Urbino. 1538.
Oil on canvas, 25⅝″ × 46⅞″.
Uffizi Gallery, Florence. Alinari/Art Resource.

Manet renewed these themes by portraying each one as a contemporary event. His decision to pattern contemporary Paris after Renaissance paintings reflected his agreement with his friend Baudelaire's call for a "heroism of modern times." Manet hoped these two paintings would combine the strength of the old with the vitality of the new.

The strategy, as noted, failed disastrously.

Manet's Artistic Offense: Severing the Connection with the Ideal World

One obvious reason for the public reaction to Manet's paintings was his seeming disregard of one of the essential qualities of Academic painting. Manet's paintings failed to present an ideal world as a goal for the present to imitate. The public did not want to see the present more clearly and vividly; they wanted to see the present reflected and softened by the rearview-mirror approach of Academic painting.

The four people in *Luncheon on the Grass* were obviously not borrowed from some idealized existence. They included, in fact, Manet's brother (Eugène), his future brother-in-law, and his favorite model, Victorine. Victorine was known to the Salon public from Manet's earlier paintings.

These three people—real people—and the figure of the woman in the background were obviously enjoying themselves in present-day Paris. Part of the pleasure apparently included the lark of posing as parts of a Renaissance painting. The scene seemed, at best, undignified. The painting gave the impression that as soon as the posing was finished, they would also thoroughly enjoy the meal that served for the moment as a marvelously painted miniature Dutch still life in the painting's lower foreground.

Manet's painting was a homage so entirely directed to the enjoyment of the present that the "ideal world" conjured up in Renaissance painting was destroyed even while it was being superficially imitated.

So, despite Manet's brilliant orchestration of traditional themes prized by Academic painting—a nude, figures in a landscape, a still life—the public accurately perceived that these elements were not being treated as elements of an ideal world. The public therefore saw the mixture as merely ludicrous.

Manet's *Olympia*: An Unwelcome "Venus" for Modern Paris

Olympia fared no better before the public or the critics in the Salon of 1865.

The contemporary art critic Ernest Chesneau—who had bought one of Manet's earlier paintings—wrote the following comments about *Olympia*:

I must say that the grotesque aspect of his contributions has two causes: first, an almost childish ignorance of the fundamentals of drawing, and then a prejudice in favor of inconceivable vulgarity. . . . He succeeds in provoking almost scandalous laughter, which causes the Salon visitors to crowd around this ludicrous creature called "Olympia."[1]

In order to appreciate what the public and the critics preferred, it is helpful to see an Academic painting from the Salon of 1865 that was hailed by the same critics who condemned Manet's two paintings as both immoral and inept. Alexander Cabanel's *Birth of Venus* (fig. 6.6) was not only a favorite of the crowds and of the professional critics, it was bought by the "first citizen" himself, Napoleon III.

The prestigious critic Paul de Saint-Victor described Cabanel's painting this way:

> We give the prize, as the public does, to that of M. Cabanel. It is a morsel from the gods and the first picture of the Salon. One cannot praise too highly the virgin purity of the neck, the simplicity of the stomach, the supple undulating turn of her hip, the pallor of her thighs, the delicate formation of her feet right down to her bent toe, to her curled fingers, as they are done by Correggio.[2]

It is difficult not to admire Saint-Victor's thoroughness of observation, which encompasses the Venus from her neck to her toes. Yet his praise makes even more clear the preconceptions that Saint-Victor and the public brought with them, preconceptions that enabled them to see Cabanel's *Venus* as nude and forced them to see Manet's *Olympia* as merely naked. Like the nudes in Academic paintings, Cabanel's *Venus* was not of the present world at all; she emerged—even if a bit wantonly—from the ideal world to which the bourgeoisie aspired.

Bouguereau, Couture, and Cabanel obligingly presented nudes ("Venuses") for fantasizing about from a safe distance. Manet's naked *Olympia* was simply too close for comfort. She was far too modern. Despite Manet's homage to the past in his openness to the present, Academic painting demonstrated again its powerful hold onto the political and social majority that Manet hoped to please.

Manet's Artistic Revolution: A New Language of Artistic Form

Manet's combining of the artistic tradition of the past with his scenes of contemporary Paris would be enough to explain his rejection by the public. His difficulties, however, were magnified by Manet's dramatic innovations in artistic form. These changes not only challenged traditional concepts of

6.6 Alexandre Cabanel. *Birth of Venus.* 1863. Oil on canvas, 2′7½″ × 4′5″. The Louvre, Paris.

color and composition but decisively broke with the central formal structure of paintings since Brunelleschi himself: the perspective-based illusion of three-dimensional form. Manet's changes, quite simply, made his paintings look flat.

Yet even this, like Manet's choice of subject matter, had originated as a response to traditional painting. Just as Manet had naively hoped to combine the old and the new in subject matter, he had also hoped to uncover an entirely new way of using color. His teacher, the famous Academic painter Thomas Couture, taught the time-honored technique of carefully blending colors to create smooth transitions from light to dark. Manet changed this. Manet believed that

light appeared to the human eye with a unity such that a single tone was sufficient to render it. . . . It was preferable, crude though it may seem, to pass suddenly from light to darkness rather than accumulate features the eye does not see and which not only weaken the force of light but accentuate the colouring of the shadows.[3]

Manet, in short, justified his bold use of color contrasts as being more natural (and thus more scientific) than the seemingly photographic illusionism of Academic painting.

The bold areas of color also looked like the photographs of the day, which usually lit the subject from the front. This kind of lighting produced little of the dramatic dark and light values, or "chiaroscuro," that had been popular in Western art since the time of Leonardo.

The curious look of Manet's work resembled another aspect of photography also; his compositions had the "unedited" look of snapshots. Manet, in other words, began to take the kind of composition seen in the earlier paintings of

6.7 Édouard Manet.
Gare Saint-Lazare. 1873.
Oil on canvas, 36¾″ × 45⅛″.
National Gallery of Art, Washington, Gift of Horace Havemeyer in memory of his mother, Louisine W. Havemeyer, 1956.

6.8 Utagawa Hiroshige.
The Hurricane, from the series, *Fifty-three Stations of the Tokaido.*
19th century.
Japanese woodcut (Edo period), Ukiyo-e school, 14⅞″ × 9¹⁵⁄₁₆″.
Cleveland Museum of Art, Gift of Mrs. T. Wingate Todd from the collection of Dr. T. Wingate Todd.

6.9 Wood-engraving block.
Smithsonian Institution, Washington. Photo # 73-1944.

6.7

Constable and Jones into the Salon. This "snapshot" composition was an important aspect of Manet's style. It conveyed the immediacy, the sense of the present, that Manet sought.

This kind of composition can be seen in Manet's painting of 1873 *Gare Saint-Lazare* (fig. 6.7); it looks remarkably like a snapshot. The woman in the painting is Victorine, the model used for *Luncheon on the Grass*. She looks up as if someone had just distracted her from her book. The puppy and the little girl keep their attention elsewhere.

This painting was accepted into the Salon of 1874, but it was criticized widely because though it was named for a Paris train station, it showed smoke but no trains. The public expected the title (as in a good Academic painting) to sum up the story of the picture. *Gare Saint-Lazare* acknowledged the ordinary quality, not the novelty, of trains. For Manet, trains were now merely a part of the background of everyday life. The attitudes of the figures in the picture were meant to be equally casual—part of the quickly changing urban scene.

Manet and Popular Art: The Mass Media Begin to Influence "High Art"

Manet's problems with critics and the public went beyond his unacceptable approach to subject matter and his unconventional way of imitating photography. He was also accused of corrupting fine art with ingredients borrowed from the wide range of popular art then flooding Paris.

Manet, like Courbet, was accused of imitating the crude, flat color effects of the popular and inexpensive images d'Epinal, the woodcuts that had been used so successfully by Napoleon's propaganda machine. Manet's work was also compared—unfavorably—to the flat color and design seen in the Japanese woodcuts that had recently become familiar in Paris. These woodcuts, like *The Hurricane* (fig. 6.8) by Utagawa Hiroshige (1797–1858) were inexpensive and popular in Japan. They were called ukiyo-e ("the passing world") prints because they depicted scenes of ordinary life.

It is important to note that photography was not a mass art form in the nineteenth century. Photographs could not be directly adapted to the new mechanized printing presses without expensive and laborious conversion into the format of an etching, engraving, or woodcut. These traditional forms of printed pictures thus provided the images that illustrated the first modern mass circulation journals and newspapers.

The adaptation of etchings, woodcuts, and engravings to the new presses was itself a complicated affair. Figure 6.9 shows an American wood engraving that is ready for the printing press. The printing surface, after being drawn on by one artist, has been cut into small sections that have been engraved by craftsmen. The image on the block has origi-

6.8

6.9

152

nally been copied from a sketch done by an artist at the scene—a Civil War campground. This is the kind of image of the Civil War that was seen by Americans in *Harper's Weekly* and other publications similar to those that Manet and his generation were reading in Paris. One of America's greatest nineteenth-century artists, Winslow Homer (1836–1910), was a visual reporter for *Harper's* whose drawings were seen by the public in the form of wood engravings (fig. 6.10).

These kinds of images are only a small portion of the printed pictures of various kinds that had become a major element of the visual environment in Paris by mid-century. The most influential form of popular art was the newly invented process of lithography.

6.10 *The Sharpshooter.*
From a drawing by Winslow Homer in *Harper's Weekly*, 11/15/1862.
Smithsonian Institution, Washington. Photo # X 1482 Exhibits.

6.11 Transition of academic painting to perspective images of the mass media.

6.12 Honoré Daumier.
Nadar Elevating Photography to the Height of Art. 1863.
Lithograph.
Courtesy of the Science Museum, London

6.10

The Lithograph: The Most Powerful of the Early Mass Media Images

Lithography was invented by Aloys Senefelder and patented in Germany in 1799. The lithograph (literally, "stone-drawing") revolutionized the process of printing images by enabling an artist to draw directly onto a stone. After treating it with chemicals, a printer could produce hundreds of copies of the image in a tiny fraction of the time required by the three older techniques, etching, engraving, and woodcutting. (See Basic Printmaking Processes in the color section.) Since, for the artist, lithography was the most direct method of working, lithographic images dominated in the flood of popular images that inundated Paris and other Western cities beginning in the 1820s.

Despite its relative directness and speed, the lithographic process required the stone to be printed separately from the presses that could print both type (words) and engraved or etched images at the same time on the same page. The main outlet for the new art of lithography was as a separate sheet circulated with the newspaper.

Honoré Daumier (1808–1879): The Public Easel of the Mass Media

The artist whose work most clearly shows the impact of the popular art of lithography on the art of Manet and his generation is Honoré Daumier. Daumier referred to the newspaper format as his "public easel," because for almost fifty years (1828–79) it gave him an audience of unparalleled size. He belonged to the first generation of artists who could address a mass audience. Until the Industrial Revolution and the massive influx of people into cities, there was no mass audience. The Industrial Revolution weakened the craft and folk art tradition that had been part of the substance of peasant life. Both the new urban middle class and the new urban proletariat needed new forms of art. Artists like Daumier used the mass media to combine the remnants of traditional folk art and religious art with new kinds of images that reflected the modern urban environment. The second quarter of the nineteenth century thus marks the beginning of the modern mass media in both its technological form and its iconic impact on a more mobile, urban population. Figure 6.11 shows how mass media imagery from this time on continues the Western tradition of perspective images.

Unlike Academic art, with its entrenched flattery, Daumier's lithographs satirized, cajoled, and even inspired the city of Paris with images that reminded all classes of the gap between their ideals and their practice.

His drawings dealt with the major issues and events of his day. The ongoing dispute about the respective merits of photography and art inspired the lithograph drawing of Nadar photographing Paris from a balloon. Daumier's title poked fun at the artistic aspirations of photographers like Nadar: *Nadar Elevating Photography to the Height of Art* (fig. 6.12).

6.12

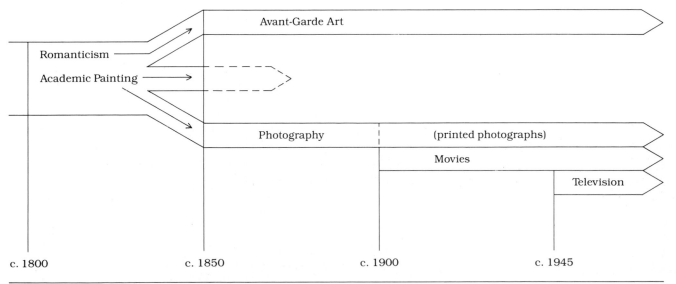

6.11

6.13

6.14

Daumier's lithographic masterpiece is probably his drawing of the murder of an innocent worker and his family in a proletarian section of Paris (near Daumier's own apartment) by government police in 1834 (fig. 6.13). Daumier made all of Paris witness to the event through the journalistic severity of his lithograph. This lithograph took three months to prepare and was sold separately from the newspapers until the stone and all copies were confiscated by the government. The only words with the image were the simplest facts identifying the atrocity in space and time: *Rue Transnonain, 15 April, 1834.*

Daumier also produced paintings that reflected urban life. Though admired only by a small number of avant-garde artists at the time, these paintings nevertheless prophesied how popular art would help to overwhelm the bastions of the Academy by its open and direct approach to contemporary reality.

The style of his 1860 oil, *The Uprising* (fig. 6.14), rooted in popular art, is remarkably different from Delacroix's painting of a similar theme, *Liberty Leading the People* (fig. 4.39). Daumier's painting, based on his direct observation of street life and his rapid method of drawing on lithographic stones, ignored classical composition and allegorical figures. He painted the furious and desperate energy of the crowd with the directness of a sympathetic witness.

Daumier produced thousands of lithographs during his long career, and Manet grew up admiring his work. Manet also saw thousands of lithographs by other artists who supplied the lucrative Paris market for printed pictures of all kinds. These images must have had a profound influence on Manet's sense of what modern subject matter should be.

The art historian Beatrice Farwell has documented this explosion of mass media images, including their influence on artists like Manet:

It must be assumed that any artist whose youth was spent in the 1830s, 1840s or 1850s grew up in the constant presence of a pleth-

6.15

images that were bound to appeal to visual sensibility and the urge to draw.[4]

Farwell cites a large number of lithographs that, long before Manet produced his shocking paintings, prefigured their themes. The lithograph in figure 6.15 was produced in 1834 by the popular artist Achille Devéria (1800–1857) and bears the same title as Manet's painting *Luncheon on the Grass.* Another lithograph by Devéria, *La Coquetterie* (fig. 6.16), shows why the public might have assumed that Titian's *Venus of Urbino* was not the only possible source for Manet's *Olympia.*

From this general background it is easy to see why the public saw the touch of popular art in Manet's work, reflected in the jibe—circulated among visitors to the Salon of 1865—that dismissed *Olympia* by calling it merely a large image d'Epinal. This connection with popular art is even more explicit in the remark made to Manet by his teacher, Thomas Couture: "You will never be more than the Daumier of your time."[5]

6.13 Honoré Daumier.
Rue Transnonain, 15 April, 1834.
1834.
Lithograph, 11¼″ × 17⅜″.
Cleveland Museum of Art, Gift of Ralph King.

6.14 Honoré Daumier.
The Uprising. c. 1860.
Oil on canvas, 34½″ × 44½″.
The Phillips Collection, Washington.

6.15 Achille Devéria.
Luncheon on the Grass. 1834.
Lithograph.
Bibliothèque Nationale, Paris.

6.16 Achille Devéria.
La Coquetterie. 1829.
Lithograph.
Bibliothèque Nationale, Paris.

6.16

156

Couture meant this as an insult. He was right, neverthe-less, in one respect: something of Daumier's all-encompassing view of Paris shines through the surfaces of both *Luncheon on the Grass* and *Olympia*.

Manet, however, had defenders even in 1867. He was pub-licly defended—and heralded—by the young writer Émile Zola. Zola's defense of Manet is part of another important ele-ment of the modern mass media that emerged during Manet's generation: the art critic in the newspapers and magazines who helped interpret the avant-garde to a gradu-ally more sympathetic public.

Manet and Émile Zola: Words to Focus the New Visual Language of the Avant-Garde

Manet's 1868 portrait *Émile Zola* (fig. 6.17) represented his tribute and his thanks to Zola for his public support of Manet's work. It was doubly appropriate that the painting showed a photograph of *Olympia* pinned on the wall above

6.17 Édouard Manet.
Émile Zola. 1868.
Oil on canvas, 4'9½" × 3'7½".
The Louvre, Paris.

6.17

Zola's desk, together with a Japanese print. Even more significant is the small book on Zola's desk entitled *Manet*—it contained Zola's defense of Manet's paintings.

These writings had originally appeared as newspaper articles. Just as newspapers had helped form Manet's sense of modern times with their writing and imagery, so also— thanks to critics like Baudelaire and Zola—newspapers helped to inject the work of Manet and other avant-garde artists into the public forum.

Zola defended Manet with a brilliant description of the painter's new approach to subject matter and artistic form; his defense and clarification of Manet's peculiarly modern vision can be seen in his comments on *Olympia.*

Zola's Defense of *Olympia:* The New Role of the Artist and the New Language of Art

Zola insisted on the presence of the personality of the artist as an integral part of the language of avant-garde art:

Each society will contribute its artists, who, in turn, will contribute their personalities . . . and our role, as judges of art works, is limited to ascertaining the language of temperaments . . . [since] the whole personality of the artist consists in the way his vision is organized.[6]

This emphasis on the personality of the artist continued the tradition established as early as Michelangelo and continued in the recent art of the Romantics and Courbet. Zola used this concept to emphasize the value of the unique eye of the artist—the intelligent eye of the artist—in contrast to the totally objective but mechanical eye of the photograph, which was producing such limiting effects in Academic art.

Zola went on to discuss Manet's new use of the basic visual language of art—color, line, and shape—in his description of Manet's highly personal use of these elements in *Olympia:*

"Olympia," reclining on the white sheets, is a large pale spot on the black background . . . details have disappeared. Look at the head of the young girl. The lips are two narrow pink lines, the eyes are reduced to a few black strokes. Now look closely at the bouquet. Some patches of pink, blue, and green. Everything is simplified and if you wish to reconstruct reality you must step back a bit. Then a curious thing happens. Each object falls into its proper plane. An accurate eye and a direct hand performed this miracle.[7]

Zola thus characterized Manet's artistic language as creating a dynamic perceptual process that flows from abstraction ("pale spot on the black background") to realism ("Each object falls into its proper plane").

Like Brunelleschi's first perspective painting, *Olympia* is a kind of artistic "miracle." Unlike Brunelleschi's painting, however, Manet's painting makes it recognizable *in spite of* and not *because of* the technique employed. Manet's approach is a direct and deliberate break with the Western tradi-

6.18 Jean Léon Gérôme.
The Slave Market. c. 1867.
Oil on canvas, 33³/₁₆″ × 24¹³/₁₆″.
Sterling and Francine Clark Art Institute,
Williamstown, Massachusetts.

tion of the painting as a perspective window. For Manet, the painting and the painted surface now had a language and an existence of their own. His art began to declare its independence from the optical world of photography and perspective.

It is important to emphasize that Manet began to abandon the objectivity of perspective and photography in order to achieve *more* realism in his art, not less. A good way to show how Manet's new language of art could generate a greater sense of realism is by comparing Manet's *Olympia* with a well-known Academic painting done at almost the same time, *The Slave Market* by Jean Léon Gérôme (fig. 6.18 and plate 12).

Gérôme's painting is particularly appropriate because it was completed only two years after *Olympia* was shown in the Salon of 1865. The same public thus saw both paintings. A comparison of the color plates of both paintings demonstrates the dramatic contrast between Academic paintings and the new visual language of Manet, just as the public reaction to each painting demonstrates the contrast in attitude between avant-garde and middle-class audiences.

Manet presented *Olympia* as a nude in the tradition of Titian's *Venus,* though in a very modern Parisian setting. Gérôme presented *The Slave Market* in the guise of a scene from nineteenth-century Islamic Egypt. He tinted it with the sense of scientific detail and detachment of a modern photographic essay. This superficial objectivity enabled Gérôme to portray the woman as a commodity for sale—she is being inspected like a horse being auctioned at a fair. The public that banned *Olympia* as immoral applauded *The Slave Market.* Like Couture's painting of the "decadent" Romans, its "scientific" accuracy was really veiled eroticism. It also supplied the added thrill to the Salon visitor of implying European superiority—Western culture forbade such treatment of women.

In terms of visual language, Gérôme's painting is so photographic that the background even appears to be subtly soft-focused in order to bring the foreground figures into greater relief. Linda Nochlin underscores Gérôme's preoccupation with photographic technique:

No other artist has so inexorably eradicated all traces of the picture plane as Gérôme, denying us any clue to the art work as a literal flat surface.[8]

By contrast, the surfaces of Manet's paintings were so flat that they seemed to press out toward the viewer. The red wall behind Olympia appears to be on the same plane and of the same color as the couch in the lower left-hand corner. Olympia herself is painted in a very flat tone that makes her figure look something like a silhouette pasted onto the painted surface. As Zola pointed out, the colors and shapes dissolve into strokes of paint.

In front of Gérôme's painting the viewer is supposed to be within the scene; in front of Manet's painting, the viewer is supposed to be aware of the painted surface that creates the scene. Manet thus emphasized precisely what Gérôme and the Academics strove most to eliminate: the awareness of the flat surface of the painting as well as of the visual language used to give this surface form and meaning.

Gérôme and other Academic painters knew that Manet was proposing totally new standards of artistic realism, and Gérôme accurately saw that Manet's style—in form and content—contradicted almost everything he and other Academic artists stood for. He publicly opposed the purchase of *Olympia* for the Louvre as late as 1902, almost two decades after Manet's death.

Manet: The Dilemma of Being Modern

It should not be difficult now to see why Manet suffered such confused reactions to his paintings. He heard his paintings described by some as verging on pure abstractions, yet condemned by others as immoral.

This rejection, as noted earlier, caused Manet great personal pain. He was not trying to destroy the tradition represented by Academic painting as much as he was trying to rejuvenate it from within. Even though recognition by the Academy gradually came his way, his career was marred by a constant air of controversy. A year before his death at the age of fifty-three, he was told that he had been admitted as a member of the Academy; his reply was brief and bitter: "It is too late."

Manet was unable to heal the crisis of realism in art. He was unable to bring the old and the new together in a peaceful transition. The price of this lag between the old and the new was the personal sense of alienation that is vividly clear in his paintings.

Two of his early paintings reflect this sense of alienation better than the more familiar *Luncheon on the Grass* and *Olympia.* In 1864 Manet painted two pictures on the theme of death: *The Dead Toreador* (fig. 6.19) and *The Dead Christ with Angels* (fig. 6.20). Both, again, were based on traditional works.

6.19 Édouard Manet.
The Dead Toreador. c. 1864.
Oil on canvas, 29⅞″ × 60⅜″.
National Gallery of Art, Washington,
Widener Collection.

6.20 Édouard Manet.
The Dead Christ with Angels. 1864.
Oil on canvas, 70⅝″ × 59″.
Metropolitan Museum of Art, New York,
The H. O. Havemeyer Collection, Bequest of
Mrs. H. O. Havemeyer.

6.21 Édouard Manet.
A Bar at the Folies-Bergère. 1881.
Oil on canvas, 3′1¾″ × 4′2″.
Courtauld Institute Galleries, London.

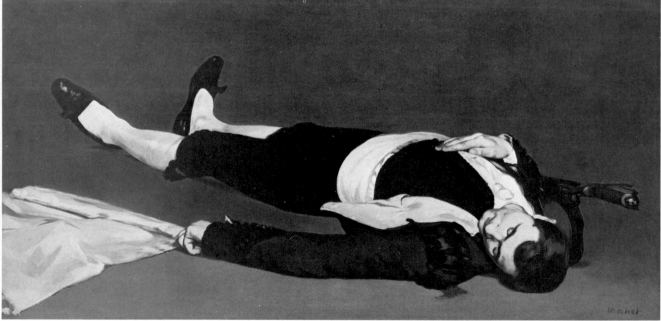

6.19

These two paintings are perhaps more shocking today than either of Manet's earlier and more famous works. It is obvious that the Christ in *The Dead Christ with Angels* is not meant to express any traditional religious belief—as Zola himself commented, it is merely a cadaver. The toreador was not painted as heroically dead, either; he seems to lie on the ground with a disturbing sense of neutrality or indifference. Death is neither proud nor conquered in these paintings; Manet presents death as merely a fact. Instead of making a comment on death, the artist merely observes.

Manet's final painting, *A Bar at the Folies-Bergère* (fig. 6.21 and plate 13) shows how his own personality was the basis of the truth of his art. The figure of the barmaid faces the viewer with the same direct stare as the nude figure in *Luncheon on the Grass*. Despite her exquisitely painted clothes and her corsage, her expression reveals her sense of detachment from the supposedly festive atmosphere. She looks trapped between the shimmering two-dimensional world of the mirror, and the counter, which supports a brilliantly painted still life of bottles and fruit.

If the mirror is compared to the flat surface of Manet's paintings, the counter—including the bottles and the fruit—can then be compared to the older traditions of art. In his paintings, Manet's personality appears, like the barmaid, to be trapped in the gap between his artistic struggle to represent modern Paris and his admiration for the older tradition of art that he found no longer sufficient.

Like many people in the nineteenth century, Manet faced in two directions. His art expressed a uniquely nineteenth-

6.20

6.21

century sense of freedom from the burdens of the past traditions, but it also expressed the modern burden of searching for new traditions. Manet's art is about this search. In his early work he searched the past; in his later work he searched the present. He was never able to completely close the gap between them.

This new sense of freedom was not limited to the avant-garde. A series of pamphlets that was popular in France from the 1830s through the 1870s expressed the new myth of the autonomous individual this way:

Serf in 1600, subject in 1789, citizen in 1793, the people were crowned emperor in 1804 . . . the man [sic] of the people will become manufacturer, artist, inventor. He will have fortune and position.[9]

It is a sign of the changes taking place in Western culture that Manet did not feel obliged to pass on meanings inherited from the past; his paintings are icons of the freedom to express, if nothing else, the truth of one's own experience. As Zola pointed out in the 1860s, *Olympia* tells us more about Manet's personality than it does about the traditional theme he used, in the literal sense of the term, as a starting point.

Despite his personal disappointments, Manet did live to see that he had won a great artistic battle. Gérôme and his followers could only fight a rearguard action against his art and that of the avant-garde. Manet had opened a new window for Western art that would not be closed, a window based on the experience and personality of the individual artist.

Perhaps the best way to describe Manet is by turning to one of his few public statements about himself. In 1867, Manet countered the disdain of the critics and the Salon by taking his work—as Courbet had done—directly to the people. He set up his own exhibition on a Paris street and issued a brief manifesto describing his intentions and his work. One particular word was singled out to summarize his work: *sincere*. *Sincere* comes from two Latin words that mean "without wax." In his day, for Manet to present art "without wax" was a radical act. After Manet it became easier, in subject matter and form, to be sincere.

The next chapter will show how the avant-garde built on the tradition of Courbet and Manet and undertook, not one, but many new approaches to resolving the artistic crisis of realism.

CHAPTER SEVEN

THE PHOTOGRAPHIC AGE III: THE AVANT-GARDE AFTER MANET

ASSESSMENTS

1. In your opinion, what does it mean to view the world through the eyes of an artist?
2. Have you ever observed how color affects your responses to your surroundings? How do color and light work together to create mood?
3. What do you think about the idea that for some artists the process of painting is more important than the product?
4. Besides the reality that can be seen with the eye (and therefore photographed), what other important aspects of reality can art represent or express? What is your response to the statement made by the artist Paul Gauguin: "I close my eyes in order to see better"?
5. What is symbolism? What things, events, or persons have important symbolic value in your life?
6. If you could adopt a culture other than your own, which would you choose? How might this culture complete your personality? As an artist, what images, rituals, beliefs would you want to integrate into your art works?

164

7.1 Cham.
Cartoon from *Charivari*. 1877.
Roger-Viollet, Paris.

7.2 Claude Monet.
Le Dejeuner. 1868.
Oil on canvas, 191.6 × 125.2 cm.
Stadelsches Kunstinstitut, Frankfurt.

7.1

Manet's paintings, despite the controversy surrounding them, consolidated the freedom to depict modern society that had been earlier initiated by artists like Courbet and Daumier.

Manet himself became a symbol of this new freedom. Throughout the 1860s a group of young artists rallied around his artistic standard. The Café Guerbois in the bohemian Montmartre section of Paris was their informal meeting place. Manet's presence at these wide-ranging discussions helped to generate a sense of mutual support against a common enemy: the artistic "old guard" of the Academy.

This group of young painters concentrated on artistic issues. The political and social dimension of Courbet's approach to avant-garde art receded, temporarily, to a secondary position.

Artistically, Manet had breached the barricade of perspective that even Courbet had honored. The young artists who followed him through the gap mapped out vast new territories of artistic structure and expression that are still being explored today.

In 1874 thirty of these artists assembled their work for a show at the studio of Paul Nadar. The list of their names is a roll call of future greatness: Cézanne, Degas, Guillaumin, Monet, Morisot, Pissarro, Sisley. They called themselves, quite accurately, the "Independents." The hostile press subsequently dubbed them "Impressionists." The second name stuck.

Even though Impressionism has become one of the most amiable and universally appealing styles of art in Western history, the barb of derision meant by the original term is evident in figure 7.1. This cartoon shows Impressionist paintings being used at the front—as weapons to terrify enemy soldiers.

Even though they had grouped themselves under one tent primarily for purposes of organization and morale, the term *impressionism* did describe their common sense of spontaneity and immediacy. The critics, if wrongly, at least reacted to the right quality. Claude Monet was the artist from this first band of exhibitors who took the basic thrust of Impressionism to its fullest expression.

This chapter will discuss Impressionism in terms of Monet and then describe the unfolding terrain of artistic reality mapped out by five other major artists: Georges Seurat, Paul Cézanne, Vincent van Gogh, Paul Gauguin, and Henri Rousseau. Even though all these artists, except Rousseau, exhibited in at least one of the eight Impressionist exhibitions held between 1874 and 1886, all of them are today grouped under the heading Post-Impressionists. It is a tribute to Impressionism that it could initially contain such a variety of artistic ideas and temperaments; the criticism of Impressionism is that, ultimately, it was not enough.

Claude Monet (1840–1926): Moving beyond Manet

Claude Monet broke with his family's wish for him to pursue a career in law, and in 1859 he left the coastal city of Le Havre to study art in Paris. In 1866 he became personally acquainted with Édouard Manet, after admiring his controversial work for several years. Though Monet learned much from Manet—and frequently depended on his financial help for survival—Monet gradually developed his own distinctive approach. Manet had given traditional themes like *Olympia* a sense of modernity and freshness. Monet left the museums entirely behind; he insisted on painting in the open air and finishing the painting "on the scene" instead of in the studio.

Manet himself was impressed by the results of the younger artist's open-air approach. *Gare Saint-Lazare* (fig. 6.7) showed that Manet was also willing to learn new things. But there were clear limits to Manet's approval of and admiration for Monet. Quite tactfully, Manet refused to show his own work in the first Impressionist exhibition of 1874. His Salon ambitions precluded too close an association with the highly diverse and struggling group of self-styled Independents.

The paintings that Monet showed at this time, however, clearly reveal both his debt to and his differences with Manet.

Monet's First Breakthrough: *Impression: Sunrise*

Monet's debt to Manet is seen most clearly in *Le Dejeuner*, painted in 1868 (fig. 7.2). This painting shows Monet's first wife, Camille, and his son in a comfortable, middle-class family setting. In terms of Monet's own life at the time, however, the painting was pure fantasy; his poverty was so severe that he had already once attempted suicide. His young wife later died from the lingering effects of malnutrition.

Le Dejeuner's clear colors and shapes mark it as a solid example of the kind of painting pioneered by Manet during the previous ten years. By itself, it would prove only that Monet was Manet's best student. Monet's uniqueness as an artist became apparent in another painting in the same exhibition, *Impression: Sunrise* (fig. 7.3).

Impression: Sunrise was painted in Le Havre in 1872 during Monet's brief stay there on his return from London, where he had gone to escape military service during the disastrous Franco-Prussian War of 1870–71 that brought down the government of Napoleon III. This defeat led to the equally disastrous socialist takeover of Paris—the Commune—whose fall resulted in Courbet's exile by the new French government.

In artistic terms, this painting shows Monet taking a decisively different direction from Manet. To the critics and

7.2

7.3

7.3 Claude Monet.
Impression: Sunrise. 1872.
Oil on canvas, 19½″ × 25½″.
Musée Marmottan, Paris.

7.4 Claude Monet.
The Terrace at Sainte-Adresse. 1866.
Oil on canvas, 3′2⅝″ × 4′3⅛″.
Metropolitan Museum of Art, New York,
Purchased with special contributions and
purchase funds given or bequeathed by
friends of the Museum, 1967.

7.5 Claude Monet.
La Capeline Rouge—Madame Monet.
c. 1870.
Oil on canvas, 39½″ × 31½″.
Cleveland Museum of Art, Bequest of
Leonard C. Hanna, Jr.

the public, the painting proved that Monet could not draw.

The critics tore into Monet with less venom but as much ridicule as they had used on Manet. One critic cautioned visitors to the exhibition to be careful because a gentleman who had visited the display earlier had suddenly gone mad and begun to bite the passersby! Cham's cartoon (fig. 7.1) was another reference to a potential for violent reaction. A less militant critic characterized Monet's canvases as wallpaper in embryonic form.

The derision is even more understandable if one compares this painting to one of Monet's finest early works, *The Terrace at Sainte-Adresse* (fig. 7.4). This painting could be called an "outdoor" Manet. Its bold color and simple forms, derived from Manet, produce a clearly lit, strikingly solid sense of space. Flowers, people, and shadows all have a remarkable freshness and clarity.

In *Impression: Sunrise,* however, everything dissolves

7.4

into a single element: light. The boats, the sun, the fog itself, become mere transmitters of light. Imagine cutting out any small section of this painting—except perhaps the sun and the small boat in the foreground—and having to identify it without the rest of the painting. The critics, insofar as they accepted photographic realism as the only form of art, certainly had a point. There is a distinct suggestion here of "embryonic wallpaper."

Yet Monet refused to budge. He even insisted that his paintings were more scientifically accurate than the photographic illusionism of Academic painting. Unlike such images, he insisted, his paintings were based on how the eye actually sees.

Monet's Impressionism: Painting as the Response of an Active Eye

Monet argued that the eye was active in its contact with nature—it did not see mechanically like a camera. Monet insisted that color, not the space of perspective and photography, was the basic content of human perception.

Since he saw nature, and therefore art, as a feast of color, Monet wanted, as he said, to see "innocently." He wanted to see without imposing any preconceived artistic composition or hierarchy of importance onto the world of experience. The term he coined to describe this quality was *instantaneity.*

"Instantaneity" could be brought about only if art was directed toward recording what Monet called *objective sensations,* the raw data, so to speak, received by the eye from nature. The best way to understand Monet's "objective sensations" and their relationship to his art is by examining his painting process itself.

While painting outdoors with the scene before him, Monet concentrated on the purely optical world. He applied his colors to the canvas in small, separate brush strokes that represented the discrete patches of color that his eye received from nature. The viewer's eye would assemble these little dabs of color into a scene in a way similar to how the eye sees nature in ordinary vision.

Monet's 1870 painting of his first wife, Camille—glimpsed as she passes the window on a winter day—illustrates the early stage of his technique (fig. 7.5). The quick brush strokes that describe the snowy branches of the tree are repeated in the strokes that suggest the pattern of light and shadow along the top of the curtains. Monet defined the wallpaper to the right of the window with similar quick touches of color. The passing figure of Camille is masterfully done. The winter cloak is a single shade of red; the expression on her face is achieved by several rapid passages of the brush. *Impression: Sunrise,* painted two years later, uses this technique throughout.

7.5

Monet's Laboratory of the Eye: Haystacks and Cathedrals

By the 1890s Monet had finally achieved financial and critical success with his paintings of the boulevards and suburban haunts of the middle class. People had begun to see their own environment with his vision.

Now, however, he made a dramatic change in his approach. He stopped painting familiar urban scenes—or any scenes with human figures. By this time, his eye did not just see, it analyzed as it saw. He began to concentrate on painting the sensation of perception itself.

Monet's increasing emphasis on perception became apparent in a remarkable group of fifteen paintings exhibited in 1891, unusual not only because of their new attention to how the eye sees color, but because they all featured the same subject—haystacks (fig. 7.6).

Monet painted the haystack series in order to explore the changing conditions of light. A major source for the idea of a series was probably the ukiyo-e color woodblocks of the Japanese artist Katsushika Hokusai (1760–1849) (fig. 7.7) whose *Thirty-Six Views of Mount Fuji* were among the Japanese prints that had influenced Paris artists since the early work of Manet.

After the haystacks, Monet produced forty paintings of the front—or facade—of Rouen Cathedral (figs. 7.8, 7.9, plates 14, 15), which he painted in different lights ranging from that of moonlight to that of midday. To study the scene properly, he rented a room across the square from the church. In these paintings, Monet used thick strokes of paint on the canvas in colors that created the impression that the light itself was forming a kind of tactile screen.

Well-publicized scientific discoveries during this period had disclosed that the human retina is a kaleidoscope of interacting colors. Color in the human eye is not only relative, it is always changing. By focusing on the same subject

7.6 Claude Monet.
Haystack at Sunrise Near Giverny.
1891.
Oil on canvas, 29½″ × 37″.
Courtesy of Museum of Fine Arts, Boston, Bequest of Robert J. Edwards in memory of his mother, 1925.

7.7 Katsushika Hokusai.
Fuji in Clear Weather. Edo period (18th–19th century), Ukiyo-e school.
Color woodblock print, 10¹/₁₆″ × 14¾″.
Cleveland Museum of Art, Bequest of Edward L. Whittemore.

7.7

7.6

7.8

7.9

through a whole series of paintings, Monet was able to concentrate on recording visual sensations themselves. The subjects did not change, but the visual sensations—due to changing conditions of light—changed constantly. The haystacks and cathedrals enabled Monet to bring into attention ordinary visual sensations that, though usually unnoticed, are part of normal vision.

Other avant-garde artists besides Monet began at this time to radically depart from the traditional notion that color was part of the objects seen in nature. Monet began to derive color from perception; other artists began to base their use of color on feeling, symbolism, or some other source. A reference point for discussing these many new ways of using color is the color wheel shown in figure 7.10 and in the color section.

7.8 Claude Monet.
Rouen Cathedral, West Facade, Sunlight. 1894.
Oil on canvas, 39½″ × 26″.
National Gallery of Art, Washington, Chester Dale Collection.

7.9 Claude Monet.
Rouen Cathedral, West Facade. 1894.
Oil on canvas, 39½″ × 26″.
The National Gallery of Art, Washington, Chester Dale Collection.

The color wheel arranges the colors of the spectrum in a circular band according to wave length. Two terms that can be illustrated by the color chart came into common use by avant-garde artists at this time: *complementary colors* and *analogous colors.*

Complementary colors are any two colors that are *opposite* each other on the color wheel (e.g., green and red, blue-violet and yellow). Analogous colors are any two colors that are *next* to each other on the color wheel (e.g., blue and blue-green, red-orange and orange). Two important conversational terms for color are *warm* for the colors that extend from red-violet to yellow-green and *cool* for the colors that extend from violet to green.

One effect of ordinary perception exploited by Monet that can be illustrated by the color wheel is called *simultaneous contrast,* the tendency to see in a given color fleeting traces of its complementary color. *Rouen Cathedral, West Facade* is built up from a flurry of brush strokes that interlace reds within greens, violets within yellows, and so on. In one sense, Monet did not paint the cathedral so much as he painted the action of the image of the cathedral on his own retina. The viewer thus sees the cathedral, not as it is in the world, but as it momentarily inhabited Monet's own eye. The two versions of the cathedral in plates 14 and 15 show that the constantly varying paintings of the cathedral were not just a perceptual game for Monet, they dramatized an objective fact: to human perception, the cathedral was never the same.

Another common visual effect he explored was the appearance of flatness that results when the viewer looks at an object lit from behind. The haystack paintings explore this effect with incredible complexity. Even the black-and-white illustration (fig. 7.6) reveals how Monet has flattened out the haystack that is lit from behind. His painting also shows the slight halo or radiance that occurs with this kind of light, as well as the tendency—seen in the front of the haystack—for such lighting to cause the object to appear to merge with its own shadow. This insistence on color as the basic building block of human perception as well as art explains why there is no black in the shadows in Monet's paintings. Since black is the *total* absence of light, all shadows have some color in them.

Monet's attention to these scientifically documented effects was not of a mechanical sort. Just as Vermeer adapted the "circles of confusion" produced by the camera lens to his own artistic purposes, Monet turned the new knowledge of perception to the concerns of his own art. Since Monet was intuitively sensitive to the process of perception, it might be more precise to say that such current scientific information enabled him to justify his own spontaneous responses to critics of his approach.

COLOR WHEEL

Hues (Showing
Complementary and Analogous
Relationships)

Complementary
Relationships

Analagous
Relationships

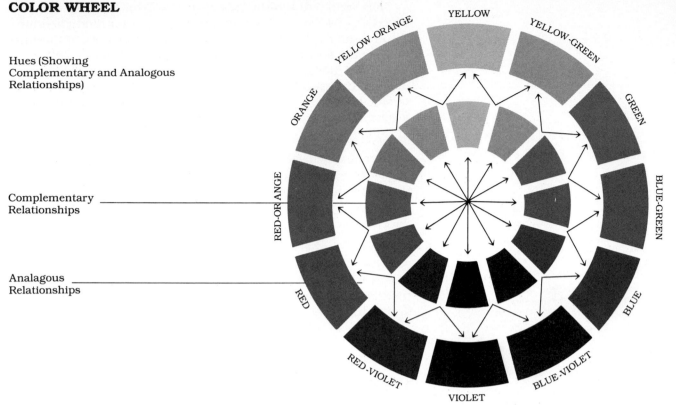

Cool and Warm Colors   Two important conversational terms for color are *cool* for the colors that extend from blue-violet to yellow-green and *warm* for the colors that extend from yellow to red-violet.

Successive Contrast   This term refers to the experience of retaining the complementary afterimage of a given color. After looking for about a minute at the yellow/violet figure, focus on the black dot in the middle of the white square on the right. You will see a slight impression of a violet square with traces of yellow. Simultaneous contrast, a less common phenomenon, is the tendency to see, within a given color, glimpses of the complementary hue of the adjacent color.

Hue and Value   The term *hue* refers to basic color—red, blue, and so forth. The term *value* refers to dark and light variations of hue. The figures below are composed of two hues, red-orange and blue-green. Note that the values of the red-orange circles are constant, but the changing values of the blue-green background make the values of the red-orange circles appear also to change.

B-V	B	B-G	G	Y-G	Y	Y-O	O	R-O	R	R-V

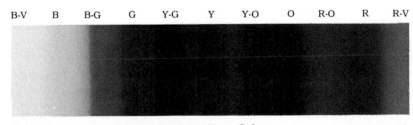

Cool Colors ⟶ Warm Colors ⟶

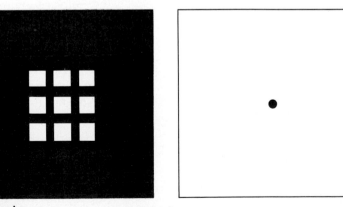

Successive Contrast ⟶

Hue: Red-orange and blue-green.
Value: Red-orange is constant in value; blue-green varies in value.

7.10 Color wheel.

His sensitivity to the perception of color at times bordered on obsession. One incident in particular disturbed him throughout his life. He had painted many portraits of Camille besides the scene of her passing by the window (fig. 7.5). When she died of a lingering illness in 1879, he painted her one last time as she lay in her casket. Later, however, he wrote about the complex emotions behind this painting. He described in a letter how he became caught up in the

act of mechanically analysing the succession of appropriate colour gradations which death was imposing on her immobile face. Tones of blue, of yellow, of grey . . . my organism automatically reacted to the colour stimuli, and my reflexes caught me up in spite of myself, in an unconscious operation which was the daily course of my life—just like an animal turning his mill.[1]

Monet, in his disciplined attention to the "objective sensations" of his perception, had become capable of separating his art from his feelings. Charles Darwin described how an unbalanced involvement with science had affected his mind, and in the same way, Monet's eye showed the potential for becoming so "objective" that it became detached from his humanity.

Monet's Water Lilies and Gardens: Seeing Nature from the Other Side of Perspective

One of the most astonishing aspects of Monet's career is how innovative and productive he was in his last years. The haystacks and cathedrals were only the halfway point in his uncovering of an artistic language tied directly to the objective processes of perception. Monet spent his last forty years on his estate at Giverny, forty miles outside Paris. Here he cultivated a network of pools and gardens that became almost the sole subject of his paintings (fig. 7.11).

At Giverny, Monet's paintings became larger—and then redoubled in size. The artist who began his career by taking his paintings outdoors to finish in one sitting ended by painting fields of vision. At the age of seventy-five he had to climb a ladder to reach the top of some of his canvases. His gardens and his canvases began to compete with each other in scale; in the final paintings at Giverny, the reach of Monet's perception closed the boundaries between nature and art. Monet's paintings became environments that rivaled nature itself.

Monet found resources in Impressionism that carried him into an immensely creative old age. He died wealthy, acknowledged as a genius, in the company of the premier of France, Georges Clemenceau.

Monet's eventual success should not obscure that Impressionism was seen as socially and politically suspect throughout the 1870s and 1880s. This is doubly surprising in view of the fact that two of the most accomplished and persistent Impressionist artists were women whose work—

7.11 Claude Monet.
Water Lilies. c. 1919–26.
Oil on canvas, 79″ × 167½″.
Cleveland Museum of Art, Purchase, John L. Severance Fund.

7.12 Mary Cassatt.
The Bath. c. 1891–92.
Oil on canvas, 39½″ × 26″.
Art Institute of Chicago.

7.11

unlike the publicly acclaimed canvases of Rosa Bonheur—consisted of painted scenes relating to motherhood and domestic life. Berthe Morisot (1841–1895) began, like Monet, as a follower of Manet, although her painting later influenced Manet's decision to adopt a more Impressionist approach to color. The American artist Mary Cassatt (1844–1926), in *The Bath* (fig. 7.12), shows her mastery of Japanese print design as well as her adaptation of the spontaneity of Impressionism to interior scenes. The art of Impressionism demonstrates that any art—no matter how innocent its intent—can be perceived as revolutionary and dangerous simply because it encourages people to see in a new way.

In one sense, however, the critics who saw Impressionism as a revolutionary force were right. Impressionism spurred a wide range of new approaches to art between 1886 (the date of the last Impressionist Exhibition) and the beginning of the twentieth century. This diverse group of artists whose work began in Impressionism became known as the Post-Impressionists.

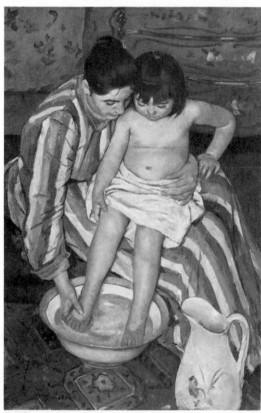

7.12

The Post-Impressionists: Artistic Search for Reality beyond the Eye

The Post-Impressionists, in addition to their debt to Impressionism, were united in their determination to take their art beyond the sensations of the optical world. Human beings also perceive reality through ideas, feelings, symbols, and dreams. The Post-Impressionists did not deny the objective world seen by the eye, but they began to explore the growing conviction that objective reality is always affected by the presence of the observer. Post-Impressionism, implicitly or explicitly, presented the world as a fusion of the human being *and* objective reality.

Georges Seurat (1859–1891): Painting with the Mathematical Dot

Georges Seurat was a young artist who was strongly influenced by the scientific theories of his day and tried to apply them directly to his art. Monet's art and visual language began with the experience in his eye, even though scientific theories might aid his perception or justify aspects of his art. Seurat's art began with the scientific theories themselves. His artistic objective was to control the spectator's response in a scientifically predictable way.

The important link between Impressionism and Seurat's masterpiece *Sunday Afternoon on the Island of La Grande Jatte* (fig. 7.13, plate 16) is the painted dot. The dot for Monet was an intuitive, gestural response to an immediate impression; the dot for Seurat was a cool, calculated mathematical point of color. Seurat used the dot like the modular beams used in the Crystal Palace: it was the prefabricated building block that supported the perfectly controlled architecture of his painting.

7.13 Georges Seurat. *Sunday Afternoon on the Island of La Grande Jatte.* 1884–86. Oil on canvas, 6'9" × 10'3⁄8". Art Institute of Chicago, Helen Birch Bartlett Memorial Collection.

There are two years of labor and over two hundred preparatory sketches behind the shimmering plane of color that covers the surface of the immense canvas of *La Grande Jatte*. The effect was both stunning and controversial when it was exhibited in 1886 at the last Impressionist exhibition. The public had by then adjusted to Monet's eye, but Seurat presented—literally—a whole new problem.

The luminous surface of *La Grande Jatte* grew from thousands of self-effacing dots applied with mathematical precision. Even color took on scientific discipline. Seurat preferred to call his approach to color "divisionism," because he broke color down further than Monet and the Impressionists. He treated each dot as if it were a sort of atom of color. If Seurat wanted a green, he would place varying numbers of blue and yellow dots next to each other. The two colors that made the green would also have small, carefully calculated dots of their complementary colors next to them: orange next to blue, violet next to yellow. The dominant color green was mixed by the viewer's eye. By dividing color into elementary dot-particles, he hoped to be able to create every possible color by mixing varying amounts of the basic colors on the color wheel. Though an unkind critic in 1886 compared the surfaces of Seurat's canvases to swarms of "colored fleas," most people admitted that he had created a startlingly luminous representation of light.

Seurat not only made sure that his dots observed such perceptual laws as simultaneous contrast, the halo effect, absence of black, and so forth, he also counted them out so that they organized space as completely as they organized color. Seurat divided his canvas and calculated the size of the figures and their relation to each other by using geometric proportions similar to those of Greek art and architecture. Even the subject matter was related to Greek art: he called *La Grande Jatte* his modern version of the Panathenaic Procession—the sculptural frieze that surrounds the Parthenon (fig. 2.22). He meant the painting to be a similar tribute to the middle-class society of modern Paris. The strangely toylike figures that people his landscape have been rounded off in order to approach the superior perfection of geometry. The curves in umbrellas and bustles find a harmonic echo in the shapes of a bent tree and the tail of a monkey. Shapes resonate as methodically as dots of color. His method aimed at redeploying the visual language of Impressionism toward the kind of grandeur he admired in classical Greek art.

The ultimate aim of this carefully plotted network of colors, lines, and shapes was an art that would alter the emotional pattern of the viewer in a predictable way. His paintings exemplify the most extreme version of the nineteenth-century optimism that every aspect of culture could be reformed and reinterpreted by science. For some, this overarching faith in science amounted almost to a religion. Hippolyte Taine, a professor at the École des Beaux-Arts at mid-century, summarized this belief in the physical basis of thought, sensation, and behavior:

Vice and virtue are products, like vitriol and sugar. Let us then seek the simple phenomena for moral qualities as we seek them for physical qualities.[2]

Behind this view is the belief that human responses could eventually be reduced to the laws of physics and chemistry and could therefore be described mathematically. Seurat wanted to use a science of human sensibility to create—through art—a technology of human feeling. With this goal of human control in mind, Seurat constructed his images the way an engineer constructs a new automobile: with blueprints, data, and trial runs.

Seurat's confidence that he could apply such an approach to art was strongly influenced by the lectures of Charles Henry, a scientist and poet at the University of Paris who was trying to bring science and art into a unified system. Henry was convinced that he could eventually develop a mathematical description of human feeling.

Seurat applied Henry's theories on the "emotional laws" of line, color, and value (light and dark). Seurat even applied Henry's "aesthetic protractor" to some of his paintings. This device resembled an ordinary geometric protractor used to measure angles. When used according to Henry's principles, the "aesthetic protractor" was meant to precisely calculate the angle for ascending and descending lines needed to trigger a desired response in the viewer.

Figure 7.14 is a line chart based on Seurat's application of his line theories to the painting *Le Chahut* (fig. 7.15) and illustrates Seurat's desire to control the image's details, down to the uplift of the conductor's mustache and the bows on the dancers' shoes.

Le Chahut is a less ambitious painting than *La Grande Jatte*, but it reveals Seurat's programmatic approach even more clearly. The dominant colors of the painting are in the yellow-orange-red range. Even the upward emphasis of the dominant colors is calculated to produce the proper "lively" disposition in the viewer.

One of Seurat's finest paintings is *Le Cirque* (fig. 7.16), the final work completed before his tragically early death from influenza in 1891 at the age of thirty-two. Note that in this work, whose rhythm lines influenced later posters and Art Nouveau designs, Seurat has painted his own frame around the image, in a further effort to control the total color effect. He preferred the frames around his paintings to be white, to ensure a properly neutral buffer zone between the outside world and the perfectly controlled world of his painting.

Seurat did not live long enough to test his theories beyond the scope of barely a half-dozen major paintings. But his importance in the development of the art of our own day is reflected in his own statement about his artistic aims.

7.14 Diagram of linear structure of *Le Chahut.*
Illustration from *Seurat and the Science of Painting,* by Wiliam Innes Homer. Cambridge: M.I.T. Press, 1964, p. 225.
Courtesy M.I.T. Press, Cambridge, Massachusetts.

7.15 Georges Seurat.
Le Chahut. 1889–90.
Oil on canvas, 66½″ × 54¾″.
Collection Ryksmuseum Kroller-Muller, Otterlo, Netherlands.

7.16 Georges Seurat
Le Cirque. 1891.
Oil on canvas, 5′10⅞″ × 4′10¼″.
The Louvre, Paris. Photo: Giraudon/Art Resource.

7.14

When an admiring critic noted a certain poetry in one of his works, Seurat denied it angrily: "They see poetry in what I have done. No, I apply my method and that is all there is to it."[3] Or, as a friend wrote of him after his death: "He believed in the power of theories, in the absolute value of methods."[4]

Seurat, in other words, sought a visual language for his art that would have the predictability and efficiency of technology. His paintings are icons that express the myth of a totally controlled and rationalized human life.

Paul Cézanne (1839-1906): Creating an Architecture of Color

Paul Cézanne was a childhood friend of Émile Zola and an informal but exhibiting member of the Impressionists in Paris in the 1870s and 1880s. By the late eighties, however, he had broken with Zola for using him as a model for the artist-hero of one of his novels. He also broke with the Impressionists, because, he said, their art lacked structure.

By 1886, when the Impressionists were having their first public success, the disgruntled Cézanne retired to the family estate near Aix-en-Provence, in the south of France. Supported by an inheritance, he led the life of a recluse. He also became a greater artist-hero than Zola could have imagined.

7.15

7.16

Cézanne proceeded to take Impressionism apart and reconstruct it into a visual language that became an influential basis for the avant-garde art of the twentieth century.

The key to Cézanne's painting is color. The Impressionists had used color intuitively, like perception itself. Cézanne was not interested in the instantaneous flash of appearances. He was also not interested in an art with the predictability of technology. He said that he wanted "to make of Impressionism something solid and durable, like the art of the museums."[5]

Cézanne nevertheless fulfilled Impressionism more than he abandoned it. Monet recorded his sensations; Cézanne reconstructed them. The world appears lighter and more radiant in Monet; it appears heavier and more solid in Cézanne.

Cézanne: Creating Light with the Density of Matter

Both Cézanne's link with Impressionism and his impending break to a new style are evident in his landscape of 1880, *Houses in Provence* (fig. 7.17 and plate 17).

At first glance, the landscape has the familiar brush strokes of Monet's work of the same period. A closer look reveals that Cézanne had already begun to discipline these strokes into nearly parallel layers of color that gave a strong sense of structural surface. Even in a black-and-white photograph, Cézanne's painting looks more like a landscape hammered into a relief sculpture than an image based on the perception of light.

Cézanne's intuitive but highly structured transformation of Impressionism resulted from his increasingly effective use of color to create structure. This effect is fully realized in his 1895 painting *The Basket of Apples* (fig. 7.18). This achievement is even more evident when compared with a highly competent Academic painting of the same theme, Carl Schuch's *Still Life with Apples* (fig. 7.19).

7.17

The most obvious difference between the two paintings is the same as that between works by Manet and Gérôme: Cézanne affirmed the surface of the canvas and the visual language used to create the image, whereas Schuch presented the illusion of a window that opens onto a three-dimensional volume of space filled with real objects.

For Cézanne, color *was* perspective. He used warm colors to make forms appear close, cool colors to make forms recede. He shared Manet's observation that objects painted in flat but bright colors seem to achieve fullness of form without the subtleties of shading.

By using tiny slabs of color that simultaneously create both structure and space, Cézanne produced paintings that took on a solidity that defies the simplicity of their initial appearance. The apples, in fact, seem to have a density many times that of ordinary apples. The apples in Schuch's painting, by comparison, seem weightless. This density even

7.17 Paul Cézanne.
Houses in Provence. c. 1880.
Oil on canvas, 25⅝″ × 32″.
National Gallery of Art, Washington,
Collection of Mr. and Mrs. Paul Mellon.

7.18 Paul Cézanne.
The Basket of Apples. c. 1895.
Oil on canvas, 24⅜″ × 31″.
Courtesy of the Art Institute of Chicago.

7.19 Carl Schuch.
Still Life with Apples. 1870–75.
Oil on canvas.
Staatliche Museen zu Berlin, Hauptstadt
der DDR, Nationalgalerie.

7.18

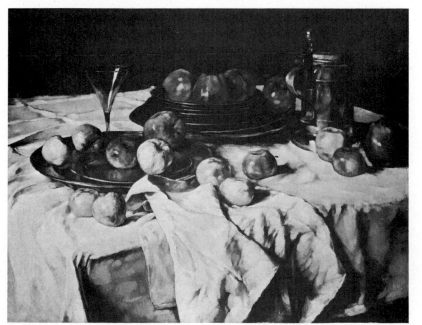

7.19

affects the light—Cézanne's painted forms do not seem to reflect light, they seem to absorb it.

Cézanne employed an equally willful geometry to hold *Still Life with Apples* together. Notice how the bottle leans slightly to the left. In order to balance the bottle, the two top pastries on the dish in the background lean up at an improbable angle and point to the right. The white tablecloth forms a secure, open triangle at the front of the canvas; this helps to counteract the edges of the table, which touch the edges of the canvas with otherwise inconsistent angles.

Cézanne's portraits and landscapes show the same willful, form-bending pressure. In the portrait of Madame Cézanne (fig. 7.20), notice how the dark stripe on the wall changes its width on either side of her chair. And despite the flattened quality of her figure, Madame Cézanne somehow seems quite comfortable in the unique space created for her by her husband, a remarkable effect of a visual language that uses color as both light and structure at the same time.

As has been noted, none of these innovations in color, shape, or geometry is part of a formula. They defy explanation. Cézanne's paintings have a feeling of intense study and labor. They reflect the flinty, meditative, introspective character of Cézanne himself. Art for him was a lonely quest. He received very little recognition for his extraordinary recasting of ordinary sight into a vision of iron but gentle certainty. Nevertheless, before he died in 1906 he received acknowledgment from the group that had interested him the most: the avant-garde.

Seurat and Cézanne each created a new basis of artistic structure that went beyond Impressionism. Even though their personalities inevitably appear through their work, the expression of personality was not their primary focus. Vincent van Gogh, Paul Gauguin, and Henri Rousseau were three Post-Impressionist artists for whom the subjective world of personal feelings, symbols, and dreams were primary artistic goals. The first of them to achieve a new visual language of subjectivity was a Dutch artist whose hero, quite appropriately, was Rembrandt: Vincent van Gogh.

Vincent van Gogh: (1853–1890): Avant-Garde Art as Self-Revelation

Vincent van Gogh's life, one of the most remarkable in the history of Western art, has since become a legend because of its persistent difficulties and tragic ending. He began his artistic career in 1880 at the age of twenty-seven. By the time of his death ten years later, he had opened up Post-Impressionist art to a radically new level of subjective expression of feeling.

Van Gogh's brief career had three distinct periods, each of which evolved in a different location: Holland (1880–86), Paris (1886–88), and Arles, in the south of France (1888–90).

7.20

Even though the paintings from the last period are his most influential works, the other periods are equally important in terms of his life and his artistic accomplishment.

Van Gogh's Apprenticeship (1880–86): Student of Life and Student of Art

By the time van Gogh turned to art he had already lost a promising sales career in an international art gallery based in The Hague. He had also served for almost two years as a religious missionary in a poverty-stricken industrial town in Belgium. These failures were due, at least partly, to his deep but impulsive idealism and the equally strong intensity of his personality.

He loved humanity but could not get along easily with individual people. He was so serious that it was difficult to tell a joke in his presence or carry on a discussion without it becoming an argument. These qualities caused him frustration in the human relationships he continuously sought throughout his life. As he himself often admitted, what he was unable to express in his relationships with people he poured into his art. Even more than Manet's, van Gogh's art and life were characterized by an indelible sincerity.

The Potato Eaters (fig. 7.21) is a good example of this characteristic sincerity. This painting dates from 1885, five years after van Gogh, with his usual fervor, decided to embark upon a career as a self-educated artist. The crude, almost cartoonlike quality of the painting makes Courbet seem like a perfumed and polished Academic. The painting nevertheless shows van Gogh's biblical concern for the poor, as well as his disdain for courting easy success by pleasing public taste. The concern and vulnerability of the painting overcome its aesthetic limitations.

7.20 Paul Cézanne. *Madame Cézanne in a Yellow Rocking Chair.* 1890–94. Oil on canvas, 31½″ × 25¼″. Courtesy of the Art Institute of Chicago.

7.21 Vincent van Gogh. *The Potato Eaters.* 1885. Oil on canvas, 82 × 114 cm. Collection Ryksmuseum Vincent van Gogh, Amsterdam.

7.21

I have tried to make it clear how these people, eating their potatoes under the lamplight, have dug the earth with the very hands which they put into the dish.[6]

Van Gogh's art was always focused on his need to communicate personal feelings about reality with the same passionate conviction clearly visible in *The Potato Eaters*.

In 1886, after reaching a point at which he was satisfied with his progress, he accepted his brother Theo's invitation to come to Paris. Theo had made a successful career for himself as an art dealer there and had been helping his brother financially since his decision to become an artist—some would say his conversion. Theo had urged Vincent to come to Paris and see the artistic revolution then under way by the Impressionists.

Van Gogh in Paris (1886–88): The Discovery and the Rejection of Impressionism

During his stay in Paris van Gogh received a rapid education in the theories and practices that had been accumulating in avant-garde art since Courbet. Since the technology for printing photographs of paintings in magazines and newspapers did not arrive until the turn of the century, avant-garde art had made little impact outside of Paris.

His 1886–87 self-portrait (fig. 7.22) reflects his enthusiasm for the new brightness of Seurat's recently exhibited *La Grande Jatte* (fig. 7.13). Only the background dots, however, stay in line. The brush strokes of the face are far too direct and forceful to qualify as Seurat's devotion to mathematically applied "technique." This portrait, with its deliberate attempt at urbanity, clearly reveals van Gogh's characteristic intensity and the subtle shadow of paranoia that so often rose to the surface. The portrait also shows why the artist who painted *The Potato Eaters* could not be contained indefinitely within the moderation of Impressionism or the grid of Seurat's hyper-controlled dot system.

By 1888, van Gogh had absorbed all the theory and done all the experimenting he needed to bring himself to the threshold of his own artistic breakthrough. With his brother Theo's continuing help, he left for the south of France to begin the final phase of his artistic pilgrimage.

Van Gogh in Arles (1888–90): The Beginning and the End

Even though he was there for only a little over a year, van Gogh's art bloomed in Arles. The sunlight there had an intensity that matched his own, yet Arles refreshed him. Its Roman ruins and its Mediterranean tolerance were a welcome escape from the combative and hurried pace of Paris. Nevertheless, van Gogh worked constantly. He drove himself

7.22

like a man who heard a clock ticking away his opportunity. The results were prodigious; he produced over two hundred paintings in two years.

The Bedroom at Arles (fig. 7.23 and plate 18) is a remarkable example of the style he evolved to answer the need for an art that expressed feelings. The breakthrough for him was his decision to use color as a completely subjective device. He wrote to his brother that he agreed with another Impressionist artist, Camille Pissarro, that color and line must be exaggerated, or a picture is no better than a photograph. He wrote, "All of my work is in a way founded on Japanese art, and we do not know enough about Japanese prints."[7]

Van Gogh in this painting used color to express and magnify his feelings, and he employed the outlined shapes and flat colors of Japanese prints. He used the same terminology for color as Monet, Seurat, and Cézanne; this painting, however, is a singularly new thing in art, a work that uses all these sources to make a statement about subjective feeling:

Well, I enormously enjoyed doing this interior of nothing at all, of a Seurat-like simplicity; . . . the walls pale *lilac*, the ground a faded broken *red*, the chairs and the bed chrome *yellow*, the pillows and the sheet a very pale *green-citron*, the counterpane blood *red*, the

7.22 Vincent van Gogh.
Self-portrait. 1886–87.
Oil on cardboard, 16⅛″ × 13½″.
Courtesy of the Art Institute of Chicago.

7.23 Vincent van Gogh.
The Bedroom at Arles. 1888–89.
Oil on canvas, 29″ × 36″.
Courtesy of the Art Institute of Chicago.

7.23

washstand *orange,* the washbasin *blue,* the window *green.* By means of all these very diverse tones I have wanted to express an *absolute restfulness,* you see, and there is no white in it at all except the little note produced by the mirror with its black frame (*in order to get the fourth pair of complementaries into it*).[8] [Italics mine, except for "absolute restfulness."]

In order to appreciate van Gogh's radical subjectivity, imagine what a photograph of the kind of room that would fit his budget would look like. The painting is a statement of van Gogh's power to hope. He shows the viewer the room as he felt when he was in it after a day of laboring at his art. He communicated what the room *meant* to him, not what it looked like.

Van Gogh was elated about his artistic breakthrough. Even though his brother had yet to sell a single one of his paintings—he eventually would sell one before Vincent died—Vincent was convinced that his approach would eventually meet with the same public approval as Impressionism was then beginning to evoke. With typical enthusiasm, he invited a brilliant artist he had met in Paris, Paul Gauguin, to come to Arles. Van Gogh's plan was simple; since they had similar ideas, they would not only share expenses and lodging, but would make progress in their art. Their personalities, however, clashed so severely that van Gogh—already overworked and probably undernourished—broke down and had the first of his seizures in December of 1888.

When he woke up in jail on the day after his seizure he was shocked to learn that he had cut off part of his ear and given it to a prostitute. He also learned that Gauguin had left Arles, but van Gogh desperately resolved to continue on his own.

His life for the next eighteen months became a tragedy. In May of 1889 he voluntarily confined himself in a mental hospital at St. Remy, not far from Arles. During his stay there he alternated between hope for a full recovery and despair at his recurring periods of illness. He nevertheless continued to paint through the entire cycle.

Ironically, before he began to have these seizures, his art had evolved to the point that his brush strokes became the direct expression of his feelings. He wrote that when he was absorbed in painting,

the emotions are sometimes so strong that one works without being aware of working . . . and the strokes come with a sequence and coherence like words in a speech or a letter.[9]

Starry Night (fig. 7.24), painted during one of his lucid intervals, is an eruption of ecstatic feeling. The universe is alive. Yellow stars wheel through a purple-blue sky. The town, peopled with carefully outlined and solid houses, is dominated by the spire of a church. It was van Gogh's dream, from his stay in the Belgian coal-mine village to the rented

rooms in Arles, to settle into a world like this, a world that offered, not only security, but epiphanies.

For van Gogh, of course, it was only a dream. The wheeling stars themselves show the swirling lines of a mind that was struggling to find, with an increasing sense of despair, an island of stability.

Starry Night was painted during his stay at St. Remy. The copy of *The Bedroom at Arles* in figure 7.23 was one of two that he made of his original painting while he was there. Since he had made no significant improvement at St. Remy after several months, he left and went north, to the town of Auvers to place himself under the care of Dr. Paul Gachet, who was a friend of Cézanne and other avant-garde artists. His efforts there also failed to halt his worsening condition, caused by a still undetermined neurological disease. In despair of ever fully recovering, van Gogh shot himself in July of 1890.

7.24 Vincent van Gogh. *Starry Night.* 1889. Oil on canvas, 29″ × 36¼″. Collection, Museum of Modern Art, New York. Acquired through the Lillie P. Bliss Bequest.

In one of his letters to his brother he summed up his experience of life:

There may be a great fire in one's soul and no one ever comes to warm himself at it, and the passersby see only a little bit of smoke coming through the chimney and pass on their way.[10]

Ironically, others had begun to see the fire in his paintings. Only a year after his death, a show of his paintings in Paris prompted the following comment in a review by the influential art critic Octave Mirbeau:

It is not possible to forget his personality, whether it be directed toward some scene from reality or toward some internal vision. It overflows his being, giving intense illumination to all that he sees, touches, and feels . . . he has absorbed nature within himself.[11]

This was van Gogh's achievement. He created an art that fused color and form with the feeling arising from his own experience of reality.

In another letter, he had written that

at moments, when I am in a good mood, I think that what is alive in art, and eternally alive, is in the first place the painter and in the second place the picture.[12]

Mirbeau's comments, coming from a man who had never met the artist, showed how successful van Gogh's apparent failure had really been.

Paul Gauguin (1848–1903): Discovering the Dream of Native Art

Paul Gauguin, like Cézanne and van Gogh, owed much to Impressionism. He admired the work of Monet, but eventually scornfully dismissed it as inadequate. Gauguin's scorn was not narrowly focused. He dismissed Seurat with even more characteristic bluntness, calling him "that little green chemist." In fact, Gauguin eventually dismissed almost everything, including all that van Gogh never achieved: a family, a career, and financial security.

Gauguin came from an affluent, middle-class background and spent many of his childhood years in Peru. As an adult, he traveled widely, including a visit to the tropical island of Martinique and a period as a laborer on the Panama Canal. With his background, he was able to establish a financial career on the Paris stock market that supported his family of six children quite comfortably. During his spare time, he painted with the Impressionists, and he was so talented that they allowed him—a stockbroker—to exhibit with them. His talents even met Academic standards: one of his paintings was accepted into the Salon of 1876.

By 1886, Gauguin had turned his back on all of this, breaking away not only from Impressionism but also from his family. With his powerful, argumentative intelligence, he

7.25 Paul Gauguin.
Self-Portrait. 1889.
Oil on canvas, 30¼″ × 20¼″.
National Gallery of Art, Washington.

7.26 Paul Gauguin.
The Vision after the Sermon—Jacob Wrestling with the Angel. 1888.
Oil on canvas, 28¾″ × 36¼″.
National Gallery of Scotland, Edinburgh.

became the informal leader of a group of painters who settled in the town of Pont-Aven in rural Brittany. Here on the remote Atlantic coast, Gauguin and his group hoped to learn how to "paint like children."

In this very religious and still pre-industrial region, Gauguin explored a style, similar to van Gogh's, that included an emphasis on flat shapes, bold color, and heavy outlining. Gauguin also added an important new element: *symbolism.* Van Gogh projected feelings into his images; Gauguin used symbolism to project the ideas that originate, as he put it, in the "mysterious centers of thought."

In his 1889 self-portrait (fig. 7.25 and plate 19), Gauguin portrays himself, quite candidly, as a man divided within himself—symbolized by the apples, the halo, and the snake borrowed from the biblical story of the temptation of Adam and Eve. Equally candid is the large nose and the mischievous and arrogant expression of the eyes. The two flat shapes that make up the torso and the background are bright yellow and red, respectively; they give the image the feeling of a playing card, including the connotation of risk-taking and chance that was a central aspect of Gauguin's character.

Gauguin's *The Vision After the Sermon—Jacob Wrestling with the Angel* (fig. 7.26) is a more complex example of Gauguin's new approach to color, line, and symbolism. The

7.25

7.26

Fatata te Miti   P Gauguin 92

7.27

colors were simplified to basic tones of red, blue, and white. Gauguin pictured a mental event as well as a physical event. Women in traditional peasant attire are shown as they listen to a sermon dealing with the biblical story of Jacob wrestling with the angel—the events described in the sermon are pictured in the background. This painting shows the avant-garde acceptance of mental events as the subject of painting. It could be used to illustrate one of Gauguin's personal mottoes: "I close my eyes in order to see better."[13]

After his brief and disastrous visit with van Gogh in 1888, Gauguin returned briefly to Pont-Aven, but then decided to leave Europe entirely in order to steep himself in the native culture of Tahiti.

Gauguin in Tahiti: Creating the Avant-Garde Myth of the Noble Savage

Gauguin arrived in Tahiti in 1891 to begin his journey away from Western civilization. His experience in Tahiti transformed his art. Some of his early paintings suggest that Gauguin found the beauty and simplicity of life that he sought in his escape from Europe. His 1892 painting *By the Sea* (fig. 7.27 and color plate 20) shows two women about to swim in the ocean. A luxuriant tree moves rhythmically across the front of the painting. In the background a man fishes in the surf with a spear. Life seems transparently clear and simple.

Other early paintings, however, involve the complex mixture of symbol and direct observation seen in *After the Sermon. La Orana Maria (We Greet Thee, Mary,* fig. 7.28), painted in muted earth colors and lush pastel tones, employs a simplified drawing style to depict a world where epiphanies and the natural environment merge. An angel with white wings stirs behind the branches of the elegant bush in the foreground as two worshipful figures advance toward the Madonna and Child figures (complete with halos). The tapestry-like background with abundant fruit completes the sense of paradisical harmony.

The halos, however, are an indication that Gauguin had not forgotten his Western roots. The painting's surface has the color and charm of a medieval painting from just before the Perspective Age. What it lacks, of course, is belief. Gauguin was neither a Polynesian nor a Christian; he was a superbly sophisticated Parisian who painted his *desire* for faith and simplicity—much as Monet painted in order to reach an "innocence of seeing."

Paintings like this, however, fueled his reputation in Paris. When he returned for a visit in 1893 after two years in Tahiti, he was welcomed by the avant-garde as a kind of Victor the wild boy in reverse: he had made the journey from civilization back to nature.

Gauguin indulged these expectations, reappearing in Paris with spears, idols, and artifacts from Polynesia. With his Javanese bride (from Montmartre) and a monkey he kept in tow, he made the rounds of his old bohemian haunts, wearing a long blue frock coat and carrying a walking stick carved with "barbaric" figures. He established his claim to the title "Gauguin the savage."

Gauguin: The Final Return to Paradise

By the end of 1893 Gauguin had again tired of Paris, so he arranged for an exhibition of his paintings in order to finance his return to Tahiti. The impression created by Gauguin's art (and personality) at this time is summed up in the introduction to this exhibition written by the playwright August Strindberg.

Who is he then? He is Gauguin, the savage who hates a wearisome civilization; something of a Titan who, jealous of his Creator, in his idle moments makes his own little creation; a child who breaks up his toys to make others; he who denies and defies the rabble, preferring to see the sky red, rather than blue, as they do.[14]

Gauguin's second, and final, trip to Tahiti took him to the Marquesas so as to escape the reach of the French colo-

7.28

7.27 Paul Gauguin.
Fatata te Miti (By the Sea). 1892.
Oil on canvas, 26¾" × 36".
National Gallery of Art, Washington, Chester Dale Collection.

7.28 Paul Gauguin.
La Orana Maria (We Greet Thee, Mary). 1891.
Oil on canvas, 44¾" × 34½".
Metropolitan Museum of Art, New York. Bequest of Samuel A. Lewisohn.

190

nial authorities, who did not approve of his influence on the native Polynesian culture. Gauguin, for his part, despised their attempts to make the natives more French.

His art here took on a deeper connection with the myths and traditions of the people around him. He began to do mural-size works as well as easel paintings. Easel paintings, which had originated during the Renaissance, were a private window for a single viewer to observe scale-model images of an objective world. Gauguin's murals created a surrounding environment instead of the illusion of a window; they seemed to offer a way back toward community, ritual, and myth.

Gauguin believed that art could change the way the artist perceived reality and, in the process, change the artist's self. For Gauguin, art had become a kind of religion, a link with mysterious and transformative energies. This attitude is especially clear in the huge painting *Where do we come from? Where are we? Where are we going?* (fig. 7.29).

Gauguin created this mural-size painting after learning of the death of his favorite daughter, Aline, in Denmark, and it reflects his mood of despair at the time. The colors of the natural background are suppressed to a cold, muted gray, even though the figures almost glow with a golden bronze. Gauguin left a lengthy description of the picture, noting that he put into it his

7.29 Paul Gauguin. *Where do we come from? Where are we? Where are we going?* 1897. Oil on canvas, 5'7" × 14'9". Courtesy of Museum of Fine Arts, Boston, Tompkins Collection, Arthur Gordon Tompkins Residuary Fund.

7.30 Paul Gauguin. *L'Appel (The Call).* 1902. Oil on canvas, 51¼" × 35½". Cleveland Museum of Art, Gift of Hanna Fund.

sufferings in terrible circumstances. . . . An intentionally large figure, which defies perspective, sits with an arm upraised and looks in amazement at the two people who dare think about their destiny.[15]

Having catalogued his despair in these ritually posed forms set in his own mysteriously glowing color, Gauguin attempted suicide by taking arsenic.

He was found, barely alive, by natives who brought him back to his house. After weeks of suffering, he recovered his

7.29

health and began a final period of productivity before his death in 1903.

Despite his continuing confrontation with French colonial authorities and his strong attachment to European links, ranging from newspapers to letters to tobacco, his paintings continued to portray the dream rather than the reality of his life in the South Seas. One of his last paintings, *L'Appel* (*The Call*, fig. 7.30), has the same calm serenity and glowing color of paintings like *By the Sea* (fig. 7.27).

Early in the twentieth century, Gauguin's art began to achieve a wide acceptance. His continuing influence on contemporary art is immense. But the most moving tribute to Gauguin came, not from those who felt the mystery of his art, but from the natives who anointed his body and mourned him in their traditional manner. They had named him Koke, the "forefather of flowers," and they said of him: "Koke is dead. There is no other man. We are lost."[16]

Henri Rousseau (1844–1910): Experiencing Innocence and Wilderness in Paris

Van Gogh and Gauguin contributed to the subjective dimension of the avant-garde art tradition by freeing color and symbolism from the constraints of the optical world. From each of them the process exacted an incalculable personal cost. Henri Rousseau accomplished a similar feat without disrupting his ordinary pattern of life in urban Paris.

Rousseau worked for twenty years as a soldier and a tax collector (thus his nickname Douanier, "tax collector"). At the age of forty-two he took an early pension and devoted the rest of his life to art.

Rousseau's art reveals a kind of innocence that is much like that sought in different ways by Monet and Gauguin. His was the interior innocence buried in each individual as the residue of the child art phase of development.

Rousseau's own baffling innocence permeated his life. He once commented that he would not work to pay for a bigger apartment than his one-room dwelling, because the first thing he saw when he awoke each day was one of his paintings—and what could be better than that? He added that, without working, every day is Sunday.

His innocence extended to his painting technique. Rousseau aimed at the photographic perfection that he saw and admired in the work of the famous Academic painters of the day, and his techniques of painting even imitated theirs: besides using photographs as source materials and as a standard of visual perfection, he devoted himself, in John Canaday's words, to an "extreme carefulness of outline, a smoothing out of the paint, a finicky blending of one tone into another, and a fascination with fine detail."[17]

This technique was similar to that of one of his favorite

7.30

painters, Jean Léon Gérôme; one of Gérôme's paintings served as inspiration for Rousseau's marvelous *The Sleeping Gypsy* (fig. 7.31). This painting has the luminous clarity of a dream. Its remarkable innocence, unmitigated by any theory or explanation, presents the shoulder of the gypsy, the mandolin, and the vase from three different viewpoints. Rousseau confounds the theories of the Academic painters and the avant-garde; he admired both and imitated their achievements. The result is inimitable.

The only art Rousseau's painting resembles at all is child art. But his child art vision has the richness of fully adult experience of the world of modern Paris. Later, twentieth-century developments like Freudian psychology, Cubism, and Surrealism would make his paintings look like prophecies.

7.31 Henri Rousseau.
The Sleeping Gypsy. 1897.
Oil on canvas, 51″ × 6′7″.
Museum of Modern Art, New York, Gift of
Mrs. Simon Guggenheim.

7.32 Henri Rousseau.
The Dream. 1910.
Oil on canvas, 6′8½″ × 9′9½″.
Museum of Modern Art, New York. Gift of
Nelson A. Rockefeller.

7.31

Rousseau's Jungle Paintings: Finding the Wilderness Within

Rousseau's finest paintings are those culled from his visits to the botanical gardens in Paris and from postcards and photographs of tropical places he visited in his imagination.

His last major painting, *The Dream* (fig. 7.32), is a kind of summation of the energies he poured into these works. This figure-landscape composition rivals the visionary myths of Gauguin. Pressed against the canvas is a forest of subtle green color and forms—like a mirthfully restored Eden. A dreamy, sensuous nude on a burgundy couch (another avant-garde *Olympia*) gazes at an ebony, Egyptianesque flute player. Two astonished lions and a partly hidden rhino gaze out from their habitat. Each plant seems to line up horizontally in an effort to achieve maximum recognition within this lush, horizontally layered apparition of forms.

It is a painting whose seemingly effortless fecundity realizes the dream of art so agonizingly fabricated by Gauguin:

Art is an abstraction. Extract from your dreams about nature and think more of the creation than of the result. The only way to approach God is to do as our Divine Master did, to create.[18]

Rousseau showed that the effort of the subjective direction of the avant-garde was not to reject civilization but to reclaim its source within the human person. Of all the artists of the nineteenth century, Rousseau affirms perhaps the most complete version of the myth of the autonomous individual. His works celebrate the importance of the inner event and the inner landscape. Rousseau took the journey of subjectivity without leaving home.

7.32

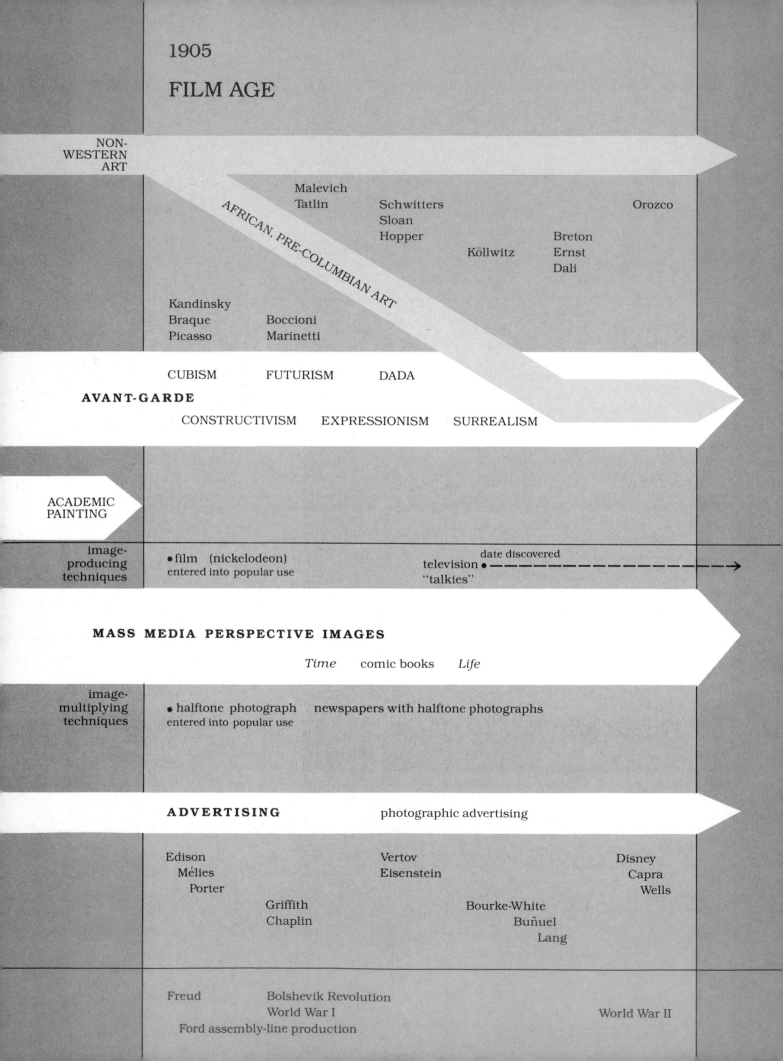

1905

FILM AGE

NON-WESTERN ART

AFRICAN, PRE-COLUMBIAN ART

Malevich
Tatlin
Schwitters
Sloan
Hopper
Köllwitz
Orozco
Breton
Ernst
Dali

Kandinsky
Braque
Picasso
Boccioni
Marinetti

CUBISM   FUTURISM   DADA

AVANT-GARDE

CONSTRUCTIVISM   EXPRESSIONISM   SURREALISM

ACADEMIC PAINTING

image-producing techniques

• film   (nickelodeon)
entered into popular use

date discovered
television •– – – – – – – – – – – – →
"talkies"

MASS MEDIA PERSPECTIVE IMAGES

Time   comic books   *Life*

image-multiplying techniques

• halftone photograph   newspapers with halftone photographs
entered into popular use

ADVERTISING   photographic advertising

Edison
Mélies
Porter
Vertov
Eisenstein
Disney
Capra
Wells

Griffith
Chaplin
Bourke-White
Buñuel
Lang

Freud   Bolshevik Revolution
World War I
World War II
Ford assembly-line production

CHAPTER EIGHT

THE FILM AGE I:
MOVIES AND PHOTOGRAPHY
TRANSFORM
THE MASS MEDIA

ASSESSMENTS

1. Recall the first movies you were aware of seeing—what were they? What impressions did you have? Do you enjoy going to movies today?
2. What specific films have made a lasting impression on you? What *types* of films do you like? Do you have any favorite film actors or actresses or directors?
3. Are you interested in seeing, hearing, or reading about celebrities? Do you wish you were a celebrity? In your opinion, what is the role of celebrities in American culture today?
4. What newspapers, magazines, or comics do you regularly read? How important are they in your daily life?
5. In what sense are the specific newspapers and magazines that you are familiar with expressing their own particular myth?

By 1905 the work of Monet, Seurat, Cézanne, van Gogh, and Gauguin had gained strong recognition within the avant-garde and was about to make a significant impact on the wider public that had supported Academic painting. Monet had become wealthy. He was then living at Giverny, painting his gardens. Only Rousseau was yet unacknowledged by either the avant-garde or the general public.

One of the most important developments for Western art at the turn of the century, however, occurred in the mass media. A convenient date to mark the beginning of this next phase of Western art is 1905, for three important reasons: the first nickelodeon (a theater devoted exclusively to the showing of movies) opened in the United States (fig. 8.1); the halftone process that allowed photographs to be printed in mass publications had been generally adopted (fig. 8.2); and the French government had dropped its sole sponsorship and dominance of the Academy and the Salon system. These combined factors illustrate the conclusion of the momentous cultural change that had begun in Manet's time: the substitution of the mass media for Academic painting as Western culture's most influential source of perspective images to reflect its basic values.

8.1 Edwin S. Porter.
The Great Train Robbery. 1903.
Museum of Modern Art, New York, Film Stills Archives.

8.2 *Daily Mirror* front page, June 24, 1924.
Smithsonian Institution, Washington. Photo #78–14217.

8.3 *Lyman H. Howe's New Marvels in Moving Pictures.* 1898.
Lithograph.
Courtesy of Library of Congress. #LC-USZ62-62048.

8.4 *Diorama of Paris.*
Mid-19th century. Daguerreotype.
Courtesy of Science Museum, London.

8.1

Before discussing the powerful impact of the mass media on avant-garde art in the next chapter, it is necessary to examine the important new cultural role of the mass media themselves. They not only continued, in a meaningful sense, the popular realism of Academic painting, they produced icons that both reflected and helped to create a radically different middle-class society from that of the nineteenth century. The most powerful new mass media art form was the movies.

8.2

The Origin of the Movies I: American Roots in Academic Painting

Even though the major contribution to the development of the movies came from America, influences and contributions from other countries were critically important. Among them, the effect of French Academic painting was direct and substantial.

Despite the importance of photography as a mass medium, it was primarily the movies that displaced Academic painting as the new standard of visual imagery. The frame around the screen in the 1898 poster *Lyman H. Howe's New Marvels in Moving Pictures* (fig. 8.3) is an attempt to relate the new medium to fine art. The cultivated upper middle class audience shown in the poster was, at this date, as fictional as the battleships on the screen. The movies, in spite of their eventually universal appeal, began as a popular art adopted by the lower class. The film historian Charles Eidsvik has commented:

The cinema, like the Academy, was born to serve the aesthetic of spectacular romantic realism that dominated the popular arts of the nineteenth century. . . . The picture on a movie screen resembles a nineteenth-century painting far more than either resembles the painting on the walls of virtually any museum of modern art.[1]

8.3

The influence of Academic painting on the development of the movies goes back to the early nineteenth century. Louis Daguerre began as an aspiring Academic painter. Lacking sufficient talent for Salon competition, he devoted his interest in realistic imagery to improving the highly popular visual spectacle called the diorama (fig. 8.4). Daguerre's dioramas were large-scale scenes painted on translucent canvas in such a way that one scene would show if light was reflected *from* the canvas and another scene would show if light was projected *through* the canvas from behind. These lighting effects and the addition of a musical accompaniment added a strong touch of drama as well as a sense of passing time. The public gladly paid admission to

8.4

see these spectacular displays of visual illusion. Dioramas were thus a major step from painting toward the movies.

It was Daguerre's quest for an increasingly convincing illusion of reality that took him beyond the diorama to collaborate with Niepce in the invention of photography.

American artists were also motivated by the urge for maximum visual illusion underlying Academic painting. After all, French Academic painters trained most of America's most important nineteenth-century artists. Thomas Cole, Frederick Edwin Church, and Albert Bierstadt were either immigrants from Europe with European training or had studied in Europe. Gérôme himself at one time had ninety American students in Paris.

The most impressive and original application of Academic painting technique to American themes is seen in nineteenth-century landscape painting. American artists created landscapes that Robert Hughes has called "pre-Cinemascope prodigies" without equal in Europe.

Frederick Edwin Church's *Twilight in the Wilderness* is a superb example of this tradition (fig. 8.5 and plate 21). The reds, yellows, and greens of the sunset are reflected in the placid blue of the water to create a peaceful symmetry. This sense of order is enhanced by the carefully observed and rendered details of the trees and clouds. The sense of quiet in the scene is as vivid as the colors. The result is both meditative and scientific at the same time. Such stunning, almost visionary landscapes combined the Academic attention to photographic detail with the strong nineteenth-century American belief in their continent as a biblical land of promise.

Many of these works were so detailed that it was com-

8.5

mon practice to use opera glasses to become absorbed within the spectacular imagery. Barbara Novak describes one particularly interesting example of this passion for visual illusion that took the form of a "moving painting" or panorama:

Henry Lewis's *Mammoth Panorama of the Mississippi River*, painted on 45,000 square feet of canvas, representing the Mississippi from St. Louis to the Falls of St. Anthony, was offered to the public view at the Louisville Theater in Kentucky in 1849. Seats were available through a box office . . . doors opened at seven forty-five and the Panorama commenced moving at precisely eight-thirty. What was in fact on offer was a moving picture with all its social appurtenances.[2]

Similar effects were used in nineteenth-century theater dramas by combining such "moving paintings" with the diorama techniques pioneered by Daguerre. All of these are examples of an emerging "pre-movie" mentality; American artists by the late nineteenth century had certainly made the public ready for the movies.

It is interesting to note that popular art lithographs, like those in France at the same time, contributed a strong note of pragmatic realism. The Currier and Ives company was the most important nineteenth-century American producer of these popular lithographs. *Across the Continent* (fig. 8.6), printed in the same decade as *Twilight in the Wilderness*, presents a more prophetic, if less biblical, view of the American landscape. A railroad splits the continent in half: on one side are public schools, Conestoga wagons heading farther West, homesteads (future suburbia), and felled trees; on the other side of the tracks are the disappearing wilderness and the figures of two astonished Indians about to be engulfed in the smoke of the onrushing train.

Thomas Eakins (1844–1916): Beyond the Academy toward the Movies

One American artist, Thomas Eakins, took the photographic realism of Academic painting and of photography itself and pushed both to their absolute limits—short of actual motion.

8.6

8.5 Frederick Edwin Church.
Twilight in the Wilderness. 1864.
Oil on canvas, 40" × 64".
Cleveland Museum of Art, Mr. and Mrs.
William H. Marlatt Fund.

8.6 Currier and Ives.
Across the Continent. 1868.
Lithograph, 17¾" × 27".
Courtesy of Library of Congress.
#LC-USZ62-1.

Eakins, a young man from Philadelphia, was so gifted that in 1866, at the age of twenty-two, he had to choose between art and medicine. With typical intensity, he went to Paris to study art under the direction of the painter he most admired, Jean Léon Gérôme, who was, in turn, so impressed with young Eakins that he avoided a government ban on foreign students at the École des Beaux-Arts by taking him in as private student in his own studio.

Eakins stayed in Paris for four years, spending long hours at the Louvre and traveling to Spain in addition to working in Gérôme's studio. He was quite sure what he wanted to do; his interest was so completely focused on Academic painting that his letters home mentioned nothing about Manet or the tumult caused by the Impressionists during his stay in Paris.

Eakins's hard work was rewarded when Gérôme acknowledged him as his best student, an assessment Eakins agreed with, as can be seen in a letter he wrote shortly before his return home: "I know perfectly what I am doing and can run my modelling, without polishing or hiding or sneaking it away to the end. I can finish as far as I can see."[3]

As his words indicate, Eakins was confident that, in approaching the mastery of a Gérôme, he was ready to make a powerful impact on American art.

8.7

Eakins in America: Too Real and Too Factual

Eakins's first major painting when he returned from Paris, *Max Schmitt in a Single Scull* (fig. 8.7), shows just how far he could finish and how far he could see. A scull is a small rowboat used at that time for a popular form of racing. Eakins's painting shows Max Schmitt, a well-known sculler, pausing in a spectacularly painted autumn scene. Eakins proudly inserted a self-portrait—the sculler in the background. Thus Eakins's work resembled the paintings of Manet and the Impressionists in the sense that he attempted to depict the "heroism" of the immediate environment—which, on America's east coast, was now far more city than wilderness.

Eakins fully expected this painting to earn him public and critical acclaim and establish for him a prominent place in American art. The critics, however, picked at its technical perfection; the public simply found it boring. Professional athletes were not a favored subject in late nineteenth-century America.

Undeterred, his next major work, *The Gross Clinic* (fig. 8.8), combined rigorously objective portraiture with the strong theatrical flavor of Academic painting. The composition centers on the famous surgeon Dr. Samuel David Gross. Eakins heightened the sense of melodrama by inserting the cringing figure of a woman—the patient's mother—in the background. The gray socks worn by the young man indicate that he was poor; the operation was therefore free, because he had agreed to become the subject of the lecture/demonstration. Dr. Gross, meanwhile—as a true hero of science—rises above the trauma to instruct the surrounding

8.7 Thomas Eakins.
Max Schmitt in a Single Scull. 1871.
Oil on canvas, 32¼″ × 46¼″.
Metropolitan Museum of Art, New York, Purchase, 1934, Alfred N. Punnett Fund and Gift of George D. Pratt.

8.8 Thomas Eakins.
The Gross Clinic. 1875.
Oil on canvas, 8′ × 6′6″.
Jefferson Medical College, Thomas Jefferson University, Philadelphia.

8.8

tiers of attentive students. Eakins was well qualified to paint this picture; he had spent two years studying anatomy, including several dissections, before taking up art as a career.

Even melodrama did not help with the critics or the public. The bloody hands of the surgeon and the undignified position of the patient (not to mention the patient's gray socks symbolizing the poorhouse) undercut any potential sentimental appeal in the melodrama.

The greatest insult came, however, when Eakins submitted the painting for display at Philadelphia's Centennial Exhibition of 1876: the jury rejected it. Eakins had to settle for a place in a display of medical equipment. Officials apparently reasoned that anyone who confronted the painting there was either professionally desensitized to its horrific realism, or was at least properly forewarned.

This public lack of enthusiasm continued to greet Eakins's paintings of contemporary life, which ranged from sporting events to urban landscapes. Despite his current reputation as one of America's truly great nineteenth-century painters, Eakins in his own lifetime received recognition primarily for his portraits, which included the leading industrialists, social figures, and politicians of his day. His uncompromisingly realistic spirit met opposition even here—many of his portraits were refused by the sitter after completion, and some were actually burned. For Gérôme, realism was a veneer, a camouflage; for Eakins, realism meant one thing: objective visual truth. This pursuit of it led Eakins to the threshold of the movies.

Eakins and Photographic Realism: Pushing Photography toward the Movies

Eakins was intensely interested in photography as a means of acquiring objective information for his painting of the human figure, landscapes, and animals. In one of his paintings, *A May Morning in the Park*, Eakins used information from photography to paint the correct position of horses' legs while they are running. This kind of visual perfection was possible only through photography, since the speed of horses' legs is not visible to the human eye.

Eakins's quest for the minutest details of visual reality brought him to experiment in recording motion through photography. He was fascinated by the rapid-succession photographs of Eadweard Muybridge (fig. 5.12) and corresponded with him. His own motion photographs include a sequential figure done in 1884 (fig. 8.9). Less than a decade after *A May Morning in the Park*, another American, Thomas Edison, put together the mechanical gears that finally made photographs move.

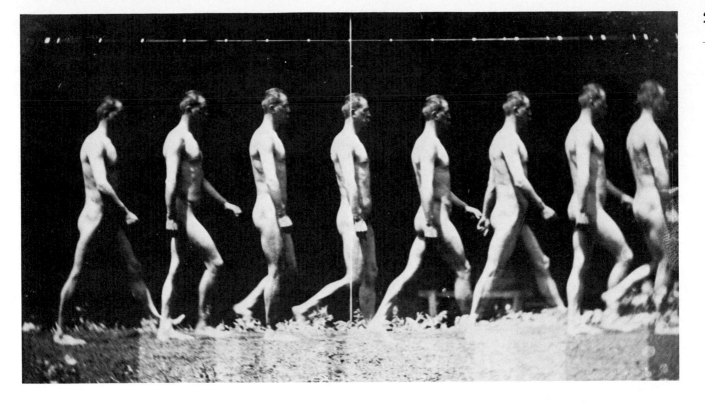

8.9 Thomas Eakins.
Marey Wheel Photograph of Jesse Godley. 1884.
Philadelphia Museum of Art, Given by Charles Bregler.

The Origins of the Movies II: Scientific Roots

The steps that led directly from photography to the movies began in the work of Eadweard Muybridge, the photographer who influenced Eakins.

Muybridge's work influenced the French photographer Étienne Marey, who had also been experimenting with ways to photograph the motion of animals and birds. Marey met Muybridge in 1872. By 1882 Marey had developed a rifle-shaped camera that could take twelve images per second on a single photographic plate. By 1892, Marey's rifle-camera process used roll film. At this point "rapid photography" was ready for the final refinement—George Eastman's more pliable roll film with sprocket holes. With this film and this background of development, Thomas Edison produced the first movies.

Viewers of Edison's first movies had to look through a peephole into a machine called the kinetoscope. By 1896 a lantern and screen arrangement enabled the film image to be projected for a group audience. Movies then quickly became a standard part of both vaudeville shows and carnivals across America.

The realism of the movies was so startling that during their first decade audiences were quite content with repetitive footage of boxers (fig. 8.10), presidents, vaudeville acts, and other predictable scenes. The artistic qualities of these first films can be judged by their early use as "chasers"—in many vaudeville houses they were shown at the end of the evening as the signal that it was time to go home.

The first filmmaker who began to explore the potential of both the form and the content of movies as a vehicle for effects unique to motion pictures was the French magician Georges Méliès. With Méliès, movies became more than a novelty; they began to take their own artistic identity as film.

Georges Méliès (1861–1938): Enter the Magicians

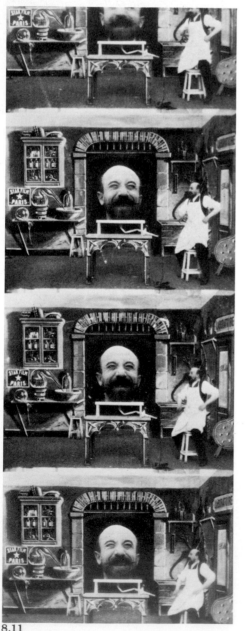

8.10

8.11

Méliès had a professional background as a caricaturist, set designer, actor, and producer when he began to apply his energy to the new art form of film. He approached the medium from the beginning as a magician and an artist. Films like *The Man with the Rubber Head* (fig. 8.11) were based on his own scripts and sets, which combined to form what he called "artificially arranged scenes."

This accurate term also describes his initial approach to the camera: his films featured no close-ups or changes of camera angle. Despite his stationary camera, Méliès enthralled audiences with his seemingly uncanny special effects—most of which derived from his career as a professional magician. By 1900 he had made over two hundred one- to two-minute films, which became the most popular screen events in America.

Méliès did more than record magic tricks on film. He discovered and then creatively applied one of the most commonly used devices in film history—the jump cut. While filming on a busy Paris street, the film jammed in his camera, and after freeing it, he resumed shooting. When he viewed the developed footage in his laboratory, the astonished Méliès saw a bus suddenly turn into a hearse! The delay in freeing the jammed film had put a bus on one frame and a hearse on the next—with no separation between them. Méliès had accidentally made a collage of time and space, and he was creative enough to turn a happy accident into a discovery.

In 1902, Méliès took a bold step toward the feature film. His masterpiece, *A Trip to the Moon* (fig. 8.12), not only more than doubled the standard two-minute-length of a film to five minutes, it also began the long march of space adventures that has led to today's *Star Wars*.

A Trip to the Moon had an enormous impact in Europe and America. It helped inspire an American filmmaker who worked for Edison—Edwin S. Porter—to go beyond Méliès's own artificially arranged scenes and film a story set in the real outdoors. Méliès's domination of film ended when Porter released his film: *The Great Train Robbery*.

8.10 *Corbett and Courtney Before the Kinetograph.*
Museum of Modern Art, New York, Film Stills Archive.

8.11 George Méliès.
The Man With the Rubber Head. 1902.
Museum of Modern Art, New York, Film Stills Archive.

8.12 George Méliès.
A Trip to the Moon. 1902.
Museum of Modern Art, New York, Film Stills Archive.

Edwin S. Porter (1870–1941): Editing Real Time and Real Space

Just as Méliès had used the magic show as a visual starting point, Porter based his first major film, *The Life of an American Fireman*, on a series of six popular Currier and Ives lithographs on the same theme.

In *The Great Train Robbery*, Porter gave America its first classic chase scene, its first illusion of riding a train, the shock of seeing a passenger shot by a bandit, and—finishing off a whole series of such thrills—the experience of a bandit turning and firing his pistol directly into the audience! (see fig. 8.1).

Even more significant than the full fifteen minutes of special effects and the sense of narrative continuity was Porter's introduction of a definitive conceptual change in the film process: editing. Instead of first conceiving the film as a play and then filming it, Porter shot a continuing sequence of scenes within a real environment and within the ongoing action. Later, after developing the film, he cut and rearranged the sections of film into the final narrative form. This later examination and reassembling of film is called editing—it is the difference between "filmed theater" and pure film.

The Movies Become Independent: *The Great Train Robbery* and the Rise of the Nickelodeon

The Great Train Robbery also signaled an entirely new era for distribution and for the cultural influence of the movies.

John Sloan's delightful 1905 etching *Fun, One Cent* (fig. 8.13) captures the end of the era when movies were viewed in the "peep show" format of Edison's original kinetoscope. A historic turning point came in 1905 when a Pittsburgh businessman, John P. Harris, opened the first nickelodeon (admission price plus *odeon,* the French word for theater). Films were now considered interesting enough to have their own theater for display and enjoyment. Harris's nickelodeon had standing-room-only audiences for several weeks with *The Great Train Robbery.*

Within a year there were thousands of nickelodeons across America. In urban areas, the huge immigrant population flocked to early films, which were understandable across the language barrier. The movies of this period were powerful icons for assimilating millions of individuals from diverse cultures into a common vision of American life.

By World War I, films had earned enough respectability to move into middle-class neighborhoods. Elegant downtown theaters like the Palace in New York were built to accomodate up to five thousand customers. Movie audiences were also ready for more sophisticated visual techniques and more interesting story lines. The stage was set for the arrival of D. W. Griffith, America's most internationally acclaimed early master of film.

D. W. Griffith: The Film as Visual Epic

D. W. Griffith was an actor and would-be writer who entered the film trade only reluctantly. His first employment in the movies came in 1906 when he accepted an acting role in one

8.13 John Sloan.
Fun, One Cent. 1905.
Etching, 5″ × 7″ (plate).
Museum of Modern Art, New York.

of Edwin S. Porter's films. Even though he considered movies a step down from the theater, by 1908 he was directing his own. Griffith's greatness lay in his ability to convert two nineteenth-century traditions into the new language of motion pictures: the realistic melodrama of the theater and the combination of grandeur and detailed observation of Academic painting. In 1915 and 1916 Griffith produced two films that often still appear on lists of the greatest films ever made. The first, *Birth of a Nation*, shows his brilliant ability to make visual melodrama. The second, *Intolerance*, is an example of adept translation of Academic painting into the language of film.

Birth of a Nation opened at the Palace Theater in New York in March of 1915 accompanied by a forty-piece orchestra and a chorus. Its 44-week run made film history. In addition, the film generated a controversy that accompanies it to this day whenever it is shown.

Griffith's film was a patriotic epic about American history, from the Old South through the period of Reconstruction after the Civil War. The plot, by itself, is vintage melodrama centered on the relationships between members of a northern and a southern family who fight on opposite sides and then find a new sense of harmony after the war. Griffith, whose father had been a Confederate officer, presented the Ku Klux Klan as a noble and patriotic group that was needed to defend public virtue against the freed but uncontrollable blacks. One subtitle reads, "The former enemies of North and South are united again in defense of their Arian birthright."

Despite being banned in several cities, the film became immensely popular. Griffith showed an amazing ability to weave the complex story and action into a unified balance of both epic and highly personal scenes. His visual techniques became standard for later filmmakers.

Epic vs. Personal

Griffith devised visual methods to personalize every aspect of the drama—including the panoramic war scenes (fig. 8.14). He transformed the black circle, or "iris" shape, traditionally used to show the end of a scene into a kind of zoom lens: one particular scene opens with the iris contracted to show only the small, sorrowful figure of a woman; as the circle of the iris opens, the screen reveals the cause of the woman's sorrow—the valley below her is filled with the tumult of battle.

Lighting

Films had previously been shot in maximum overall light. Griffith shot scenes at night, by campfire light, in semidarkness, and so on.

8.14

Natural Landscape

He used the backgrounds in *Birth of a Nation* to create specific moods. To suggest the epic nature of the Civil War battles, for instance, Griffith shot panoramic scenes from distances of up to four miles. These landscapes were significant also because, instead of Georgia, they were shot in southern California. Griffith is the filmmaker who established California as the movie capital of the world.

Color Tinting

Griffith added emotional drama by dyeing sections of the film; he dyed the burning of Atlanta sequence in *Birth of a Nation* to a flaming red.

Camera Movement

One of Griffith's greatest innovations was in the way he used the camera. He understood that the director's role in the moving of the camera was as important as the directing of the actors and actresses.

Despite the box-office and critical success of *Birth of a Nation,* Griffith was so stung by the charges of racism that he devoted his entire earnings from the film to a 1916 extravaganza aimed at exposing the vicious nature of prejudice. He called the film *Intolerance.*

Intolerance presented four stories that illustrated injustice and prejudice in four periods of history: ancient Babylon, the time of Christ, seventeenth-century France (the Huguenots), and the modern industrial era. Despite Griffith's efforts, the public did not respond. The film's length (three and a half hours), the confusing changes of scenes, and the amount of bare flesh in the Babylon sequence distracted from the quality of moral outrage that Griffith hoped to communicate. Also, its strongly pacifist sentiment was ill-timed for a period of rising public agitation for America to enter World War I.

Despite its failure with the public, *Intolerance* shows Griffith's more intense efforts to achieve the grandeur of Academic painting. The attention to archaeological detail rivaled that of a historical painting by Gérôme. The set for the city of Babylon featured a wall that was three hundred feet high and a mile long.

Griffith used several Academic paintings as models for individual scenes from the Babylon sequence. The seven-and-a-half-minute "Babylonian marriage market" scene (fig. 8.15) is a particularly good example. The action in this section involves an unwilling maiden about to be sold into marriage. She is ultimately saved by the courage of an enamored, and appropriately unprejudiced, prince. Griffith based the entire composition—from figure groupings and details of the auction platform to the the pattern of the tiles on the wall—on *The Babylonian Marriage Market*, a Salon painting by Edwin Long.

8.15

Griffith took sixty shots in this sequence to take in every detail of the human emotions and physical environment. As in *Birth of a Nation*, he made the crowd more than a spectacle by cutting to shots of individual faces, whose contrasting expressions of greed, fear, and lust heightened the involvement of the viewer. The setting and its historical details had been already given by the painting; Griffith's genius lay in being able to amplify the potential of the painting into the heightened realism of film.

Griffith's intention to insert his motion pictures into the grand tradition of Academic painting is clearly seen in a publicity photo from *Intolerance* (fig. 8.16). The image is surrounded by an ornate frame. A small plaque on the bottom identifies the scene; another plaque on the top of the frame reads: D. W. Griffith: INTOLERANCE.

8.16

210

Birth of a Nation and *Intolerance* educated movie audiences to the epic potential of film. They also solidified the appeal of film to all audience levels and, as the next chapter will show, provided the starting point from which European filmmakers created the first avant-garde films.

The filmmaker who successfully consolidated the potential of the Hollywood film to entertain all levels of American society was Charlie Chaplin.

Charlie Chaplin (1889–1977): The Film's Mythic Autonomous Individual

If Griffith approached film with the sentimental and epic scope of Academic painting, Chaplin leaned toward the sharply sketched but affectionate caricature of Daumier's lithographs. Chaplin presented the common man not only coping with mechanization, bureaucracy, and a wide variety of superior-acting people, but often gaining temporary, but gratifying, triumphs over them. To a movie audience still dominated by the experience of immigration, it was a popular message. His raggedy image of "the little tramp" (fig. 8.17) had a far closer connection with early twentieth-century movie audiences than the figure who appeared in the IBM computer commercials of the early 1980s. The film critic Richard Schickel has described Chaplin's irrepressible film character this way:

He was eternally the average man at his best: hopeful, inventive, constantly at war with his environment, constantly acting out the dream so many of us share—the dream of being able to escape simply by setting off down the road to find a better life when things get too tough.[4]

For fifteen years Chaplin films were the undisputed epitome of film possibility—especially in terms of individual expression.

The late 1920s, however, brought changes that eclipsed even the film genius of Charlie Chaplin. One change was the addition of sound to the movie image; another was the de-

8.17

scent of American society into the horror of the Great
Depression.

"Talkies": Hollywood Upholds the American Dream

Chaplin's 1936 film *Modern Times* was a success with the
public even though the only sound in it was its own musical
sound track. Nevertheless, "the little tramp's" lighthearted
and successful subterfuges against bureaucracies and
would-be aristocrats began to lose their appeal for the American people during the Great Depression. As President Roose-
velt so decisively understood, people had a single overwhelming need: the need for hope.

At the same time, technical innovations, including
sound and the increased mobility of the camera that enabled
it to follow the director's eye, brought the sensual and imag-
inative impact of film to a new level of sophistication and
realism. Millions of people who had the twenty-five cents for
admission could escape for three hours from the spectacle
outside the theater of an America turned upside down.
Edward Hopper (1882–1967), a great painter of America's
urban scene from the 1930s through the sixties, caught the
mixture of loneliness and tranquilizing illusion typified by
the movie theaters during the depression years in his *New
York Movie* (fig. 8.18). The immense size of the theater also
implies the social and artistic growth of the movies since the
peep show era seen in Sloan's etching (fig. 8.13).

Statistics show that during the depression years the
average American saw two films a week. Hollywood cranked
out more than a movie a day (470) in its peak year, 1936.

8.18

8.17 Charlie Chaplin.
The Tramp. 1915.
Museum of Modern Art, New York, Film
Stills Archive.

8.18 Edward Hopper.
New York Movie. 1939.
Oil on canvas, 32¼" × 40⅛".
Museum of Modern Art, New York.

What did people see in these projected dreams? Not the grim reality of the depression, of course, but comedy—Marx Brothers' slapstick, Cary Grant's high-society high jinks—romance—musicals by Busby Berkeley—and upbeat personalities like Fred Astaire and Shirley Temple. When the depression intruded into these films, it was vanquished (in innumerable variations) by the heroism of the common man or woman.

Two filmmakers in particular represented the iconic or culture-building role of Hollywood during the crisis that accompanied the depression: Walt Disney and Frank Capra.

Walt Disney (1901–1966): From Free-Form Fantasy to Imagineering

Walt Disney's short cartoons were the direct heirs of Méliès's magical films, as well as the early twentieth-century newspaper comic strips. The newspapers had already produced a famous mouse, Ignatz, from the "Krazy Kat" strip, which ran from 1910 to 1944. Ignatz was feisty and suspiciously anarchistic. His favorite pastime was hurling bricks at Krazy Kat; his constant task was to avoid being jailed by Offisa Pup.

Like Méliès, Disney created a visual world of unlimited possibility. This was especially true of his early black-and-white animations, including the immediately popular cartoons starring Mickey Mouse.

In these early cartoons Mickey was the hero of a fantasy world that was unpredictable, full of surprises. In the midst of it all, Mickey somehow survived, with a kind of Chaplinesque indestructibility.

In *The Opry House* (1929), the piano Mickey is playing comes to life and kicks him out of the theater. In *Traffic Troubles* (1930), Mickey's cab bites another car to get a parking space. In the 1928 cartoon *Steamboat Willie* (fig. 8.19), a goat eats Minnie Mouse's sheet music, and she twists its tail like a crank as the goat's mouth opens and projects out the sounds (with notes drawn in the air) of "Turkey in the Straw."

But this world of open-ended and sometimes sinister surprise lost its appeal as the grim surprise of the 1930s ground American society to a halt.

As early as 1932, *The Three Little Pigs*, Disney's first color cartoon (which earned him his first Academy Award), showed Mickey's free-wheeling fantasy world coming down to earth. Mickey, in this film, became more respectable—more middle class. In subsequent films he took on the role of a leading man in a whole series of boy-meets-girl mini-dramas. Mickey was definitely headed for Main Street.

Disney began to employ his increasing technical mastery to teach a single overriding lesson: individualism is to be channeled by close attention to society's rules, without anarchy.

In *The Tortoise and the Hare* (1934), the anarchistic

8.19

hare loses the race. In *The Flying Mouse* (1934), the brash mouse pilot (not Mickey) who scares people with his stunts and maneuvers has to be saved from evil bats by the intercession of a good witch, who intones to the grounded individualist, "You learned your lesson. Do your best. Be yourself. And life will smile on you." The true depth of Mickey's conversion is seen in *Pluto's Revenge* (1935), when Mickey berates Pluto (his dog) for chasing a cat! How conservative can a mouse get?

Disney, with a deliberation of purpose that deserves his self-chosen term—"*imagineering*"—had by the mid-1930s accepted the role of cultural mythmaker, determined to reanimate and brightly color the badly faded image of the American dream.

This approach took epic scope as Disney began to do to animation what Griffith had accomplished for the live-action drama film: he created sentimental narrative epics whose visual detail and richness of color rivaled the accessibility and appeal of the Academic paintings of the Photographic Age. In *Snow White and the Seven Dwarfs,* which won an Academy Award in 1939, and *Pinocchio* (fig. 8.20 and plate 22) in 1940, Disney reached a level of animation art that he never again achieved. After World War II, Disney devoted his energies to creating a global entertainment empire anchored in television and theme parks.

8.20

Frank Capra (1897—): Reconstructing Main Street

Frank Capra's films of the 1930s show a remarkable similarity to Disney's mythic evolution during the same period.

Capra's plots are fantastically improbable, yet the messages of the stories are pragmatic and hopeful: the common man can make the system work; friends will come through in the clutch; and so on.

The titles of three of his films from this period suggest their upbeat emphasis on politics and the average citizen. *Mr. Deeds Goes to Town* (1936), *Mr. Smith Goes to Washington* (1939), and *Meet John Doe* (1941). In these films the support for the hero—Gary Cooper in *Mr. Deeds,* Jimmy Stewart in *Mr. Smith* (fig. 8.21)—comes from the people as much as from the beautiful heroine. They also showed that the wealthy and powerful were not necessarily benign; they ranged from sinister businessmen to corrupt politicians whom the hero—representing and backed by the people—had to either reform or oppose.

8.21 Frank Capra.
Mr. Smith Goes to Washington. 1939.
Museum of Modern Art, New York, Film Stills Archive.

8.22 Enlarged section of a printed halftone photograph.

8.23 Edwin Forbes.
The Bucktail's Last Shot: Pennsylvania Reserves, Bethesda Church, Va. June 8, 1864.
Pencil drawing.
Courtesy of Library of Congress.
#LC–USZ62–13758.

8.24 *The True Defenders of the Constitution.*
Wood engraving (from sketch by James Walker).
Courtesy of the Library of Congress.
#LC–USZ62–33842.

8.25 T. H. O'Sullivan.
Gettysburg. July 1863.
Courtesy of Library of Congress.
#LC–165–SB–36.

8.21

The message of Capra's films at the time was clear. The average person counts; the people will find their leaders among themselves. Power, both economic and political, can be controlled. Or, as Walt Disney films put it at about the same time, the system—with a little bit of imagination and postponed gratification—works. Beyond the makeshift colonies of drifters and unemployed on the fringes of every major city (called Hoovervilles) was the promise of Disneyland—and Disneyworld.

However, the motion picture was not the only radically new type of image that achieved new iconic power and presence during the Film Age. The photograph took on an entirely new presence in newspapers and magazines beginning at almost the same time as *The Great Train Robbery* was playing on and on in America's new nickelodeons. The basis of this new power was the halftone dot.

The Halftone Dot: The Photograph Becomes a Mass Media Icon

The halftone dot technique had been used to print limited numbers of photographs since the 1880s, but standardization of the halftone process meant that photographs could be printed in newspapers and magazines even more easily than the printed etchings and engravings of the nineteenth century. By 1905, major metropolitan newspapers were printing halftone dot photographs on a regular basis.

The halftone process broke down a photographic image on a metal plate into a series of dots. Since each dot carried ink, it was the size of the dots in each area of the image that determined the blackness of that area (fig. 8.22); this distribution of varying sizes of dots corresponded to the different shades of black and grey in the original photograph. The dots are still clearly visible in today's newspaper photographs.

When the dots appeared in 1905 they caused a technical and iconic revolution. The importance of the halftone process for the icon function of photographs is best seen in what newspapers, before 1905, did *not* show to the public.

Figure 8.23 shows a drawing of a dead Civil War soldier drawn by an artist on the scene. Figure 8.24 shows how drawings like this appeared after being redrawn onto blocks, cut by the engravers, and then printed in weekly newspapers with an accompanying text. Figure 8.25 shows the kind of image people could have seen during the Civil War if the halftone dot process had been available. Even though, as noted earlier, great artists like Winslow Homer sent drawings from the front for the newspapers and magazines of the era, the artist's eye (and hand) could not record journalistic fact with the same objectivity as the camera.

When the photograph began to replace artists' hand-drawn lithographs and engravings as the dominant mass media image, it created a change in public expectations as dramatic as the change brought about by the introduction of perspective woodcuts in the illustrated books of the fifteenth century.

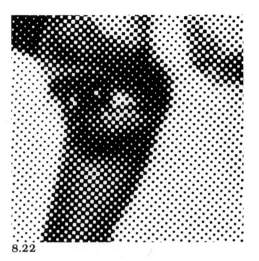

8.22

8.23

THE TRUE DEFENDERS OF THE CONSTITUTION.—[DRAWN BY MR. JAMES WALKER.]

8.24

8.25

The Mass Media Photograph: The Myth of the News

The man who most clearly understood and applied the visual and the mythic possibilities of the modern newspaper illustrated by halftone photographs was William Randolph Hearst. One of the most innovative and influential films in American movie history—Orson Welles's *Citizen Kane* (fig. 8.26)—bears a close resemblance to Hearst's career. Figures 8.27 and 8.28 show the difference in impact between a nineteenth-century illustrated newspaper and the front page of Hearst's New York *Daily Mirror.* Under Hearst, the halftone photograph began to compete in importance with the printed words themselves. Hearst began a process that would eventually end today with news meaning, for most people, *pictures* of the news—on television.

8.26 Orson Welles.
Citizen Kane. 1940.
Museum of Modern Art, New York, Film Stills Archive.

8.27 *Frank Leslie's Illustrated Newspaper.*
October 22, 1864.
Smithsonian Institution, Washington.
Photo #73–5232.

8.28 *Daily Mirror* front page, June 24, 1924.
Smithsonian Institution, Washington.
Photo #78–14217.

8.27

8.26

By 1905, Hearst's papers served the same audience that was flocking to the movies—the masses of urban workers and immigrants.

Newspapers during the Film Age continued the visual tradition begun by artists like Daumier; besides political cartoons, they expanded to include a new art form, the comics. Hearst printed cartoon strips like "The Yellow Kid" and the "Katzenjammer Kids," which appealed to ethnic roots as well as portraying the conflicts between rich and poor in the exploding city.

The comics drew upon visual techniques from a range of sources, from Hollywood movies to the art of the avant-garde. Windsor McCay's fantasy drawings for the "Little Nemo in Slumberland" comic strip (begun in 1905) used perspective and fantasy to a degree that rivaled the artistic inventiveness of the avant-garde art of the time. By the late 1920s, Hal

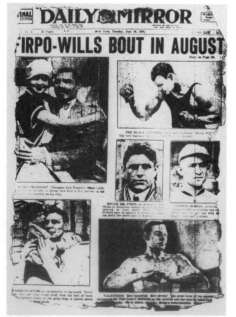

8.28

Foster's "Tarzan" comic-strip adventure featured a remarkably polished Academic drawing style. Foster went on to draw the "Prince Valiant" series. Burne Hogarth continued "Tarzan" with an equally detailed illustrative technique. These comic artists, along with Alex Raymond, who drew the "Flash Gordon" adventure series, added the popular realism of the Academic tradition to the "public easel" of the modern newspaper.

For the newspaper of the Film Age, however, the basic pictorial element was news. Hearst operated on the motto: If there's no news, make news! In his effort to get a conflict with Spain going over Cuba, he wired the famous artist Frederic Remington in Havana, "You furnish the pictures and I'll furnish the war!" He practically invented the headline (a kind of shout in print), his most famous one being "Remember the Maine!" He was no stranger to the modern cult of celebrity and the public relations pseudoevent: Hearst went ashore in Cuba from a longboat. He waded through the surf, brandishing two six-shooters, and then forced two half-drowned Spanish sailors to kneel and kiss the American flag—in front of a camera.

Hearst, Joseph Pulitzer, and other big-city publishers soon made the halftone photograph the focus of the daily newspaper's billboard of ads, sports, comics, and sensationalistic journalism. In this new context, the photograph had a powerful new iconic impact. Compared with the nineteenth-century newspaper illustrated with wood engravings and/or accompanying lithographs, the newspaper illustrated with photographs brought the world to the individual with a dramatic new sense of objectivity. Explorers at the North Pole, revolutionaries in Russia, or murders in the Bronx—all these events became a private, subjective spectacle for the individual reader.

But the icon effect of the newspaper photograph can also be manipulated, and it is this aspect of its impact in the early twentieth century that is described by Marshall McLuhan:

By posing as a Jack-the-Giant-Killer, this sort of press can give the ordinary reader an heroic image of himself as capable of similar feats, while it tacitly assumes Barnum's view of the public as a sucker.[5]

Time Magazine: Focusing the Image of the News

A second means by which the photograph assumed new iconic power was within the format of the mass-circulation magazine.

Henry Luce decided in the early 1920s that the interested, educated person was too busy to take the time to sort things out from all the sensationalism of the newspapers, and in 1923 he founded *Time* magazine. *Time* sorted the news, written in a clear, concise style, into "departments." There was consistent emphasis on people—and, of course, photographs.

The following quotation is from the writing style book given to *Time* staff writers during its first year.

The basis of good TIME writing is narrative, and the basis of a good narrative is to tell events: (1) in the order they occur; and (2) in the form an observer might have seen them, so the readers can imagine themselves in the scene.[6]

This writing style could be called "perspective news"—it is the verbal parallel of Brunelleschi's painting in front of the Florence Baptistry. Its purpose, supported by the photograph, is to create the impression that the individual is the subjective center of an objective world.

Luce's pioneering work on *Time* enabled him to found later a magazine in which photographs were more important than copy. In his next magazine, *Life*, photographs *were* the news.

Life Magazine: A Photographic *Mappa Mundi*

Life was based on the public familiarity with film as much as it grew out of *Time* and the photo newspapers. *Life* was thematic like film—and almost as visual. Like the films of

8.29 Margaret Bourke-White. *Untitled* (smokestacks). c. 1927–29. Cleveland Museum of Art, Gift of Mrs. Albert A. Levin.

Disney and Capra, Luce's *Life* had uplift. Despite its photographs of global disaster, suffering, and war, the context was ultimately consoling: American optimism, know-how, and ingenuity somehow overshadowed any limitations implied by the devastating impact of the news photographs.

Photographic features on art, celebrities, and entertainment implied a world better than the sordid, out-of-control documentary world so often covered by journalism. *Life* projected a photographic world that was nearly as much purely aesthetic as journalistic. A good photograph, in other words, would automatically find space in *Life*.

Life introduced some of the greatest photographers of the twentieth century to a mass audience: Edward Weston, Jr., Margaret Bourke-White (fig. 8.29), Paul Strand, Ansel Adams, and others.

Life's photographs ranged from the grotesque, to the wonderful (the first cover of *Life* showed a baby being born), to the newest miracles of science. *Life* offered photo essays on art from all ages. It provided views of exotic peoples around the world, important sporting events, and life in mythic middle America.

Life mixed its cover photographs of famous men with the beautiful faces of America's celluloid sweethearts: movie stars, hometown cheerleaders, bathing beauty contestants— *Life* integrated the "cheesecake" photograph into its visual model of the world. Luce was quite explicit about such photographs:

Pretty girls are as much a part of today's life as the irrational bloodiness of war, the unrealities of some contemporary art, and the devious channels of international politics.[7]

There's no denying the devious channels of international politics, although Luce's reference to the "unrealities of some contemporary art" showed that the mass media had not only taken over an iconic function similar to that of Academic painting but also continued in the Academy's tradition of opposition and distrust of avant-garde art.

Life, like Academic painting, used the powerful appearance of objectivity provided by photography to make credible its presentation of a world glamorized by celebrity lives, important events, progress, opportunity, and advertisements.

Advertising images reached a new level of graphic power in *Life*. The gleaming smiles of the men and women in the ads made the pages of *Life* brim with good cheer along with technical marvels. In the gloom of the Depression, such sumptuous images added up to a spectacle as meaningful as that on the ceiling of a Baroque church, with its vision of heaven and its revelation of glory-bound heroes, angels, and oceans of light. The advertising in *Life* was the culmination of a class of images that was causing a revolution in America— the revolution of consumer capitalism.

Icons of Revolution: "Coca-Cola" or Karl Marx

Advertising was the final important segment of mass media art set in place during the Film Age. The images produced by Hearst, Disney, and Luce had cultural and artistic connections with the images of popular realism in the Academic painting tradition; the advertising images of the Film Age are important for their radical newness. Though advertising probably has existed to a certain extent in all cultures, it took on a qualitatively new existence and power during the Film Age.

The role of advertising stemmed from the nineteenth-century divisions that caused Western culture's social and artistic crisis of realism. Karl Marx had predicted in the nineteenth century that workers in capitalist countries would eventually revolt because of continuing conditions of poverty and exploitation. Two steps significantly cut off such a revolution in twentieth-century America. One was the decision by industrialists—pioneered by Henry Ford—to raise wages to the point that the worker could become a consumer (Marx had predicted a cycle of increasingly lower wages). The second was the magnification of advertising to the point that it could motivate workers to increased productivity—and to increased consumption.

The possibilities of consuming as a way of life were spread by the increasingly pictorial ads in the photo-based newspapers and magazines of the Film Age.

Calvin Coolidge (1872–1933): Advertising and the Civilization of Desire

By 1926, advertising had reached sufficient importance to merit a major address by the president of the United States. According to the president, the basic function of advertising was education.

As we turn through the pages of the press and the periodicals, as we catch the flash of billboards along the railroads and the highways, all of which have become enormous vehicles of the advertising art, I doubt if we realize at all the impressive part that these displays are coming more and more to play in modern life. . . .

We see that basically it is that of education. . . . It makes new thoughts, new desires, new actions. . . . Rightfully applied, it is the method by which desire is created for better things.

Desire, in turn, is the crucial element separating the civilized from the uncivilized:

The uncivilized make little progress because they have few desires. The inhabitants of our country are stimulated to new wants in all directions. In order to satisfy their constantly increasing desires they necessarily expand their productive powers. They create more wealth because it is only by that method that they can satisfy their wants. It is this constantly enlarging circle that represents the increasing circle of civilization.[8]

President Coolidge saw the importance of advertising images in the modern economy, in which need must keep up with industrial output—even if need itself has to be artificially stimulated by the new industry of advertising. Advertising images became icons that began to open up a new dimension of the myth of the autonomous individual, an economic dimension that increasingly identified freedom with consumption.

Desire is clearly the subject of the advertisement in figure 8.30, aimed at the people who were the underlying subject of President Coolidge's speech—the largely immigrant working class, who were the potential equivalent, in America, of Europe's nineteenth-century proletariat. The image contains all

8.30 Heart's Desire advertisement. 1928. Published by the Association of American Soap and Glycerine Producers, Inc., to aid the work of the Cleanliness Institute.

the elements of Coolidge's speech: the circle of civilization, desire, productivity, and progress. It also shows the trodden-down bodies of those who do not quite make the grade in such a competitive system. The civilization of desire can also become a civilization of greed.

Advertising: Icons against Marxism

Just as President Coolidge's description of advertising implied its central cultural and political role, American corporations were aware of its power to undercut the appeal of Marxism, especially during the labor unrest of the period. This dimension of American advertising is the literal content of the Chevrolet advertisement shown in figure 8.31:

Every owner is in effect a railroad president. . . .

The once poor laborer and mechanic now drives to the building operation or construction job in his own car. He is now a capitalist. . . . His wages have been increased from $1.50 or $3.00 a day to $5.00 or $15.00 a day. . . .

He has become *somebody!* . . . How can Bolshevism flourish in a motorized country. . . ?[9]

Bolshevism could not, as American political and business leaders both knew. Karl Marx had no idea of the power of advertising.

Again, the importance of Film Age advertising art was not in its artistic merit but in its radically new culture-building effect. Advertising images, regardless of their minimal artistic merit, were the decisively new icons that emerged in the Film Age.

But just as Karl Marx could not have foreseen the political and cultural impact of modern advertising (or the productive capacity of modern industry), Calvin Coolidge could not have foreseen the possibility of a form of advertising that would have more iconic power than the magazines and billboards of his day, and, in addition, claim to being an art form: the 30- to 60-second television commercial.

Before discussing the Television Age, however, it is important to complete the description of the Film Age by examining the artistic alternative to the mass media provided by the avant-garde.

for Economical Transportation

CHEVROLET

The Psychology of the Automobile

The automobile 14,000,000 strong, has in truth become our most numerous "common carrier."

Every owner is in effect a railroad president, operating individually on an elective schedule, over highways built and maintained chiefly at the expense of himself and his fellow motorists.

What has been the effect of the automobile on our composite national mind?—on our social political and economic outlook?

The once poor laborer and mechanic now drives to the building operation or construction job in his own car. He is now a capitalist—the owner of a taxable asset. His wages have been increased from $1.50 or $3.00 a day to $5.00 or $15.00 a day. Before or after acquiring the automobile he has begun paying for a suburban home of his own, and is interested in local improvements, consolidated schools, highways, and community service of various kinds. As a *direct* taxpayer, he votes with care and independence.

Evenings and Sundays he takes his family into the country or to the now near town fifty to one hundred miles away. He has become *somebody*, has a broader and more tolerant view of the one-time cartoon hayseed and the fat-cigared plutocrat.

How can Bolshevism flourish in a motorized country having a standard of living, and thinking too high to permit the existence of an ignorant, narrow, peasant majority?

Is not the automobile entitled to the major credit in this elevation of our standard of citizenship?

Chevrolet Motor Co. Detroit, Michigan
Division of General Motors Corporation

8.31 General Motors advertisement. 1924. In *Auto Ads,* by Jane Stern and Michael Stern. New York: David Obst Books, Random House, 1978.

CHAPTER NINE

THE FILM AGE II:

FROM ABSTRACTION

TO CULTURAL

REVOLUTION

ASSESSMENTS

1. Is there any area in your life in which you have deliberately broken with convention or the status quo? Why, and in what way? What have been the positive and negative effects of this break with convention?
2. What do you like or dislike about avant-garde art? Why?
3. How would you define creativity? How is it a part of your life? Who in particular do you associate with the idea of creativity? Why?
4. In what ways can art contribute to political and social change? Can you cite any specific examples? What made the art successful in communicating its political/social messages?
5. How could your dreams become the material for an art work? What qualities would the art work have?

When the Film Age began, movies, newspapers, and magazines replaced not only the mass media art forms of the nineteenth century, but also Academic painting as the standard of visual realism. Movies presented historical epic and romantic melodrama; newspaper and magazine photographs pictured the world as an arena of factual drama. Advertising, which reached a new level of prominence through the mass media, pictured consumer goods and commodities in a way that invited the working class to participate in the "circle of civilization" centered on the autonomous individual. All these images became effective icons for helping to resolve the social divisions of the nineteenth century by bringing the working class into full participation in a revolutionary form of consumer capitalism.

By 1905, the mass media was also having a powerful effect on avant-garde art. Figure 9.1 is a photograph of the painting *Madame Matisse (The Green Line)* by Henri Matisse (1869–1954), one of several Matisse paintings that caused a sensation at the Salon d'Automne in 1905. The full impact of Matisse's paintings came from something new for the avant-garde: some of them appeared as photographs in the Paris newspaper *L'Illustration*. Matisse's paintings will

9.1 Henri Matisse.
Madame Matisse (The Green Line).
1905.
Oil on canvas, 16″ × 12¾″.
Statens Museum for Kunst, Copenhagen.

be discussed in detail later in the chapter. For now, it is sufficient to note that in 1905 the halftone photograph gave avant-garde art, for the first time, the kind of public arena that had previously belonged only to Academic painting.

In order to appreciate the new opportunity halftone photography provided for avant-garde art, it is important to recall that in the nineteenth century artists could make accurate engraved or lithographic copies of Academic paintings. The accuracy of the engravings of Bonheur's *The Horse Fair* (fig. 5.20) was so good that people who had seen the work when it first appeared in the Salon noticed minor changes she had made in the background when they saw the painting during its tour. As noted in Chapter 5, such prints helped confirm and establish the imagery of Academic painting as the norm—the highest form—of illusionistic imagery.

Avant-garde art was in just the opposite position before 1905. Even if the public had been interested, imagine someone trying to make an engraved or lithographic copy of one of Monet's haystacks (fig. 7.6) or cathedrals (figs. 7.8, and 7.9)—or of Seurat's *La Grande Jatte* (fig. 7.13). Remember that van Gogh had to travel to Paris to obtain an accurate idea of Impressionism. Before the appearance of the halftone photograph, *Madame Matisse* would have looked like a crude woodcut without the most intense and laborious efforts of a master craftsperson.

With the arrival of inexpensive mass media photography, the public—even if they disliked avant-garde paintings—at least began to see them reasonably accurately.

The imagery of the mass media was so powerful in its own right, so environmental in its presence, that its photographic realism could be called a "new Academy." In this sense, one of the main challenges facing the avant-garde was to continue its traditional role of demonstrating that human sight and creativity extended beyond the limits of photographic realism.

The Film Age Avant-Garde: The Journey to Abstraction and the Search for Icons of Cultural Revolution

The story of the Film Age avant-garde can be told in terms of two sequential developments. The first, occurring between 1905 and 1912, was the journey to abstraction. Two different roads led there. Pablo Picasso developed an objective style of abstraction that became known as Cubism; independently of Picasso, Wassily Kandinsky created a form of abstraction based on subjective feeling and intuition.

After discussing the highly individual achievements of Picasso and Kandinsky, the rest of this chapter will describe the second phase of the Film Age avant-garde, which lasted from 1912 until World War II. This period is marked by the highly diverse application of avant-garde art to social criticism and cultural revolution by movements known as Futurism, Constructivism, Dada, German Expressionism, and Surrealism.

Pablo Ruiz y Picasso (1881–1973): The Avant-Garde Art School of Bohemian Paris

Pablo Picasso was well equipped to complete the avant-garde journey to abstraction. Since his father was an art teacher in Barcelona, Picasso mastered Academic painting techniques at an early age, and when he arrived in Paris in 1901 at the age of nineteen, he immediately began to absorb the lessons of van Gogh, Cézanne, and Gauguin. He was also influenced by more recent avant-garde artists, like Toulouse-Lautrec (fig. 9.2), who still used the bohemian Montmartre section as their social and artistic center.

9.3

9.2

Picasso's early paintings in Paris were relentlessly melancholic. A 1903 painting seems to pantomime its title, *The Tragedy* (fig. 9.3). Many of these works were dominated by a blue tone laced with the garish colors appropriate to the sordid and desperate circumstances of his early struggle to establish himself. His subjects included prostitutes, destitute young lovers, beggars—he even painted the funeral portrait of a friend who had committed suicide over a love affair.

By 1904 Picasso's painting had begun to bring him some financial success. His work then took on a lighter tone and included circus scenes, harlequins, and lovers who seem to have a future. *Family of Saltimbanques* (fig. 9.4), despite its barren landscape and figures who are isolated by their private poses and gestures, has a new sense of openness and humor.

In 1905, however, Picasso saw Matisse's *Madame Matisse* at the Salon d'Automne. He also saw paintings in a similar style by the group of young artists who followed Matisse. The public that saw these works only as black-and-white photographs in the newspapers might have been sur-

9.4

9.2 Henri de Toulouse-Lautrec.
Monsieur Boileau at the Cafe. 1893.
Gouache on cardboard, 31½" × 25½".
Cleveland Museum of Art, Hinman B. Hurlbut Collection.

9.3 Pablo Picasso.
The Tragedy. 1903.
Oil on wood, 41½" × 27⅛".
National Gallery of Art, Washington, Chester Dale Collection.

9.4 Pablo Picasso.
Family of Saltimbanques. 1905.
Oil on canvas, 83¾" × 90⅜".
National Gallery of Art, Washington, Chester Dale Collection.

prised that the critics called Matisse and his followers wild beasts, or *fauves*. Picasso, and others who saw the original canvas, understood the term very clearly.

Madame Matisse is dominated by shocking complementary values of red and green, ranging from large, abstract background shapes to the bright green stripe connecting the the forehead and the nose. In between the clashing greens and reds are streaks of yellow, blue, and purple. Matisse and the other Fauves had seen a recent exhibition of van Gogh's works, and they took his bold but emotionally powerful color to a stage of total freedom from any purpose other than artistic expressiveness. In Fauve paintings, the figure itself began

228

to crack and give way under the volcanic pressure of pure color, shape, and line.

Picasso was impressed. Instead of following the lead of the Fauves, however, he continued to absorb the lessons of the avant-garde in his own way. It was not until 1907 that Picasso produced a painting that showed that his own avant-garde education was complete. This same painting brought him to the border of Cubism—and also brought him all the discomforts of confronting the unknown.

Picasso's *Les Demoiselles d'Avignon:* The Beauty of the Ugly

Les Demoiselles d'Avignon (fig. 9.5 and color plate 23) is one of the strangest paintings in the history of Western art. It is really Picasso's incomplete meditation on the nature of painting itself. The story of this work provides an illuminating glimpse into the creative process involved in all avant-garde art.

Picasso normally painted rapidly and without preliminary sketches, yet he worked on this painting for almost six months before he would allow anyone to see it. His studio became littered with half-finished drawings. He painted over much of his original idea. Most unusual of all, he was not sure, even after six months, of what he had done.

The biggest disappointment came when he invited close friends to see the painting. Most of them thought it was ugly, or improbable. Matisse—Picasso's lifelong rival—thought it was a hoax or a practical joke. The famous critic Felix Feneon responded with some advice for Picasso: "It's interesting, my boy. You ought to devote yourself to caricature."[1]

The painting, in a word, was ugly—and remained so.

Fortunately, another young painter, Georges Braque (1882–1963), was so stunned by the painting, ugly or not, that he began to work closely with Picasso and helped produce the Cubist revolution.

Also among the few people invited to see the intimidating group of painted ladies was the American writer Gertrude Stein. She immediately sensed that Picasso had created something more important than a beautiful painting; she saw that *Les Demoiselles* was a prototype for a new phase in art. Later, she wrote:

Picasso said once that he who created a thing is forced to make it ugly. In the effort to create the intensity and the struggle to create this intensity, the result always produces a certain ugliness.[2]

The process that went into the painting reflects Picasso's inner struggle to find its proper form.

The painting originally included several figures gathered around a still life that included a skull. The crouching form at the right originally was a sailor.

9.5

Then it began to change.

The figures became female nudes with flat, angular outlines. Then the faces began to change. They now showed artistic ancestries that ranged from Egypt to the native art of Africa. The two almost "doglike" faces, painted long after the painting was started, reflected Picasso's introduction to African art through some examples owned by Matisse and Picasso's own study of the African art in the Musée de l'Homme (The Museum of Man) in Paris.

9.5 Pablo Picasso.
Les Demoiselles d'Avignon. 1907.
Oil on canvas, 8′ × 7′8″.
Museum of Modern Art, New York,
Acquired through the Lillie P. Bliss
Bequest.

The colors, too, kept changing until—unlike the brilliant colors of all previous avant-garde art—they settled into drab earth colors flavored with some flat areas of blue and pink.

Picasso labored for six months on the painting; then he simply stopped working on it. *Les Demoiselles* remained in his studio for another thirteen years before he would allow it to be shown in public. By that time, Cubism had already altered the course of avant-garde art.

Les Demoiselles d'Avignon: A Problem, Not a Solution

Perhaps the simplest explanation of *Les Demoiselles* is that it was not a solution for Picasso as much as the statement of a problem.

Its perplexing combination of forms posed the final phase of the question that had preoccupied painting since Manet: What is a painting if it is not a perspective window onto the world? Van Gogh, Seurat, and other artists had moved painting quite a distance away from photographic realism, but the basic question still remained: Could a painting exist only in terms of its own language of color, line, and shape? Could art, like music, be totally free of the objective world of appearances?

Picasso did not answer this question immediately. His paintings of the next few years nevertheless show how he, like an archaeologist probing through level after level of sediment, finally reached a layer that became one of the basic languages of twentieth-century art—the layer now known as Cubism.

Beyond *Les Demoiselles d'Avignon:* Picasso Discovers Rousseau and Cézanne

One of the things that helped Picasso during this period of personal discovery—besides the encouragement of Gertrude Stein and the virtual partnership of Georges Braque—was his discovery of the art of Henri Rousseau.

Picasso bought some Rousseau paintings that he discovered in a junk shop. Many of his acquaintances found his enthusiasm for Rousseau as puzzling as his new direction in painting. Picasso, however, was quite convinced that Rousseau was more than an amusing eccentric. What he admired in Rousseau was precisely what he himself was trying to do in his own art: ignore visual conventions in order to see and paint more directly.

Another contemporary artist whose work helped Picasso in his search at this time was Cézanne. Picasso especially admired the solidly structured landscapes that he had seen in Cézanne's Paris retrospective exhibition in 1904.

In the summer of 1909 all these influences came together. The austere clarity of Cézanne, the direct simplicity of Rousseau, and the bold material expressiveness of African art gave Picasso the ingredients for the resolution of the artistic problem stated but unresolved in *Les Demoiselles d'Avignon.*

The Summer of 1909: Picasso's Journey to Objective Abstraction (Analytic Cubism)

Picasso spent the summer of 1909 in Spain. When he returned to Paris in the fall, he took back several landscapes he had painted of Spanish hillside villages (fig. 9.6). Gertrude Stein later noted her observations about these landscapes and their role in Picasso's discovery of Cubism:

These three landscapes were extraordinarily realist and all the same the beginning of Cubism. Picasso had by chance taken some photographs (fig. 9.7) of the village that he had painted and it always amused me, when everyone protested against the fantasy of the pictures, to make them look at the photographs, which made them see that the pictures were almost exactly like the photographs.[3]

9.6 Pablo Picasso.
Houses on the Hill, Horta de Ebro.
1909.
Oil on canvas, 31⅞″ × 25¼″.
Private collection (photo courtesy Giraudon/Art Resources).

9.7 Pablo Picasso.
Houses of Horta de Ebro. 1909.
Photograph.
Copyright SPADEM, Paris/VAGA, New York.

9.7

9.6

This remarkable passage illustrates the kind of creative vision that underlies all great art. Picasso's search for Cubism resulted in his finding Cubism in the real world—he could literally see it there in the stark Spanish landscape. Like the painters before photography and the artists before the movies, Picasso's involvement with Cubism shows that there had to be a certain readiness or predisposition before a new way of seeing (and making images) could occur.

Another way to understand Picasso's approach to Cubism is to compare it to the action of the human eye. In looking at someone's face, for instance, the eyes do not focus (as implied in the structure of a perspective image) on a single point. The eyes move constantly around the face, or any other subject, and keep assembling detailed glances into an ongoing composite. Picasso's famous portrait of Gertrude Stein is based on this kind of multiple viewpoint. Typically, when someone remarked that it didn't look much like her, she replied, "Don't worry, it will." She was confident that people would learn to see Cubist art just as they had learned to see perspective art.

9.8 Pablo Picasso.
Ma Jolie. 1911–12.
Oil on canvas, 39⅞″ × 25¾″.
Museum of Modern Art, New York,
Acquired through the Lillie P. Bliss
Bequest.

9.9 Pablo Picasso.
Nude Woman. 1910.
Oil on canvas, 73¾″ × 24″.
National Gallery of Art, Washington, Ailsa
Mellon Bruce Fund.

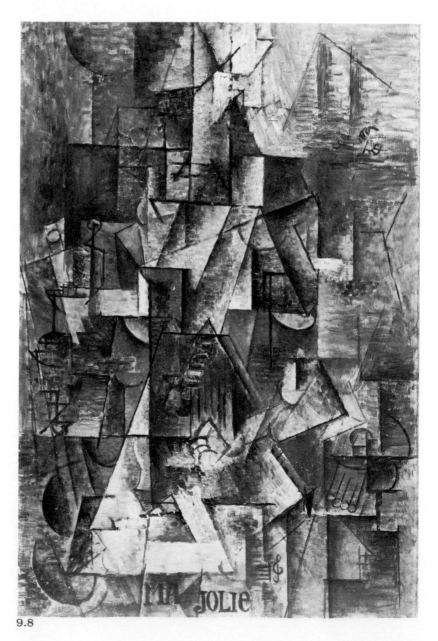

9.8

Picasso's landscapes of 1909, however, had not yet reached the basic layer of pure line, color, and shape. His paintings still clung, even if only by the puckish sleight of hand of Picasso's photographs, to the external world.

"Orville and Wilbur": The Flight to Abstraction

From 1909 until 1912 Picasso worked so intensely and closely with Braque on the final phase of Cubism that they called themselves "Orville and Wilbur," after the Wright brothers.

Despite the movement toward abstraction, some Cubist paintings—with the help of their titles—enabled the viewer to see bits and pieces of recognizable form and meaning. *Ma Jolie* (fig. 9.8), for instance, has surprisingly concrete references despite its highly abstract form. *Ma Jolie* was a romantic tribute to Picasso's new love, Eva (Marcelle Humbert), the title a phrase from a then popular cabaret song—note the fragmented musical notation in the painting. Also at the bottom of the composition is a part of Gertrude Stein's calling card left at his studio while Picasso was working on the painting. These apparently random elements thus form a concrete pattern closely connected to Picasso's personal experiences at this time.

Other paintings from this period verge on total elimination of both subject and subjectivity. The painting in figure 9.9 has the flattened, dull surface of hammered bronze. Even its title, *Nude Woman*, helps only slightly. Appropriately, Picasso and Braque left many of their paintings from this period unsigned. Many of them are indistinguishable in origin to this day. Picasso and Braque thus underscored the intense objectivity of the visual language they were creating: it had nothing to do with the experience of feeling; it dealt so completely with structure that it approached anonymity. Because of this determination to analyze painting in its essentials, this phase of Cubism has become known as Analytic Cubism.

Synthetic Cubism: Putting the Subject back into the Painting

By 1912, however, Picasso drew back from the point of pure abstraction and began to incorporate fragments of words, bits of torn wallpaper, and so on into his paintings. This period of "putting the subject back into the painting" has been called Synthetic Cubism.

One of Picasso's friends from this period, Fernand Olivier, later recalled an incident that helped turn Picasso toward Synthetic Cubism. A French naval officer, brought by another friend, visited Picasso's studio and told a story about how astonished some African tribesmen were when they

9.9

were shown a photograph of themselves. The Africans responded by doing a drawing of the officer in their native art style. After starting to give the drawing to the officer, the artist suddenly took it back and quickly drew in the gold buttons: encircling the head! He placed the stripes alongside the arms and over the head. Then he gave the officer the drawing. Picasso enjoyed the story immensely.

It was at that time that Picasso began to add strips of newspaper, glass, and different materials to his paintings. He had already painted names and letters, but at that time Cubism took on a more concrete reality.[4]

Guitar (fig. 9.10) is composed of pieces of a newspaper advertising page, wallpaper, and various drawing media. In 1921, *Three Musicians* (fig. 9.11) included an entire environment of figures, furniture, and a room reintegrated into the flat, but highly readable, space of Synthetic Cubism.

9.10

9.11

The scraps of the real world that began to filter back into Cubist painting did not compromise its newly won independence. However, Western painting, having reached the zero point, would never again be the same. The ripped theater tickets and bits of labels and newspapers simply proved that Cubism could survive—and make beauty—with scraps from the mass media images that were creating Western culture's picture of reality.

But Cubism was not the only abstract language of painting that developed at the beginning of the Film Age. A totally different road to abstraction—a road based on the subjectivity of personal feeling—was taken by the Russian artist Wassily Kandinsky.

Wassily Kandinsky (1866–1944): The Journey to Subjective Abstraction

The decisive years for Kandinsky's artistic journey were 1909 to 1912, almost the years of Analytic Cubism's "heroic" period. Kandinsky's search, like Picasso's, was inspired by a wide variety of artistic sources. Unlike Picasso, however, he talked and wrote about his sources with enthusiasm.

In 1912 he and a German artist, Franz Marc, published an almanac of illustrations and essays called *The Blue Rider (Der Blaue Reiter),* which revealed and discussed these sources. This compendium of illustrations included examples of children's art from Europe and Arabia, Russian icons and folk art, archaic Greek sculpture, Japanese prints, nineteenth-century German folk art, as well as over fifty illustrations of European avant-garde art since the Impressionists.

This book is a remarkable example of how the mass media presented almost unlimited sources of visual language for avant-garde artists. Kandinsky used these sources to create abstract paintings that were radically different from Cubist works. His more lyrical abstract forms had something of the freedom and spontaneity of music. He wanted to use the elements of art—line, shape, and color—in the same intuitive way that the musician used harmony, tempo, and rhythm. From 1907 to 1912, his work, like a slow-motion film, moved gradually from representation to lyrical abstraction. With his 1912 painting *Improvisation with Green Center, #176* (fig. 9.12), Kandinsky indicated that he felt he had achieved his goal: he titled this painting in the traditional way musical compositions are named.

Even though Kandinsky's step to completely abstract painting depended on the combined influence of folk art, popular art, and avant-garde art, it was a thoroughly personal achievement. He was overwhelmed by the expressive power of abstraction:

This solution liberated me and opened up new worlds. Everything "dead" trembled. Not only the stars, moon, woods, flowers of which the poets sing, but also a cigarette butt lying in the ashtray, a patient white trouser button looking up from a puddle in the street . . . everything shows me its face, its innermost being, its secret soul. . . . Thus every still and every moving point (= line) became equally alive and revealed its soul to me.[5]

The remarkable thing about this passage, written in 1913, was Kandinsky's emphasis on his new, vivified awareness of the concrete, physical world around him. "Abstract" thus did not mean Kandinsky was cut off from nature;

9.12

9.10 Pablo Picasso.
Guitar. 1913.
Charcoal, crayon, ink, and pasted paper, 26⅛″ × 19½″.
Collection, Museum of Modern Art, New York, Nelson A. Rockefeller Bequest.

9.11 Pablo Picasso.
Three Musicians. 1921.
Oil on canvas, 6′7″ × 7′3¾″.
Collection, Museum of Modern Art, New York, Mrs. Simon Guggenheim Fund.

9.12 Wassily Kandinsky.
Improvisation with Green Center, #176. 1912.
Oil on canvas, 43¼″ × 47½″.
Arthur Jerome Eddy Memorial Collection, Courtesy of the Art Institute of Chicago.

rather, by focusing directly on his emotional responses, abstraction intensified his awareness of nature's impact. It is in this sense that he called his art spiritual—that is, an art based primarily on an inner human reality instead of on the observation of the external world.

Another difference between the abstract paintings of Kandinsky and those of Picasso is that Kandinsky wanted his paintings to have a specific kind of impact. He hoped his paintings would help people break through visual conventions and habits reinforced by the omnipresent images of the mass media.

Regardless of the intent of either artist, however, Picasso and Kandinsky presented Western artists with a radical new opportunity: abstraction, by 1912, existed in both objective and subjective forms; artists could apply these languages to whatever purposes and goals they chose.

Almost immediately, groups of artists began to apply the full range of this language to social issues. The first of these groups was the movement known as Futurism.

Futurism: Transforming Cubism into the Visual Language of the Machine

The Futurist movement began—before Cubism was born—at the turn of the century, with the writing, funding, and recruiting efforts of the wealthy Italian writer and poet Filippo Marinetti, who wanted to unmire Italy from what he considered to be its stifling preoccupation with its glorious past. Futurism therefore sought an art that would actively embrace artist, spectator, and art object in an acceptance of the emerging machine-dominated society of the early twentieth century. Marinetti's mechanized vision had been articulated as early as 1900:

We declare that the world's splendor has been enriched by a new beauty: the beauty of speed. . . . We shall sing of the great crowds excited by work, pleasure, and rebellion; we shall sing of . . . the factories suspended from the clouds by the twisted strings of their smoke . . . of broad-chested locomotives pawing at the rails like huge steel horses bridled with steel tubes; and of the gliding flight of aeroplanes.[6]

Futurists, quite simply, wanted to create icons that conveyed the experience of the individual absorbed into a machine-dominated world.

The Futurist Myth: The Autonomous Individual as Mechanized Superman

The Futurist world of science and the machine held out new and radical possibilities for the individual. The artist Umberto Boccioni (1882–1916), Marinetti's most brilliant follower, summarized the Futurist admiration for science by urging the contemporary individual to "draw support from the tangible miracles of contemporary life just as our ancestors drew support from the religious atmosphere which surrounded them."[7]

From the tangible miracles of contemporary life, the Futurists hoped would emerge a new kind of individual. Ultimately, Marinetti looked forward to a kind of superman who would be "mechanized . . . with replaceable parts."[8]

Futurist theory, however, lacked a new visual language to express the dynamism of its ideas.

The Artistic Language of "Universal Dynamism": Futurism Discovers Cubism

In 1911 the Futurist artist Gino Severini saw the Cubist experiments of Picasso and Braque. Despite the totally apolitical isolation of "Orville and Wilbur," Severini immediately urged Marinetti and other Futurists to come to Paris. He knew they would agree with him that Cubism was the visual language they had been seeking. The small group of Futurists who took the train to Paris in the fall of 1911 began the transformation of Futurist art by adopting the language of Cubism.

Boccioni was the most talented and versatile of the Futurist artists; his work before 1911 came closest to the dynamic energy of Futurist theory. *The City Rises* (fig. 9.13), painted in 1910, captured the spirit of workmen and horses rhythmically united in heroic labor. Only the line of the building roofs along the top of the painting linked this image with the realism of the past.

9.13 Umberto Boccioni. *The City Rises.* 1910. Oil on canvas, 6'6½" × 9'10½". Museum of Modern Art, New York, Mrs. Simon Guggenheim Fund.

9.14

In *The Laugh* (fig. 9.14), Boccioni painted over an earlier image and broke the canvas into the angular forms of Cubism; only the face of the laughing lady remains from the original work.

Boccioni gave equally brilliant artistic form to his sculpture titled *Unique Forms of Continuity in Space* (fig. 9.15). This work exhibits the forceful beauty, as well as the disturbing contradictions, within Futurist theory. The figure's armorlike anatomy strides toward the future with an aggressive and warlike determination that accurately reflects the sense of motion, mechanization, and pure force so avidly sought by the Futurists as the deepest essence of modern life. The language of Cubism has certainly freed this sculpture from Italy's classical past; it would be virtually inconceivable outside the twentieth century. Boccioni's sculpture also lacks any sense of human personality. Its title could equally well describe a diagram or an experiment in physics. The human face has disappeared.

Icons of "Universal Dynamism": Art as Propaganda for Violence, Speed, War

The Futurists took the art-for-art's-sake attitude of Cubism as an absurdity. Futurist artistic ambition aimed at a cultural revolution, the artistic renovation of Western culture

9.15

from architecture to clothing to children's toys. With this agenda in mind, it is not surprising that the Futurists became the first group to consciously use the new mass media as exhibition space for their art and ideas.

By 1913 the Futurists had confronted London, Brussels, Munich, Amsterdam, Berlin—and even Chicago—not only with their art, but also with public "manifestos," or statements, spelling out their radical ideas and goals. The "Manifesto on the Reconstruction of the Universe," for instance, envisioned the production of toys that would train children for war—the maximum condition of "universal dynamism's" total expression of human and cosmic energy:

> With plastic complexes we will construct toys that will accustom the child . . . to physical courage, to fighting and to war (with enormous and dangerous toys that will work outdoors).[9]

With admirable consistency, the Futurists welcomed World War I. They directed their art just before the outbreak of the war to ridiculing Italy's reluctance to enter the conflict, and as war approached, Marinetti exhorted his artists to "live the war pictorially."

The Futurists went beyond living the war pictorially— several enlisted. Boccioni and two other Futurists, the architect St. Elia and the musician Russolo, died during the conflict. Marinetti himself survived the war, but he apparently did not learn its pictorial or its human lessons. In 1929 he became the minister of culture for Benito Mussolini.

Futurism hoped, without success, to initiate a cultural revolution through art. Another movement of avant-garde art, also using a language based predominantly on Cubism, came close to success just at the time Futurism ceased to exist: the Constructivist avant-garde of the Russian Revolution.

Constructivism: Russia Welcomes the Avant-Garde

Unlike the Italian Futurists, Russian avant-garde artists found themselves in the midst of a political revolution that involved the entire fabric of Russian culture. Nevertheless, by the time the Russian Revolution occurred in 1917, the avant-garde revolution had already arrived. Kandinsky had crossed the threshold into pure abstraction by 1910, and he returned to his native Russia to teach art in one of the new state-sponsored schools.

Another Russian artist, Kasimir Malevich (1878–1935), had visited Paris for a month in 1912 and then returned to Russia as a Cubist. By 1913 Malevich had pushed Cubism further than either Picasso or Braque. *Suprematist Composition: White on White* (fig. 9.16) was his statement of absolute artistic purity. It represented the style "Suprematism," the supremacy of feeling over fact.

Vladimir Tatlin (1885–1953) performed the same function for Constructivism that Boccioni and other artists had

9.14 Umberto Boccioni.
The Laugh. 1911.
Oil on canvas, 43⅜″ × 57¼″.
Museum of Modern Art, New York, Gift of Herbert and Nannette Rothschild.

9.15 Umberto Boccioni.
Unique Forms of Continuity in Space. 1913.
Bronze, 43⅞″ × 34⅞″ × 15¾″.
Museum of Modern Art, New York, Acquired through the Lillie P. Bliss Bequest.

9.16 Kasimir Malevich.
Suprematist Composition: White on White. 1918.
Oil on canvas, 31¼″ × 31¼″.
Museum of Modern Art, New York.

9.16

for Futurism. In 1913 he visited Paris and met Picasso. Tatlin admired the objectivity of Cubist abstraction and its bold affirmation of materials. Tatlin used Cubism as the basic language for icons of the Russian Revolution. Its geometric impersonality enabled Constructivist art to represent the values of the new regime without the confusion of traditional symbolism.

This same impersonality served the even more important iconic need for an art that eliminated the traditional Western myth of the autonomous individual, which Lenin dismissed as "bourgeois anarchist-individualism." In America, as the last chapter described, the working class was absorbed into the middle class (bourgeoisie)—as consumers. The Soviet Union found a different resolution of the nineteenth-century crisis of realism: the middle class was eliminated. Under the new cultural myth, freedom was—by definition—service by the individual to the state. Cubism's impersonality and its angular, machinelike forms made it ideally suitable to a society based on a scientific view of history in which technology was to be the ultimate organizing principle in all areas of life.

Tatlin and his fellow artists attempted to apply the visual language of Constructivism to the full range of practical and political concerns of the state. From 1917 until the early twenties, avant-garde art and revolutionary politics were dedicated, if uneasy, comrades.

Nothing illustrates the ardor and compatibility of the brief alliance of these artistic and political revolutionaries more than the monument proposed by Tatlin for the Third International in 1919 (fig. 9.17).

Tatlin took eighteen months to perfect the design and model of a spiral structure that would jut 1300 feet into the

9.17 Vladimir Tatlin.
Monument for the Third International. 1919.
Photograph courtesy of Moderna Museet, Stockholm.

9.18 Dziga Vertov.
The Man with a Movie Camera. 1929.
Museum of Modern Art, New York, Film Stills Archive.

9.17

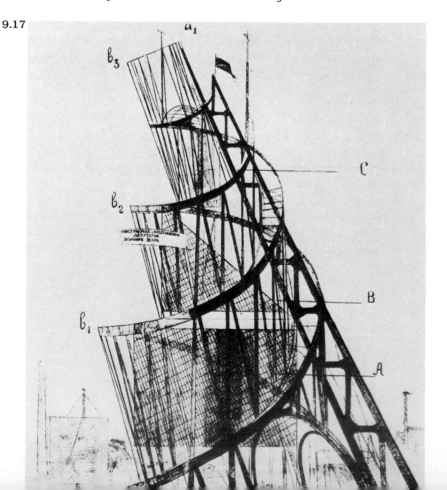

sky above Moscow and, by a slightly tilted angle, point toward the pole star (thus symbolizing the constancy and cosmic importance of the Revolution).

Inside the spiral structure were to be three glass buildings, one on top of the other. The top building was to be a sphere that would rotate once an hour and broadcast radio, telegraph, and loudspeaker messages as well as project giant images—weather permitting—onto the clouds. The middle building was a cube-shaped office building that would rotate once a month. The bottom building, shaped like a cone, would rotate once a year; it would house assemblies and congresses.

This visionary structure was never seriously considered for construction by Soviet authorities. Nevertheless, the model was displayed in Moscow and Petrograd and toured rural Russia, where villagers carried it in processions like the traditional icons of saints. Its image was printed on postage stamps. Tatlin's design, in Russia and the West, gradually became a generally recognized symbol of the aspirations, if not the achievements, of the new Soviet state.

Constructivism had its most practical impact on Soviet society through graphic design. Abstract posters advertised everything from the quality of Soviet baby-bottle nipples to the imminent arrival of electricity for every Soviet home. The Constructivists, like the Futurists, also submitted designs for clothing—appropriate attire for the "new Soviet man."

Constructivist art also reached the Russian streets and byways. In 1918, Red Square in Moscow was often decorated in brightly colored Constructivist imagery for public ceremonies. During the following few years, trains and boats decorated in Constructivist style made their way through rural Russia carrying "agitprop" (agitation-propaganda) teams to lecture and convert the peasants to the virtues of socialism, Bolshevik-style. Never mind that behind the Constructivist agitprop teams of peaceful persuasion were armed troops shooting peasants who insisted on un-socialist ideals like protecting reserves of grain and cattle.

The Soviets, however, realized that the greatest propaganda device was film. Lenin himself was quite specific: "For us the cinema is the most important of all the arts."[10] Constructivists produced films for the revolution, and many were shown in special cars attached to agitprop trains. Dziga Vertov's (1896–1954) film *The Man with a Movie Camera* (fig. 9.18) included scenes of him filming scenes in the film, scenes of audiences watching parts of the film, and so on. Like a Cubist painting, the Constructivist film made the viewer aware of the material (film) and the process (inserts, camera angles, etc.) used to create the final work. The viewer is asked to see the movie *as a movie* and not be swept away in the illusion of a real-life experience. Vertov wanted to unite the viewer with the very mechanics of filmmaking, because it was symbolic of other relationships between human being

9.18

and machine. The intended icon impact of Vertov's film is revealed in his own words:

We discover the souls of the machine, we are in love with the worker at the bench, we are in love with the farmer at his tractor, the engineer on his locomotive. We bring creative joy into every mechanical activity. We make peace between man and the machine. We educate the new man.[11]

The Russian public, however, did not find much joy in Vertov's films. Even before the death of Lenin in 1924, the work of Vertov, Tatlin, and other Constructivists had ceased to please the party hierarchy. Under Josef Stalin, Lenin's successor, photographic realism—renamed Socialist Realism—was installed as the official visual language of Soviet art and propaganda. The Soviet artistic revolution thus retreated back to a style of art similar to that favored by nineteenth-century bourgeois capitalists. Constructivism was gradually retired to the museums. Kandinsky left Russia in 1921; Malevich lingered on in Russia, but in total obscurity.

The Russian Revolution did produce one major artist whose work has remained as honored in the West as in Russia—the filmmaker Sergei Eisenstein. Eisenstein's films, however, were not based on avant-garde art but on his admiration for and study of the films of D. W. Griffith.

Sergei Eisenstein (1898–1948): Learning Film from the American Master

Eisenstein based his films primarily on expanding the editing process, which had been mastered by Griffith. Eisenstein called his careful assemblage of sequences of frames montage. He worked on the premise that two well-edited frames can create an effect together that far surpasses the sum of their individual impacts.

9.19 Sergei Eisenstein.
Potemkin. 1925.
Museum of Modern Art, New York, Film Stills Archives.

9.20 Käthe Kollwitz.
Death Seizing a Woman. 1934.
Lithograph, 20″ × 14⁷⁄₁₆″.
Collection, Museum of Modern Art, New York, Purchase fund.

9.21 Fritz Lang.
Metropolis. 1926.
Museum of Modern Art, New York, Film Stills Archive.

9.19

Eisenstein's *Potemkin* was made in 1925 to commemorate the 1905 revolt of the crew of the *Potemkin*—a revolt that failed, but nevertheless temporarily rallied the people of the port of Odessa into opposition to the czar. Eisenstein's most famous montage sequence in the film is the one showing the relentless progress of the czar's troops down the Odessa steps, firing into the crowd of civilians (fig. 9.19). Even more effectively than Griffith, Eisenstein succeeded in personalizing an epic event by moving the camera from close-ups of individual faces to sweeping scenes of chaotic activity. The sequence evokes the horror and efficiency of Goya's *The Third of May* (fig. 4.34).

Eisenstein survived Stalin's purges and made several more films. He even journeyed to Hollywood in the late twenties in the hope of learning more about cinema in the movie capital founded by D. W. Griffith. Paramount Studios signed him to a contract, but even though studio executives admired his script for the popular muckraking novel *An American Tragedy,* by Theodore Dreiser, they would not allow a Soviet director to shoot such a politically sensitive film. Eisenstein, disillusioned, returned to Russia.

Germany between the Wars: German Expressionism Protests the Social Nightmare

The Russian Revolution was only one part of the turmoil that swept through Europe in constant waves of unrest from the end of World War I to the beginning of World War II. In Germany there was a gradual drift toward the organized terror of Hitler. Artists like Käthe Kollwitz (1867–1945) (fig. 9.20) developed a form of subjective expressionism similar to that of van Gogh but with a strong sense of specific social concern and anguish. German Expressionist artists like Kollwitz, Ludwig Kirchner, Max Beckmann, and others were banned from exhibiting. Many of them migrated to the United States and later contributed to America's postwar artistic prominence.

German films between the end of World War I and the rise of Hitler were the most successful at adapting avant-garde painting styles to film. An early classic, Ernst Lubitsch's *The Cabinet of Dr. Caligari* (1920), effectively combined the visual texture of German Expressionist painting and the abstract forms of Cubism in a compelling visual and narrative whole.

Another masterpiece of this period of German avant-garde film was Fritz Lang's *Metropolis* (fig. 9.21). Lang constructed sets that pictured a futuristic world in which workers live and labor in underground factories while owners live on the surface of the earth surrounded by luxury. The extremely simple plot is sustained by the stunning visual impact of Lang's sets and his use of the camera. The stark simplicity of the story line nevertheless reflected the social

9.20

9.21

unrest and political violence that threatened all parts of Europe after World War I. It was this permanent state of incipient chaos that produced the art movement known as Dada.

Dada: The Avant-Garde Turns against Culture

As early as 1916, a group of artists and writers met regularly at the Cafe Voltaire in Zurich, Switzerland (Switzerland accepted those from other European countries who fled the Great War), and discussed the calamity that surrounded them. The common theme of their writings, their art, and their philosophy was that the traditional culture had to be discredited and brought down. It would have to be reduced to rubble before any new culture could be envisioned. This sense of returning to an absolute beginning is perhaps one reason for the choice of "Dada"—the nonsensical (at least to adults) sound of baby talk—as the name for a highly diverse and fluid movement that spread from Switzerland throughout Europe after the Great War ended.

The best description of Dada would probably be a page of randomly selected words and photographic snippets, with an overlay of graffiti. The tone of Dada can also be seen in the gesture of Dada's leading theoretician, Marcel Duchamp, in exhibiting a urinal as a piece of sculpture—and signing it "R. Mutt." Nevertheless, despite the destructive tone of Dada, it is clear in retrospect that Dada explored approaches to art that have contributed as heavily to the art of our day as any of the other avant-garde movements of the Film Age. Three specific contributions of Dada have become especially important: art as performance (or happening); art as environment; and art as the chance combination of industrially produced objects and images (assemblage). One Dada artist who associated his work with all these approaches to art was Kurt Schwitters.

Kurt Schwitters (1887–1948): "Everything the Artist Spits Is Art"

Kurt Schwitters was a poet as well as an artist. By 1918 he was painting abstract pictures, but—unlike Kandinsky—he was so disillusioned with the possibilities of art in the service of culture that he decided to join the Berlin Dada group that had been formed in 1918.

The Berlin Dada group, however, turned Schwitters down; they feared he was too middle class and too unpolitical. Schwitters went on to prove them wrong.

Schwitters maintained contact with the group and gradually persuaded confirmed Dada writers and artists to contribute to the magazine he founded, which he called *Merz*, a word he lifted from a letterhead, "Kommerzbank," that appeared in one of his collages. The collages (fig. 9.22) of

intense color and graphic impact Schwitters made from scraps of mass-produced photographs, cardboard, packaging materials, and so on were icons of Dada; they asserted that rubble and debris—the junk of the inherited culture—were the necessary sources for art to find a new way.

Merz, for Schwitters, meant an entire way of life based on involvement with chance and fragments instead of the traditional, ordered world. He literally built over the rooms of his house in Hannover with scraps of discarded building materials, until the house's interior became a three-dimensional collage. He thus lived within a Merz environment, which he called a Merzbau. When his home in Hannover was destroyed in World War II, he built a second one in Norway (also destroyed) and had a third Merzbau in progress in England when he died.

Schwitters not only created collages, a magazine, and environments based on the principles of chance and non-art becoming art, he also took part in performances in which Dadaists gave ad-lib lectures in cafes and other public places and took part in a Dada tour of Holland.

9.22 Kurt Schwitters.
Cherry Picture. 1921.
Collage on gouache and cardboard,
36⅛″ × 27¾″.
Museum of Modern Art, New York,
Mr. and Mrs. A. Atwater Kent, Jr., Fund.

Schwitters's work thus touches all the areas of the Dada experience. When his various Merz art forms first appeared, they struck the public as hardly more than the rubbish they began with. Their only brilliance seemed to be that of the brilliant light they cast on the dark center of European culture itself. They were icons of de-construction.

Dada, by its own definition, had to move on. A movement that accepted the dark center illuminated by Dada but also embraced a way to create a new culture out of this irrationality came next: Surrealism.

Surrealism: Exploring the Inner World through Art

Surrealism sought a way out of the entire cultural pattern that had produced the blind alley of the Great War. Unlike Futurists, however, Surrealists placed no faith in the machine or in technology in general. They saw cultural revolution as possible only by beginning in the consciousness of individuals.

Like the Futurists, the Surrealists had a new model of the human person (culture requires an "enlarged humanity" to build on) based on science. Instead of physics, however, their model was based on the psychoanalytic theories of Sigmund Freud.

Freudian Psychology: Evolution and Revolution Lie Within

Futurism saw the human person and the cosmos linked by the expression of energy—outward. Surrealism accepted the Freudian view that linked the human person to the cosmos through the inner biological structure of consciousness itself.

In this theory, the mind has three layers or dimensions: the superego, the ego, and the id (fig. 9.23).

The superego can be described as the level of awareness that is first given to the individual by parents and then society as the individual matures. The superego is experienced as the "voice of conscience" that tells us what to do and what not to do. It can also be described as the pattern of conformity inevitably accompanying participation within a culture.

The ego can be described as the "real" self, although it experiences tension whenever there is conflict between the parental/cultural values and the individual's own ingrained perceptions and preferences. This discontent between the superego and the ego is, according to Freud, unavoidable. Abnormal persons are those who are unable to adjust to the tension resulting from this conflict.

The id refers to the subconscious (ordinarily inaccessible to conscious thought). The most basic human drives—

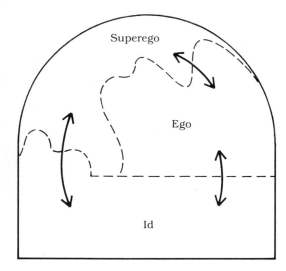

9.23 Diagram showing dynamic relationship between Freudian concepts of Id, Ego, and Superego.

unseen and unknown—operate in this primordial wilderness of the mind. These drives normally find expression through the acceptable patterns permitted by the ego and the superego. In psychotics, these drives rip through both outer layers and discharge their energies in ways that defy the patterns approved by the culture as a whole.

An appreciation of the Freudian model of personality (simplified as it is here) is necessary in order to appreciate what the Surrealists wanted to do with their art. To begin with, even though the Surrealists accepted Freud's basic model, they rejected his psychological goal for people: adjustment to normal, middle-class (bourgeois) society.

To the Surrealists, normalcy was a lie; the war had proved it. The Surrealists wanted to escape from bourgeois life in order to uncover a more real ("surreal") state of existence, or at least of consciousness. Art was part of the process of uncovering and, if necessary, creating, this surreal form of consciousness.

André Breton, like Marinetti for Futurism, was the theorist and poet who assumed doctrinal leadership of the Surrealist movement. His 1924 "Surrealist Manifesto" summed up their cultural goals:

To discover America, Columbus had to sail with a shipload of madmen. Just look around you and see how that madness has taken shape and endured. . . . I believe in the future resolution of those two states, apparently so contradictory, that we know as dream and reality, their resolution into a sort of absolute reality or superreality ("surrealism").[12]

Surrealism: Techniques for the Shuttle to Inner Space

This unknown continent desired by Breton and his followers had already been vividly seen in the work of Henri Rousseau. But Rousseau was a kind of Victor the wild boy stumbling out of the woods—he was already there. The problem for the Surrealists was to find a way to take themselves into the unknown—and then back. Gaëtan Picon described their intention this way:

The Surrealists landed on an unknown continent, but there was no question of their settling there; what they did rather was to organize a shuttle between the old world and the new.[13]

And what was this shuttle? It was any technique that enabled an artist to descend into the subconscious and then return to the surface of ordinary reality with art (or writing) based on the experience. Hypnosis, starvation, boredom, drugs, were all tried—sometimes in combination. The two most successful techniques turned out to be the collage and the dream.

248

Max Ernst (1891–1976): The Visual Shuttle of Collage

Even though most people have made collages before they leave grammar school, few have made collages with the intensity or purpose of Max Ernst.

Ernst's collages are especially significant because they originated in response to the mass media environment. He traced his interest in collage to a particular rainy day in 1919 when he was idly flipping through the pages of a catalogue of scientific instruments. His reaction resulted in an amazing description, first, of media overload and, second, of the creative process responding to this overload:

The sheer absurdity of this assemblage [of catalogue images] caused a sudden intensification of my visionary faculties and brought forth a hallucinating succession of contradictory images, double, triple, and multiple images overlaying each other with the persistence and rapidity peculiar to love memories and the visions of half-sleep.

Ernst was able to turn this totally unsought experience into art:

All I had to do was to add to these catalogue pages, painting or drawing over them . . . what I could see within me. . . . What before had been banal pages of publicity was transformed into dramas revealing my inner-most desires.[14]

Figure 9.24 is an example of Ernst's manipulation of illustrations from a scientific catalogue. Figure 9.25 shows his interest in collages made from nineteenth-century engravings. In short, Ernst not only turned mass media im-

9.25

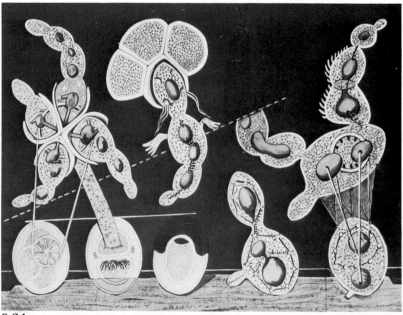

9.24

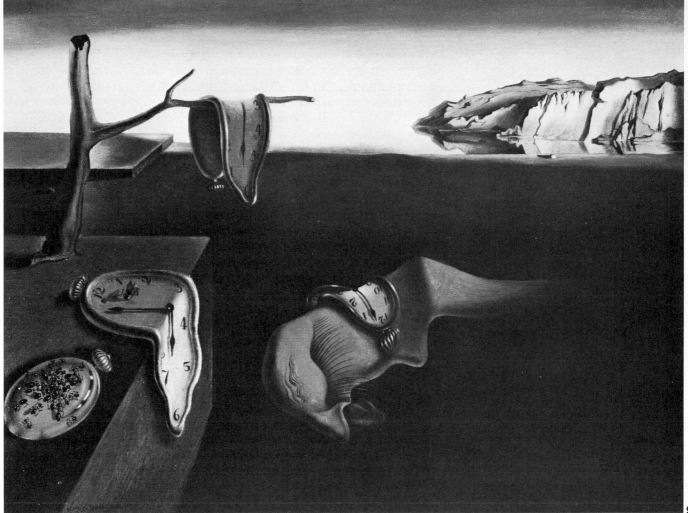

9.26

ages into his own personal language, this language told him about his own subconscious self.

The mass media image was the bait that enticed the forms that lay deep in the subconscious to rise to the surface and become art. Once made into art, the subconscious becomes part of conscious awareness. This was the cultural revolution envisioned by Surrealism: a society built on individuals who lived in this kind of vital contact with their own inner selves.

Salvador Dali (1904—): The Visual Shuttle of the Dream

Another kind of shuttle to the unconscious was brilliantly designed and operated by a young Spanish painter, Salvador Dali, who began his involvement with the Surrealists in Paris in 1928. Dali's technique was very direct: he simply painted his dreams—in perfect perspective.

The Persistence of Memory (fig. 9.26) is an early example

9.24 Max Ernst.
The gramineous bicycle garnished with bells the dappled fire damps and the echinoderms bending the spine to look for caresses. Cologne, 1920 or 1921.
Botanical chart altered with gouache, 29¼″ × 39¼″.
Collection, Museum of Modern Art, New York, Purchase.

9.25 Max Ernst.
Jean Hatchet and Charles the Bold, or *The Young Prince.* 1929.
Collage, 9⅝″ × 7⅞″.
Cleveland Museum of Art, John L. Severance Fund.

9.26 Salvador Dali.
The Persistence of Memory. 1931.
Oil on canvas, 9½″ × 13″.
Museum of Modern Art, New York, Given anonymously.

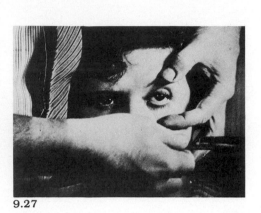

9.27

of Dali's style. Despite its small scale (9½ by 13 inches), it has the perspective depth of the Academic painting tradition Dali admired. Its overbright colors also reflect Dali's enthusiasm for the popular colored lithographs of the nineteenth century. Dali has referred to his paintings as "hand-colored photographs," but he nevertheless subverted photographic realism by turning inward into the world of dreams, where watches melt and unnamed creatures emerge from alien landscapes.

Dali teamed with another Surrealist, Luis Buñuel, to produce a remarkable film, *An Andalusian Dog (Un Chien Andalou)* that captured the radical vision of Surrealism by its bizarre and unpredictable cuts, dissolves, and double images. In addition to several irreligious and erotic scenes, it shocked the public with a scene of a woman's eye being cut by a razor (fig. 9.27).

Dali's early work also demonstrated his talent for publicity. He extended subconscious imagery into real life with stunts like arriving nude in a sports car filled with cauliflower in front of the Paris Opera. After the major Surrealist Exhibition in Paris in 1938, Breton expelled him from the movement. Even for Surrealism, Dali simply showed too much ego.

Dali: Catholicism, Science, and Spain

Dali's paintings after World War II switched from Freudian orthodoxy to a bizarre yet equally zealous commitment to paintings based on Roman Catholicism, modern science, and Spanish nationalism.

Dali's *The Sacrament of the Last Supper* (fig. 9.28 and plate 24) is one of a large number of remarkable paintings on religious themes from this period of his life. Despite the common theme, all that relates this painting to Leonardo's famous mural is the superbly executed linear perspective. The Dalian *Last Supper* allegedly takes place in the center of the carbon atom, with a view of the Mediterranean coast near

9.28

Dali's home. Other religious paintings of this time show an equally subjective iconography—the many paintings that include the Virgin Mary, for instance, all have Dali's wife, Gala, as a model.

Dali's personal and artistic withdrawal into mere eccentricity represented the almost tragic outcome of Surrealism as a movement: the impact of its individual artists exceeded the accomplishments of the movement in moving the larger culture in a direction opposite to the madness that had produced World War I. Breton himself underscored this lack of cultural influence:

Surrealism can only be historically understood in terms of the war—from 1919 to 1938—in terms of the war from which it started and the one to which it returned.[15]

Perhaps the most fitting image to conclude this description of avant-garde art from 1905 to World War II is a painting by Picasso, whose Cubism had such a powerful impact. Picasso had worked on developing Cubism with a monkish sense of detachment from anything outside of the painterly realm of the canvas, but his 1937 masterpiece *Guernica* (fig. 9.29) turns the cool, objective forms of Cubism into screams of anguish. Guernica was a Spanish town that Nazi bombers reduced to rubble in April of 1937. The grays, whites, and blacks of the painting, when combined with the stippled marks dotting many of its brutally stereotyped shapes, suggest a uniquely twentieth-century experience: witnessing distant and terrible events through the impersonal halftone photographs and printed words of the newspaper.

9.27 Salvador Dali and Luis Bunuel. *Un Chien Andalou*. 1928. Museum of Modern Art, New York, Film Stills Archive.

9.28 Salvador Dali. *The Sacrament of the Last Supper*. 1955. Oil on canvas, 65⅝″ × 105⅛″. National Gallery of Art, Washington, Chester Dale Collection.

9.29 Pablo Picasso. *Guernica*. 1937. Oil on canvas, 140⅜″ × 312¾″. Museo del Prado, Madrid. SPADEM/ New York.

9.29

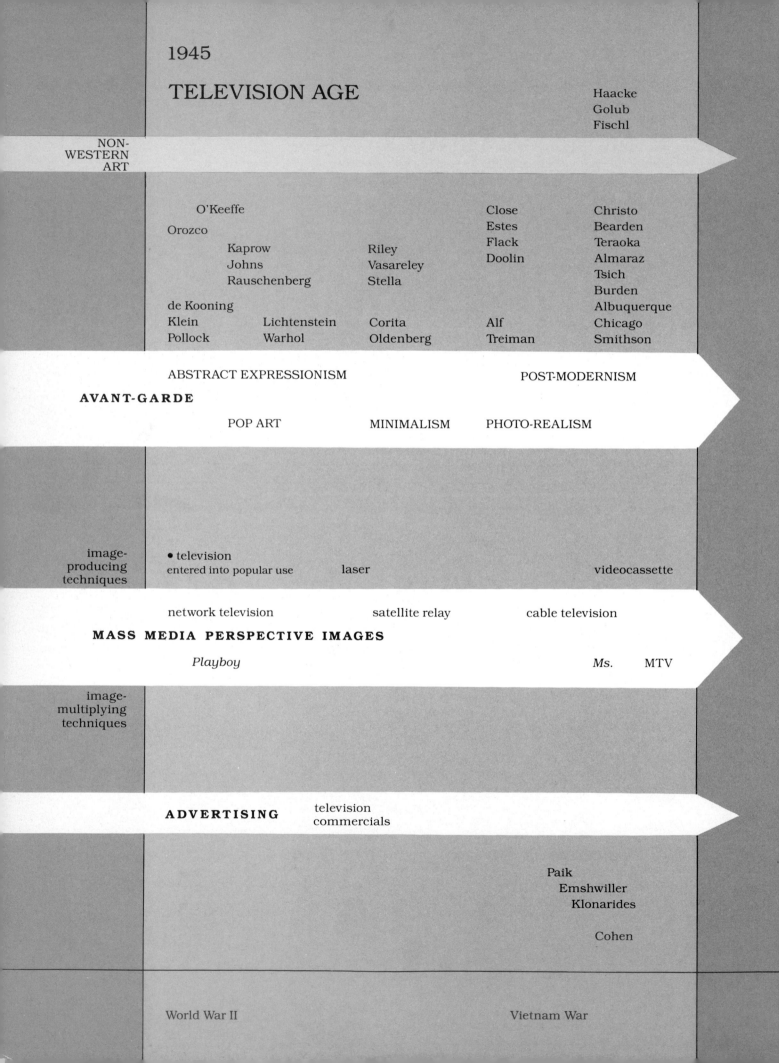

1945

TELEVISION AGE

Haacke
Golub
Fischl

NON-
WESTERN
ART

O'Keeffe
Orozco
Kaprow
Johns
Rauschenberg
de Kooning
Klein
Pollock

Riley
Vasareley
Stella

Lichtenstein
Warhol

Corita
Oldenberg

Close
Estes
Flack
Doolin

Alf
Treiman

Christo
Bearden
Teraoka
Almaraz
Tsich
Burden
Albuquerque
Chicago
Smithson

ABSTRACT EXPRESSIONISM

POST-MODERNISM

AVANT-GARDE

POP ART

MINIMALISM

PHOTO-REALISM

image-
producing
techniques

• television
entered into popular use

laser

videocassette

network television

satellite relay

cable television

MASS MEDIA PERSPECTIVE IMAGES

Playboy

Ms.   MTV

image-
multiplying
techniques

ADVERTISING   television
commercials

Paik
Emshwiller
Klonarides

Cohen

World War II

Vietnam War

CHAPTER TEN

THE

TELEVISION AGE I:

TELEVISION AS THE

CULTURAL CENTER

ASSESSMENTS

1. Recall your early memories of television. What programs stand out? How old were you then? What kinds of information did you obtain from watching television? Has television contributed to your sense of yourself? How?
2. What are some of the visual and auditory ways that television and films are similar/dissimilar?
3. What is a stereotype? Do you see stereotyping in television programming?
4. Do you watch television news? What awareness have you gained about people and events from television news that you could not have gained from just reading newspapers or magazines? Has watching television made you more sensitive or less sensitive as a person? Explain.
5. Do you watch music videos? What do you like/dislike about videos? Would you consider videos avant-garde in any way? If so, why?
6. Do you own a VCR? If you do not, would you like to own one? How does the VCR change the context of viewing and producing movies, including their themes?

10.1

Despite the vision of cultural revolution underlying much of the art of the Film Age avant-garde, it was the mass media popular arts, including advertising, that had a radical effect on Western culture before World War II. The arrival of television after World War II made the icons of the mass media even more powerful. Television has changed the perceptual base of Western culture and has profoundly influenced the development of other mass media popular arts. It has also changed the avant-garde. The structure and icon function of network television will be discussed in this chapter. The final three chapters will discuss the development of avant-garde art as well as the art of advertising in the new context of the Television Age.

The main reason for the cultural and artistic impact of television is easy to identify: for the first time in Western history, the primary source of culture-building images is located within the home itself. Television has produced images ranging from the Felix the Cat doll (fig. 10.1) used in NBC's experimental broadcasts before World War II to the live shots of an American setting foot on the surface of the moon (fig. 10.2) to belated scenes of the invasion of Grenada (fig. 10.3). These three images suggest the almost unimaginable quantitative and qualitative range of images that have appeared during television's first half-century of existence.

These few examples also show why television images are

10.2

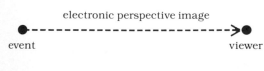

electronic perspective image

event   viewer

10.4

so powerful. They are the most real in the ongoing tradition of perspective images created by Western art and science since the time of Brunelleschi: they are instant, moving perspective images, the most powerful icons in Western history (fig. 10.4).

For most Americans today, television's home-based, factual and fictional images form the basic picture of social,

10.1 Felix the Cat.
Plastic toy used in NBC experimental television broadcasts before World War II.
Photo courtesy of the National Broadcasting Company, Inc.

10.2 Television monitor shot of Neil Armstrong making first step onto lunar surface. 1969.
Photo courtesy of the National Broadcasting Company, Inc.

10.3 Television monitor shot of Grenada invasion. 1983.
Photo courtesy of the National Broadcasting Company, Inc.

10.4 "Pure" television: instant, unmanipulated transmission of the television image to the viewer.

10.5 Kennedy/Nixon debate. October 7, 1960. Host, Frank McGee, NBC News.
Photo courtesy of the National Broadcasting Company, Inc.

economic, and political reality. Television today is so powerful that, in the opinion of the sociologist George Gerbner, television *is* the culture:

Today television is, for all practical purposes, the common culture. Culture is the system of messages that cultivates the images fitting the established structure of social relations. Television thereby becomes the common basis for social interaction. . . . As such, it can only be compared, in terms of its functions, not to any other medium but to the pre-industrial notion of religion.[1]

This statement remains valid even for people who do not watch television at all. For example, television, since the 1960 Nixon-Kennedy debates (fig. 10.5), has dominated our political process; beyond the political arena, it affects the attitudes, perceptions, and behavior of so many people in our culture that even those who avoid it live lives surrounded by a culture that is based on the effects of television.

The power of television is not due only to its position inside the home, but to its inherent ability to store and retrieve art forms and experiences of all kinds. Our experience of reality now includes the instant replay as well as the instant news bulletin. Saturn, the earth, and the moon are on tape; so is the death of Lee Harvey Oswald and the marriage of Tiny Tim.

Yet such television experiences, unlike real events and live performances, have no context outside television itself. Real events have a precise time and space context; video events can go forward and backward in time and are subject to unlimited manipulation.

The powerful realism of the television image coupled with its equally obvious potential for manipulation has made it a source of controversy from its postwar beginnings. Sev-

10.5

eral important films have dealt with the impact of television. *Network* satirized the social impact of network television's drive for ratings through ever more drastic levels of violence. *Being There* was a brilliant parable about a man who becomes a leading politician because the only phrases and gestures he knows come from television, not from contact with real people, making him, therefore, a perfect communicator—on television. *Videodrome* pictured a perverse science fiction world in which television experiences literally take over the perception and response capacities of those who watch.

The potential of television's capacity to record, retrieve, and manipulate reality is still provoking controversy. Video cameras could be whirring in every American home, sending their live images to a central storage bank where anyone's home life could be called up and replayed at any time. Or, in a switch on Michael Crichton's film *The Terminal Man*, a video camera could be transplanted into the eye of a person and his or her whole life experience be transmitted, stored, and retrieved. As was noted in Chapter 1, some robots today have their own television eyes.

The underlying theme of such films and observations is that television has a radically new power, only partially realized, to merge reality and fiction. Even though it is the third kind of image derived from Western perspective image–making machines, it is far more powerful than its predecessors, the photograph and the film. In a television-dominated society, each person must develop the ability to create his or her own context for the unavoidable flow of images. This ability to control one's imagery is a basic standard of visual literacy.

Neither Brunelleschi nor the Academic painters could have dreamed it would turn out like this.

Pure Television: Nothing but the Facts

Unlike the complex journey required for Cubism to uncover the basic structure of "pure" paintings, however, making "pure" television is very easy. All one need do is go into a bank or a store and watch a television monitor as it scans the environment and whirs mindlessly on.

Pure television is pure boredom. Fortunately, we do not see "pure" television. Before television images enter our homes and build our culture, they go through an intervention and manipulation process as involved as that of shaping a lump of clay into a vase or transforming random color into a painting.

This chapter will discuss how the hands of artists and technicians shape television's perspective images. A later chapter will discuss the crucial manipulative role of sponsors and advertising. Two terms will help to clarify this manipulative quality of the television image: *event* will refer to the original fact or process that occurs, or has occurred in the past, in front of the television camera; *filter* will refer to all the means by which the original event is edited or otherwise manipulated in any way before it appears as an image on the television screen in front of the viewer (fig. 10.6).

Network television programming has three major filters that inevitably manipulate the viewer's perception of the images that appear on the television screen. The first and most important filter has already been mentioned—it is the home. The other two filters that alter broadcasted events are part of the television image itself—the filters of drama and personality.

Manipulating the Television Image I: The Home as Filter

Many people admit to the habit of walking into their home or apartment and turning on the television set, whether they intend to watch it or not. It is simply there. More than 97 percent of American homes today have at least one television set (exceeding the percentage of homes with a refrigerator).

The home as a filter gives television images a context of everyday familiarity that subtly integrates them into our daily experience. As has been noted earlier, other art forms have their special limitations of time, place, and attention. Television is always there within reach. It's "family."

Even the cathedral, the most unified social, artistic, and political art form in the Western tradition, required the individual to enter into its special space at special times. By contrast, people have been known to leave home merely to get *away* from television and its incessant flow of images. Television images are simply part of the environment of the American home. As seen in the Taft Broadcasting Company advertisement (fig. 10.7), the television industry is quite aware of the power of the home as a filter.

The Home as Filter: Childhood Ends

The home as a filter for the television image not only gives it an environmental presence, it also radically affects the relationships between people within the house. The "TV dinner" is a symbol of the many subtle changes in family relationships that have come from television. Parents hush children during the news. People schedule weekends around the NFL or make a daily ritual of "Donahue" or "the soaps." Individual Americans watch television for an average of over four hours each day. Children watch more.

Children not only have their own programming, they also watch the programs the adults watch; in fact, many children prefer adult programs. As the communication specialist Joshua Meyerwitz has observed:

Everyone, regardless of age, tends to watch similar programs. In 1980, for example, "Dallas," "The Dukes of Hazard," "Love Boat,"

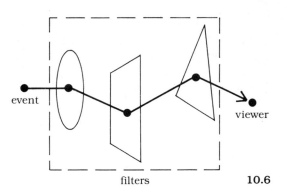

filters   **10.6**

10.7

10.6 Network television: television image reaches viewer bearing manipulative effects of "filters" (home, drama, personality).

10.7 Joseph Csatari.
Painting used in Taft Broadcasting Company advertisement.
Courtesy of Taft Broadcasting Company.

and "The Muppets" were among the most popular programs in the country, including ages 2 to 11.[2]

The education professor Neil Postman extends this observation to include a comparison with the condition of children in the Middle Ages. Medieval children, before the printing press required literacy, became absorbed in the realities of the adult world as soon as they could speak and work. Later, literacy and the necessity for schooling created the barrier between adulthood and childhood that in modern times has become accepted as normal. Today, television is tending to erase that distinction.

According to Postman, medieval paintings that depict children as tiny adults (fig. 10.8) accurately reflect the situation of the medieval child-adult, one that is returning in our culture because television

10.8

presents information mostly in visual images. All we have to do is look, which children do in our culture at an average of 27 hours a week. And, as noted above, they watch what adults watch.

This means that all adult secrets—social, sexual, physical, and the like—must be revealed. . . . It is even more than the revelation of secrets. It is the ultimate trivialization of culture.[3]

The open-window familiarity of the television image, because of the filter of the home, thus has a particularly strong impact on children. Much of the adult behavior they see would previously have appeared only to adults. Today, television not only makes the home itself a theater, it also uses the family as the main subject matter for its dramas.

The Family: The Main Subject of Television Drama

Television has evolved an amazingly wide variety of group relationships that can be seen as variations of the family unit. Over the years, four general types of television families have evolved: the nuclear family (Ma, Pa, and the kids), the splintered family (single parent plus kids), the unorthodox family (living together in nonsexual but supportive relationship, no kids), and "almost family" (groups who do not live together but are bound by extraordinary closeness). Entries in these categories vary from year to year; classic examples of each are, for the nuclear family, "The Waltons" and "Family Ties"; for the splintered family, "Diff'rent Strokes" (fig. 10.9) and "One Day at a Time"; for the unorthodox family, "The Odd Couple" and "Three's Company"; for the "almost family," "M.A.S.H." and "Cheers."

These fictional series are self-contained dramas; they are productions that could exist as either plays or movies outside of television. The term *drama* can apply in a more general sense to virtually all network television productions, whether fictional or not. Drama is a second powerfully manipulative filter built into the network television image. A good way to see how the filter of drama works is by examin-

10.9

ing a type of programming that is basically nonfictional: the filter of drama is powerfully evident even in the most factual kind of network broadcast, the news show.

Manipulating the Television Image II: The Filter of Drama

The network news show is a drama, that is, a dramatic presentation of facts. It follows a recurring narrative structure and theme with as much predictability as an effective prime-time fictional series. All network news shows are equally dramatic, but the discussion that follows will take the "NBC Nightly News" for its example.

Before 1985, NBC's opening logo pictured an image of the world spinning toward the viewer. The accompanying high-tech sound effects also dramatically suggested the scope of information about to emerge above the viewer's horizon. The current NBC logo is equally dramatic but far more patriotic: it presents a helicopter view of the Statue of Liberty accompanied by a stately orchestral theme titled "The Mission."

Following the opening logo, the "star" of the story, Tom Brokaw (fig. 10.10), looks directly into our living rooms and says, "Good Evening." The papers he folds in his hands suggest that he has just caught up with the last-minute facts that are pouring in from television cameras stationed across the world—which appears in the spread-out map that was designed into the "Nightly News" set (fig. 10.11).

All this has taken about thirty seconds. Now, the news.

Brokaw first describes the lead international story—or domestic disaster—and then the image on the screen switches to an on-the-spot reporter. If the lead story is complicated, the coverage will switch to a second correspondent after a maximum of about two minutes. Television news keeps the pictures—and audience's attention—moving.

After Tom Brokaw wraps up the story, a graphic menu appears on the screen to create interest in what is coming up next. Even television news has to be careful to keep its drama competitive with the dramas about miraculous tires, lost travelers' checks, and upset stomachs that regularly appear as part of the news show format—the commercials.

The drama of the news then continues with stories of lessening importance broken up by graphics reminding us to stay tuned through the commercial breaks.

Throughout the program, the sets, the graphics, and the environmental sounds are all dramatically orchestrated to enhance the credibility of the visual facts. A reporter will stand in front of the White House or another significant place to read comments that could just as easily—and a lot more comfortably—be read from an easy chair at home (fig. 10.12). The location shot, however, gives the report an on-the-spot touch of drama.

10.10

10.11

10.12

10.8 Simone Martini.
Christ on the Way to Calvary.
c. 1340.
Oil on wood, 9⅞" × 6⅛".
The Louvre, Paris.

10.9 "Diff'rent Strokes" (Dana Plato, Todd Bridges, Gary Coleman, Conrad Bain).
Photo courtesy of the National Broadcasting Company, Inc.

10.10 Tom Brokaw. "NBC Nightly News."
Photo courtesy of the National Broadcasting Company, Inc.

10.11 Set for "NBC Nightly News."
Photo courtesy of the National Broadcasting Company, Inc.

10.12 John Chancellor, NBC News. Beirut, 1982.
Photo courtesy of the National Broadcasting Company, Inc.

260

10.13 Tom Brokaw. "NBC Nightly News."
Photo courtesy of the National
Broadcasting Company, Inc.

The overall dramatic effect proceeds from chaos (bad news) to order (light news). The final wrap-up is usually a human interest story. It could be a story about the first girl to play Little League baseball in Keokuk, or someone who won a million dollars in the New York lottery. Or it might be another story about the plight of China's pandas. Whatever it is, it helps to turn the tragedy of the news into a "comedy" of hope.

The news can then end with a good-natured smile or wink from Tom Brokaw and a ritual "Good night from all of us at NBC news" (fig. 10.13). A closing set of graphics and high-tech sounds completes the dramatic cycle from chaos to order with reassuring familiarity. There will be another story tomorrow night. The world will hold together. In the meantime, right after a commercial break, the prime-time family shows will begin.

The iconic impact of these images is remarkably similar to that of the medieval *mappa mundi*. It is a picture story of the world, but, instead of Christ, it is held together by the personality of the anchorperson and, implicitly, the marvels of technology. It thus provides the viewer with an ingenious updated version of Western culture's most basic traditional myth: the experience of the autonomous individual who is at the center of the world. The motto of ABC News is very specific about this iconic effect: "ABC News—uniquely qualified to bring you the world."

This description of the news show as an iconic picture of the world has already referred to the third major filter of network television, the filter of personality.

Manipulating the Television Image III: The Filter of Personality

Personality is a filter that operates in virtually all network television programming. That it is present even in the national news show, when the programming is supposedly "nothing but the facts," is a measure of its importance.

The personality of the anchorperson is crucial to the news show—as is reflected by his or her "star" status and yearly salary. Walter Cronkite (formerly with CBS), Tom Brokaw (NBC), and Peter Jennings (ABC) have publicly commented on the difficulty of keeping news objective and factual in light of the pressure for high ratings, ratings heavily dependent on the personality that the anchorperson(s) give to the show. The script of the half-hour evening news show could fit easily on the front page of a newspaper and could be read in much less than thirty minutes. The presence of the anchorperson makes one huge difference: the viewer hears the news from *someone*. The filter of personality gives the dramatic chaos-to-order structure of the news show an important extra dimension: it changes drama into *personal* drama.

Television, perhaps more than any medium before it, demonstrates the artistic principle that was discussed earlier in terms of Baudelaire, Courbet, and Eakins: facts and events alone are not enough. The drama critic Martin Esslin has described the process by which television imagery merges fact, drama, and personality:

We are not primarily getting facts [in the television image], we are getting drama. . . . Drama is always that of human beings. In drama we experience the world through personality.[4]

The problem in television, as in the fact-versus-feeling dilemma in nineteenth-century art, is not the presence of personality and feeling but the ultimate effect of the mixture of fact, personality, and feeling. With a result similar to the oversentimentality of Academic painting, the television journalist can dominate the broadcast by his or her personality, even if unintentionally. Joan Lunden, one of ABC's national correspondents, described her earlier role as television reporter on ABC's New York affiliate this way:

People watch "Eyewitness News" just as much to find out what Roseanne did today and what JJ did today and what so-and-so is wearing and what their feelings are that day, as they are tuning in to get the news. It is almost like a continuing soap opera, a serial.[5]

Lunden goes on to describe the "Eyewitness News" practice of running promotions—television commercials for the news show—that build up the image of each reporter as a specific personality type.

Lunden's candid evaluation of her relationship to her audience does not mean that the news she presents is false. It means that she is aware of how her personality—whether she likes it or not—becomes a filter that manipulates the viewer's perception of the images television is presenting.

The filter of personality is so familiar and so interwoven into our experience of television that it seems as natural as the facts themselves. The networks, of course, are keenly aware of its effect. At least one attempt has been made to evaluate the effect of a network broadcast without the filter of personality—an experiment that proved how decisively important it really is.

Removing the Filter of Personality: Television as Pure Fact

In December of 1981, the NBC producer Don Ohlmeyer decided to broadcast the season-ending NFL football game between the Miami Dolphins and the New York Jets without the normal crew of two or three commentators hovering over each play.

Ohlmeyer went to great lengths to eliminate personality. Technicians duplicated the sound environment of the stadium as closely as possible. Instead of the enthusiastic voices of the announcers, people at home heard crowd noises, loudspeakers, sounds from the playing field—and little else.

The result was one of the dullest games—or rather, television programs—ever broadcast. The most devout opponents of sports announcers admitted that the game was almost impossible to watch. The viewers felt alone—inside the stadium visually but somehow outside the event. Even though the images were as factual as ever, the missing filter of personality took away much of their interest. The public reaction to this "purely objective" broadcast resembled the public reaction to Eakins's *Max Schmitt in a Single Scull* (fig. 8.7). It was seen as so objective that it lacked any human connection, any feeling or drama.

The Background of the Television Image: Breaking the Closed Circle of Television

The emphasis so far on the three major filters of network television might suggest that network television is total manipulation. Television, however, is obviously not this powerful. One important reason is that, because they are able to transmit images of the real world in a more direct way than any previous form of perspective image, television images have an innate quality that limits the ability of any technician (or sponsor) to totally control what people see. This revolutionary quality of the television image is an element that can be called *background.*

Background refers to the unintended and uncontrollable glimpses of reality that unexpectedly, yet inevitably, intrude into television imagery, regardless of the filters bracketing the event or the objectives of the sponsor.

All earlier forms of perspective images totally controlled background. A movie, for instance, has a background as controlled as that of a Renaissance painting. The script and editing process eliminates the possibility for background to intrude into the planned sequence and meaning of the images it presents.

Television, because of its electronic base and rapid distribution, is qualitatively different. The editing that can be applied to television is not as complete as that applied to movies or to magazine photography.

Background intrudes even into the virtually closed system of Soviet television programming. A Soviet woman answered an American reporter's question about why the Russian people do not totally believe their government's picture of America by describing a documentary she had seen on television about drug problems in America. She forgot about the drugs, she said, but she was very impressed by the quantity and variety of goods on display in American drug stores. This, she said, contradicted other government documentaries on poverty in America.

For Americans, background is particularly evident in television news programs. One of the best examples of background occurred during coverage of one of the most important events of the Television Age: the 1969 flight of Apollo 11.

The Uniqueness of the Television Image: The Background Emerges

Millions of Americans watched the flight of Apollo 11 on television sets that are as common in American homes as vases were in the homes of ancient Greece. Over a hundred million Americans watched the astronauts, like the figures clearly etched against the backgrounds of those vases, float with serenity and confidence against the black background of space (fig. 10.14).

10.14

10.14 Astronaut tethered outside space shuttle *Challenger*. 1983. Courtesy of NASA.

10.15 Apollo 11 photograph of lunar surface. 1969. Courtesy of NASA.

When the command capsule entered its phase of flying behind the moon, however, the serenity suddenly vanished. The disappearance of the capsule left the picture empty except for the utterly still and barren lunar landscape pressed against the television screen (fig. 10.15). For a few moments there was absolute quiet from the command module, from NASA, and from the network correspondents.

For people around the world watching their sets, all that was left on the screen was background—an unmanipulated and "unframed" picture of the reality of the moon. The surface of the moon was so powerful by itself that it swallowed up the awareness of the recent chattering of the commentators. All the filters disappeared. Only the fact remained, the fact of the moon.

The stunning reality of sitting on earth and examining the surface of the moon overwhelmed everything else. The

10.15

experience was pure television: a perspective image transmitted with the speed of light directly from the "event" to the viewer.

Very soon, however, the filters closed in on the mystery. Footage of a simulated lunar capsule drifting behind a simulated moon appeared on the screen. Accompanied by expert commentary and interrupted by commercial breaks, this sequence filled the gap until the astronauts reappeared.

Despite the epic quality of this example, it is true that the most important effects of the background of the television image have occurred on earth. As a recurring dimension of television imagery, these background effects are proof that television, despite its powerful filters, is not an entirely closed system of images. The social effects of background became especially apparent in the late 1950s and early 1960s when Americans became involved in the Civil Rights movement.

Television Background: The Shock of the News

During the 1950s American society was subjected to the cultural shock of seeing images of itself on television in addition to the familiar context of the movies. On the movie screen, as was noted earlier, people were pictured like characters in a novel, completely rounded-off, consistent, and moving within a carefully plotted story and environment.

The background of the television image changed this. Television, at first gradually, and then with sudden flashes of disturbance, showed images of Americans without the epic and narrative context of film: Americans saw themselves, live and (since 1960) in color. One of the first changes of perceptions involved the image of black Americans.

Television Background and the Civil Rights Movement: From Stereotypes to Real Images

Before television, blacks had achieved prominence and recognition in the fields of jazz and (though it was outside the major professional leagues) sports. Blacks were either excluded from or simply invisible in every other field. When it came, television, to an astonishing degree, was an all-white world. Where blacks were visible, they were visible only as stereotypes. Stereotypes, as applied to people, are fixed pictures or ideas about how a particular group (ethnic, religious, or racial) thinks or behaves, a picture that simplifies, often to the point of caricature, and prohibits the recognition of individual, personal uniqueness.

Black stereotypes had remained unchanged in American popular art from the nineteenth-century Currier and Ives lithographs (fig. 10.16) to the movies of the 1930s (fig. 10.17) and the sitcoms of the Television Age. Blacks were shown as

10.16 Currier and Ives.
The Old Barn Floor.
Lithograph. 1868.
Currier and Ives.
Courtesy of the Library of Congress.
#LC-USZ62#12333.

10.17 Shirley Temple and Bill "Bojangles" Robinson in *The Little Colonel.* 1935.
Collection, Museum of Modern Art, New York, Film Stills Archive.

10.16

slow-moving (except when they danced), talented only at menial tasks (except for sports), and—most of all—very happy with having the world managed by white folks.

Suddenly, on the television news, background began to interfere with the stereotypes. In the late fifties and early sixties, black faces began to appear with increasing frequency on the news. Unlike the stereotypes of the sitcoms, variety hours, and movies, however, they were not content. Via television, black Americans stepped out of their stereotypes right into the same living rooms where they had been seen for years in the late-evening time slots, on "The Jack Benny Show," "Beulah," and "The Amos 'n Andy Show."

Television suddenly presented civil rights demonstrators on the same screen as the stereotypes. The stereotypes became increasingly unacceptable to most black or white Americans as the civil rights activity grew from isolated events to a national movement. The background of television made the tradition of black stereotypes *look like stereotypes,* that is, narrow and offensive caricatures.

10.17

This example brings out a principle of television programming that arises from the effect of background: fact tends toward fiction and fiction tends toward fact. Even though stereotypes, to a certain extent, are necessary in all forms of visual and dramatic art, the intrusion of background initiates a process that forces the creation of newer, more up-to-date stereotypes. For the civil rights movement, this principle meant that once the perceptions of blacks had been changed by the news programs, fictional portrayals of blacks also had to change.

Fiction Tends toward Fact: New Stereotypes to Fit the News

The changes in television's fictional portrayal of blacks be-

10.18

10.19

10.18 Diahann Carroll and Marc Copage, in "Julia." 1968.
Photo courtesy of the National Broadcasting Company, Inc.
10.19 Mr. T and George Peppard, "The A-Team." 1984.
Photo courtesy of the National Broadcasting Company, Inc.

gan in the mid-sixties. The 1965 show "I Spy" featured Bill Cosby in an equal role alongside white actors without having to dance, crack jokes, or wait on tables. "Mission Impossible," "Julia" (fig. 10.18), "The Outsiders," "Sanford and Son," "The Jeffersons," "Diff'rent Strokes," "Benson," and "The Bill Cosby Show" are among the shows starring blacks that have appeared in the last two decades. "Roots," one of television's first miniseries, was one of the highest-rated programs in television history. Even though the eighties have seen a narrowing of fictional roles for blacks back toward sitcom humor or Mr. T's comic book ghetto-tough image (fig. 10.19), the revolutionary change in the images of blacks on television cannot be denied. The same period has already produced another breakthrough series for Bill Cosby, "The Cosby Show," which depicts a middle-class black family in which both parents are professionals: one a lawyer and one a doctor. Compared to television in the 1950s, this is a totally new world.

Fiction Tends toward Fact: New Stereotypes for Women

The history of the stereotypes of women on television forms an equally clear example of how fictional roles on television adapt to changing facts in society.

In the 1950s, women's social and fictional television roles seemed to be in total sync: women were housewives and mothers who served as happily in a man's world as blacks did in a white world. The only power women showed was either in pure fantasy shows like "I Dream of Jeannie" and "Bewitched" or in sitcoms where the humor was based on women's absurd attempts to show themselves as capable as their husbands, as in "I Love Lucy" and "I Married Joan." The most famous woman professional in a 1950s prime-time series was Eve Arden's character in "Our Miss Brooks," a high school teacher. Miss Brooks's most basic concern, however, was prowling the halls in an eternally unsuccessful effort to marry the dim-witted biology teacher.

By the early sixties, over half of American marriages were ending in divorce, and almost half of all American women had jobs outside the home. This reality, plus the impetus to protest and change generated by the civil rights movement, produced a dramatic shift of fiction toward fact in the portrayal of women on television. Shows like "That Girl," "The Mary Tyler Moore Show," "Alice," and "One Day at a Time" pictured women coping with divorce and single parenting and entering into careers and professions instead of mere jobs. Despite the increased complexity of character and role of these new fictional women, the fictional world they moved in—perhaps best symbolized by "Charlie's Angels"—was dominated by men.

The fictional television roles of women in the eighties have again shown fiction tending toward fact. In the 1973 season, for example, almost thirty percent of prime-time shows had no regularly appearing actresses. In 1984 almost half the characters on prime-time shows were women, many of them in starring roles. Nine of the twenty-one new network shows in 1984 starred women in career roles. All these shows presented women not only as powerful, but as *the* power in their respective social worlds. These roles featured down-to-earth characters, in marked contrast to earlier fantasy roles like Wonder Woman and The Bionic Woman or the fashion model chic of Charlie's Angels. Power for women in the eighties, in other words, no longer depended on miraculous circumstances.

Despite the lightweight and frivolous character of almost all television fictional heroes, their images are important icons: fictional stereotypes tell people, at least in fantasy, what they can expect to become. In order to achieve a goal, it is first necessary to be able to imagine it. Linda Lavin, the star of the long-running series "Alice," traced prime-time television's increased realism in portraying women to television news, that is, to background: "News influences entertainment . . . the link between women and activists and reporters who care about women's issues grows stronger each year."[6]

There is still criticism of the limited roles that minorities play in a medium in which almost two-thirds of the people who appear on screen are white males. Nevertheless, the process of change in fictional roles that arises from the effect of background is an example of how television, despite its powerful filters, opens our culture to the possibility of change.

There is, however, one more aspect of the network television image that has a potentially powerful, though less frequent, effect on society. In the history of television there have been several instances of the background within a television broadcast being itself deliberately manipulated by people outside the television system. This deliberate manipulation of background is sometimes called *feedback*.

Two incidents from the crucial year of 1968, when American society was wrenched almost to the breaking point, illustrate the principle of feedback and its potentially powerful effects. One event is the Tet offensive in Vietnam. The other event is the Democratic National Convention in Chicago.

Manipulating Background: Feedback from Vietnam

The Tet offensive began on January 30, 1968, and lasted for less than two weeks. It was a surprise attack on the major cities and military outposts throughout South Vietnam by the Vietcong and North Vietnamese troops. The suicide attacks were a surprise because they came during a period of truce that had been agreed to by both sides in previous years.

The attacks were futile from a military point of view, as

President Johnson quickly assured the American public in his televised address to the nation. He predicted that all military gains would be reversed almost immediately. The president was right. Militarily.

What was never regained, or rather, what was lost by America during the brief Tet offensive, was the will to fight—and ultimately the war itself.

General Giap, the North Vietnamese commander, had correctly assumed that Americans would not tolerate for long the spectacle of their young men dying—in numbing detail—on their television screens (fig. 10.20). The pictures did not need the shaken commentary of the frightened correspondents. The background effect of death was overwhelming. No evening of "Bonanza," "Ironside," or "The Dean Martin Show" (all part of the NBC lineup in 1968) could begin to dull the impact or manipulate the message of the live horror show from Vietnam.

10.20 David Burrington, NBC News correspondent in Vietnam. 1966.
Photo courtesy of the National Broadcasting Company, Inc.

10.21 Farewell to "M.A.S.H." *Newsweek* cover. Feb. 28, 1983.
Courtesy of *Newsweek* magazine.

10.22 Salvador Dali.
Apparition of a Face and Fruit Dish on a Beach. 1938.
Oil on canvas, 3′7½″ × 4′9″.
Courtesy of Wadsworth Atheneum, Hartford.

10.20

10.21

The Tet offensive had been planned from the beginning as a video event, as an image to turn off the war in American homes. The ritual pattern of the news show had been broken—no order followed the initial chaos, and no amount of personality could make the news bearable.

Seven years later Americans watched the final chapter of the war: Americans and South Vietnamese clinging to the skids of helicopters lifting off from the American embassy as Saigon opened the gates to the Vietcong and the North Vietnamese.

Besides dramatizing the principle of feedback, the Vietnam War illustrates the principle that fiction tends toward fact. "M.A.S.H." (fig. 10.21), despite its setting in Korea in the early fifties, met with unparalleled public acceptance because of the public's perception of the absurdity of the Vietnam War—a perception in turn based on the images seen on television.

Another important example of feedback occurred later in 1968 at the Democratic National Convention in Chicago.

Feedback in Chicago: Commercials for the Revolution

The Democratic convention came at the end of a period of political violence that had included the assassinations of Martin Luther King, Jr., and Robert Kennedy. Along with the convention proceedings, Americans watched violence in the streets as police and demonstrators clashed outside. This was feedback—the battles had been planned as video events. Abbie Hoffman led the Yippies! and other antiwar groups into the streets in order to appear on television. He later wrote a book about the plan, *Revolution for the Hell of It*.

Hoffman explained what went on in Chicago by referring to a painting by Salvador Dali, *Apparition of a Face and Fruit Dish on a Beach* (fig. 10.22). Just as Dali manipulates the viewer's perception among competing images of a face, a dog, and a still life, Hoffman and the Yippies! manipulated the television images of the convention so that the real message of the event was not what the Democratic party had planned: "Support the war and business as usual." Their message, made into a slogan for easy consumption, was "End the war and dump the Hump" (Hubert Humphrey, the Democratic presidential nominee).

Thus, as in Dali's painting, the background switched to the foreground with disconcerting results—for the convention sponsors. Hoffman described the Yippie! strategy in terms of normal network programming:

10.22

> Our actions in Chicago established a brilliant figure-ground relationship. The rhetoric of the convention was allotted the fifty minutes of the hour, we were given the ten or less usually reserved for the commercials. We were the advertisement for revolution. Watching the convention play out its boring drama, one could not help but be conscious of the revolution being played out in the streets.[7]

As Salvador Dali once said, "The only difference between me and a madman is that I'm not mad."

Feedback, though infrequent, is a potentially devastating element unique to the television image. In a more recent example Iranians held Americans hostage. This event took the course it did only because the Iranians saw the advantage in having daily television publicity for their revolution. The spectacle of Americans held hostage by Iranian revolutionaries became a daily drama played on worldwide television for over a year. Without the television cameras, it would have been an almost meaningless event.

10.23

The 1985 Beirut hostage crisis was a more recent example of feedback. American television coverage was a major objective of the incident. Despite the tragedy of a murdered American sailor, the situation eventually took on the shrewdly calculated format of a global talk show, sponsored and hosted by constantly smiling Amal militia.

A fiction-follows-fact example of feedback is "Special Bulletin" (fig. 10.23), a superb television drama produced for NBC by Don Ohlmeyer in 1983. "Special Bulletin" was based on a terrorist attempt to use feedback in a plan to force a move toward nuclear disarmament. The terrorists demanded a live feed on network television to address the American people about their objectives; their threat was to trigger a nuclear device that would destroy Charleston, South Carolina. As in the hostage crises cited above, the real effort of the terrorists was to seize the background of the television image from the networks and use it for their own ideological drama.

The Impact of Television: New Forms for the Popular Arts

Television has not just created its own audience and its own "space" within the mass media; its presence has altered the form and content of all other mass media art forms. Radio used to produce prime-time variety shows and dramas. Today radio plays music, news blips, and commercials.

Movies used to provide general entertainment that supported basic cultural myths for mass audiences. Today's Hollywood movies, except for a small number of high-tech and/or big-name productions, aim at specialized audiences, which has opened up to filmmakers a far wider range of themes and approaches. The last decade has also seen a dramatic increase in movies made *for* the networks. Steven Spielberg is an important director who first won acclaim for a 1972 movie made for television, *Duel*.

Magazines used to provide the major perspective images of news and human interest. Under the impact of television, *Life*'s global pictures and pinups were displaced by innumerable magazines, each appealing to a specialized audience. *People* is a kind of pictorialized gossip version of *Life* itself. *Playboy* (fig. 10.24), symbolized by the centerfold, achieved dramatic success with its soft-focused view of a world of eroticized commodities available to image-conscious male consumers. *Cosmopolitan* and *Ms.* reflect segments of the highly specialized women's audience. Perhaps the most spectacular examples of specialized magazines geared to narrow audiences are the scores of computer magazines now overwhelming the racks at bookstores and newsstands.

Television thus did not replace the popular art forms that had provided the dominant icons of the Film Age. Forced to take on more specialized formats, these popular arts have extended their reach and increased their profitability.

10.24

Television, having caused such drastic changes in other mass media art forms, has begun to feel the urgency for change in its own structure; it is at the beginning of a period of change that could transform its role in society as drastically as its own appearance affected the other media.

Television beyond the Networks: Toward Video Democracy, or Video Segregation?

The key adjective throughout this chapter has been the word *network. Network* television implies two concepts that, until the early 1980s, were for all practical purposes unchallenged and seemingly unchangeable: *network* implied both "national" and "free." Network television wired all geographic sections and all economic levels of America to the same core programming of news, sports, prime-time entertainment, and—as Chapter 12 will discuss—advertising. From the 1950s through the 1970s, network television provided a system of icons as well as the general picture of the world to an almost seamless community of viewers.

In the late 1970s, extending into the early 1980s, however, network television's "seamless" audience began to—as the networks describe it—erode. From 1978 until 1983, the three networks lost over 10 percent of the national television audience—even though because of population growth, the number of people watching network television has not diminished. Nevertheless, network television has begun to meet its first challenge since it began to enter American homes after World War II. The challenge is coming from two sources: access to alternative programming sources through cable, and changes in video programming resulting from increased personal ownership of videocassette recorders, or VCRs.

Cable television has multiplied access to nonnetwork programming to over 60 percent of American homes, bringing specialized stations like the all-news network based in Atlanta, CNN (fig. 10.25). CNN does not have superstar anchorpersons. CNN prides itself on covering events that the networks, because of their profitable daytime soap operas, will not cover. One such event was the trial of CBS's "Sixty Minutes" libel suit (fig. 10.26). In 1984, only CNN covered both the Republican and the Democratic national conventions from gavel to gavel.

MTV, the 24-hour music channel launched in 1981, is another specialized channel available by cable. It draws a huge youthful audience with its visual dramatizations of recorded and taped music. MTV has produced one of television's own art forms, the "video," which already has its own classics, including Michael Jackson's "Thriller" (1983), Culture Club's "War Song" (1984), and Dire Straits's "Money for Nothin'" (1985). Videos have in turn influenced Hollywood movies and network television. *Flashdance* is a 1983 movie hit with a strong video style. NBC inaugurated a television

10.23 "Special Bulletin" (David Clennon and David Rasche). Rebroadcast Nov. 1984.
Photo courtesy of the National Broadcasting Company, Inc.

10.24 *Playboy* cover. Sept. 1983.
Reproduced by Special Permission of PLAYBOY magazine, Photography by Steve Wayda. Copyright 1983 by PLAYBOY.

10.25 Photo courtesy of Turner Broadcasting System, Inc.

10.26 CNN coverage of Dan Rather/"Sixty Minutes" trial. 1983.
Photo courtesy of Turner Broadcasting System, Inc.

10.25

10.26

series, "Miami Vice," whose video style has attracted the young audience being visually educated by MTV.

Videos have been widely criticized for their overemphasis on sex and violence. This criticism apparently led MTV to cut three-fourths of its heavy metal video programming in 1985. Videos have also been criticized for implanting a visual formula that deprives the listener of his or her own fantasy response to the music. Since MTV is already available in over 40 percent of American homes and attracts many viewers who do not watch network television, it is an important development in American mass media popular art (the impact of videos on avant-garde art will be discussed in Chapter 13). As an art form, the videos featured on MTV fall somewhere between commercials and feature films; in fact, many directors of commercials and films have also directed videos. The rock video is, in this sense, an example of the influence of the television commercial on American culture.

The final crack in the monopoly of network broadcasting is the VCR; sales skyrocketed in the early 1980s. The VCR enables its owner to program his or her own video entertainment schedule. This independence in television viewing offered by the VCR will be discussed again in Chapter 13 in terms of its potential effect on avant-garde video.

When the viewing time for cable and self-programmed VCRs is added to network viewing time, it is clear that America is watching more television in the 1980s, not less.

The world is also watching more television, with increasing possibilities for simultaneous global video events. The 1984 Olympics and the 1985 Live Aid broadcast showed the new potential provided by satellite communication networks. Michael Mitchell, who supervised the media formats of both the Olympics and Live Aid, claims that these events are just the beginning of television's global impact. He is planning, with backing from the United Nations, a live 24-hour broadcast in which all ninety-seven nations with satellite uplinks will participate. The media, says Mitchell, provide the ". . . only tool that has the ability to create a non-threatening, non-boundary-producing sense of family."[8]

The Television Age: New Forms and New Opportunities for the Avant-Garde

This chapter has outlined some of the ways in which television, by its powerful influence on our picture of the world and of ourselves, produces a "television" culture. Television cannot be seen as just another perspective machine whose images take their place alongside more traditional ones; it has displaced and altered all previous Western art forms. The next chapter will discuss the role of avant-garde art in the Television Age.

CHAPTER ELEVEN

THE

TELEVISION AGE II:

COMPLETING THE AGENDA

OF MODERNISM

ASSESSMENTS

1. What is implied in the statement "I want to express my feelings instead of illustrating them"? What kinds of colors, lines, and shapes would you choose to draw the emotions of love, anger, sadness, hope, joy?
2. Can you imagine yourself being inside one of the paintings in the following pages? Do you respond to the idea of being "inside" the painting rather than "outside" of it?
3. How might the scraps of paper in your purse or pocket—or the glove compartment of your car—become elements in a painting or collage?
4. What are optical illusions? How might optical illusions become art?
5. Recall your experience with comic strips. Which were your favorites? Did comics contribute to the formulation of your personal and social values? Do you still read or collect comics?

274

Roy Lichtenstein's *Little Big Painting* (fig. 11.1) graphically summarizes the position of American art in the Television Age. Though not without its critics, American art is at the global center of both mass media (fig. 11.2) and avant-garde art. Lichtenstein's painting transforms the gestural brush stroke symbolizing America's first postwar art movement, Abstract Expressionism, into an image suggesting both a triumphal flag and a comic book emblem. His painting accurately projects the historical importance of Abstract Expressionism, as well as the mass media's powerful tendency either to absorb other forms of art or to force them into its own terms.

11.1

11.2

This chapter will discuss the development of American avant-garde art from its postwar beginnings until the early 1970s. At that point the influence of the mass media and the very success of avant-garde art created a unique set of problems that inaugurated a distinctive new phase of the avant-garde. The development of the avant-garde art from the early seventies to the present will then be discussed in Chapter 13.

The art movement that ushered in the postwar triumph of American art, Abstract Expressionism, is most closely associated with an artist named Jackson Pollock.

The Avant-Garde in America: Jackson Pollock (1912–1956)

Jackson Pollock, as he liked to remind people, was born "out West" in Cody, Wyoming. Although he grew up in a family that was torn apart by the Great Depression, his strong-willed mother managed to keep her five children together despite the family's incessant drift from one temporary location to another. Eventually they settled in Los Angeles long enough for Pollock, regardless of frequent conflicts with teachers and administrators, to graduate from high school.

In 1930, Pollock moved to New York's bohemian Greenwich Village. He studied at the Art Students' League under Thomas Hart Benton, whose paintings of rural American folklore echoed Pollock's own strong populist sentiments.

Pollock was also interested in radical political ideas and painting based on social consciousness. During the thirties he was especially impressed by the works of the great Mexi-

11.3

11.1 Roy Lichtenstein.
Little Big Painting. 1965.
Oil on canvas, 68″ × 80″.
Collection of Whitney Museum of American Art, Gift of the Friends of the Whitney Museum of American Art, New York.

11.2 "What the World Thinks of America."
Newsweek cover. July 11, 1983.
Photo courtesy of *Newsweek*.

11.3 José Clemente Orozco.
Hispano-America, from the murals *Quetzalcoatl and the Sopiratims of Mantina.* 1932–34.
Hood Museum, Dartmouth College.

can artist, José Clemente Orozco (1883–1949), who had become internationally known for his murals depicting the Mexican revolution. Orozco came to the United States in the thirties and painted a series of murals at Dartmouth College in New Hampshire, dealing with his favorite theme, the poor triumphing over institutionalized injustice. Figure 11.3 shows a section of the Dartmouth mural titled *Hispano-America.*

Pollock's most important encounter in the thirties, however, was with his own alcoholism. He was hospitalized several times, including one period of voluntary commitment. By 1939, he was desperate. As he struggled to avoid continuing deterioration, he became increasingly drawn to the more inner-directed art of Surrealism. Breton and other Surrealists were in New York at this time, having fled Hitler, and Pollock had become familiar with their ideas as well as their art.

In 1939 Pollock decided to undergo psychotherapy under the direction of Dr. Joseph Henderson. During the year of therapy, Dr. Henderson encouraged Pollock to express his feelings as directly as possible in quick, spontaneous drawings. This process of direct drawing based on intense feeling not only helped heal Pollock's inner confusion but also enabled him to transform Surrealism into his own highly personal style.

276

From Therapy to Art: Private Rituals Become Public Myth

The first phase of Pollock's paintings from the early forties reflects the highly figurative and symbolic imagery uncovered by his drawings during therapy. *The She-Wolf* (fig. 11.4) at first looks like a field of scrambled calligraphy or graffiti. The title, however, helps the viewer discover the she-wolf figure, outlined in strong black and white lines, that faces to the left and dominates the entire width of the painting. Like other paintings of this period, the image is built on an interplay between a partly veiled image that emerges from weaving lines moving through fields of solid color.

11.4 Jackson Pollock.
The She-Wolf. 1943.
Oil, gouache, and plaster on canvas,
41⅞″ × 67″.
Museum of Modern Art, New York,
Purchase.

11.5 Jackson Pollock.
Number 27, 1950.
Oil on canvas, 49″ × 106″.
Collection of Whitney Museum of
American Art, New York. Purchase.

11.4

This kind of highly personal, partly veiled imagery gradually gave way in the late forties to Pollock's unique form of abstraction: Abstract Expressionism, or Action Painting. These paintings are so intimately connected with the process of painting them that the process itself must be described with as much detail as the paintings.

Pollock's "Action Paintings": Dancing Out the Inner Man

Pollock's technique for producing his Action Paintings reveals an ingenious adaptation of elements that range from the abstract work of Kandinsky and Navaho sand-painting to, more obviously, psychotherapy and Surrealism.

Pollock approached painting with the movement of his whole body instead of just his eye and hand. He abandoned the paintbrush and stretched canvas. Using various kinds of paint, including enamel, he either poured them out or dripped them from a stick as he moved across the huge canvases stretched out on the floor of his studio. In a way, he danced his paintings into existence.

On the floor I am more at ease. I feel nearer, more a part of the painting, since this way I can walk around it, working from the four sides, and literally be in the painting.[1]

Though related to the ritualized painting of native American art, Pollock's approach was totally personal and subjective. It involved drawing forth his own inner myth instead of a public, community myth like that of the Navaho or other native cultures.

Pollock was also unlike native American artists (as well as most Western artists throughout history) in that he had no preconceived image when he began his painting ritual.

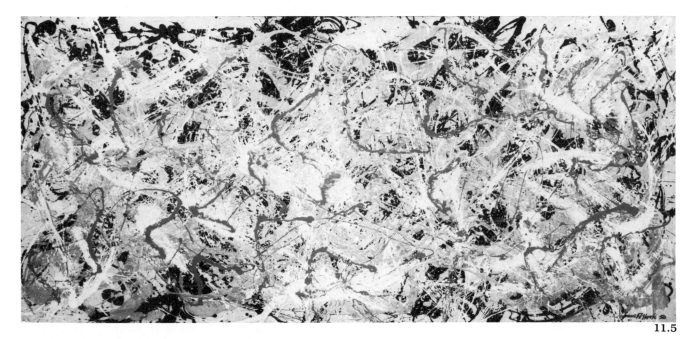

11.5

As he had done with the drawings for Dr. Henderson, Pollock wanted to "express his feelings rather than illustrate them." He wanted to discover the look and the meaning of the painting only after he had produced it. The following description of Breton's "automatic writing" comes close to describing Pollock's approach, if the word *painting* is substituted for *monologue* and *executed* for *spoken:* Automatism is . . . a monologue spoken as rapidly as possible without the intervention of the critical faculties.[2]

Two paintings from 1950 illustrate the results of Pollock's attempt to immerse himself directly in the painting process. *Number 27, 1950* (fig. 11.5), shows the kind of shallow space that Pollock's technique produced. The moving streams of yellow, black, red, and white enamels each appear to flow on top of each other. Each thus creates a different spatial layer within the painting. The effect is of a very thin or shallow space filled with brilliant energy, color, and form.

The paradoxical quality of Pollock's "drip paintings" is that they capture a sense of change or motion itself as their main subject matter.

A second painting from 1950, *Number 1, 1950 (Lavender Mist)* (fig. 11.6 and color plate 25), is almost seven by ten feet. Even though it too is formed by the dripping and pouring technique, it is quite different from *Number 27, 1950*. The lines are leaner and form a more complex pattern. As the title implies, an opening appears to be forming in the middle of the painting, like the center of a cloud that is about to dissolve and reveal the space behind it. Both of these paintings resemble the late water lily paintings of Monet in their visual richness and monumental scale. Unlike Monet's paintings, Pollock's works seem to dip just below the threshold of ordinary perception to suggest the pattern of energy underlying natural forms.

This quality of verging on a recognizable or natural image was important to Pollock. He insisted that his paintings had a connection to the real world. When a well-known artist remarked to Pollock at this time that he should do more drawing directly from nature, Pollock's reply was direct and simple: "I am nature."[3]

If the artist is nature, what the artist paints from within himself or herself is already, to some degree, a picture of nature. The marks, lines, and drips, in other words, will take care of themselves. The nature that is visible in Pollock's paintings is nature glimpsed through the filter of his own

11.6 Jackson Pollock. *Number 1, 1950 (Lavender Mist).* Oil, enamel, and aluminum on canvas, 87″ × 118″. The National Gallery of Art, Washington, Ailsa Mellon Bruce Fund.

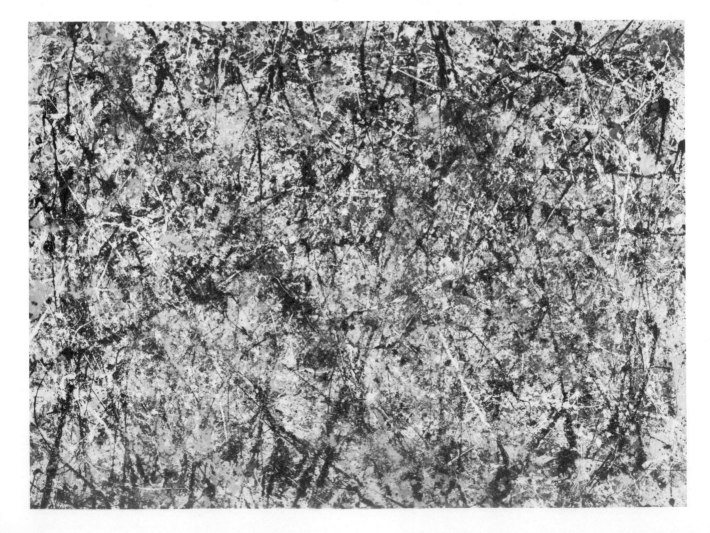

consciousness and personality. This is precisely what Zola said about Manet's work. Kandinsky, whose paintings Pollock had seen at New York's Guggenheim Museum in 1945, had also insisted that subjective abstraction produced a direct contact with nature. Pollock had thus produced another version of the subjective abstraction of the avant-garde tradition.

Pollock and the Mass Media: The Public Myth Destroys the Private Self

Jackson Pollock, however, was unable to keep the precarious grasp on his inner world represented by the vulnerable web-like patterns of his paintings. The avant-garde in the Television Age had become *news.* Pollock suddenly became a celebrity. The unraveling of his inner life began in 1948, when *Life* magazine installed him and his paintings in a three-page spread with color photographs under the headline "Jackson Pollock: Is He the Greatest Living Painter in the United States?"

This is the same *Life* magazine that only a decade earlier had lumped the "unrealities of modern art" alongside the "irrational bloodiness of war" and the "devious channels of politics" as the main scourges of modern life.

Other magazines and newspapers followed with a glare of publicity. Ironically, it was this publicity that apparently trapped Pollock in a mirror of his own creation: his own carefully projected public image. Pollock had been something of an outsider since high school, when he was expelled for fighting with a coach. From the time he arrived in New York, he had liked to swagger around bars; he had played the role of a kind of bohemian cowboy powered by a reputation for hard drinking and hard living (he once tried to demolish a friend's sculpture with his car). Pollock's image, in other words, was ready and waiting when the media discovered him.

Unfortunately, Pollock could not handle the tension between the greatly magnified public self in the media and his private self. The delicate balance he had worked out through therapy and a discipline he achieved through the support of his artist-wife, Lee Krassner, was destroyed, and his alcoholism returned. He died in an automobile accident in 1956. Pollock's public image apparently had become more powerful than his inner one.

Pollock's art, his readily available public image, and his tragic death have placed him as the most prominent symbol of Abstract Expressionism. Other artists, however, contributed to the energy and the depth that sustained Action Painting as an international avant-garde movement. Two other prominent Abstract Expressionist painters were Franz Kline and Willem de Kooning.

280

Abstract Expressionism: The Personal Abstractions of Franz Kline (1910–1962) and Willem de Kooning (1904—)

Franz Kline incorporated the influence of Japanese art in his painting style. He was strongly influenced by the work of Mark Tobey, an American artist who had studied Zen Buddhism in Japan. Kline's paintings had the size and directness of Pollock's. The massive strokes of black on white in his 1956 painting *Mahoning* (fig. 11.7) show how his austere linear imagery suggests a fusion of Zen spontaneity within the gigantic grid patterns and steel girders of the New York urban environment.

Another artist who developed a strong personal approach to Action Painting was Willem de Kooning, who was born in Holland but moved to the United States in 1926. De Kooning manipulated abstract shapes rather than the linear elements of Pollock and Kline. In the early fifties he began a series of paintings of women. In *Woman I* (fig. 11.8) a wide-eyed and garish woman's face breaks through the ambiguity of the painted surface with something of the fierceness of an exorcism or an alchemist's magic. The woman's face seems to be forcing itself to the surface of the paint. De Kooning's

11.7

struggle with the highly figurative female image within his work at times included torn bits of magazine photographs of women. In this sense, de Kooning was an artistic prophet. The next movement in American art involved a dramatic fusion of Abstract Expressionism with a return to clearly recognizable subject matter.

Robert Rauschenberg (1925—): The Subject Returns

The art of Jackson Pollock and other Abstract Expressionists was intensely personal and intensely private. It stood in absolute contrast to the constantly expanding postwar television, photograph, and advertising imagery of the mass media. Instead of instant recognition, it required intense personal involvement on the part of the viewer. Even though Abstract Expressionist painting made news and made painters into celebrities, even in newspaper and magazine photographs it challenged the viewer with its open-ended possibilities of meaning. There was no clear-cut message. Abstract Expressionism was about mystery, not clarity.

In the late 1950s, the work of Robert Rauschenberg, Jasper Johns, and other New York artists began to combine

11.8

11.7 Franz Kline.
Mahoning. 1956.
Oil on canvas, 80″ × 100″.
Collection of Whitney Museum of American Art, New York. Gift of the Friends of the Whitney Museum of American Art.

11.8 Willem de Kooning.
Woman I. 1952.
Oil on canvas, 6′3⅞″ × 58″.
Collection, Museum of Modern Art, New York, Purchase.

abstraction with clearly defined subject matter, including three-dimensional objects. Rauschenberg began to make art out of discarded fragments and pieces of the urban environment itself. He called his works "combine/paintings."

His first major combine/painting was a full-size bed on whose surface Rauschenberg added a layer of flung and dripped paint. This Pollock-like surface was a mildly irreverent reference to the notoriety that Abstract Expressionism had achieved by the late fifties. Instead of using abstraction to create a unique object, Rauschenberg used abstraction—which had become a standardized cliché through the mass media—to draw attention to the uniqueness of manufactured items already in the environment. Rauschenberg thus used a new stereotype created by the mass media (the familiarity of Abstract Expressionism) to salvage an old stereotyped object—a mass-produced bed.

The new source for Rauschenberg's art was not the "nature within" of Abstract Expressionism, but whatever was going on outside his New York window:

I actually had a kind of house rule. If I walked completely around the block and didn't find enough to work with, I could take one other block and walk around it—but that was it. The works had to look at least as interesting as anything that was going on outside the window.[4]

Jasper Johns's *Target with Four Faces* (fig. 11.9) combines plaster faces, a wooden box, and the thickly painted surface of a target into a work that also combines found objects and the touch of Abstract Expressionist brushwork.

In the sixties, however, Rauschenberg's art moved from contact with the physical man-made environment to the world of television. In 1962, he described his reaction to television this way:

I was bombarded with TV sets and magazines by the refuse, by the excess of the world. . . . I thought that if I could paint or make an honest work, it should incorporate all of these elements, which were and are a reality.[5]

Retroactive I (fig. 11.10) combines the kind of images that make up the mass media environment. The replay and retrieval cycle of the mass media in the Television Age keeps such images familiar to a wide public. Besides a strong debt to synthetic Cubism and the collages of Ernst, these works also continue the tradition of American realism, which produced remarkable still lifes as well as the landscapes discussed in Chapter 8. A comparison of Rauschenberg's *Retroactive I* and John Frederick Peto's 1894 painting *Card Rack with Jack of Hearts* (fig. 11.11) indicates the difference between the density of the image environments of the nineteenth century and postwar America.

Shortly after Rauschenberg began to receive attention for his object/combines and his found-image paintings,

11.9 Jasper Johns.
Target with Four Faces. 1955.
Encaustic on newspaper over canvas, 26″ × 26″, surmounted by four tinted plaster faces in wood box with hinged front. Box, closed, 3¾″ × 26″ × 3½″.
Collection, Museum of Modern Art, New York, Gift of Mr. and Mrs. Robert C. Scull.

11.10 Robert Rauschenberg.
Retroactive I. 1969.
Silkscreen, 96″ × 72″.
Courtesy of Wadsworth Atheneum, Hartford. Photographer: Joseph Szaszfai.

11.11 John Frederick Peto.
Card Rack with Jack of Hearts.
c. 1894.
Oil on canvas, 30″ × 25″.
Cleveland Museum of Art, Purchase from the J. H. Wade Fund.

11.9

11.10

avant-garde art embraced the mass media as the main subject matter, in the movement known as Pop Art.

Pop Art: The Avant-Garde Embraces
the Mass Media

Even though the first Pop Art images are generally credited
to British artists in the late 1950s, the movement achieved
international prominence in an exhibit entitled "The New
Realism" at the Sidney Janis Gallery in New York in 1962.
Artists like Rauschenberg and Jasper Johns had already
used mass media images and familiar symbols like flags (fig.
11.12) and targets as basic forms to which they applied the
tactile, personalizing patina of Abstract Expressionism.
Their art resided in a kind of halfway space between the
avant-garde and mass-produced art and objects.

11.11

11.12

11.12 Jasper Johns.
Three Flags. 1958.
Encaustic on canvas, 30⅞″ × 45½″
× 5″.
Collection of Whitney Museum of
American Art, New York, 50th Anniversary
gift of the Gilman Foundation, Inc., the
Lauder Foundation, A. Alfred Taubman, an
anonymous donor, (and purchase).

11.13 Andy Warhol.
Marilyn Monroe. 1962.
Acrylic and silkscreen on canvas,
81″ × 66¾″.
Photo courtesy of Leo Castelli Gallery, New
York.

11.14 Andy Warhol.
Liz Taylor. 1964.
Lithograph, 21⁵⁄₁₆″ × 21⁵⁄₁₆″.
Cleveland Museum of Art, Gift of Mr. and
Mrs. Henry Steinberg in memory of
Katherine C. White.

11.15 Andy Warhol.
100 Soup Cans. 1962.
Casein on canvas, 72″ × 52″.
Photo courtesy of Leo Castelli Gallery, New
York.

11.16 Andy Warhol.
Chairman Mao. 1975.
Oil on canvas, 26″ × 22″.
Collection of Whitney Museum of
American Art, New York, Gift of Mr. and
Mrs. Peter M. Brandt.

11.17 Andy Warhol.
Nineteen Cents. 1960.
Oil on canvas, 71¾″ × 53¾″.
Photo courtesy of Leo Castelli Gallery, New
York.

Pop Art closed the gap between the mass-produced image and art. Pop Art transferred the mass media image,
sometimes without even a change of clothes, directly into
the gallery and the museum. This approach is particularly
clear in the work—and the career—of Andy Warhol.

Andy Warhol (1930—): Celebrities as Commodities, Commodities as Celebrities

Warhol's art reflects his interest in the processes of the mass
media as well as its imagery. He was a successful commercial artist in New York before his fine-art gallery debut, an
exhibition of drawings of shoes "customized" to reflect personalities of celebrities like Jackie Kennedy and Mae West.
This first exhibition embodied one of the continuing themes
of Warhol's work: the process by which the mass media
turns the celebrity into a kind of commodity.

Warhol used commercial printing processes like silkscreening, in which ink is forced through a fabric or screen
by pulling a squeegee across its surface (see Appendix A).
Paper or other material is used as a stencil under the screen.
This process is commonly used to make the bold signs in
store windows and supermarkets.

Warhol used the silk-screen technique to make portraits of celebrities. The flat colors and the multiple images he obtained with this stencil method of applying ink or paint gave the faces of *Marilyn Monroe* (fig. 11.13) the mass-produced quality that is part of the celebrity image. When Warhol produced the lithographic portrait of Elizabeth Taylor (fig. 11.14), he deposited the mascara and lipstick in the impersonal style of the silkscreen process used for *Marilyn Monroe*. In these paintings and prints of celebrities, the public image seems about to slide off the person's face—like a label that is coming unstuck. Warhol's work compares the celebrity's image to the same production processes that produce *100 Soup Cans* (fig. 11.15).

This also explains why both Chairman Mao (fig. 11.16) and a can of beef noodle soup (fig. 11.17) are subjects for paintings: they are both celebrities (and, reproduced in the media, they are both commodities). These two paintings also illustrate Warhol's attitude toward individuality, one of the traditional values associated with avant-garde art since Courbet:

Everybody looks alike and acts alike and we're getting more and more that way.

I think everybody should be a machine.
I think everybody should like everybody.[6]

In Warhol's view, objects, images, and people all aspire to the ultimate and equivalent reality of being a celebrity. He once commented that he hoped our society would eventually reach a point where "everyone would be famous for fifteen minutes." Everyone would then be a celebrity and, presumably, happy.

In the meantime, his art continued to show how easy and how accessible celebrity status, and art, could be. *Do It Yourself* (fig. 11.18) is self-explanatory. Warhol stood by his principles, since he often allowed friends who drifted into his studio (The Factory) to color in sections of his paintings.

Warhol not only recycled images of celebrities and celebrity-objects from the mass media, he also created his own celebrities. He made his own movies and his own movie stars. Unlike Jackson Pollock, Warhol knew the mass media well enough to manipulate it for his own ends. Once he him-

11.13

11.14

11.15

11.16

11.17

11.18

self became famous, his eye could make others famous. People, things, and their interactions became celebrities because Warhol pointed his camera at them. Edie Sedgewick, Ultraviolet, and Valeria Solano all appeared in Warhol's films, and by doing so, became celebrities—at least for the required fifteen minutes. Warhol also experienced some of the anguish of media fame. One of his superstars, Valeria Solano, shot and seriously wounded him on the same day in 1968 that Robert Kennedy was assassinated. Warhol survived.

Warhol's films, besides elevating ordinary people to celebrity status, tended to downgrade established celebrities. His film *Empire State Building* showed the Empire State Building from the viewpoint of a single stationary camera for eight hours. Unlike Monet's discovery of splendor in the ordinary existence of Rouen cathedral through the normal cycle of light and time, *Empire State Building* simply recorded what happened in front of the deadpan eye of the camera. For the viewer, boredom eventually made incidents like lights going on in windows or pigeons flying from window sills into highly dramatic events. Another film, *Haircut*, consisted of thirty-three minutes of footage of a friend getting a haircut.

Warhol's sometimes bludgeonlike emphasis on mass media processes inevitably makes the viewer more conscious of media processes and the power of media images. Warhol's work is both cynically humorous and starkly realistic in its reflection of how the mass media—especially television—tend to reduce everything to equal importance and thereby mash perception into a kind of pulp. Television switches from Wimbledon to "Celebrity Bowling," after a thirty-second drama about a couple who have lost their travelers' checks. It switches from agonizing scenes of starvation in Africa to a commercial for a soft drink that ends with the jingle "You can't pinch an inch!" Warhol's silk-screened paintings of automobile wrecks, the electric chair (fig. 11.19), and other disasters therefore make a cruel kind of sense. They are lifted, like Liz Taylor and the soup cans, from the same source: the newspaper, the television set, the magazine. We see them there every day.

11.18 Andy Warhol.
Do It Yourself. 1962.
Liquitex on canvas, 72″ × 54″.
Photo courtesy of Leo Castelli Gallery, New York.

11.19 Andy Warhol.
Electric Chair. 1967.
Acrylic and silkscreen enamel on canvas, 54″ × 73″.
Photo courtesy of Leo Castelli Gallery, New York.

11.20 Roy Lichtenstein.
Cubist Still Life. 1974.
Oil and magna on canvas, 90″ × 68⅛″.
National Gallery of Art, Washington, Lila Acheson Wallace Fund.

11.21 Roy Lichtenstein.
Self-Portrait. 1978.
Oil and magna on canvas, 70″ × 54″.
Photo courtesy of Leo Castelli Gallery, New York.

11.19

Warhol's blatant and caustic realism illuminates this process, even though he accepts it without any visible emotional connection or personal judgment. The mass media, to Warhol, is all we have, life *is* public relations: "I am everything my scrapbook says I am."[7]

As the art historian Lucy Lippard has commented:

Warhol . . . refuses to comment, and aligns himself with the spectator who looks on the horrors of modern life as he would look at a TV film, without involvement, without more than slight irritation at the interruption by a commercial. . . . In this respect Warhol is true to the attitudes of our technological society.[8]

Roy Lichtenstein (1923—): Avant-Garde Art as "Newspeak"

Roy Lichtenstein, another Pop artist, extended Warhol's perception of celebrities and commodities to avant-garde works themselves. Impressionism (fig. i.4), Cubism (fig. 11.20 and plate 26), and Action Painting (fig. 11.1) are shown as either halftone dot photographs or as comic stereotypes reproduced in the gallery of the mass media. These paintings illustrate what Lichtenstein calls the *industrialization* of art. The original art object, once it is pumped into the mass media, becomes yet another stereotype or cliché among all the others.

If the viewer ever does see the original art object, it is seen through the masks and labels already provided by the media. Art reproductions in books and magazines make us all like tourists visiting famous places: if we eventually have the opportunity, we cannot help comparing the original to the photograph. The impact of Lichtenstein's art is verified by anyone who has approached a famous painting like Leonardo's *Mona Lisa* (fig. 3.29) in the Louvre. One is forced to elbow through a bustling crowd armed with headsets and cameras only to find the art object cloistered in a vault protected by thick glass. As Warhol has already implied, what the viewer really sees is not so much an art object as yet another celebrity.

Pollock's life exemplified the new difficulty of the artist as celebrity; Lichtenstein suggests that the art object in the Television Age has a similar problem. By the late 1960s the mass media had welcomed and begun to absorb the avant-garde as part of its own appetite for entertainment, news, and celebrities. How can the individual art object, which has traditionally represented the individuality of the artist, have any real meaning if it is multiplied indefinitely in the mass media? The viewer's mind can easily become, as Lichtenstein's *Self-Portrait* (fig. 11.21) candidly illustrates, a kind of mirror reflecting clichés that have all the familiarity of a famous brand name or label.

Warhol and Lichtenstein are especially important because their art vividly illustrates what is true for all avant-

11.20

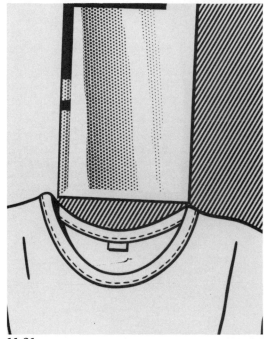

11.21

11.22

garde art in one way or another. Nevertheless, other artists have used the mass media and mass-produced products as the means for creating far more personal statements.

Claes Oldenburg, for example, has a unique gift for viewing everyday objects with an almost sensuously creative vision. To him, objects are extensions of the human beings who first imagined and then produced them. Oldenburg takes the dream a step further: an ordinary clothespin becomes a 45-foot steel sculpture in Philadelphia; a giant three-way electrical plug greets visitors to the St. Louis art museum; three ascending yellow-painted steel hats preside over a park in the California town of Salinas. Figure 11.22 shows Oldenburg's rendering for a cathedral in the form of a faucet. Oldenburg's art attempts to restore a sense of individuality, mirth, and celebration to America's involvement with, and devotion to, things: "I'd like to turn people on to the fact that the world is form, not just function and money."[9]

Another Pop artist who uses mass-media imagery for her own personal statements is Corita Kent. During the 1960s she produced silk screen prints that subverted mass-media clichés into traditional religious meanings. In 1984, she chose a billboard format for her statement "We can live without war" (fig. 11.23). In this case, the mass-media format became the perfect medium for the message.

After Pop Art: Painting Completes Its Language of Abstraction and Realism

During the early 1960s, American art fairly exploded with painting styles based on the precedents of Abstract Expressionism and Pop Art. Abstract art passed through objective styles called Minimal Art and Op Art. Pop Art's emphasis on subject matter was followed by the photographic style of Photo-Realism.

Minimal Art and Op Art: What You See Is What You Get

Whatever their differences, the common theme of all Pop artists was a heightened perception of mass media images and processes. The Minimal and Op Art movements created paintings that constricted attention to the painting surface as a self-contained entity. Minimal Art turned the painting into a self-defining object of artistic form. Op Art toyed with the perceptual illusions that can result from human perceptual processes. Both movements created abstract works that did not depend on any subject matter outside the painting. Unlike Abstract Expressionism, they seemed to have little to do with the artist's subjective feelings.

Frank Stella is one of the pioneers of Minimal Art. His work began in the early sixties with sets of paintings whose

11.22 Claes Oldenburg.
Proposal for a Cathedral in the Form of a Colossal Faucet, Lake Union, Seattle. 1972.
Pencil, colored pencil, and watercolor, 28¹⁵/₁₆″ × 22⅞″.
Collection of Whitney Museum of American Art, New York, Gift of Knoll International (and purchase).

11.23 Corita Kent.
We Can Live Without War. 1985.
Billboard on Highway 1, Morro Bay, Calif.
Photo: Mary Hall-Pelfrey.

11.24 Frank Stella.
Gran Cairo. 1962.
Synthetic polymer, 85½″ × 85½″.
Collection of Whitney Museum of American Art, New York, Gift of the Friends of the Whitney Museum of American Art.

11.25 Frank Stella.
Sanbornville III. 1966.
Flourescent alkyd and epoxy paint on canvas, 104″ × 146″.
Collection of Whitney Museum of American Art, New York, Promised and Partial Gift of Joseph A. Helman, New York.

11.26 Frank Stella.
Agbatana I. 1968.
Synthetic polymer on canvas, 120″ × 180″.
Collection of Whitney Museum of American Art, New York, Gift of Mr. and Mrs. Oscar Kolin.

11.23

11.24

linear patterns reflected the shape of the canvas itself. The interior squares of *Gran Cairo* (fig. 11.24) step symmetrically to the painting's center. *Sanbornville III* (fig. 11.25) is a later work over ten feet wide. Its asymmetrical outer shape is defined by the interior triangles and parallelograms formed by large color bands.

By 1968 Stella's painting had expanded to an even larger scale. *Agbatana I* (fig. 11.26 and plate 27) is one of a series of giant paintings whose rounded shapes contained arching bands of striking colors that loop and thread through each other in a sporting, lyrical dance of fascinating precision.

These works are brilliant examples of paintings conceived as self-contained objects referring to nothing beyond

11.25

11.26

290

themselves. Stella summarized the intent of his paintings this way:

My painting is based on the fact that only what can be seen there is there. It really is an object. . . . All I want anyone to get out of my paintings, and all that I ever get out of them, is the fact that you can see the whole idea without any confusion. . . . What you see is what you get.[10]

This degree of objectivity was new to Western abstract art. Picasso left clues to the material world. Kandinsky's abstraction referred to his own "spiritual states." The material honesty of Constructivist abstraction reflected the objectivity of science and the new order of the Russian Revolution. Just as Warhol's art virtually merged with the mass media, Stella's art took painting to an extreme degree of pure language and pure detachment. An art based on such a pure reference only to itself is also a definite break with one of the basic themes of Western art, one that goes back to ancient Greece: "Man is the measure of all things." Stella's paintings measure only themselves. They are brilliant icons of the technological mentality, which tends to reduce all phases of life to a series of self-contained problems that have their own independent solution.

Op Art: Exploring the Uncertainty of Seeing

Op Art developed in the 1960s as part of the same intense interest in visual objectivity seen in Stella's pursuit of the painting as a pure object. Op Art, however, was not as "pure" as Stella's work—Op imagery implied the perceptual presence of the human eye. Bridget Riley's *Balm* (fig. 11.27) is an

11.27

almost eight-foot-square painting that deliberately teases the observing eye into seeing its dotted surface as simultaneously curved and flat. Both the shapes and the colors challenge the eye to become aware of its own processes, and to enjoy the experience. The self-consciousness of the eye's perceptual processes give Op Art a connection with the paintings of Seurat. In one sense, they look like gigantic enlargements of small sections of his carefully plotted canvases.

Another well-known French Op artist, Victor de Vasarely (fig. 11.28), bases the perceptual variations of his images on his own mathematical systems of relating colors and shapes. One of Vasarely's image formulas was once programmed into a computer, which printed out an incredible number of minutely varied designs. Vaserely looks forward to the time when "painting machines" will take over the production of art entirely.

Minimal Art and Op Art took abstraction to the limits of the self-contained art object. During the early seventies, another art movement, Photo-Realism, explored the objective limits of representational art by returning painting to one of the original sources of the nineteenth-century avant-garde, the photograph.

Photo-Realism: Processing Photographic Information into Art

Photo-Realist artists use a variety of approaches to their photographic sources. Chuck Close, for instance, makes paintings from photographs of his friends' faces. He began his career by painting in the Abstract Expressionist style and

11.27 Bridget Riley .
Balm. 1964.
Oil on canvas, 76¾" × 76¾".
National Gallery of Art, Washington, Gift of Mr. and Mrs. Burton Tremaine.

11.28 Victor de Vasarely.
Kalota. 1963.
Oil on canvas, 200 × 109.9 cm.
St. Louis Art Museum, Funds given by Henry B. Pflager and the Schoenberg Foundation.

11.28

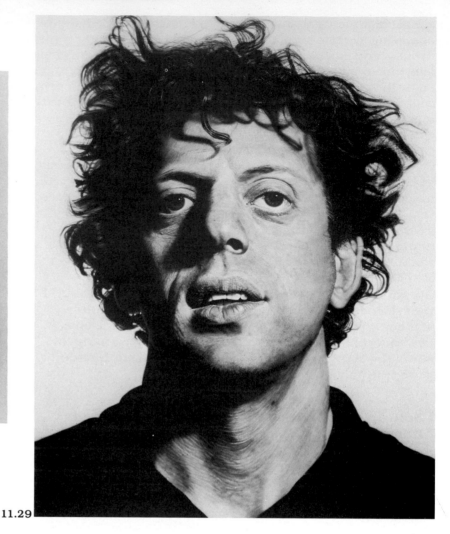

11.30

11.29

turned to Photo-Realism in a deliberate attempt to eliminate what he called "art marks"—a kind of gesture or mark that would be recognized as personal to the artist.

Phil (fig. 11.29), Close's 1969 airbrushed painting, illustrates the results of this fastidious process. Paintings like this one, which is over eight feet tall, take Close over a year to complete. The grid system originally drawn on the canvas to help redraw the photograph contains thousands of squares, each a tiny area where the painting process—with brush strokes or spray-painted dots—occurs.

By keeping the painting focused on the precise objective image in the photograph, Close found himself able to invent tiny innovative gestures within each grid section. His marks in each grid were nevertheless disciplined by having to add back up to a precise piece of cheek or hair to match the corresponding grid section in the photograph. In this way, whatever personality or signature that might be in the tiny marks making up the painting becomes absorbed into the overwhelming scale of the photographic image. Objectivity thus wins over subjectivity.

Phil/Fingerprint II (fig. 11.30) is a second portrait of the same person done nine years later. This time Close used pencil, a stamp pad, and his own fingerprints to create the image.

Audrey Flack (1931—) is a Photo-Realist artist who has based her paintings on photographic sources since the mid-sixties. By the seventies, her style had matured into a technique of incredible refinement achieved by spray-painting layers of primary colors onto still life images enlarged to a monumental scale. Flack's Photo-Realist images also have a unique emphasis on feeling. *World War II, April 1945* (fig. 11.31 and plate 28), for instance, is a still life centered on a photograph of a group of Jewish prisoners of war, based on a photograph by Margaret Bourke-White. The Star of David, the rose, and the candle are tributes to the dead. The book passage reads, "You can take everything from me—the pillow from under my head, my house—but you cannot take God from my heart."

The overripe pear and the clock, as in the realistic still life paintings from seventeenth-century Holland, are naturalistic symbols of mortality.

The Photo-Realist paintings of Richard Estes feature the city. *Ansonia* (fig. 11.32) was produced by his usual method, shooting several rolls of film of a given area of the city to use as a basis for his painting. He does not just copy the photograph, however:

The camera is like one eye and it really deals only with values. And painting is trickery, because you can make people respond by guiding their eyes around the picture. The photograph doesn't have ideas. It can only reproduce, so you have to use a lot of trickery.[11]

The black and white illustration of *Ansonia* shows how Estes guides your eye around the painting in a way that a straight photograph would not do. For instance, he painted the reflections in the window in darker values than a photograph would show, and they are also crisper and clearer than they would be in a photograph. Estes thus reinterprets the photograph to suit his own needs as a painter.

11.31

11.31 Audrey Flack.
World War II, April 1945. 1976–77.
Oil on canvas, 96″ × 96″.
Photo courtesy of Louis K. Meisel Gallery, New York. *WWII* by Audrey Flack incorporates a portion of the Margaret Bourke-White photograph *Buchenwald, 1945.* Copyright Time, Inc.

11.32 Richard Estes.
Ansonia. 1977.
Oil on canvas, 48″ × 60″.
Collection of the Whitney Museum of American Art, New York. Gift of Frances and Sydney Lewis.

11.32

Another remarkable example of using photographic sources without duplicating the camera is Jim Doolin's painting *Shopping Mall* (fig. 11.33 and plate 29). Doolin's painting took four years to complete. He took hundreds of photographs of people, cars, buildings, and other elements of the Santa Monica Mall. He then translated each photographic image into the space of a 7½-foot-square canvas in which each person is approximately an inch tall (fig. 11.34). The detail he achieves by using the photographic sources extends to a coat hanger being visible through the back window of a car.

Doolin's painting "guides the eye" even more than Estes's *Ansonia*. Despite the photographic look of the painting, it is not in photographic (linear) perspective; this is not how the mall would look from the air. Notice that the intersecting streets are parallel instead of converging. Doolin wanted all the figures in the painting to have equal detail and individu-

11.33 James Doolin.
Shopping Mall. 1973–77.
Oil on canvas, 90″ × 90″.
Courtesy of the artist.

11.34 James Doolin.
Detail of *Shopping Mall.*

11.33

ality. *Shopping Mall*—despite its dependency on photography—therefore returns to the kind of parallel perspective used in Oriental art and discussed in Chapter 3 in terms of Greek and Roman art.

Avant-Garde Art in the Seventies: The Dilemma of Success

By the early seventies, the success of avant-garde art had brought it to a qualitatively new position in society. It was inescapable that the mass media had accepted avant-garde art as news and entertainment. As the career of Andy Warhol illustrates, the avant-garde artist was welcomed as a very usable celebrity package. Lichtenstein's art commented on the degree to which the idea of the unique art object has been eroded by the spectacular success of postwar color printing processes that multiply images of art objects into the millions.

Minimal Art and Photo-Realism had brought the language of avant-garde art—which had begun to move away from photographic realism in the work of Manet in the 1860s—full circle. Photo-Realism used photography as a base with as much rigor as the most demanding nineteenth-century Academic painter. Minimal Art and Photo-Realism signaled the end—in the sense of completion—of painting as the leading edge of innovation in the avant-garde. The language of painting had, so to speak, no more worlds to conquer.

Lastly, its increasing success threatened to end the traditional role of the avant-garde as an alternative visual system to that of the established social order. Beginning with Abstract Expressionism, the avant-garde had become acceptable to a network of museums, galleries, and universities and the public they served. As noted in the Introduction, over a million people saw the Picasso retrospective at the Museum of Modern Art in New York in 1981. In the phrase of Harold Rosenberg, avant-garde art had become a "tradition of the new." In contrast to the reception of the earlier avant-garde, the tradition's next move was eagerly awaited. For the first time in its history, avant-garde art presented the opportunity for a highly lucrative career.

This last point is a crucial one. One of the major icon roles of the avant-garde since its beginning has been that of creating an alternative system of images to that of the dominant culture. Such alternative images, including the personal and social values they embodied, ranged from the socialism of Courbet and the anarchy of Futurism to the psychic independence of Surrealism and the intense individuality of Pollock. Even the Impressionists, during their first twenty years, were regarded as revolutionaries, because their images challenged the Academic painting that was approved by the government and the dominant classes in France.

11.34

296

11.35 Billy Al Bengston.
Mahana Draculas (as used in
advertisement for First Los Angeles
Bank). 1981.
Acrylic on canvas, 76″ × 80″.
Courtesy of the James Corcoran Gallery,
Los Angeles, Billy Al Bengston, artist.

Avant-garde art, in other words, was always about a different way to think, feel, or see than that offered by the establishment. Recall that before World War II, *Life* magazine lumped the "unrealities of contemporary art" with the "irrational bloodiness of war."

Avant-garde art today is a prime emblem of establishment institutions: business, government, education. Phillip Morris sponsors major exhibitions of contemporary art; its ads for such exhibitions often carry the tag line "It takes art to make a company great." ARCO is the major contributor to the new wing of contemporary art at the Los Angeles County Museum of Art. Atlantic-Richfield Company's logo will thus sit on the wall of the museum like the label on a pair of designer jeans: every work of art that appears will add to ARCO's corporate luster. First Los Angeles Bank says in its ads, "Like Modern Art, Our Bank Dares to be Different." To prove it, the advertisement features a painting by contemporary artist Billy Al Bengston (fig. 11.35, plate 30).

Some artists and critics regard this acceptance of the avant-garde as the much-desired return to the normal condition of art in all cultures—that of affirming and sustaining the culture's basic values. Michelangelo supported the dominant cultural institution of his day—the Church—and so did Rembrandt, even though he was treated as an outsider. But the modern state—whether capitalist or socialist—is built on an entirely new kind of culture. Since the time of the French and American Revolutions (and the myth of Frankenstein and of the Natural Man), Western culture has seen itself as man-made: it no longer represents a higher, sacred order beyond itself. Culture could be changed, but—without the element of dissent—it could also become a closed system. Maintaining this "openness" had been one of the major historical roles of the avant-garde. As artist and critic Suzi Gablik has put it:

Our culture is perhaps the first completely secularized culture in human history . . . the artist is an outcast who stands for another way of life than the established one, whose purpose as a religious, spiritual or moral hero is to create a symbolic life that will have a meaning for others—has been reduced to the same kind of mechanical order and bureaucratic fixity that engulfs other professions in our society and tends to stifle the free self-possessed personality. "Why do people think artists are special?" asks Warhol, "It's just another job."[12]

This need for art, and for the special role of avant-garde art, in our culture is best seen in terms of the simultaneous impact of the most powerful icon system in our culture—the icons of the art of advertising.

CHAPTER TWELVE

THE

TELEVISION AGE III:

THE IDEOLOGY AND IMAGERY

OF ADVERTISING

ASSESSMENTS

1. Do you like or dislike television commercials? What do you find yourself being aware of first—color, subject matter, sound, something else?
2. Do you think you have allowed your personality, likes/ dislikes, behaviors, preferences, and so on, to be molded in any way by the advertisements you have seen in the media? How?
3. How important is advertising in creating values in our society?
4. Since advertisements can be considered as icons, look at all of the advertisements in one issue of a magazine and decide what they say to you about the roles of men and women within our society.
5. What magazine advertisement can you immediately recall because of its appeal or interest? What kind of "power" does the advertisement seem to promise? What visual elements are used to give this sense of power?
6. Have you ever bought a product because of an experience evoked by an advertisement? What was the product and what was the experience evoked by the advertisement?

298

12.1

12.1 IBM advertisement. 1984.
Courtesy of Lord, Geller, Federico, Einstein, Inc.

12.2 Charlie Chaplin.
Modern Times. 1936.
Museum of Modern Art, New York, Film Stills Archive.

12.3 Footprint of Apollo 11 astronaut Neil Armstrong on the moon. July 20, 1969.
Courtesy of NASA.

12.4 "It's hard to tell where you leave off and the camera begins."
Minolta camera advertisement.
Courtesy of Bozell and Jacobs, Advertising.

America does not run, aesthetically, on avant-garde art. America runs on the art of advertising. Chapter 8 noted advertising's historical and crucial role in helping to transform the working class into consumers—into the "civilization of desire" described by President Coolidge. Quite simply, the working class became the middle class. Since World War II, however, advertising has taken on a qualitative new power in shaping American culture. Symbolized by the television commercial, advertising is arguably the most powerful form of art in our society today. The postwar role of advertising, in turn, has stemmed from the parallel growth of technology.

After World War II, America moved beyond factory-oriented industries and became the first society based primarily on new organizational and informational technologies. The Television Age is an age of triumphant expansion of technology into every aspect of Western culture. As noted in the last chapter, American popular and avant-garde art have accompanied this spread of the influence of American technology over all the globe.

The importance of advertising is directly linked with the increasing role of technology in American life. An IBM commercial of the early eighties (fig. 12.1) captured this change beautifully: "Charlie," once the heroic outsider who often battled with technology, (fig. 12.2), became a prosperous businessman. Appropriately, the commercial shows that Charlie's transformation is in large part due to the friendly help of postwar technology.

12.2

Technology, however, is not just "there." It expresses our basic cultural myth as clearly as houses and village and masks express the Dogon culture described in Chapter 1. Technology expresses the myth of the autonomous individ-

12.3

ual by transforming the physical environment to conform with our needs, wishes, and desires. This transformation is not seen only in our giant buildings, freeways, and dams. On a cosmic scale, it is the footprints of American astronauts that will lie forever on the surface of the moon (fig. 12.3). On a microcosmic scale it is human intervention at the genetic level of biology and the atomic level of matter.

Despite its complexity, our technological culture depends upon advertising art for the same thing that native arts provide for their cultures: advertising images provide meaning, the kind of meaning that comes from the experience of myth—the meaning given by the icon aspect of art.

Advertising art attempts to connect the technological environment of products, organizations, and programming to *personal* patterns of perception and use. This connection happens in two phases: in the first phase, the advertisement attaches a sense of power and personality to the product, organization, or program; in the second phase, it attempts to connect this sense of power and personality—in however small a degree—to the personality of the individual who experiences the advertisement. To the extent that this sense of power and personality do transfer from image to viewer, the personal, mythic connection is made.

Advertising Art I: Power and Personality for Technological Products

The Minolta camera in Figure 12.4 perfectly illustrates this process. First, the camera is pictured as an extension of the eye; the caption reads: "It's hard to tell where you leave off and the camera begins." Second, the caption identifies the camera with the person: "Minolta—When you are the camera and the camera is you."

It's hard to tell where you leave off and the camera begins.

12.4

12.5

12.6

12.7

The 1983 advertisement for Saab automobiles (fig. 12.5) takes a slightly different approach. This image accomplishes the first phase of the advertising process by directly fusing the car (the technology) with the personality of the individual. The approach is obviously meant to be humorous, but it is only funny because it dramatizes in a blatant way what we all expect from ads in more subtle terms: "This car (an object) is an extension of you (a person)."

This shrewd image is calculated to have a powerful appeal to people who enjoy seeing the structure of advertising ridiculed in its mythic and psychological pretensions. The ad nevertheless does the same thing that it parodies: it connects a certain type of personality (sophisticated, intelligent) with a particular product of technology (the Saab automobile). Its underlying message is: people with superior knowledge of advertising and automobiles choose Saab.

Even if we as individuals actually purchase very few objects or products because of ads like these, they still function as icons for technology in general. They keep us fine-tuned to what is out there, just waiting for our mythic response. The theme of the Timex ads expressed it very well: "We make technology beautiful."

Advertising Art II: Power and Personality for Organizations

Organizations do more than advertise their products and services; they also use advertising art to counteract any negative effects of the way they must use people to achieve their particular goals (making automobiles, extracting oil, etc.). These advertisements, like the others, also have a two-stage process: first, they present images that portray the organization as a single "big person"; second, they portray its concern for the welfare, happiness, and freedom of each "little person"—you—as primary.

Until the oil glut of the early 1980s, America's giant oil companies had been severely criticized for the negative ecological and economic impact of some of their policies. Advertising icons helped correct this negative impression. Note how the ad in figure 12.6 shows us that the giant hands of ARCO are gently restoring our environment to its unspoiled condition. Meanwhile, we can relax at home while ARCO brings "Cosmos" into our living rooms (fig. 12.7).

Texaco, meanwhile, announced "good news for all living things on this earth" (fig. 12.8). "Good news" is another name for the Christian gospel message. The distinctly messianic tone of this advertising icon becomes even more clear when it is compared with a famous nineteenth-century American painting that, through Currier and Ives lithograph copies, became immensely popular (fig. 12.9). It presented virtually the same scene as the Texaco ad. Its title, *Peaceable Kingdom,* refers to the biblical description of the messianic

12.5 Saab advertisement.
Courtesy of Ally & Gargano, Inc.,
Advertising.

12.6 "Explore without spoiling."
ARCO advertisement.
Courtesy of Foote, Cone, & Belding.

kingdom when "the lion will lie down with the lamb." Texaco, evidently, is an even bigger and better "person" than ARCO.

12.9

12.8

Notice, however, that neither of these big persons has yet said anything about selling oil.

Lastly, figure 12.10 shows an advertisement for the high-tech Japanese firm Hitachi. As an icon, this ad invites Americans to overcome any hostility they may feel toward Japanese economic and technological dominance by experiencing what the title, with remarkable simplicity, describes: "I am you." Hitachi, that is, is people; people have families; the people at Hitachi give service, not unemployment, to America. Hitachi is therefore lovable—just like you.

Advertising art's icons for organizations thus strive to present them as benign persons, large but lovable, pursuing on a gigantic scale what we each pursue as individuals: individual freedom. Famous personalities: Bob Hope for Texaco, Cliff Robertson for AT&T, Cheryl Tiegs for Sears—increase this mythic sense of corporate personality. And what is the mythic bond or feeling these icons would like us to experience in relation to these organizations? One ad puts it quite nicely: "You're in good hands. . . ."

The Television Commercial: Ideological Center of Television

The most powerful personalizing and mythmaking form of advertising is the television commercial. Insofar as television *is* the culture in the sense described in Chapter 10, the ideological center of American network television itself is the commercial. The American thirty- to sixty-second commer-

12.10

12.7 "Cosmos."
ARCO advertisement.
Courtesy of Foote, Cone, & Belding.

12.8 "Texaco announces some good news."
Texaco advertisement.
Courtesy of Texaco, Incorporated.

12.9 Edward Hicks.
Peaceable Kingdom. 1846.
Oil on canvas, 24" × 31¾".
Phillips Collection, Washington.

12.10 "I am you."
Hitachi advertisement.
Courtesy of Hitachi America Ltd.

cial is so integral a part of network television programming that its impact is comparable to the filters of home, drama, and personality.

The rest of this chapter will discuss how the television commercial has incorporated aspects of both avant-garde and popular art traditions and will also try to help clarify the important role, and the specific difficulties, of avant-garde art today.

The Thirty-Second Television Commercial: A Basic Icon of American Culture

Like all forms of advertising, commercials promote the buying of products as well as create "images" that personalize products and organizations. The television commercial, however, does more than this. Increasingly, the television commercial has lent its methodology—especially its techniques of packaging an "image"—to every facet of American life.

Presidential campaigns are defined by commercials that package the slogans and the look of the candidate with the same techniques used to market products. In 1984, the Reagan and Mondale campaigns spent over sixty million dollars on commercials. For the first time in the history of America's national political conventions, a major party's nominee for president was introduced by a film—a "supercommercial" (made by the agency that produces Coca-Cola commercials) later cut into smaller segments and shown as commercials during the Reagan campaign. Geraldine Ferraro later capitalized on her fame as America's first woman nominee for vice-president by starring in a commercial for Pepsi. This commercial caused as much interest as the 1984 commercial that featured Michael Jackson and, according to Pepsi president Roger Enrico: "demonstrated our total commitment to place Pepsi on the leading edge of American lifestyles."[1] Mr. Enrico's company, with over five million dollars invested in the Jackson commercials alone, understands the icon value of commercials very clearly.

Almost every organization and important issue eventually crystallizes its image in the format of a television commercial. The voice of Pope John Paul II has been used in a commercial against nuclear war. Brooke Shields has warned teenagers about the dangers of smoking. And other countries are imitating the American pattern. The Venezuelan government uses commercials to stimulate parents to attend to the educational potential of their children.

In America, however, children's Saturday-morning television approaches the condition of a single continuous commercial. Products and dolls have always followed in the wake of popular movies and television shows. The development of children's shows *after* the product is in existence is a more recent, and a qualitatively different, issue. The National Association for Better Broadcasting took the Los Angeles channel KCOP-TV to court in 1984, charging that the children's show "He-man and the Masters of the Universe" was nothing more than a 23-minute commercial based on an already existing line of Mattel toys.

Commercials today are powerful enough to create folk heroes and renew the lagging careers of former celebrities. The Miller Lite commercials are sometimes more interesting than the sporting events they help to sponsor. Rodney Dangerfield and John Madden have expanded their careers on the basis of this series of commercials. Former football stars Bubba Smith and Dick Butkus went on to star in their own prime-time series .

Michael Crichton, whose films deal with the intricacies of our technological culture, based his 1981 film *Looker* on the potential for commercials to manipulate personal behavior. The mastermind behind a commercial-making empire at one point makes a speech to his colleagues that includes the statement that the average American will spend fifteen years of his or her life watching television. The speech continues:

And the average American spends more than one and a half years of his life just watching television commercials. Fifty minutes a day, every day of his life, watching commercials. What power![2]

The impressive power of the commercial stems in large part from its ability to absorb earlier forms of Western art and ingeniously redirect them into producing icons of consumerism. A few examples will illustrate the structure of the television commercial, beginning with one of the most successful commercials ever broadcast—"1984."

"1984": The Commercial as Movie, Myth, and Personal Experience

The commercial "1984" appeared on network television on January 22, 1984, during the broadcast of Superbowl XVIII. The impact of this commercial was so strong that it evoked almost as much postgame comment as the football game itself. It has become a classic example of the complexity, effectiveness, and iconic appeal of the television commercial.

Like most commercials, "1984" was not a videotape; it was a movie made for television. As a movie, it had a complete plot, a hero, and a happy ending. Figure 12.11 shows the initial storyboard for the commercial. Its production costs exceeded half a million dollars.

The opening scene of "1984" showed lines of men filing into a huge hall set somewhere within a massive, bunkerlike futuristic structure (fig. 12.12). All of the men's heads were shaved, and all wore drab gray clothes.

Once seated somewhere inside the structure, all the men gazed up at a huge television screen that was filled by the stern, emaciated face of a dictatorial leader. The leader's face looked troubled despite his triumphantly shouted propa-

12.11 "1984" storyboard.
   Courtesy of Chiat/Day Advertising, Los Angeles.
12.12 "1984" photo (from commercial).
   Chiat/Day Advertising, Los Angeles.

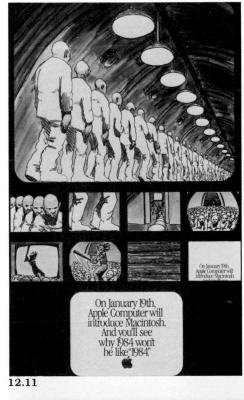

12.11

12.12

12.13

On January 24th,
Apple Computer will introduce
Macintosh.
And you'll see why 1984
won't be like "1984."

12.14

12.13 "1984" photo (from commercial). Chiat/Day Advertising, Los Angeles.

12.14 "1984" photo (from commercial). Chiat/Day Advertising, Los Angeles.

ganda slogans, which themselves appeared graphically on the screen beside his face.

Then the action suddenly cut to a scene outside the hall, an athletic young woman dressed in white-and-red track clothes racing down a corridor leading to the hall. Her face had an expression of unstoppable determination, and she carried a large sledgehammer.

Scenes then began to switch from the face on the screen to the rows of men to the onrushing figure of the woman. As she entered the hall she began to swing the sledgehammer over her head. When she reached the front of the room she pivoted in a single graceful, powerful motion and hurled the hammer into the face on the television screen. There was an explosion of light. The camera showed the drab faces of the men in the hall suddenly illuminated with a sense of liberation (fig. 12.13).

Only then did the faces at home break into (somewhat milder) expressions of enhanced understanding as the following words appeared on the screen (fig. 12.14):

On January 24th,
Apple Computer will introduce
Macintosh.
And you'll see why 1984
won't be like "1984."

The entire movie drama took sixty seconds.

The effectiveness of this commercial is reflected in the fact that, despite only one showing of "1984" on national television, Apple sold out its stock of Macintosh computers on January 24, the first sales day following the commercial's broadcast.

Commercials draw on the entire tradition of film (which includes photography and painting). All the techniques discussed in Chapter 8, from the jump cut to the flashback, are included in commercials, plus the techniques that have been developed in film since that early period.

The director of "1984," Ridley Scott, is one of many directors who produces both commercials and feature films. His films *Alien* and *Bladerunner* show the same kind of rich environmental detail seen in "1984."

The title "1984" refers back to George Orwell's famous novel of that name. A fine Hollywood film of the novel came out later in the same year, but the plot and imagery of the commercial played on the whole tradition of movies about totalitarian societies. The overall mood and the scene of the men filing into the building, for instance, bear a strong resemblance to scenes in Fritz Lang's underground city in *Metropolis* (fig. 9.21) referred to in Chapter 9.

As "1984" did, commercials often recycle themes from popular movies. During the same Superbowl broadcast that featured "1984," IBM presented one of its commercial mini-movies, starring an updated version of Charlie Chaplin, that shows the organization *saving* the "common man." During

1984 alone, Pepsi aired commercials based on three Steven Spielberg films, *Close Encounters of the Third Kind, E.T.,* and *Jaws.*

Unlike the tradition of the movies that it builds on, the commercial is neither pure drama nor pure entertainment. Its purpose, as seen in "1984," is a double one: first, to create a compelling experience for the viewer; second, to link that experience with a product, an organization, or an idea.

The Commercial: Dramas for Experiencing Commodities

The dreamlike yet fast-paced quality of "1984" provides a classic example of how the experience built into the commercial is calculated to link the viewer and the product in an emotional bond.

Despite its mere sixty-second length, "1984's" narrative embodies several highly emotional themes: the individual versus tyranny, human strength versus technology, and women's liberation versus male domination. By choosing a beautiful, athletic woman it also used sex appeal.

Who would not want the emotional charge from the dramatic experience of such themes connected, even if only subconsciously, with their product?

This principle explains why no Macintosh computer appeared in the entire sequence of images—no picture of a computer was needed. The purpose of the commercial was not to provide information about the computer. Its purpose was to fuse the emotional experience of the commercial with the product name, Macintosh. The commercial was, quite simply, an experience that carried a label—like a pair of designer jeans. The experience of the commercial, unlike the jeans, is worn on the *in*side of the person.

The emphasis on *experience* rather than *information* is a critical dimension in most successful commercials; "1984" was unique in having only one national showing. Most commercials rely on the ritual of repeated viewings, updated with a series of related commercials, to keep the desired experience resonating in the viewer. McDonald's, for instance, has always produced commercials that are based, not on hamburgers, but on the American Way of Life.

The Big Mac: The Experience of Patriotism, Family, and Fun

The Big Mac is a hamburger. Through the constant visual ritual of its commercials, however, it eventually becomes—especially for children—a hamburger wrapped in the experience of fun, friendliness, and the American Way of Life. People in McDonald's ads—old people, young people, black people, white people—are always enthusiastic and always smiling. The direct appeal to children is illustrated in the lyrics of an especially effective commercial called "Fries":

You
You're the one.
You are the only reason.
You
You're the one.
We taken pride in pleasin'.
You're why a McDonald's fry
Is crisp and golden brown.
You're what they're famous for
Why they're the best french fries in town. . . .
(chorus)
You deserve a break today. . . .[3]

That's a lot to get with an order of fries.

This "all-American" tradition of McDonald's found its maximum expressive force in the series of commercials made exclusively for the 1984 Olympics. The theme of each minimovie was "When the U.S.A. Wins, You Win!" Americans thus saw, sandwiched between gymnasts and rowers and updates on the quest for the gold medals, a series of fantasies that showed Dad, Mom, and the kids fusing their identities with the Olympian heroes. Although the vision of the gold medal, by the end of the commercial, turned out to be only a dream, the experience packaged in the commercials aimed at coloring the next order of burger and fries with a bit of the aura of patriotism, family, and fun—and winning.

The commercial shown in figure 12.15 was also strikingly effective. It pictured the swimming stadium donated to the games by McDonald's. A diver climbed up the ladder and dived into the pool, but his face was never shown: the hero was the pool. The McDonald's logo in the commercial helped turn the Olympics itself into an advertisement for McDonald's.

Diet Pepsi: The Product as Erotic Experience

Another experience often wrapped up with the imagery of the commercial is sex appeal. The Diet Pepsi commercials in the early eighties were a classic example of linking sex appeal to a product.

These commercials (fig. 12.16 and 12.17) presented a succession of quick-cuts showing extremely shapely bodies, mostly of women, either in close-up detail or with partly covered faces. They key to the image sequence in each commercial was the last shot: it showed a can of Diet Pepsi posing alongside a final shot of a beautiful model.

Besides the obvious appeal to male and female viewers to get thin by drinking Diet Pepsi, these commercials included a more subtle appeal to motivate women to see their own bodies as sex objects. The commercial also sought to

12.15

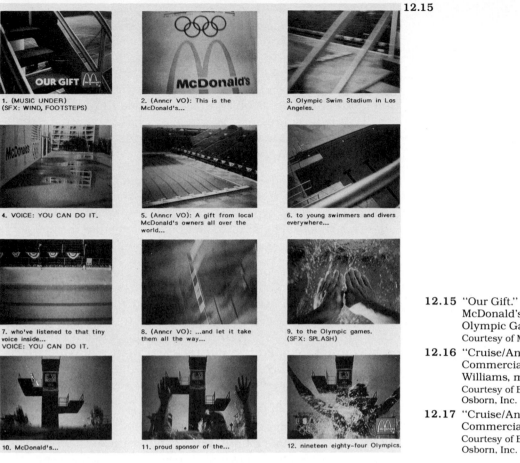

1. (MUSIC UNDER)
(SFX: WIND, FOOTSTEPS)

2. (Anncr VO): This is the McDonald's...

3. Olympic Swim Stadium in Los Angeles.

4. VOICE: YOU CAN DO IT.

5. (Anncr VO): A gift from local McDonald's owners all over the world...

6. to young swimmers and divers everywhere...

7. who've listened to that tiny voice inside...
VOICE: YOU CAN DO IT.

8. (Anncr VO): ...and let it take them all the way...

9. to the Olympic games.
(SFX: SPLASH)

10. McDonald's...

11. proud sponsor of the...

12. nineteen eighty-four Olympics.

12.15 "Our Gift."
McDonald's commercial for 1984 Olympic Games.
Courtesy of McDonald's Corporation.

12.16 "Cruise/Anthony."
Commercial for Diet Pepsi. Gail Williams, model.
Courtesy of Batten, Barton, Durstine, & Osborn, Inc.

12.17 "Cruise/Anthony."
Commercial for Diet Pepsi.
Courtesy of Batten, Barton, Durstine, & Osborn, Inc.

give women the experience of seeing themselves, so to speak, through the admiring eyes of men—and also through the envious eyes of other women. The message of the commercial was not only for a woman to become a sex object, but to enjoy the experience.

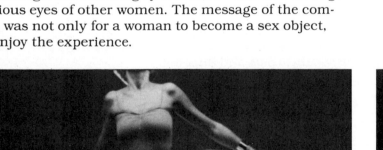

12.16

12.17

The Television Commercial: Absorbing the Western Artistic Tradition

Commercials reveal a strong connection with avant-garde films as well as with the Hollywood film tradition. Robert Breer, who became involved in avant-garde filmmaking in order to control and review the processes in his own paintings, had this comment to make on the relationship between commercials and avant-garde films:

Avant-garde inventions are often picked up first by the people who do TV commercials: they're always on the lookout for new techniques and effects to hype a product. From commercials, the techniques are adopted by narrative film-makers, whether they're willing to admit it or not.[4]

The television commercial is also rooted in the Western painting tradition. The eroticism of commercials, like the Diet Pepsi commercials just described, goes back to Academic painting's own exploration of veiled but exploitative eroticism. The art historian Linda Nochlin has commented on how much Academic painting's "strategies of concealment" anticipated the current use of sexual imagery in the mass media. She specifically referred to Gérôme's *The Slave Market* (fig. 6.18):

Works like Gérôme's . . . are valuable and well worth investigating not because they share the aesthetic values of great art on a slightly lower level, but because as visual imagery they anticipate and predict the qualities of incipient mass culture.[5]

Commercials reflect an even stronger connection with avant-garde painting. The most casual glance shows that Surrealism—directly or indirectly—has been an ongoing source of both inspiration and instruction for American advertising artists and directors.

The world of the thirty- to sixty-second commercial is a world of imagery that realizes Breton's Surrealist vision of fusing reality and dream. Commercials present a world where watches melt and dinosaurs become oil before our very eyes. Cars and other objects defy time, space, and matter with a frivolity and abandonment that can only exist in the world of dreams—and desire.

The world of dreams evoked by the television commercial, however, is not the same world as that sought out and explored by the Surrealists.

Tony Schwartz, who has made over five thousand ads and commercials, is one of America's most important authorities on commercials. His description of the crucial role of "experience" within the advertising icon reveals how the television commercial, instead of liberating the individual's subconscious, (the Surrealist ideal), strives to achieve a kind of image-transplant:

When the consumer sees the product in the store, whether he or she consciously remembers it or not, the product may evoke the experience of the commercial. If that experience was meaningful, and there is a need, the consumer is likely to buy the product.

The critical task is to design our package of stimuli so that it resonates with information already stored within an individual and thereby induces the desired learning or behavioral effects.[6]

The world of commercials also realizes to an astonishing degree the Futurist objective to intimately connect the technological and objective world with the human personality. Like the Saab advertisement discussed earlier, many commercials show the object merging with the person.

Even Constructivism's brief alliance with Marxist revolution pales before the iconic impact of the television commercial on American culture. As the drama critic Martin Esslin has commented, the American television commercial has used psychological research for ideological purposes more effectively than the most ingenious of Marxist dramatists, including a playwright whose works are often performed in the West, Bertolt Brecht:

Brecht advocated the use of drama as an instrument of social engineering, a powerful teaching tool to change people's lives. . . . It is ironic that the truest fulfillment of Brecht's postulates of a didactic drama designed to convert mankind to communism . . . should have come in the television commercials of capitalism.[7]

The art form of the television commercial thus absorbs elements from the Western artistic tradition from Academic painting to Hollywood movies to avant-garde art. It fuses these borrowed elements, however, into an objective that is less ambitious but far more specific and attainable than anything sought by the revolutionary art of Futurism, Constructivism, and Surrealism: the cultivation of oneself as an image, based on purchasing the appropriate commodities. Commercials are icons that, in an image-conscious society, urge us to assemble our own selves.

This basic appeal to image, for the viewer to see his or her personality reflected and fulfilled in the commercial, is one of the crucial motivating factors in our culture.

The Tradition of the Avant-Garde: High Priority on Personal Expression

The importance of personality—in terms of both artist and viewer—is not unique to advertising art. The appeal to personality is *why* advertising art works so well. Art in all cultures ultimately creates its meaning and vitality by connecting the individual with persons or forces greater than himself or herself. Native art uncovers a sense of personality everywhere, even in inanimate objects. As in the horned puffin mask shown earlier (fig. 1.11), the spirit of the animal reveals itself in the Eskimo bear mask shown in figure 12.18.

12.18 Inua (Eskimo) bear mask. 19th century.
Smithsonian Institution, Washington.

The cathedral personalized the entire cosmos. The importance of the artist's own personality, however, has been an aspect of avant-garde art since its beginning. It is a basic theme that goes back to Courbet:

I have studied the art of masters and the art of the moderns, avoiding any preconceived system and without prejudice. I have no more wanted to imitate the former than to copy the latter; nor have I thought of achieving the idle aim of art for art's sake. No! I have simply wanted to draw from a thorough knowledge of tradition the reasoned and free sense of my own individuality.[8]

Zola defended Manet's expression of personality in his work. Van Gogh felt that personality is what ultimately enlivens art. Pollock's style developed from his interest in "expressing" his feelings instead of illustrating them. The sense of personality is largely what has given avant-garde art its authenticity.

To show that this sense of personality is part of both advertising art and the avant-garde as well as to show the difference in their approaches to personality, this chapter will conclude with a comparison between a famous advertisement and a well-known avant-garde work: the Virginia Slims series of advertisements and Judy Chicago's *Dinner Party*.

Virginia Slims: Attaching the Myth of Personality to a Product

The Virginia Slims ads of the past decade or more are outstanding examples of successful advertising art. The series portrays women's liberation through episodes that illustrate the historical record of male domination.

Almost every Virginia Slims ad shows a "before" and an "after" scene. One ad presented the theme of work this way: the photograph showing "his work" featured a paunchy middle-aged man relaxing with a cigar in his mouth and his feet on the desk. The adjacent photograph showing "her work" pictured a woman bending over a mop and bucket. The bucket, in turn, was surrounded by a dozen or so other objects: a pot, a broom, a feather duster, and so on. These objects, presumably, would still be there long after "his work" with the cigar was finished.

These "before" and "after" snapshots were done in monochrome color of very old photographs. They represented yesteryear.

"Today's woman" appeared in the large, white open space below the drab-colored photographs. She was shown—as she is always shown in the Virginia Slims ads—as energetic and happy: she was smiling and, as always, dressed in high-fashion clothes (the name of the designer is usually on the side of the ad). She was also smoking.

This series of ads is crafted with remarkable skill to appeal to any woman who is sensitive to women's grievances against men. The ads not only document women's monochrome, victimized past, they show with ritually reinforced precision how to achieve a liberated present: through high fashion, the right cosmetics, and, of course, the right cigarette. All it takes is money and the right commodities. The series hints that smoking itself just might be the best revenge against male-dominated history.

312

12.19

12.19 Judy Chicago.
The Dinner Party. 1979.
Mixed media. 47′ × 47′ × 47′.
Copyright Judy Chicago 1979. Photo:
Michael Alexander.

12.20 *Placesetting for Judith.* 1979.
Mixed media, 30″ wide.
Copyright Judy Chicago. Executed by Judy
Chicago, Juliet Myers, Terry Belcher. Photo:
Beth Theilen.

This ad series exemplifies the mythic process underlying advertising art: the image first links a product to a personality within the advertisement; second, the experience of the image links the product-personality to the intended viewer (a woman who smokes and is sympathetic to the theme of women's liberation).

Judy Chicago's *Dinner Party* (fig. 12.19), by contrast, is an avant-garde work that invites the viewer to reflect in a very different way on his or her feelings about the present and historical role of women in our culture. It takes a radically different approach to the viewer's personality.

Judy Chicago's *Dinner Party:* Making History into Herstory

Dinner Party is a triangular table, each side forty-five feet long. It is covered with thirty-nine individual place settings, each consisting of a unique ceramic plate and accompanying linens that bear the name and identifying symbols of an individual woman. In order to see the work, the viewer must move around the table and look down, one by one, at the names, symbols, and decorations that record how each woman made a mark on her times. Figure 12.20 (plate 31) shows the plate designed to honor Judith, the heroic Jewish

12.20

woman from the Bible who beheaded Holofernes, a Syrian general whose army threatened to destroy Israel.

The momentary pauses at each plate become, one by one, symbolic retrievals of each woman from the obscurity of standardized history. Viewing *Dinner Party* is almost a liturgical service, an artistic meal that is both a summing up and a celebration of new possibilities.

The Dinner Party, with its mixture of fun and solemnity, generated a good deal of controversy and discussion about its ideological and artistic merits. No one, however, disputed the indelible stamp of Judy Chicago's personality or of her work's powerful affirmation of the creative potential in every woman. The process of making each plate and hand-sewing each place setting also reaffirmed the artistic contribution made throughout history by women's traditional crafts. This kind of personal creativity contrasts with the Virginia Slims heroine, whose liberation is defined partly by the fact that she can buy her clothes from a designer.

The Dinner Party does not personalize commodities; it brings its viewers, including men, into a personal connection with what women have experienced and what women can experience as unique identities.

However, the differences between avant-garde art and advertising art are not absolute at any level. The artistic process of *The Dinner Party* resembles that of the Virginia Slims ad series in that *The Dinner Party* was also a group effort (led by Judy Chicago) and made use of publicity as part of its effectiveness. They both nevertheless appeal for radically different responses from the viewer. The difference is ultimately seen in the viewer's expectations: one approaches avant-garde art expecting to be challenged to see or experience or think in a new way; one approaches advertising art expecting to be "sold."

To confront avant-garde art as a viewer requires risk, the risk of making contact with another person—the artist. We can sense Judy Chicago behind her *Dinner Party.* Who is behind the Virginia Slims ads (besides the commodities)? Advertising art does not involve risk for the viewer. No matter how skillfully it is done, it involves the viewer with a prepackaged "image" or "aura" of personality that is itself often the commodity known as "the celebrity." By contrast, the sense of personality within the avant-garde art object is, in one sense, the nakedness of the artist. The viewer is often asked to respond in kind.

Avant-Garde Art in the Television Age: Icons of Individuality and Openness

The television commercial, despite its obvious power, cannot influence behavior to any predictable degree. For every campaign like Apple's "1984" commercial for the Macintosh computer, there are commercials like the ones during the same year for Atari computers, which even the acting and producing skills of Alan Alda ("M.A.S.H.") could not help.

The most important aspect of commercials, however, is not their effectiveness individually but their cumulative effect as part of the environment of television. Despite their immense variety in form and content, commercials surround us with icons that constantly affirm a specific set of basic values: that buying is a prime exercise of personal freedom, that happiness is a by-product of commodities, and that half-truths well packaged are the most valuable and effective forms of communication. Advertising, as one writer has recently demonstrated, has something like the propaganda role of Socialist Realism in Marxist societies.[9]

Despite its environmental impact, advertising is not a closed system. Among other factors, advertising art must coexist with the alternative art of the avant-garde. The last chapter described how the phenomenal success of American avant-garde art created the danger of its becoming absorbed into advertising and becoming subject to the priorities of business. The next chapter will describe how the avant-garde, in an era dominated by the television commercial, has responded to the challenge of the mass media and to the dilemma created by its own success.

CHAPTER THIRTEEN

THE

TELEVISION AGE IV:

THE CHALLENGES OF

POST-MODERNISM

ASSESSMENTS

1. Do you see areas of American culture—sports, politics, religion, etc.—under pressure to change as a result of commercial influences?
2. Which do you consider more important, the artistic process (the experience of making art) or the artistic product (the art object)? Why?
3. Who are the women artists you are most familiar with? Is all work done by women artists Feminist Art?
4. Do you watch music videos? If so, which art movements do you think have influenced music videos?
5. If you were an avant-garde artist, what statement would you want to make? What materials would you use?

The last chapter was, in a way, a commercial break, which emphasized the power of advertising art as a source of icons that reflect and create American culture. The evolving power of the television commercial also illustrates the ongoing process by which the popular arts borrow, and sometimes invert, aspects of avant-garde art.

Another aspect of the television commercial is its disclosure of the astonishing capacity of American culture to turn everything into a form of profit. As noted in Chapter 11, many artists during the early seventies began to wonder whether avant-garde art itself was becoming merely another form of advertising even if the message was more subtly expressed than Warhols's *Green Coca-Cola Bottles* (fig. 13.1). The art critic Peter Fuller has described the situation as one in which

the Fine Arts had become only a small strand . . . in "the mega-visual tradition" of monopoly capitalism. Here, I am referring to such phenomena as photography, mass-printing, billboards, neon signs, television, video, holography, and so on with which we are constantly surrounded.[1]

13.1 Andy Warhol.
Green Coca-Cola Bottles. 1962.
Oil on canvas, 82¼″ × 57″.
Whitney Museum of American Art, New York. Gift of the Friends of the Whitney Museum of American Art.

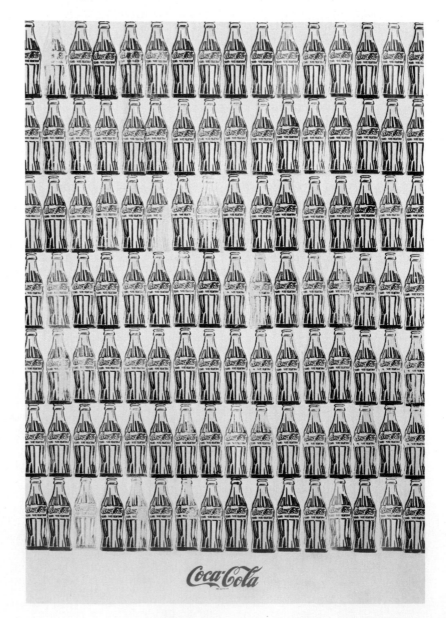

Of particular concern to many artists was the controlling influence of corporate, gallery, and mass media institutions. Their combined influence threatened to become a kind of "art industry" that could turn out art objects and artist-celebrities in a way similar to production in other sectors of the American economy.

Robert Hughes singled out the vast and highly publicized exhibition at the Museum of Modern Art in New York in 1972 entitled "New York Painting and Sculpture: 1940–1970" as the event that most dramatically illustrated the new condition of avant-garde art:

It [the MOMA exhibition] declared the union of new art, capital, and official power to be indissoluble, and crystallized the dissatisfactions that many artists felt with the interlocking, market-based system. . . . To be ahead of the game now seems pointless, for the game—under the present rules—is not worth playing.[2]

This widely felt concern in the art world paralleled the social unrest surrounding the civil rights movement and the Vietnam War, which had brought a general questioning of American values and institutions.

By the early seventies there appeared a consensus among many artists and critics that the entire tradition of avant-garde art from Manet to Minimalism and Photo-Realism had reached a stage of completion, and potential exhaustion. This long tradition, despite its great diversity, can be included under the general term *Modernism*. *Modernism* is a term that recognizes that avant-garde art from Manet to the early seventies followed a logical development of both style and subject matter that culminated in the simultaneous extremes of Minimalist art and Photo-Realism. Since these last two types of art represented a kind of absolute abstraction and absolute realism, respectively, the logic of Modernism seemed to offer no further stages to explore.

Post-modernism was the term that was then applied to describe the avant-garde art since the early seventies, when both the cultural context of avant-garde art and its own logic of artistic development had reached a point of critical change. Like the term *Post-Impressionism*, *Post-Modernism* does not describe what Post-Modernist artists have done so much as it states that it is no longer Modernism.

Post-Modernism: Experimental, Encyclopedic, and Eclectic

Post-Modernist art maintains the avant-garde tradition of experimentation. It differs from Modernism by an aggressive willingness to borrow from and combine with past styles of art rather than constantly searching for "the next step" in a logical evolution of styles. Past art styles therefore form a kind of encyclopedia for creating new art. Post-modernism's eclectic approach is to combine disparate styles of past art into a singular new form.

13.2

13.2 John Portman, architect.
The Bonaventure Hotel, Los Angeles,
California.
Photo: Robert Pelfrey.

13.3 Ad Reinhardt.
Abstract Painting, Number 33. 1963.
Oil on canvas. 60″ × 60″.
Collection of the Whitney Museum of
American Art, New York. 50th Anniversary
gift of Fred Mueller.

Perhaps the best example of these Post-Modernist tendencies working together is in contemporary architecture. For more than forty years, the skyline of the American city has been dominated by steel and glass skyscrapers based on the severely functional avant-garde architecture that originated in the Bauhaus design of early twentieth-century Germany. For the past decade, American cities have begun to sprout new buildings with highly experimental and eclectic designs borrowed from the entire encyclopedia of historical architectural styles.

The architect John Portman's Bonaventure Hotel (fig. 13.2), for instance, looms above Los Angeles freeways in the novel form of four cylindrical towers. The interior lobby of the Bonaventure is a visually exciting space that is several stories high and features the equivalent of a quarter-acre lake. New York's AT & T building is a more conventional skyscraper, except for its monumental top section, which has the shape of a Chippendale grandfather's clock. In San Francisco, a city ordinance has cleared the way for equally Post-Modernist architecture by severely limiting future construction of Modernist glass-box skyscrapers.

It is significant that these examples are taken from architecture; in the Post-Modern period painting is no longer the cutting edge of avant-garde art. During the Modern period, from Manet to Minimalism, painting tended to set the pace and define the agenda of avant-garde art.

A major concern of Post-Modernism is to confound the boundaries and the logic of inherited artistic ideas and materials, including the inheritance of Modernism. The brief history of Post-Modernism since the early seventies has already covered a tremendous diversity of artistic approaches to materials, behavior, and ideology. This chapter will discuss the Post-Modernist era in terms of Concept Art, Earth Art, Feminist Art, painting, and video. The roots of these approaches, however, can be traced back to the 1950s.

The Roots of Post-Modernism: Questioning the Rectangles

As seen in the life and work of Jackson Pollock, the potentially stifling effects of the mass media on the individual artist had become evident by the early fifties. A few artists at that time had already attempted to meet this challenge in a personal way. One Abstract Expressionist, Clifford Still, simply stopped painting. This left the media nothing to absorb, but it also left out art.

Another Abstract Expressionist painter, Ad Reinhardt (1913–1967), created paintings that were small, square, and painted in subtle tones of black (fig. 13.3). Such paintings, he hoped, would elude the photograph and therefore the mass media.

But the media adapted quite nicely. Reinhardt corres-

13.3

ponded with the famous poet and Trappist monk Thomas Merton about art and mysticism. Since many of the paintings contained faintly visible crosses, Reinhardt was dubbed the "black monk" of Abstract Expressionism. The black paintings therefore became interesting news items.

The New York artist Allan Kaprow (1912—) found an approach radically different from Still's silence and Reinhardt's black voids. All art, he pointed out, was made

in a rectangular studio, to be shown in a rectangular gallery, reproduced in a rectangular magazine, in rectangular photographs, all aligned according to rectangular axes, for rectangular reading movements and rectangular thought patterns.[3]

Even Abstract Expressionism, despite its immensely personal and intuitive approach, was tamed by the art industry rectangles. No matter how emotional and subjective the statement, it was easily coded and slotted to fit into rectangular media and gallery spaces. The art industry could easily process even Pollock's environmental-sized canvases.

During the early sixties Kaprow and other New York artists—including many Pop artists—began to create "environments," entire rooms that were turned into art by being filled with sculpted and painted forms. These were social and convivial extensions of Schwitter's isolated Merzbau constructions. The rooms, however, were really rectangles in disguise—three-dimensional rectangles. Even though people could walk into such environments, and often add to them,

320

the environments themselves were still part of the rectangular system.

Kaprow concluded that the real problem was that the Western tradition—especially since the privately owned easel painting had become a privileged artistic format during the Renaissance—had trained both artists and public to carry the rectangle around in their heads. In an effort to throw off these mental and physical rectangles, the environments went outdoors and became "happenings."

Happenings: Art Becomes Process instead of Product

Happenings are difficult to describe. Happenings stressed a minimum of direction and a maximum of participation. Kaprow, or whoever "supervised" the happening, would provide the basic performance directives and materials, but people would be free to improvise as their mood dictated. Happenings merged drama, painting, music—and whatever else fit. In the happening, the boundary between life and art closed. The happening's problem, that of life itself, was its fragility. The experience stayed with the individual participant; the happening disappeared.

It did provide a solution to the problem of the commercialization of art. The happening was not an object, nor was it a commodity that could be sold. In one sense, however, the rectangle did creep back in. Happenings could be photographed. The photographs could be displayed and sold as commodities. The experience—and whatever art it contained—was nevertheless primarily located within the individuals who participated in it.

The happening was an invaluable process in the art of the sixties. Its process orientation and environmental scope led to one of the most significant contributions to Post-Modernist thinking about art, the Earth Art projects of Robert Smithson.

Robert Smithson (1938–1973): Harnessing the Art to Processes beyond Art

Robert Smithson began from a point of view almost identical with Kaprow's: "A work of art when placed in a gallery loses its charge, and becomes a portable object or surface disengaged from the outside world.[4] The same old rectangle.

Smithson began with drawings of "sites"—ways of interacting with the earth. He experimented with ways of bringing the earth into gallery space itself, making the gallery into a site (fig. 13.4).

Wanting to avoid what he called the "little boxes" (galleries) where artists do their "tough little tricks" like rats in a behavioral maze, he decided to go beyond the rectangles of

13.4 Robert Smithson.
Installation shot, Dwan Gallery, 1969.
l to r: Gravel Mirro with Cracks and Dust;
Double Nonsite—California and Nevada.
1968.
Photo courtesy of John Weber Gallery, New York.

13.5 Robert Smithson.
Spiral Jetty with Sun. 1970.
Pencil on paper. 11⅞" × 9".
Collection Nancy Holt. Courtesy of John Weber Gallery, New York.

13.6 The Great Serpent Mound in Adams County, near Peebles, Ohio.
Courtesy of Smithsonian Institution, Washington. Photo #49,808.

13.5

13.4

the art industry and tap into the processes that would connect his art with the geological time/matter dimensions of the earth. Smithson thus began a series of projects within the natural environment that became known as Earthworks or Earth Art.

Smithson's best-known Earth Art piece was his 1969 *Spiral Jetty with Sun.* As seen in his drawing in figure 13.5, it was a spiral-shaped strip of rubble that stretched almost a quarter of a mile into Utah's Great Salt Lake.

The *Spiral Jetty* extended from a section of shoreline littered with the remains of abandoned oil drilling equipment. Smithson recycled materials from this ravaged landscape into a spiral shape to symbolize the destructive aspects of such technological interventions into nature. By drawing attention to negative processes, Smithson wanted to stress the need to subordinate technology to natural as well as human purposes:

13.6

The farmer's, miner's or artist's treatment of the land depends on how aware he is of himself as nature. After all, sex isn't all a series of rapes. If strip miners were less alienated from the nature in themselves and free of sexual aggression, cultivation could take place.[5]

Smithson, like Pollock, saw his art as an affirmation of the presence of nature *within* the human being. This subordination of technology and art to human and natural processes is seen in his willingness to abandon his earthwork to the natural erosion of the Great Salt Lake, which, as he foresaw, has now swallowed up the *Spiral Jetty.* Like the native American earth mounds (fig. 13.6) that could be seen only from the sky (by the gods) or the sculptures of medieval cathedrals that are placed where no one can see them,

Smithson's *Spiral Jetty* acknowledges powers beyond human perception—though he did not name them.

In 1973 his plane crashed during a flight to view a later project, Amarillo Ramp, near Amarillo, Texas. Despite his tragically early death, Smithson's extension of art into the environment and the processes of nature became one of the most important models for the Post-Modernist efforts to create new social and artistic formats for art. His works not only sparked a continuing interest in Earthworks, they had a powerful effect on the art that became known as Concept Art.

Concept Art: Art Is as the Artist Does

Concept Art emerged in the early seventies and specifically addressed both the social and artistic questions inherent in Post-Modernism: What is the role of art, and what is the role of the artist in a highly commercial and technological society? Concept Art encompasses quite a diverse range of artists, situations, and behaviors. The single element all Concept artists share is a determination to produce a form of artistic statement that does not fit into the comfortable category of "art object" that could, through the established media and sponsorship system, become a commodity.

The happenings of the sixties were group-oriented and had the quality of spontaneous festivals. They were also usually orchestrated by artists like Oldenburg or Rauschenberg who had already established themselves with traditional art forms and continued to produce such art in their established patterns. Concept Art is characterized by its independence from normal art materials and its absolute dependence on the will and whimsy of the artist's personality. Concept artists have therefore produced a far more significant body of stories than of observable and collectible objects—some approaching the status of legend.

Tehching Hsieh, for instance, is a Taiwanese artist who lives in New York. Hsieh's art consists in committing himself to living "life-styles" for the period of one full year, with each year symbolizing a complete life cycle. The following are Hsieh's projects for the years 1979 through 1981: a year living in a cage in his New York loft, with no books, television, or radio; a year punching a time clock each hour, twenty-four hours a day; a year living totally outdoors in New York City. Hsieh's art, in addition to the effects of his own perception, provides an alternate to the "life-styles" conveyed in the images of the mass media.

Jonathan Borofsky, at age twenty-five (in 1967), initiated a Concept piece called *Counting*, his response to the "realization that the flow of thought was more important than any art object." *Counting*, when exhibited in 1973, consisted of a stack of 9,350 eight-and-a-half-by-eleven sheets of paper. The sheets of paper contained the entire sequence of numbers from *1* to *2,067,515* along with any random comments that came to Borofsky's mind as he inscribed the numbers onto paper. *Counting,* at the time of its exhibition as a three-foot-six-inch stack of papers, had been part of a daily ritual that had gone on for five years. Like Hsieh, Borofsky attempts to erase the boundaries between life and art.

Chris Burden is an artist who exhibits himself in conditions of physican and/or mortal danger. He has crawled naked over a gallery floor covered with glass, displayed himself in a gallery tied down between buckets of water and plugged-in electrical appliances, and had himself nailed through the palms (crucified) onto the top of a Volkswagen. He once had a friend shoot him in the arm from twelve feet away with a .22-caliber rifle. Most of Burden's experiences are documented on videotapes and photographs.

The German artist Hans Haacke has made a speciality of exhibiting works whose "content" is the analysis of the connections between social and business interests and the art world, symbolized by museums. His 1974 *Manet Project* exhibited panels that listed the people who had bought and sold Manet's 1880 painting *Bunch of Asparagus* until its acquisition (for 1,360,000 deutsche marks) by the Wallraf-Richartz Museum in Cologne, West Germany.

Haacke's panels showed that the Wallraf-Richartz Museum Board of Trustees included collective membership on nineteen other corporate boards. The public documentation linking art and corporate business interests resulted in the museum refusing to exhibit Haacke's project. It achieved wide media attention, however, and—in the gallery of the mass media—asked the precise question Haacke intended: since the decision to exclude the work was based on pleasing the board of trustees of the museum, whose interests did the museum ultimately serve?

The work of Hans Haacke has the clear purpose of clarifying the connections between the art world and the business world. The other behaviors just described might sound less like art than insanity. One way to evaluate these bizarre behaviors is by noting their striking parallel in the religious traditions of Western and other cultures. Early Christian monks, for instance, performed feats of legendary absurdity in order to stress a similar independence from dominant cultural norms of their day. Saint Simeon Stylites lived for over twenty years on top of an enormous column in the Syrian desert. Two American Buddhist monks in the late seventies made a journey from Santa Monica, California, to the Oregon border in an equally unusual style. They walked the entire distance performing the following ritual: after taking three steps they knelt, kissed the ground, and uttered a prayer (fig. 13.7). The monks averaged a little over a mile a day on their four-year pilgrimage.

Even though it is impossible to separate an unrestrained desire for publicity from the purity of concept in these actions, there is the possibility that the Concept artists' actions are—like the actions of the monks—not only in some way

13.7 Buddhist monk on ritual pilgrimage from Santa Monica, California, to the Temple of the Ten Thousand Buddhas, Oregon, 1976–78. Video by Robert Pelfrey. Photo: Mary Hall-Pelfrey.

personally liberating, but meaningful to others. Burden's public encounters seem to border on the psychotic, until one thinks of the scores of shows that present a kind of candy-coated violence as entertainment each evening on prime-time television. The pain and risk Burden undergoes is shockingly real. Because it is real, watching him imperil himself produces a real, though unwelcome, emotion. Even though he has been accused of making violence the basis of his own career, his "art" can be seen as an antidote to the artificial violence that permeates our mass media popular art.

Whatever the particular judgments regarding the artists described above, Concept Art dramatizes questions through the authenticity, not of a skillfully produced object, but of a lived experience. They become heroic stories of perception and endurance in which art is reduced to the person of the artist—who is not a commodity. Concept Art seemed to be an irrefutable reply to Warhol's, "Being an artist is just another job."

As noted earlier, Concept artists' behavior and events inevitably become documented by videotape or photography. Even when the art object loses its pre-eminence, the media continues to be the exhibition space for the Post-Modernist avant-garde.

Feminist Art: More than More Women Artists

Another social movement of the sixties that has coalesced into a powerful expression in the art of the seventies and eighties is art based on the issue of women's equality; Feminism has had a powerful effect on Post-Modernist art. One of the most important events in Feminist Art—and in the writing of art history—was the 1971 essay by Linda Nochlin entitled "Why Have There Been No Great Women Artists?" Nochlin's essay described the ongoing social and institutional biases that have inhibited participation by women in the making of "fine art" and, simultaneously, prohibited recognition of the kinds of traditional art that have been mastered by women.

Nochlin's essay crystallized long-standing issues and helped to clarify the future agenda of women in art. Some women artists, like Bonheur, Morisot, and Cassatt in the nineteenth century did achieve wide recognition. Many twentieth-century women artists such as Georgia O'Keeffe (1887—) had also managed to achieve prominence before World War II despite institutionalized barriers. *Morning Glory with Black* (fig. 13.8) is an early example of O'Keeffe's exploration of images based on enlarging and simplifying natural forms. Such paintings were later admired by both abstract and realist American painters of the post-war generation.

After World War II, women artists found some improvement in their access to the art world. Lee Krassner and Helen Frankenthaler, for instance, became prominent among Abstract Expressionist painters. Frankenthaler then emerged as a leader in developing the Minimalist art of the sixties. Audrey Flack was recognized as one of the originators of Photo-Realism. Joyce Treiman's painting *Degas, Cassatt, and Me* (fig. 13.9 and plate 32), manifests this determination of women artists for a fuller reading of art history as well as a fuller participation in the artistic present. By painting herself and Mary Cassatt as subjects of the same painting, Treiman connects the past and the present through a gently humorous artistic dialogue.

By the early seventies, however, many women artists began to articulate and explore a different approach to art based on specifically feminist principles. Feminist artists did not merely strive to achieve equal competitive footing with male artists; they took an especially critical stance toward the overemphasis on art without social or human relevancy— "art for art's sake." Lucy Lippard has commented that the greatest contribution of Feminist Art has been its insistence on defecting, so to speak, from the evolutionary logic of Modernism.

Feminism's greatest contribution to the future of art has probably been precisely its *lack* of contribution to modernism. Feminist methods and theories have instead offered a socially concerned alternative to the increasingly mechanical evolution of "art about art."[6]

13.9

13.8

13.8 Georgia O'Keeffe.
Morning Glory with Black. 1926.
Oil on canvas, $35^{13}/_{16}"$ × $39^{5}/_{8}"$.
Cleveland Museum of Art, bequest of Leonard C. Hanna, Jr.

13.9 Joyce Treiman.
Degas, Cassatt, and Me. 1979.
Oil on canvas, 70" × 70".
Courtesy of Tortue Gallery, Santa Monica.

This willingness to use new materials and give new meaning to art had already begun before Feminism achieved a definitive artistic formulation. Eva Hesse, who died in 1970 at the age of thirty-seven, had begun to introduce nontraditional materials like latex, rope, and fiberglass into sculpture. Carolee Schneemann made films and appeared in performances that centered on her own nudity—in order not only to affirm the right of women to their own sexual fantasies but to reclaim the "image" of the female body from the highly visible context of pornography and other common imagery that views the female body as a commodity. Feminist Art has attempted to gather these strands together into a coherent ideology as well as a basis for dialogue regarding the role of both sexes in our culture.

The art work that sums up most completely Feminist Art principles remains Judy Chicago's *The Dinner Party,* discussed in the last chapter. It summarizes the Feminist determination to re-evaluate the artistic as well as the social history of women. *The Dinner Party* is also another example of the Post-Modernist tendency to challenge the dominance of painting as the privileged form of art: *The Dinner Party* was deliberately fabricated in art forms and with materials historically associated with women—and historically relegated by male art historians to the status of "minor arts," weaving, china painting, pottery, needlework, and so on.

Many women artists link their art with Feminism without stressing women's themes in an ideological or exclusive way. Lita Albuquerque, for instance, has extended the Earthwork direction of Robert Smithson in a way that incorporates the emphasis on human relationships, ritual, and mythic associations stressed in *The Dinner Party.*

All of her art reflects what she describes as the change in consciousness that has resulted from our landing on the moon and from our new perception of the earth, as Albuquerque puts it, "from the outside in" (fig. 13.10).

Inconceivable Mansions is a piece performed on the dunes of the central California coast in 1981. The title refers

13.10

13.11a

b

to a Buddhist text, "the seat of the soul resides where the inner and the outer world meet."[7] All her works since 1977 reflect the earth itself as that meeting point. Figure 13.11 (plate 33) shows the dancing process that produced the sand drawings.

The monumental spiral, the circles, and the triangle represent geometric shapes within the earth that can be felt but not seen. This idea connects with Greek, medieval, and Renaissance beliefs in the geometric connection between art and nature. The drawings are filled with pigments that also have symbolic meaning: blue, the universe; copper, the reflectivity of the planet; red, the energy source of the earth.

Post-Modernist Painting: The Search for Subject Matter

As noted earlier, Post-Modernist painting uses an eclectic approach to earlier styles of avant-garde art; one of its common themes, however, is a stronger emphasis on subject matter

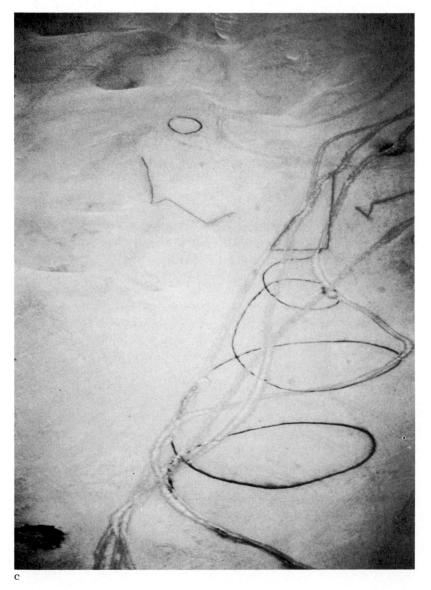

c

13.10 The Earth as seen from Apollo 11. 1969.
Courtesy of NASA.

13.11 Lita Albuquerque.
Inconceivable Mansions. 1981.
Environmental process piece, Arroyo Grande, California.
Photos courtesy of Lita Albuquerque.

than most earlier styles of Modernist painting.

This retrieval and consolidation of the avant-garde painting tradition and its application in individual ways is seen in the work of painters who create art based on ethnic or social roots. The upheavals of the sixties brought the issue of ethnic identity into special focus. Some recent artists whose paintings express their personal ethnic backgrounds are Romare Bearden, Masami Teraoka, and Carlos Almaraz.

Romare Bearden (1914—): Collaging the Black Experience

Romare Bearden is an artist who mixes painting and collage to depict the experience of being black in America.

Like Thomas Eakins, Bearden gave up a possible career in medicine to study art; his breakthrough came during the early sixties, when the flood of photographic images documenting the civil rights movement triggered his interest in exploring being black in America. By working photographs into collages, he achieved a range of imagery that reflected his deepest experiences.

Bearden's collage paintings emphasize faces. They abound in images of trains and other elements that signify the black experience of endless journeying. They often reach back and touch themes that are common to black and to European history. Above all, their abrupt shifts in imagery and harmonizing areas of color have a distinct connection with the blues music that has always been part of Bearden's life.

The Return of Odysseus (Homage to Pintoricchio and Benin) (fig. 13.12) shows all these elements. The painting refers to a story from the life of Odysseus (better known by his Roman name, Ulysses). After ten years in the Trojan War and ten more years of wandering the Mediterranean, he finally reached home. He then avenged himself on the men who had tried to take away his ancient rights and property. His wife, Penelope, had waited faithfully during his years of absence.

This story has been rendered by artists throughout Western history (see fig. 2.6). Bearden's painting resembles both Greek vase art and Picasso's Synthetic Cubism. Each figure is in a stylized pose and simplified into clean geometric shapes. The painting is composed of bright paper shapes and sections of painted color. The heroic face of Odysseus is framed by a window that opens onto a peaceful Mediterranean scene. Penelope, on the left, sits at her loom, whose frame juts in front of the window. Her face shows the frontal eye and profiled head of Egyptian art—another link between black art and history and Western culture. The figure in the right-hand corner of the painting—a courtier or servant—has the self-consciously graceful pose typical of figures from Renaissance paintings (Pintoricchio). The visual language of this painting is witty and playful; it evokes a sense of the

mythic grandeur that was a dominant concern of earlier periods of Western art.

Besides its "journey home" theme, the painting also reflects Bearden's own interrupted artistic journey and his belated but successful claim for artistic recognition. Its complex resolution of white and black culture is incorporated in the title itself: Pintoricchio was a Renaissance painter; Benin is the name of an African tribe renowned for their artistic tradition, established long before European culture penetrated into Africa. Bearden's highly personal work thus becomes a symbol of the universal experience of black Americans.

13.12 Romare Bearden.
The Return of Odysseus (*Homage to Pintoricchio and Benin*). 1977.
Collage on masonite, 44″ × 56″.
Courtesy of Cordier and Ekstrom Gallery, New York, and the Art Institute of Chicago.

Masami Teraoka (1936—): Painting in the Space between East and West

Masami Teraoka was brought up in Japan and graduated from a Japanese university, where he studied art history, philosophy, and other subjects. In 1964, at the age of twenty-five, he went to Los Angeles and began to make his own art.

Originally, Teraoka's artistic interest was in abstraction. By the early seventies, when he became interested in exploring his own background through his art, he turned to the ukiyo-e woodcuts that influenced the avant-garde painters of nineteenth-century Paris.

Teraoka, however, transformed the ukiyo-e style of imagery by adding elements of Pop Art, including its focus on standardized commercial images. Teraoka develops his paintings in a meticulous and subtle watercolor technique that demands scores of preliminary drawings.

Hanauma Bay Series/Video Rental II (fig. 13.13 and plate 34) is an example of Teraoka's fusion of Japanese and American themes. The watercolor shows a Japanese tourist, with video equipment and samurai sword, who has been enjoying Hawaii's Hanauma Bay by taping its wonders with his portable video camera. He and his geisha assistant, however, have just become aware of the wave that is about to engulf their project in mid-frame.

13.13

13.13 Masami Teraoka.
Hanauma Bay Series/Video Rental II. 1982.
Watercolor, 28¾″ × 40⅝″.
Courtesy of Space Gallery, Los Angeles.

13.14 Carlos Almaraz.
The Bridge. 1984.
Oil on canvas, 54″ × 96″.
Courtesy of Janus Gallery, Los Angeles.

13.15 Carlos Almaraz.
The Shootout! 1984.
Oil on canvas, 36″ × 48″.
Courtesy of Janus Gallery, Los Angeles.

One of Teraoka's recurring themes is the unbounded love for technology that, as in the relatively minor example illustrated in *Video Rental,* tends to blind people to its effects on the larger environment. Other Teraoka paintings depict McDonald's, Baskin Robbins, and other American companies "invading" Japan—and the Japanese accepting it all with unbridled enthusiasm.

Teraoka, like Bearden, is not retreating from the perils of modernity. Teraoka finds American culture "adventurous and dynamic." He paints himself and his friends as the characters of his dramas. He shows the difficulties of coping with the culture shock that is inescapable in an age dominated by television and an explosion of other technologies.

Because the humor is self-directed, it invites the viewer to consider his or her own "Hanauma Bay" experiences.

Carlos Almaraz (1941—): Expressionism from the Barrio

A final example of an artist whose work reflects the application of ethnic concerns in Post-Modernist painting is Carlos Almaraz. Almaraz was born in Mexico City and later received his education in New York and California universities. In the early seventies, Almaraz was a political activist in the barrio of East Los Angeles. Among other activities, he directed a city-sponsored mural program that decorated urban walls with spectacular scenes reinterpreting and combining Mexican, Indian, and American myths and folklore.

In the late seventies, Almaraz directed his energy away from the public forum to his own canvases. In the last several years his work has become identified with one of the few overarching styles of Post-Modernist painting, Neo-Expressionism, which borrows from the fervor and abandonment in the tradition of van Gogh, the Fauves, and Abstract Expressionism.

Almaraz's paintings stand out from Neo-Expressionism not only by the radiance of their color but also by their remarkably concrete sense of place. *The Bridge* (fig. 13.14 and plate 35), for instance, glows with his typical palette of hot reds, violets, yellows, and greens. The gestural brush-work of its palm tree skyline captures Los Angeles's mixture of ozone and neon, of boredom and desire, with a striking clarity, despite its aura of Surrealism.

13.14

Almaraz's paintings often show the freeways, beaches, and dingy streets of Los Angeles with the same passion. His *The Shootout!* (fig. 13.15) displays a visionary grit that combines elements of documentary and dream.

Post-Modernist painting includes far more than the specific ethnic focus represented by Bearden, Taraoka, and Almaraz. Artists' concerns range from public moral concern

13.15

13.16

to private fantasy. Leon Golub (1922—) (plate 36) paints large, unstretched canvases that feature scenes of terror and brutality derived from images seen in daily newspaper and television reports. The awkward, crude coloring and drawing of these paintings suggest the half-human world of the characters depicted within them. Eric Fischl (1948—) (fig. 13.16), by contrast, applies sensuous color and facile painting skills to evoke images that suggest the private erotic fantasies encountered in suburban dreams. The half-naked woman on the bed facing the viewer is a provocative image in the tradition of Manet's *Olympia*; the dog, however, adds a disquieting note. The differences in painting style and in approach to subject matter in the works of Golub and Fischl illustrate the diverse recycling of artistic traditions that characterizes all the arts today.

Christo (1935—): Fusing Earth, Technology, and the Mass Media

Another strong direction in contemporary art is toward an aggressive interaction with electronic media, including the mass media. The prime example of this approach of using the mass media as part of the art process—a kind of artistic feedback strategy—is the work of the Bulgarian-born American artist Christo.

Christo delights in involving mass media, business, technology, and government bureaucracies in a single art process. This interest stems from his experience in Bulgaria where, as an art student, he worked on Communist agitprop teams that fanned out into the countryside to urge workers and farmers to ever greater efforts for the state. He also painted billboards that gave a touch of scenic interest along the tracks of the Orient Express, an experience that gave him a permanent taste for group efforts and bureaucracies, even though it killed his interest in Marxism.

Christo left Bulgaria and arrived in Paris just as the Pop Art boom reverberated there from New York and London. He began to exhibit wrapped objects of various kinds as well as drawings of possible wrapped projects on a much larger scale, like wrapped buildings (fig. 13.17). In 1962, close to the anniversary of the construction of the Berlin Wall, he built an iron curtain of 204 oil drums that blocked off a Paris street. This was the first of his "temporary monuments."

Christo moved to New York in the early sixties. Like many Europeans before him, he was overwhelmed by the scale of America. In 1969 he wrapped two and a half miles of Australian coastline; in 1974 he strung a bright yellow-orange curtain across Rifle Gap in Colorado. In 1976 he completed one of the most formidable art projects of the twentieth century, the *Running Fence*.

13.17

Project *Running Fence:* Linking Ocean, Land, Bureaucracies, and the Mass Media

Christo's concept for *Running Fence,* stated in his own still-evolving English, sounds simple:

Fence should start in ocean and cross rolling hills. Not many tree. There must be roads, farmhouses, other kind of fences for animals—cow and sheeps. And at other end it must cross freeway.[8]

The completed project consisted of an eighteen-foot-high white nylon fence that crossed the California landscape north of San Francisco from the Pacific Ocean to Highway 101, twenty-four miles inland (fig. 13.18). The materials for *Running Fence* included over twenty-four miles of eighteen-foot-wide white nylon ("as high as five cow"), two thousand poles to mount the nylon, and one hundred miles of steel cable. The cost, more than two million dollars, was covered by Christo's sale before the project was begun of photographs of the area with his drawings of the fence on the landscape. When completed, the fence was in place for a total of two weeks.

The two weeks of "art time" was preceded by over three years of planning and politicking. Besides town, county, and state agencies, fifty ranchers had to give their permission for

13.16 Eric Fischl.
The Master Bedroom. 1983.
Oil on canvas, 84″ × 108″.
Courtesy of Mary Boone Gallery, New York.

13.17 Christo.
Whitney Museum of American Art Packed, Project for Whitney Museum, New York. 1971.
Lithograph with collage, 27⅞″ × 21⅞″.
Collection of Whitney Museum of American Art, New York, Gift of Mr. and Mrs. B. H. Friedman.

13.18 Christo.
Running Fence, Project for Sonoma County and Marin County, California. 1976.
Collage, pastel, charcoal, engineering data, cloth, and tape. 22″ × 28″.
Collection of Whitney Museum of American Art, New York. Paul Rewald Memorial Fund.

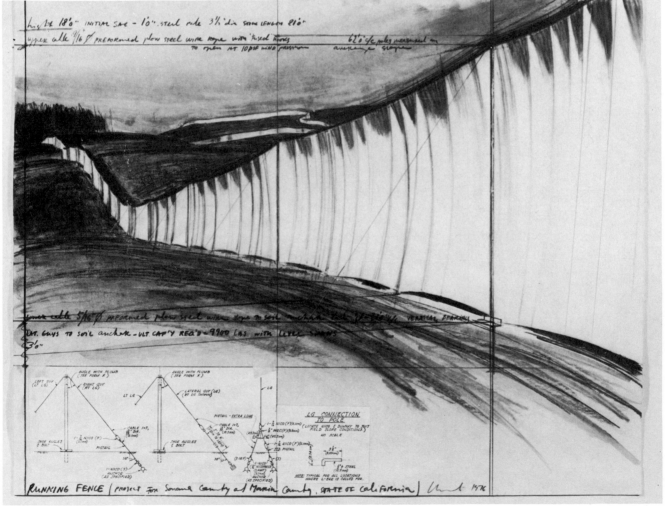

13.18

access and use of their land. Amazingly, only one rancher refused permission—there was therefore a gap in the fence—and only a last-minute Coastal Commission ban threatened to block the fence from entering the ocean. Christo put the fence into the water anyway.

For two weeks, American television and magazines spread the amazing pictures of a fence that erased private property and restored the continuous contours of the hills. The project united groups as diverse as college art students, ranchers, county supervisors, and highway patrolmen in a festive experience of the interconnectedness of natural and social processes.

In May of 1983 Christo's next project, *Surrounded Islands,* surrounded eleven islands in Miami's Biscayne Bay with 6.5 million square feet of pink fabric. The fabric extended for two-hundred feet from the shoreline of each island. This, too, lasted for two weeks and involved bureaucracies, the media, and the Miami public. Though much less accessible than *Running Fence,* it made much better color television pictures and was therefore seen by even more people. Christo was pleased with the networks' aerial television pictures of the pink "lily pads" floating in the deep blue of the water. It was, he said, his "homage to Monet."

Christo thus brings the network television image, the surface of nature, bureaucracies, and even bankers into collaborative works that do not totally eliminate the rectangles of the art industry, but definitely mix them up into new frames of perception.

A final area of increasing growth in the Post-Modernist period is video art.

Avant-Garde Television: The Era of Portable Video Begins

During the fifties, television's technological complexity and costliness placed it out of the reach of individual artists. With the introduction of the portable video deck and camera in 1965, many artists predicted the dawn of a video revolution. Portable video had great appeal: it recorded an image instantly; it recorded sound and image; it could be played back immediately; sound could be dubbed; and it could record image under much lower light conditions than any film. Two of the most important video artists currently practicing, Ed Emshwiller and Nam June Paik, have work that goes back to the early video era.

Ed Emshwiller (1925—): From Painted Images to Video Images

Ed Emshwiller moved to video after a lengthy apprenticeship in painting and film. He was an Abstract Expressionist painter from the early fifties until the mid-sixties. During this period he made time-lapse films of his painting process. When the first Portapaks arrived in the mid-sixties, Emshwiller was fascinated by video's "immediacy and its facility to combine and transform image." The Portapak, however, did not have the color and editing flexibility he wanted for his films.

The reputation of his films, however, brought him an invitation to join an experimental video project sponsored by New York's public television station WNET in 1972. Access to sophisticated editing equipment, a Moog synthesizer, and a computer provided Emshwiller with the means to accomplish the kind of visual transformations that had been the basis of his earlier paintings.

With video, I can readily combine the inner world, the fantasy world, the subjective world, with the external world. To me, that inner landscape is as important as the external landscape. One of the beauties of video is that it is probably the most immediate and most effective documenting medium for capturing reality. But, simultaneously, it has a great capacity for dealing with fantasy and combining real images in unreal ways.[9]

"Sunstone" is a three-minute 1979 video that combines Emshwiller's experiences in both painting and video. It opens with a gray, slablike image of a face. The face then goes through a series of transformations involving a kaleidoscope of color before returning to its original form. Figure 13.19 shows one of the images from the middle of the video, in which the face is rotated through a perspective sequence resembling the Surrealist world of Dali.

"Sunstone" is Emshwiller's video legacy to his experience as a painter and an illustrator of science fiction stories. His other tapes are real events remembered with the mind and eye of a painter. Emshwiller often uses drama and dance events as a starting point for his tapes and then transforms these recorded events through electronic color, overlay, and editing into statements that express his own personal imagination and feeling.

Emshwiller's work, even when it involves the complexity of several monitors, is nevertheless self-contained and packaged, to a certain extent, like a painting. Another early video

13.19 Ed Emshwiller.
Sunstone. 1980.
Color video. 3:00.
Photo courtesy of Electronic Arts Intermix, Inc., New York.

artist, Nam June Paik, has always approached television more as a performance.

Nam June Paik (1932—): Video as Happening

Though a Korean, Nam June Paik graduated from a Japanese university. Like that of Masami Teraoka, his degree reflected a wide interest in aesthetics and philosophy. Paik pursued his interest in twentieth-century music in Europe and the United States and became involved with Allan Kaprow and other New York artists during the 1960s. In 1963 Paik began his career in video by buying thirteen used television sets and using them in installations he called "video sculptures" of prepared television as parts of participatory environments or happenings. When he bought a Portapak in 1965, the camera enabled him to create his own programming for the monitors. Paik exhibited his first videotape on the same day that he bought the camera. Since 1965, he has continued to stress video as an environmental process, but he also produces his own programming and imagery.

Two of Paik's most important collaborators have been an engineer, Shuya Abe, and a musician, Charlotte Moorman.

Abe provided a radio-controlled robot, K–456, who walked and talked in Paik's performances (and sometimes on New York streets). Abe also collaborated with Paik to produce the Paik/Abe Video Synthesizer (1969), which enabled Paik to transform representational images into abstract forms as well as generate entirely unique abstract imagery.

Moorman has played a cello in many of Paik's performances. At times the sound of her cello is translated on monitors into abstract video images; at other times Moorman and her cello become involved in performances varying from submersion in a tank of water to surrounding herself with monitors that showed live images of her performance, electronically modulated by the sound of her cello (fig. 13.20 and plate 37).

13.20 Nam June Paik.
Global Groove. 1973.
Color video. 30:00.
Photo courtesy of Electronic Arts Intermix, Inc., New York.

13.21 Nam June Paik and Shigeko Kubota.
"Allan 'n Allen's Complaint." 1982.
Color video. 30:00.
Photo courtesy of Electronic Arts Intermix, Inc., New York.

13.20

The key to Paik's approach to video is that it extends into and creates the environment as much as it records it. This quality extends to Paik's style of exhibiting his videotapes: he has hung videotapes from the ceiling, projected video images onto walls, and set up installations in which the video is created by the sounds of the visitors themselves activating and modulating images on the screens.

Paik's preoccupation with environmental video is that television is already the major dimension of our environment. A 1973 piece, "TV Garden," consisted of thirty-three monitors planted, face up, among potted flowers so that the viewer could see video imagery literally competing with nature. Another work humorously probed the mystical reach of television: "TV Buddha" (1974) featured a bronze statue of a Buddha sitting before a television monitor that played back the "live" image of the Buddha—the Buddha contemplates himself on television.

Paik's humorous, open-ended, and technically experimental approach to video does not exclude personal feeling. His 1982 video, "Allan 'n Allen's Complaint" (fig. 13.21) features a very moving "conversation" between poet Allen Ginsberg and his deceased father. Paik mixed high-tech visual and sound effects with scenes of Ginsberg's friends—including one of Allan Kaprow walking on water on the Sea

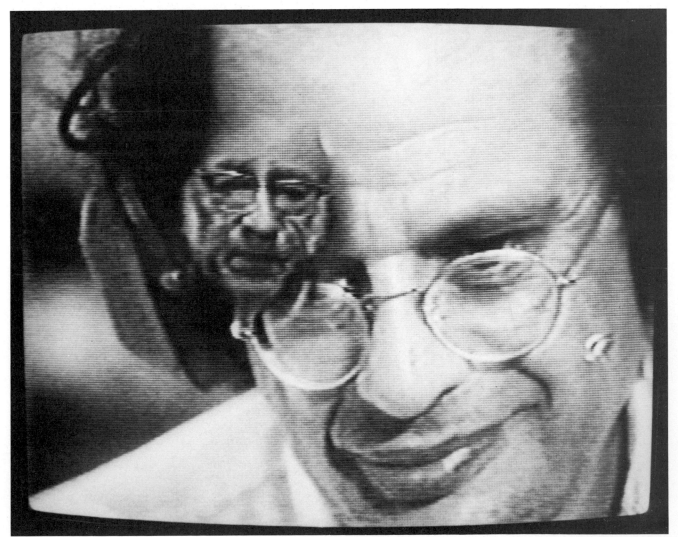

13.21

of Galilee in Israel. The half-hour tape constantly cuts back to the scenes of the elder Ginsberg commenting on the trials, joys, and dilemmas of being father to the Allen Ginsberg who has been a poetic gadfly in America since the beat generation days of the fifties.

Ginsberg is seen and heard as he reacts to the tape of his father. Since his father had already died when the tape was made, the conversation between the video images of the living poet and the dead father become a disquieting but deeply moving confrontation with the reality of death and the complexity of human relationships. Paik's zany and unpredictable cuts, images, and sounds generate a context in which this intensely personal dialogue takes place while still enabling the viewer to keep the entire sense of life—of life going on—intact. The tape, despite the revelation of sadness, ends up being a kind of celebration.

MTV and the VCR: A New Audience and a New Generation of Artists

Paik and Emshwiller represent two established artists whose involvement with video goes back to the sixties. The potential for avant-garde video has taken on new possibilities in the eighties with the explosion of personal VCR ownership. Another potential influence may come from the popularity of MTV.

Despite the criticisms that can be made of rock videos (mentioned in Chapter 11), music videos use a far more adventurous visual language than network television. They are in some ways an extension of the surprisingly experimental tradition of record album cover art.

The combination of the music video art form and the MTV distribution system has produced a kind of clearing house in which the best and the worst of the full range of popular and fine art meet. There is plenty of exploitation of visual sex and violence; there is a lot of hype and repetition. Videos are as close to commercials as they are to feature films. Yet they also have a tremendous flexibility and freedom of visual movement and fantasy that can combine film, photography, computer-generated video, drama, dance, performance, and so forth. It is the prime area for the influence of today's avant-garde.

Most videos are heavily indebted to Surrealism for their combination of fantasy and reality, along with a shrewd touch of Dada anarchy. Paul Simon put out a 1984 video whose song and visuals paid homage to the Surrealist artist René Magritte. Bob Dylan's 1984 video "Jokerman" presented a collage of visuals ranging from Renaissance art to modern abstract paintings. Andy Warhol has directed and appeared in a video by The Cars,"Hello Again." Italian avant-garde filmmaker Federico Fellini has directed a video. One group not only took its name directly from the title of a Futurist manifesto—*The Art of Noise*—they produced a brilliant video that illustrated the Futurist call for a nontraditional form of music, "Close to the Edit."

John Sanborn, a prominent video artist whose work has been exhibited in museums and on PBS television, has commented that avant-garde video should aim at a larger audience than the traditional museumgoers. Music videos are helping to prepare such a potential audience:

Video artists can't just retreat into the shelter of museums and exhibition spaces. . . .

That's why you can't ignore MTV. It's having a huge effect on a whole new video audience's visual literacy. So the video artists who care about their work and don't just see it as another job have to find a way to get that exposure too and start broadening everyone's horizons.[10]

Music videos are probably too closely linked to the promotional demands of record companies to become a prime arena for avant-garde initiative. They nevertheless have a tremendous potential for becoming a bridge linking the open-ended language of the avant-garde with a medium that has been dominated by the far more conservative corporate interests of the major networks. Videos provide another example of the powerful potential of the popular arts of the mass media to influence avant-garde art, and vice-versa, in such a way that both are enriched.

Carol Ann Klonarides and Michael Owen: Bridging the Gap between Avant-Garde and Commercial Video

One of the most interesting examples of a personal use of commercial and avant-garde forms of video is seen in the work of Carol Ann Klonarides and the producer Michael Owen. Owen has worked in commercial video ranging from political commercials to industrials to music videos. Klonarides, with a background in New York gallery management, teamed up with Owens in order to produce videos that approach the artist in such a way as to translate the artist's work into specifically video terms.

Klonarides' video, "Laurie Simmons—A Teaser," for instance, is a remarkably crisp and poetic three-and-a-half-minute video that shows the photographer Laurie Simmons photographing women swimmers underwater (fig. 13.22 and plate 38). Klonarides' video technique is remarkably simple: the camera does not move. As in the first films of Mélièes, it becomes a stationary window. Simmons, with her camera and fins, twists and moves in a constant unchoreographed ballet to photograph the swimmers. The swimmers glide through the water with the strangely random quality that nevertheless has a sense of naturalness calculated to resemble that of the photographs that Simmons herself takes.

13.22

13.22 Carol Ann Klonarides and Michael
Owen.
"Laurie Simmons—A Teaser." 1980.
Color video. 5:00.
Photo courtesy of Electronic Arts Intermix,
Inc., New York.

13.23 Carol Ann Klonarides and Michael
Owens.
"Cindy Sherman—An Interview."
1980.
Color video. 10:00.
Photo courtesy of Electronic Arts Intermix,
Inc., New York. Copyright MICA—TV for the
Artists' Television Network.

Besides bubbly underwater sounds and a slow, rhythmic musical tone, one hears the voice of Simmons commenting on her interest in such underwater photographs. Her fascination with them stems from her desire to create "images of women in an interior filled with blue light." She notes that the women she photographs are her friends, who enjoy the experience immensely. Simmons sees her photographs as images that contain figures in a blue light in the same way that the blue water of the pool contains the swimmers. Klonarides's video has the same effect.

Klonarides used the same simplicity in her interview with photographer Cindy Sherman. Sherman takes photographs of herself in roles, costumes, and environments that resemble stills from Hollywood "B" movies (fig. 13.23). She does not document a specific role or make herself up as an exact likeness of a particular star; instead, she combines her outfit, makeup, and environment (often produced by projecting a slide as a background) into an image that strikes the viewer as an illusive "déjà vu" flash of recognition based on the atmosphere, her facial expression, and the overall mood of the photograph. A Sherman photograph, in other words, becomes an entire production and characterization compressed into the format of a single evocative image—the photograph becomes a stage for Sherman to experience the idea of a movie, a star, and an era. Sherman thus personalizes her experience of the media to move in and out of identities that she can experience for a time and then, through the photograph, share with herself and others.

Klonarides' video showed her in the role of a gallery manager interviewing Cindy Sherman about her photographs. It has the same direct quality as the Simmons tape. The only change in camera comes in closeups of Sherman's face as it suddenly changes to become the same face seen in the photograph under discussion. The video reflects the same process of identity change as Sherman's photographs.

Klonarides and Owen deliberately borrow, mimic, and otherwise alter conventional television formats. They used the commercial format to present the work of artist-designer R. M. Fischer. Without the cynicism of Warhol's earlier Pop Art uses of mass media formats, these videos make the viewer conscious of the way network television uses similar programs (and an elaborate combination of filters). The fresh approach to these network formulas produces a new video experience that reveals something of both the artist and his or her work and the nature of the medium of television itself.

13.23 a

Video artists like Emshwiller, Paik, Sanborn, and Klonarides are able to show their work in museums, in university settings, and on many public television stations. Distribution of avant-garde video is also possible through sources such as the San Francisco International Video Festival or Electronic Arts Intermix, a New York organization that handles video art nationwide. There is also an Artists' Television Network in

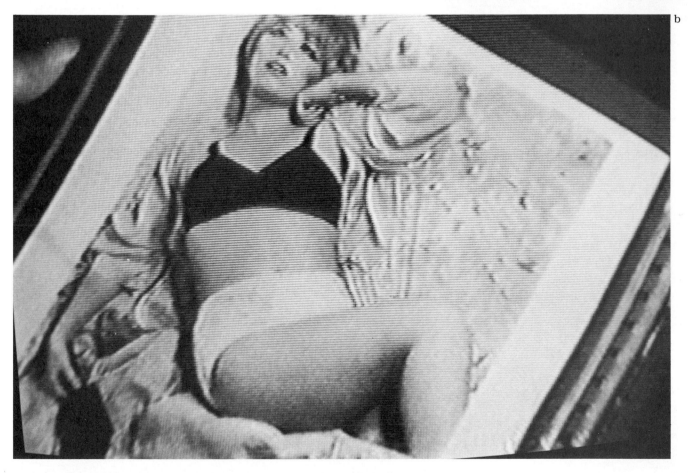

b

New York, which is pioneering the concept of setting up a kind of video gallery within the broadcast system itself.

As noted earlier in terms of commercial television, the most significant breakthrough for video artists may come from the VCR and MTV. If MTV is developing a broader sense of video language, the VCR holds out the potential for people to begin to regard videocassettes as formats of art, entertainment, and information equivalent to books that can be privately bought and saved. According to the video artist and critic Les Levine:

> If an individual artist can sell 1,000 video cassettes at $50 apiece, an economic basis for the production exists. It isn't necessary for the video artist to broadcast to everyone in America. It's only necessary for him or her to be able to reach that limited group which is interested in art. . . . Within five years, most videotape stores will have video art sections in them.[11]

Network television is a communal and public art that can be compared to the stained glass windows and mural tradition that dominated medieval culture; video art on cassettes is likely to have an effect resembling that of easel paintings in oil (and perspective) when they were introduced into Western culture during the Renaissance: it could transform video into a far more individually produced, individually owned, and individually programmed kind of art. Video—with its potential for summing up, recycling, and reinterpreting the visual language of art from all periods and cultures—could then enter a dramatically new era in its role as the primary source of icons for a far richer version of the myth of the autonomous individual.

Just as video is beginning to broaden its contact with avant-garde art, another Western image-making machine is already strongly affecting the way we think and feel about ourselves. The final chapter is a brief series of comments—an "afterword"—that suggests some of the artistic and cultural impact of the computer.

TOWARD THE

COMPUTER AGE

ASSESSMENTS

1. Do you see the computer having as great an impact on art and artists as the introduction of photography in the nineteenth century?
2. Are you aware of computer images when you see them on television or in films? What quality or qualities do they have? How do they differ from previous kinds of artistic images?
3. Do you own a computer? If not, would you like to? How do computers affect your life today?

344

The need for the alternative vision of avant-garde art is perhaps even greater today because of the transition our culture is making from the Television Age to the Computer Age. The computer is leading a revolution that is already changing the way we think and feel about ourselves.

In addition to its other information and image-producing possibilities, the computer is also the next generation of Western art's perspective machines.

Computer art, as noted in Chapter 3, was already implicit in the drawings of Paolo Uccello at the beginning of the Perspective Age. The computer surpasses all previous forms of Western perspective machines in that it does not need to have (or "see") an image to draw from. All it needs is information, bits of information. The computer, as the experts say, "crunches numbers." It then applies Brunelleschi's formula with the speed of light and can feed back perspective images ranging from the inside of the body to unseeable stars in space. Information from a Voyager space probe, for instance, enabled a computer to generate images not only of Saturn, but of Saturn's rings (fig. a.1)—including a picture of a typical cross section of its composition (fig. a.2). The first entirely computer-generated commercial, meanwhile, has already been made (fig. a.3 and plate 39). The first comic book in which the art and lettering were both created on the same computer appeared in 1985 (fig. a.4).

Recent movies have shown us a mind-boggling range of perspective images and their potential uses as derived from the computer.

Star Trek II: The Wrath of Khan contained a two-minute sequence of computer-generated imagery that displayed the evolution of life on an entire planet. *Tron* (fig. a.5 and plate 40) brought Disney Studios's animation into the computer age by integrating live actors into an entirely computer-generated environment. *Looker,* mentioned earlier, was based on the idea of developing computer-generated images of actors and

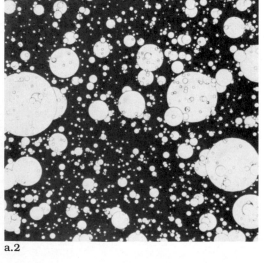

a.2

a.1

actresses by feeding statistics scanned from near-perfect specimens. These computer-generated actors and actresses would then be used to make commercials that had irresistible persuasive power.

Science has already found applications for computer-generated perspective images that rival these fictional ones. The biological structures of some animals have now been computerized completely enough to enable their use in experiments in place of live animals. Science has produced computer-generated pictures of the hydrogen atom, a feat previously considered impossible since light could not penetrate into the "space" of the atom without altering its structure in the process.

Data from spy satellites can produce computer-generated images of license plates in Red Square. American tanks can now launch missiles on the battlefield that can orbit the area until their scanning video eye "sees" an enemy tank, which the missile then pursues and attacks.

Commercial airline pilots flying in conditions of low visi-

a.1 Saturn's rings. Voyager mission. 1981.
Courtesy of NASA.

a.2 Computerized image of typical cross section (room-size) of Saturn's outermost ring. 1981.
Courtesy of NASA.

a.3 "Futureworld."
Pentel commercial. 1982.
Courtesy Triton Advertising, Inc.

a.4 *Shatter*, comic book.
Art by Mike Saenz; story by Peter B. Gillis; published by First Comics. 1985.
Trademark and Copyright 1985, First Comics, Inc.

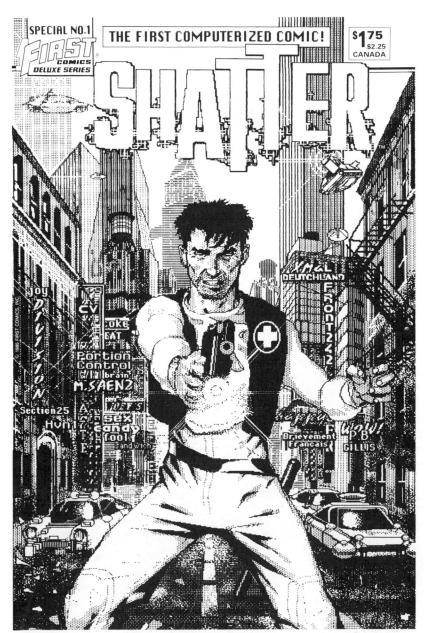
a.4

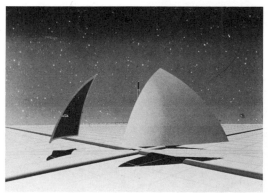
a.3

346

bility can be provided constantly updated perspective drawings of the terrain below them.

Many avant-garde artists have begun to venture into the possibilities of making art in collaboration with the computer. Some artists use newly developed "paintbrush" programs in order to essentially duplicate on a computer printout or on a video monitor the same kind of images they already produce in other media. Keith Haring has created images similar to the graffiti art shown in figure i.1. Philip Pearlstein, a New York painter known for his detached way of painting nudes, has adapted his work—virtually intact—to the computer.

At least one avant-garde artist has made a significant effort to make art that derives from the unique potential of the computer itself. Harold Cohen was an established British painter whose work had already been shown in international avant-garde exhibitions when he went to the University of California San Diego campus as a visiting professor in 1968. During that year Cohen learned computer programming; he is still in California today. He is also still producing art, undoubtedly avant-garde art. But he now has a collaborator, AARON, a computer.

Cohen equipped AARON with a kind of flexible extended arm that can move freely and make marks with a felt pen. He then programmed AARON with twenty basic rules that guide the movements of the arm (the arm unit is called the turtle). These twenty rules and their possible combinations require the same memory and computing scale as a computer programmed to play grand master-caliber chess.

The twenty rules are basic to art and sound incredibly simple. They include such concepts as the difference between inside and outside, closed and open, image and background, overlap, large and small—concepts that normally appear in child art at about the age of three. AARON, however, never gets tired and never repeats an image (he also never forgets one).

Cohen's fascination with AARON's output sparked his decision to collaborate: his role is to take AARON's drawings and color or otherwise modify them. Cohen says he actually does very little modifying, other than color, since AARON's work has its own sense of "personality" (fig. a.6).

Cohen's work raises intriguing possibilities for the avant-garde and art. It also raises some intriguing questions about the difference between personality in human beings and personality in machines.

This question is vitally important, because of our tendency to see ourselves as reflections of our technologies. How often do you hear people speak of their own thought or behavior in terms of feedback, input, data, programming, output, and so on? Computers *process data,* people *think*— as artists constantly remind us—with their bodies, senses, and minds.

Personality and the computer has also been a major

a.5 *Tron.* 1982.
Walt Disney Productions.
Copyright 1982 Walt Disney Productions.

a.6 Harold Cohen.
"Black and White Drawing." 1985.
India ink on paper, 22″ × 30″.
Photo: Becky Cohen.

theme in important films. *Star Wars* presented the computer as the benign and vulnerable personalities of R2D2 and C3PO. *2001—A Space Odyssey* presented a different computer personality—Hal, who had to be unplugged.

The question of personality and the computer, however, raises a question that only a person—not a computer personality—can answer: Who am I? Computer images of stars, of molecules, or of human organs functioning below the skin are marvelous extensions of human perception. But the image a person develops of himself or herself is through an ongoing quest that leads to the indefinable inner self. It is a picture, in other words, that the information-bit pointillism of computer art cannot put totally into focus.

The computer as an image maker thus reflects a problem similar to that of the photograph as it entered Western culture as an icon in the nineteenth century. The camera, like the computer, made images from facts. The computer is essentially a closed universe; it can only deal with facts, facts translated into numbers. In the human universe, as the avant-garde reminded Western culture for 150 years—facts simply are not enough.

A major role of Western art—from the avant-garde or elsewhere—will therefore be to continue producing icons (including computer-generated icons) that sustain our culture's myth of the autonomous individual. To do this, such icons must reflect personality. The human person must be powerful in art if it is to have a powerful effect in culture. The

a.6

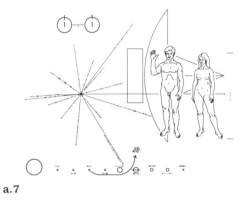

a.7

human person, as Thomas Aquinas said in the Middle Ages, "is a kind of spiritual universe."

Perhaps the appropriate image to end this text is that of the only artist-drawn image that exists beyond our solar system: the engraved image borne on a plaque on the Pioneer 10 (fig. a.7) space probe that left our solar system on June 12, 1983, on a mission to "wander through the Milky Way forever, encountering another star system every million years or so." As the *Newsweek* article continued, this image

shows a man and a woman, the location of our solar system and such basic points of science as the hydrogen molecule. Unless it makes contact with new life forms, however, Pioneer will encounter only the loneliness of the long-distance space traveler.[1]

This text, however, cannot end without criticizing this image exhibited before the cosmos on Pioneer 10. There should be a second image that complements this one, an image for instance, like Marc Chagall's *Horse and Chariot* (fig. a.8). Such an image would show any other intelligence encountering Pioneer 10 that our experience includes the inner space of the human person—the space, as Chagall's art shows, in which cows (and horses) can jump over the moon. As Chagall comments: "Our whole inner world is reality— perhaps even more real than the apparent world."[2]

a.8

NOTES

Introduction

1. Michael Real, *Mass-Mediated Culture*, (Englewood Cliffs, N.J.: Prentice-Hall, 1977).

Chapter 1

1. Martha Alf, letter to author, May 1984.
2. Rhoda Kellogg, *Analyzing Children's Art* (Palo Alto, Calif.: National Press Books, 1970).
3. Howard Nilis, "The Creative Spark," *Harvard Business Review* (January 1980), p. 33.
4. Betty Edwards, *Drawing on the Right Side of the Brain*, (Los Angeles: J. P. Tarcher, 1979), p. 76.
5. Ibid, p. 72.
6. Clifford Geertz, quoted in *The Ascent of Man*, ed. John F. Henahan (New York: Little, Brown, 1975), p. 19.

Chapter 2

1. Plato, *The Republic*, bk. II, sec. 369, l. 53.
2. José Ortega y Gassett, *The Revolt of the Masses* (New York: W. W. Norton, 1932), p. 151.
3. Christine Havelock, "Art as Communication in Ancient Greece," in *Communication Arts in the Ancient World*, ed. Eric A. Havelock and Jackson B. Hershbell. (New York: Hastings House Publishers, 1978), p. 109.
4. Jerry Jordan Pollitt, *Art and Experience in Classical Greece.* (Cambridge: Cambridge University Press, 1975), p. 78.
5. Ibid, p. 78.
6. Plato, quoted in E. H. Gombrich, *Art and Illusion* (Princeton, N.J.: Princeton University Press, 1960), p. 126.
7. Plato, quoted in Ibid, p. 126.
8. Robert Grosseteste, quoted in Otto von Simson, *The Gothic Cathedral*, (Princeton, N.J.: Princeton University Press, 1956), p. 214.
9. Otto von Simson, *The Gothic Cathedral*, p. 214.
10. Abbot Suger, quoted in Erwin Panofsky, "Abbot Suger of St. Denis," in *Meaning in the Visual Arts.* (Garden City, N.Y.: Doubleday, 1955), p. 127.
11. Kenneth Clark, quoted from the television series, *Civilisation*, program no. 2, "The Great Thaw," Time-Life Films, Inc., 1973.
12. Thomas Aquinas, quoted in Jacques Maritain, *The Person and the Common Good* (Notre Dame, Ind.: University of Notre Dame Press, 1966), p. 61.

13. Villard de Honnecourt, quoted in Jean Gimpel, *The Medieval Machine: The Industrial Revolution of the Middle Ages* (New York: Penguin Books, 1977), p. 130.
14. Roger Bacon, quoted in Ibid, pp. 144, 145.
15. Roger Bacon, quoted in Samuel Y. Edgarton, Jr., *The Renaissance Rediscovery of Linear Perspective* (New York: Harper & Row, 1975), p. 12.

Chapter 3

1. Samuel Y. Edgarton, Jr., *The Renaissance Rediscovery of Linear Perspective* (New York: Harper & Row, 1975).
2. Giorgio Vasari, *The Lives of the Artists*, trans. George Bull (New York: Penguin Books, 1965), p. 104.
3. Leon Battista Alberti, quoted in William M. Ivins, Jr., *On the Rationalization of Sight* (New York: Da Capo Press, 1973), p. 22.
4. Elton Davies, *Arts and Cultures of Man* (San Francisco: International Textbook Co., 1972), p. 370.
5. Ibid, p. 370.
6. Leonardo da Vinci, *The Notebooks of Leonardo da Vinci*, ed. Robert N. Linscott (New York: The Modern Library, 1957), p. 79.
7. Ibid, p. 35.
8. Ibid, p. viii.
9. Ibid, p. 37.
10. Michelangelo, quoted in Svetlana Alpers, *The Art of Describing: Dutch Art in the Seventeenth Century* (Chicago: University of Chicago Press, 1983), p.xxiii.
11. Giovanni Pico della Mirandola, *On the Dignity of Man*, trans. Charles Glenn Wallis (Indianapolis, Ind.: Bobbs-Mcrril Educational Publishing, 1965), p.5.
12. William M. Ivins, Jr., *Prints and Visual Communication* (Cambridge: M.I.T. Press, 1969), pp. 2, 3.

Chapter 4

1. Lawrence Gowing, *Vermeer* (New York: Barnes & Noble, 1961), p. 14.
2. Roland Barthes, *New Critical Essays* (New York: Hill & Wang, 1980), p. 25.
3. Aldous Huxley, *Heaven and Hell* (New York: Harper & Row, 1971), p. 46.
4. Charles Baudelaire, "The Salon of 1859," in *The Mirror of Art*, trans. and ed. Jonathan Mayne (Garden City, N.Y.: Doubleday Anchor, 1956), pp. 238–39.

5. Peter Galassi, *Before Photography* (New York: Museum of Modern Art, 1981).

6. Louis Jacques Mande Daguerre, "Daguerreotypie," in *Classic Essays in Photography* ed. Alan Tractenberg, (New Haven, Conn.: Leete's Island Books, 1980), p. 13.

7. John Constable, quoted in Helen Gardner, *Art Through the Ages,* ed. Horst de la Croix and Richard G. Tansey (New York: Harcourt Brace Jovanovich), p. 590.

Chapter 5

1. Paul Délaroche, quoted in Helen Gardner, *Art Through the Ages,* p. 708.

2. Gisèle Freund, *Photography and Society* (Boston: David R. Godine, 1980), p. 58.

3. Ibid, p. 57.

4. Theophile Gautier, quoted in Aaron Sharf, *Art and Photography* (London: Penguin Press, 1968), p. 111.

5. Robert Hughes, "Will the Swollen Art Market Burst?" *The New York Review of Books,* Dec. 6, 1984, p. 23.

6. Leo Rosenthal, quoted in Charles Rosen and Henri Zerner, "The Unhappy Medium," *The New York Review of Books,* May 1982, p. 50.

7. Nikolas Pevsner, *Pioneers of Modern Design* (New York: Viking/Penguin, 1964), p. 40.

8. Ibid, p. 40.

9. Ibid, p. 40.

10. Ibid, p. 42.

11. Charles Dickens, *Coketown,* quoted in J. Bronowski, *The Ascent of Man* (Boston: Little, Brown, 1975), p. 177.

12. Charles Baudelaire, "The Salon of 1846," quoted in *The Mirror of Art: Critical Studies by Baudelaire,* trans. and ed. Jonathan Mayne (Garden City, N.Y.: Doubleday Anchor, 1956), pp. 38–39.

13. Charles Darwin, quoted in Walter Kerr, *The Decline of Pleasure* (New York: Simon and Schuster, 1962), p. 67.

14. Gustave Courbet, quoted in Helen Gardner, *Art Through the Ages,* p. 758.

15. Pierre Proudhon, quoted in *Realism and Tradition in Art,* ed. Linda Nochlin (Englewood Cliffs, N.J.: Prentice-Hall, 1966), p. 52.

16. Charles Baudelaire, "The Salon of 1859," in *The Mirror of Art: Critical Studies by Baudelaire,* p. 242.

17. Ibid, pp. 230, 233.

Chapter 6

1. Ernest Chesneau, quoted in *Realism and Tradition in Art,* ed. Linda Nochlin (Englewood Cliffs, N.J.: Prentice-Hall, 1966), p. 82.

2. Paul de Saint-Victor, quoted in Ian Dunlop, *The Shock of the New* (New York: American Heritage Press, McGraw-Hill, 1972), p. 33.

3. Édouard Manet, quoted in Ibid, p. 21.

4. Beatrice Farwell, *The Cult of Images: Baudelaire and the 19th-Century Media Explosion.* (Santa Barbara, Calif.: University of California, Santa Barbara Art Museum, 1977), p. 14.

5. Thomas Couture, quoted in John Canady, *Mainstreams of Modern Art* (New York: Holt, Rinehart & Winston, 1981), p. 167.

6. Émile Zola, quoted in *Realism and Tradition in Art,* ed. Linda Nochlin, p. 77.

7. Ibid, p. 72.

8. Linda Nochlin, "Imagining the Orient," *Art in America,* May 1983, p. 122.

9. Anne Coffin Hanson, *Manet and the Modern Tradition* (New Haven, Conn.: Yale University Press, 1977), p. 193.

Chapter 7

1. Claude Monet, quoted in Linda Nochlin, *Realism* (New York: Penguin Books, 1971), p. 63.

2. Hippolyte Taine, quoted in ibid, p. 23.

3. Georges Seurat, quoted in John Rewald, *Post-Impressionism,* 3rd ed. (New York: The Museum of Modern Art, 1978), p. 83.

4. Teodor de Wyzewa, quoted in ibid., p. 397.

5. Paul Cezanne, quoted in Ariane Ruskin, *Nineteenth Century Art* (New York: McGraw-Hill, 1973), p. 186.

6. Vincent van Gogh, *Dear Theo,* ed. Irving Stone (New York: New American Library, 1969), p. 290.

7. Ibid, p. 364.

8. Vincent van Gogh, quoted in Hershel B. Chipp, *Theories of Modern Art* (Berkeley: University of California Press, 1968), p. 42.

9. Vincent van Gogh, *Dear Theo,* p. 391.

10. Vincent van Gogh, quoted in Ariane Ruskin, *Nineteenth Century Art,* p. 193.

11. Octave Mirbeau, quoted in Bogomila Welsh-Ovcharov, *Van Gogh in Perspective* (Englewood Cliffs, N.J.: Prentice-Hall, 1974), p. 66.

12. Vincent van Gogh, *Dear Theo,* p. 324.

13. Paul Gaughin, quoted in John Rewald, *Post-Impressionism,* p. 172.

14. August Strindberg, quoted in George Boudaille, *Gauguin* (London: Thomas & Hudson, 1964), p. 209.

15. Paul Gauguin, quoted in Raymond Charmond, *Gauguin* (New York: Barnes & Noble, 1965), p. 78.

16. Ibid, p. 83.

17. Ibid, p. 15.

18. John Canaday, *Mainstreams of Modern Art,* 2nd ed. (New York: Holt, Rinehart & Winston, 1981), p. 390.

19. Paul Gauguin, quoted in John Rewald, *Post-Impressionism,* p. 178.

Chapter 8

1. Charles Eidsvik, *Cineliteracy* (Boston: Random House, 1978), pp. 112–13.

2. Barbara Novak, *Nature and Culture: American Landscape and Painting, 1825–1875* (New York: Oxford University Press, 1980), p. 23.

3. Thomas Eakins, quoted in Thomas Sewell, *Thomas Eakins, Artist of Philadelphia* (Philadelphia Museum of Art, 1982), p. 5.

4. Richard Schickel, *Movies: The History of an Art and an Institution* (New York: Basic Books, 1964), p. 67.

5. Marshall McLuhan, *The Mechanical Bride* (New York: Vanguard, 1951), p. 5.

6. Britton Hadden, quoted in James Playsted Wood, *Magazines in the United States* (New York: The Ronald Press, 1971), p. 210.

7. Henry R. Luce, quoted in James Playsted Wood, *Magazine in the United States,* p. 218.

8. Calvin Coolidge, quoted in Frank Presbrey, *The History and Development of Advertising,* (Westport, Conn.: Greenwood Press, 1961), p. 619.
9. Quoted in Jane Stern and Michael Stern, *Auto Ads* (New York: David Obst Books, Random House, 1978), p. 21.

Chapter 9

1. Felix Feneon, quoted in Janine Warnod, *Washboat Days* (New York: Grossman Publishers, 1973), p. 122.
2. Gertrude Stein, *Picasso* (Boston: Beacon Press, 1959), p. 9.
3. Ibid, p. 8.
4. Jane Warnod, *Washboat Days,* p. 209.
5. Wassily Kandinsky, "Reminiscences," reprinted in *Modern Artists on Art,* ed. Robert L. Herbert (Englewood Cliffs, N.J.: Prentice-Hall, 1964), pp. 23–24.
6. Filippo Marinetti, quoted in Maryanne W. Martin, *Futurist Art and Theory* (Oxford: Clarendon Press, 1968), p. 39.
7. Umberto Boccioni, quoted in Ibid, p. 45.
8. Ibid, p. 130.
9. Giacomo Balla and Fortunato Depero, "The Futurist Reconstruction of the Universe," quoted in *Futurist Manifestos,* edited by Umbro Apollonio, translated by Robert Brain (New York: The Viking Press, 1978), p. 199.
10. Nikolai Lenin, quoted in D. J. Wenden, *The Birth of the Movies* (New York: E. P. Dutton, 1974), p. 106.
11. Dziga Vertov, quoted in Norbert Lynton, *The Story of Modern Art* (Ithica, N.Y.: Cornell University Press, 1980), p. 111.
12. André Breton, quoted in William S. Rubin, *Dada, Surrealism, and Their Heritage* (New York: Museum of Modern Art, 1968), p. 64.
13. Gaëtan Picon, *Surrealists and Surrealism* (New York: Rizzoli International Publishers, 1983), p. 63.
14. Max Ernst, quoted in Ibid, pp. 11, 12.
15. André Breton, "Surrealism Between the Wars," speech given at Yale University, published in the magazine *VVV* (March 1943).

Chapter 10

1. George Gerbner, "The Dynamics of Cultural Resistance," in *Women in the Mass Media,* ed. Gaye Tuchman, Arlene Kepler-Daniele, and James Benet. (New York: Oxford University Press, 1978), p. 47.
2. Joshua Meyerwitz, "Where Have the Children Gone?" *Newsweek,* August 30, 1982, p. 13.
3. Neil Postman, "The Day Our Children Disappear: Predictions of a Media Ecologist," *Phi Delta Kappan,* vol. 62 (Jan. 1981), p. 385.
4. Martin Esslin, *The Television Age* (San Francisco: W. H. Freeman, 1982), pp. 22, 27.
5. Joan Lunden, quoted in Robert Scheer, "The Rise of Joan Lunden: News Sense Unimportant," in *Los Angeles Times,* May 29, 1977.
6. Linda Lavin, quoted in Penny Pagano, "Strong Gains Seen in Image of Women on TV," *Los Angeles Times,* Dec. 6, 1984.
7. Abbie Hoffman, *Revolution for the Hell of It,* (New York: Dial Press, 1968), pp. 137–138.

Chapter 11

1. Jackson Pollock, quoted in Jack Hobbs, *Art in Context* (New York: Harcourt Brace Jovanovich, 1975), p. 286.
2. André Breton, quoted in *André Breton and the Basic Concepts of Surrealism,* by Michel Courrouges, translated by Maura Prendergast, S.N.D. (Alabama: University of Alabama Press, 1974), p. 101.
3. Jackson Pollock, quoted in Harold Rosenberg, "Hans Hoffman: Nature into Action," *ArtNews,* May 1957, p. 24.
4. Robert Rauschenberg, quoted in Robert Hughes, *The Shock of the New* (New York: Alfred A. Knopf, 1981), p. 334.
5. Ibid, p. 335.
6. Andy Warhol, quoted in Lucy Lippard, *Pop Art,* (New York: Frederick A. Praeger, 1966), p. 98.
7. Andy Warhol quoted in Robert Hughes, "Only in America," *The New York Review of Books,* Dec. 20, 1979, p. 20.
8. Lucy Lippard, *Pop Art,* p. 97.
9. Ralph Graves, ed., "The Master of the Soft Touch," in *Life* 67, no. 21 (November 21, 1969): 64c.
10. Frank Stella, quoted in Richard Whelan, "Frank Stella: All Dressed Up with No Place to Go," *ArtNews,* Feb. 1980, p. 78.
11. Richard Estes, quoted in Howard Smagula, *Currents, Contemporary Directions in the Arts* (Englewood Cliffs, N.J.: Prentice-Hall, 1983), p. 59.
12. Suzi Gablik, "The Art Job, or How the Avant-garde Sold Out," *Art in America,* April 1980, p. 11.

Chapter 12

1. Roger Enrico, quoted in Fred Danzig, "Pepsi Cola Gambles on the Young," *Advertising Age,* March 15, 1984, p. 3.
2. Quoted in the screenplay of the film *Looker,* by Michael Crichton, Oct. 1980, p. 112.
3. Quoted in Bruce Kurtz, *Spots: the Popular Art of American Television Commericials* (New York: Arts Communications, 1977), p. 18.
4. Robert Breer, quoted in Charles Solomon, "Aspects of the Avant-garde—a First for the Academy," *Los Angeles Times,* Oct. 10, 1981.
5. Linda Nochlin, "Imagining the Orient," *Art in America,* May 1983, p. 189.
6. Tony Schwartz, *The Resonant Chord* (New York: Doubleday Anchor, 1973), pp. 21, 22.
7. Martin Esslin, *The Television Age* (San Francisco: W. H. Freeman, 1982), p. 53.
8. Gustave Courbet, quoted in Linda Nochlin, *Realism and Tradition in Art* (Englewood Cliffs, N.J.: Prentice-Hall, 1966), p. 36.
9. Michael Schudson, *Advertising, the Uneasy Persuasion* (New York: Basic Books, 1984), p. 222.

Chapter 13

1. Peter Fuller, *Aesthetics After Modernism* (New York: W. W. Norton, 1983), p. 33.
2. Robert Hughes, *The Shock of the New* (New York: Alfred A. Knopf, 1981), p. 325.

NOTES

3. Allan Kaprow, "The Shape of the Art Environment," *Artforum* (Summer 1968), p. 33.
4. Robert Smithson, "A Sedimentation of the Mind: Earth Project," *Artforum*, Aug. 15, 1972, p. 40.
5. Robert Smithson, quoted in Lucy Lippard, *Overlay* (New York: Pantheon Books, 1983), p. 229.
6. Lucy Lippard, *Get the Message? A Decade of Art for Social Change* (New York: E. P. Dutton, 1984), p. 149.
7. Lita Albuquerque, letter to author, Sept. 1984.
8. Christo, quoted in "Onward and Upward with the Arts," *The New Yorker*, March 28, 1977, p. 56.
9. Ed Emshwiller, quoted in Victor Ancora, "Ed Emshwiller: Combining Inner and Outer Landscapes," *Videography*, Sept. 1983, p. 72.
10. John Sanborn, quoted in "Sanborn's 'Video Panorama' Eyed," by Patrick Goldstein, *The Los Angeles Times*, (January 13, 1984), part VI, p. 16.
11. Les Levine, "SATV—Small Audience TV," *Video-Arts Quarterly*, Spring 1985, p. 18.

Afterword

1. "From Here to Eternity," *Newsweek*, June 13, 1983, p. 56.
2. Marc Chagall, quoted in Judith Michaelson, "Chagall, Artist of Joy and Suffering, Dies," *Los Angeles Times*, March 29, 1985.

BIBLIOGRAPHY

General Art and Art History

Berger, John. *Ways of Seeing*. London: The British Broadcasting Corporation, and Penguin Books, 1972.

Clark, Sir Kenneth. *Civilisation: A Personal View*. New York: Harper & Row, 1969.

Edwards, Betty. *Drawing on the Right Side of the Brain*. Los Angeles: J. P. Tarcher, 1979.

Elsen, Albert E. *Purposes of Art* (4th ed.). New York: Holt, Rinehart & Winston, 1982.

Gardner, Helen. *Art Through the Ages*. 6th ed. Edited by Horst de la Croix and Richard G. Tansey. New York: Harcourt Brace Jovanovich, 1980.

Gombrich, E. H. *Art and Illusion*. Princeton, N.J.: Princeton University Press, 1960.

————. *The Story of Art*. 12th ed. London: Phaidon, 1972.

Gregory, R. I. *Eye and Brain: The Psychology of Seeing*. 2nd ed. New York: McGraw-Hill, 1972.

Hauser, Arnold. *The Social History of Art*. New York: Alfred A. Knopf, 1961.

Janson, H. W. *History of Art*. Rev. ed. Englewood Cliffs, N.J.: Prentice-Hall and Abrams, 1969.

Kellogg, Rhoda. *Analyzing Children's Art*. Palo Alto, Calif: National Press Books, 1970.

Lowenfeld, Viktor, and W. Lambert Brittain. *Creative and Mental Growth*. 7th ed. New York: Macmillan, 1982.

Preble, Duane, and Sarah Preble. *Artforms* (third edition). New York: Harper & Row, 1985.

Native Art

Goldwater, Robert. *Primitivism in Modern Art*. New York: Harper & Row, 1958.

Kirk, Malcolm. *Man as Art: New Guinea*. New York: Viking, 1981.

Rubin, William, ed. *"Primitivism" in 20th Century Art: Affinity of the Tribal and the Modern*. New York: Museum of Modern Art, 1984.

Spini, Tito. *Togu Na*. New York: Rizzoli International Publications, 1976.

Thompson, R. F. *African Art in Motion: Icon and Act*. Washington: National Gallery of Art, 1974.

Greek and Medieval Art

Boardman, John. *Greek Art*. New York: Oxford University Press. 1973.

Branner, Robert, ed. *Chartres Cathedral*. New York: W. W. Norton, 1969.

Clark, Kenneth. *Civilisation: A Personal View*. New York: Harper & Row, 1969.

Gimpel, Jean. *The Cathedral Builders*. New York: Grove Press, 1961.

————. *The Medieval Machine: The Industrial Revolution of the Middle Ages*. New York: Penguin Books, 1977.

Goldstein, Thomas. *Dawn of Modern Science*. Boston: Houghton Mifflin, 1980.

Haynes, Denys. *Greek Art and the Idea of Freedom*. London: Thames & Hudson, 1981.

Mâle, Emile. *The Gothic Image: Religious Art in France of the Thirteenth Century*. Translated by Dora Nussey. New York: Harper & Row, 1972.

Mark, Robert. *Experiments in Gothic Structure*. Cambridge: The MIT Press, 1984.

Needleman, Jacob. *A Sense of the Cosmos*. New York: E. P. Dutton, 1965.

Panofsky, Erwin. "Abbot Suger of St. Denis." In *Meaning in the Visual Arts*. Garden City, N.Y.: Doubleday, 1955.

Pollitt, Jerry Jordan. *Art and Experience in Classical Greece*. Cambridge: Cambridge University Press, 1975.

————. *The Art of Greece: 1400–31 B.C.* Englewood Cliffs, N.J.: Prentice-Hall, 1965.

Simson, Otto von. *The Gothic Cathedral*. Princeton, N. J.: Princeton University Press, 1956

Renaissance and Baroque

Alpers, Svetlana. *The Art of Describing: Dutch Art in the Seventeenth Century*. Chicago: University of Chicago Press, 1983.

Baxandall, Michael. *Painting and Experience in Fifteenth-Century Italy*. Oxford: Clarendon Press, 1972.

De Tolnay, Charles. *The Art and Thought of Michelangelo*. New York, Pantheon, 1964.

Edgarton, Samuel Y., Jr. *The Renaissance Rediscovery of Linear Perspective.* New York: Harper & Row, 1975.

Gowing, Lawrence. *Vermeer.* London: Faber & Faber, 1952.

Ivins, William J., Jr. *On the Rationalization of Sight.* New York: Da Capo Press, 1973.

Kitson, Michael. *The Age of the Baroque.* New York: McGraw-Hill, 1968.

McLuhan, Marshall, and Harley Parker. *Through the Vanishing Point: Space in Poetry and Painting.* New York: Harper & Row, 1968.

Muller, Joseph-Emile. *Rembrandt.* Trans. by Brian Hooley. New York: Harry N. Abrams, 1969.

Vasari, Giorgio. *The Lives of the Artists.* Translated by George Bull. New York: Penguin Books, 1965.

Vinci, Leonardo da. *The Notebooks of Leonardo da Vinci.* Edited by Robert N. Linscott. New York: Modern Library, 1957.

White, Christopher. *Rembrandt and His World.* London: Thames & Hudson, 1964.

White, John. *The Birth and Rebirth of Pictorial Space.* New York: T. Yoseloff, 1958.

Romanticism, Realism, and Academic Painting

Boime, Albert. *The Academy and French Nineteenth-Century Painting.* London: Phaidon, 1971.

Brion, Marcel. *Art of the Romantic Era.* New York: Frederick A. Praeger, 1969.

Dunlop, Ian. *The Shock of the New.* New York: American Heritage Press, McGraw-Hill, 1972.

Friedlander, Walter F. *From David to Delacroix.* Cambridge: Harvard University Press, 1952.

Galassi, Peter. *Before Photography.* New York: Museum of Modern Art, 1981.

Gowans, Alan. *The Restless Art: A History of Painters and Painting, 1760–1960.* New York: J. P. Lippincott Co., 1966.

Hanson, Anne Coffin. *Manet and the Modern Tradition.* New Haven, Conn.: Yale University Press, 1977.

Klingender, Francis D. *Art and the Industrial Revolution.* Rev. ed. London: Evelyn, Adams, and MacKay, 1968.

Mayne, Jonathan, ed. *The Mirror of Art: Critical Studies by Baudelaire.* Garden City, N.Y.: Doubleday Anchor, 1956.

Nochlin, Linda. *Realism.* New York: Penguin Books, 1971.

Novak, Barbara. *Nature and Culture: American Landscape and Painting, 1825–1875.* New York: Oxford University Press, 1980.

Pevsner, Nikolaus. *Academies of Art, Past and Present.* Cambridge: Cambridge University Press, 1940.

Picon, Gaëtan. *The Birth of Modern Painting.* New York: Rizzoli International Publications, 1978.

Reff, Theodore. *Manet and Modern Paris.* Washington: National Gallery of Art, 1982.

Sewell, Darrel. *Thomas Eakins, Artist of Philadelphia.* Philadelphia: Philadelphia Museum of Art, 1978.

Impressionism and Post-Impressionism

Badt, Kurt. *The Art of Cézanne.* Trans. by Sheila A. Ogilvie. Berkeley and Los Angeles: University of California Press, 1965.

Canaday, John. *Mainstreams of Modern Art.* New York: Holt, Rinehart, Winston, 1981.

Homer, William Innes. *Seurat and the Science of Painting.* Cambridge: M.I.T. Press, 1964.

Rewald, John. *The History of Impressionism.* Rev. ed. New York: Museum of Modern Art, 1967.

———. *Post-Impressionism.* 3rd ed. New York: Museum of Modern Art, 1978.

Shattuck, Roger. *The Banquet Years: The Origins of the Avant-garde in France 1885–World War I.* Rev. ed. New York: Random House, 1968.

Stone, Irving, ed. *Dear Theo.* New York: New American Library, 1969.

Welsh-Ovcharov, Bogomila, ed. *Van Gogh in Perspective.* Englewood Cliffs, N.J. Prentice-Hall, 1974.

Wichmann, Siegfried. *Japonisme: The Japanese Influence on Western Art in the 19th and 20th Centuries.* New York: Harmony Books, 1981.

Wildenstein, Daniel. *Monet's Years at Giverny: Beyond Impressionism.* New York: Metropolitan Museum of Art, 1978.

Cubism, Futurism, Constructivism, Surrealism

Barr, Alfred H., Jr., ed. *Masters of Modern Art.* New York: Museum of Modern Art, 1955.

Elgar, Frank, and Robert Maillard. *Picasso.* New York: Frederick A. Praeger, 1956.

Guerman, Mikhail. *Art of the October Revolution.* New York: Harry N. Abrams, 1979.

Kandinsky, Wassily. "Reminiscences." Reprinted in *Modern Artists on Art,* edited by Robert L. Herbert. Englewood Cliffs, N.J.: Prentice-Hall, 1964.

Lynton, Norbert. *The Story of Modern Art.* Ithica, N.Y.: Cornell University Press, 1980.

Malraux, André. *Museum Without Walls.* Translated by Stuart Gilbert and Francis Price. Garden City. N.Y.: Doubleday, 1977.

Martin, Maryanne W. *Futurist Art and Theory.* Oxford: Clarendon Press, 1968.

Penrose, Roland. *Picasso: His Life and Work.* Rev. ed. New York: Harper & Row, 1973.

Picon, Gaëtan. *Surrealists and Surrealism.* New York: Rizzoli International Publishers, 1983.

Richter, Hans. *Dada: Art and Anti-Art.* New York: Abrams, 1970.

Rickey, George. *Constructivism: Origins and Evolution.* New York: Braziller, 1967.

Stein, Gertrude. *Picasso.* Boston: Beacon Press, 1959.

Warnod, Janine. *Washboat Days.* New York: Grossman, 1973.

Abstract Expressionism, Pop Art, Minimalism, Photo-Realism

Cowart, Jack. *Roy Lichtenstein 1970–1980.* St. Louis: St. Louis Art Museum, 1981.

Frascina, Francis, and Charles Harrison, eds. *Modern Art and Modernism.* New York: Harper & Row, 1982.

Friedman, Bernard Harper. *Jackson Pollock: Energy Made Visible.* New York: McGraw-Hill, 1972.

Hughes, Robert. *The Shock of the New.* New York: Alfred A. Knopf, 1981.

———. "Only in America." *The New York Review of Books,* Dec. 20, 1979.

Lippard, Lucy. *Pop Art.* New York: Frederick A. Praeger, 1966.

Rose, Barbara. *American Art Since 1900.* New York: Praeger Publishers, 1967.

Rosenberg, Harold. *The Tradition of the New.* New York: Horizon Press, 1959.

Seuphor, Michel. *Abstract Painting: Fifty Years of Accomplishment from Kandinsky to Jackson Pollock.* New York: Dell, 1964.

Wysuph, C. L. *Jackson Pollock: Psychoanalytic Drawings.* New York: Horizon Press, 1970.

Post-Modernism

Battcock, Gregory. *Idea Art.* New York: E. P. Dutton, 1973.

Broude, Norma, and Mary D. Garrard, eds. *Feminism and Art History.* New York: Harper & Row, 1982.

Chicago, Judy. *Embroidering Our Heritage: The Dinner Party Needlework.* Garden City, N.Y.: Doubleday, 1980.

Fuller, Peter. *Aesthetics After Modernism.* New York: W. W. Norton, 1983.

Gablik, Suzi. *Has Modernism Failed?* New York: Thames & Hudson, 1984.

Huxtable, Ada Louise. *The Tall Building Artistically Reconsidered.* New York: Pantheon Books, 1982.

Jencks, Charles, and Baird, George, eds. *Meaning in Architecture.* New York: George Braziller, 1970.

Lippard, Luch. *Overlay.* New York: Pantheon Books, 1983.

———. *Get the Message? A Decade of Art for Social Change.* New York: E. P. Dutton, 1984.

Nochlin, Linda. "Why Have There Been No Great Women Artists?" In *Art and Sexual Politics,* edited by Thomas B. Hess and Elizabeth C. Baker. New York: Collier, 1971.

Slatkin, Wendy. *Women Artists in History: From Antiquity to the Twentieth Century.* Englewood Cliffs, N.J.: Prentice-Hall, 1985.

Smagula, Howard. *Currents: Contemporary Directions in the Arts.* Englewood Cliffs, N.J.: Prentic-Hall, 1983.

Tompkins, Calvin. "Onward and Upward with the Arts." In *The New Yorker,* March 28, 1977.

MASS MEDIA AND POPULAR CULTURE

General

Barthes, Roland. *Mythologies.* New York: Hill and Wang, 1972.

Benet, James, Arlene Kaplan Daniels, and Gaye Tuchman, eds. *Hearth and Home: Images of Women in the Mass Media.* New York: Oxford University Press, 1978.

Boorstein, Daniel J. *The Image: A Guide to Pseudo-Events in America.* New York: Harper & Row, 1961.

Ewen, Elizabeth, and Stuart Ewen. *Channels of Desire.* New York: McGraw-Hill, 1982.

Gans, Herbert J. *Popular Culture and High Culture: An Analysis and Evaluation of Taste.* New York: Basic Books, 1974.

Hammel, William M., ed. *The Popular Arts in America: A Reader.* New York: Harcourt, Brace, Jovanovich, Inc., 1972.

Kuhns, William. *Environmental Man.* New York: Harper & Row, 1969.

McLuhan, Marshall. *Understanding Media.* New York: McGraw-Hill, 1964.

Real, Michael. *Mass-Mediated Culture.* Englewood Cliffs, N.J.: Prentice-Hall, 1977.

Rosenberg, Bernard, and David Manning White, eds. *Mass Culture: The Popular Arts in America.* New York: The Free Press, 1964.

Sontag, Susan. *Against Interpretation.* New York: Dell, 1966.

Printed Images

Benjamin, Walter. "The Work of Art in the Age of Mechanical Reproduction," in Hannah Arendt, ed., *Illuminations.* New York: Schocken Books, 1969.

Carlin, John, and Sheena Wagstraff. *The Comic Art Show: Cartoons in Painting and Popular Culture.* New York: Whitney Museum of American Art, 1980.

Dawson, John, ed. *The Complete Guide to Prints and Printmaking.* New York: Simon & Schuster, 1981.

Dorfman, Ariel. *The Empire's Old Clothes.* New York: Pantheon Books, 1983.

Farwell, Beatrice. *The Cult of Images: Baudelaire and the Nineteenth-Century Media Explosion.* Santa Barbara, Calif.: University of California Santa Barbara Art Museum, 1977.

Horn, Maurice, ed. *The World Encyclopedia of Comics.* New York: Chelsea House, 1976.

Ivins, William M., Jr. *Prints and Visual Communication.* New York: Plenum, 1969.

Jussim, Estelle. *Visual Communication and the Graphic Arts: Photographic Technology in the Nineteenth Century.* New York: R. R. Bowker, 1983.

Mukerji, Chandra. *From Graven Images: Patterns of Modern Materialism.* New York: Columbia University Press, 1983.

Nichols, Bill. *Ideology and the Image.* Bloomington, Ind.: Indiana University Press, 1981.

Shapiro, Meyer. "Courbet and Popular Imagery." In *Modern Art: Nineteenth and Twentieth Centuries.* New York: Braziller, 1982.

Wood, James Playsted. *Magazines in the United States.* New York: Ronald Press, 1971.

Photography

Chiarenza, Carl. "Notes Toward an Integrated History of Picturemaking." In *Reading into Photography: Selected Essays, 1959–1980,* edited by Thomas F. Barrow, Shelley Armitage, and William E. Tydeman. Albuquerque, N.M.: University of New Mexico Press, 1982.

Coke, Van Deren. *The Painter and the Photograph.* Albuquerque, N.M.: University of New Mexico Press, 1964.

Freund, Gisèle. *Photography and Society.* Boston: David R. Godine, 1980.

Galassi, Peter. *Before Photography.* New York: Museum of Modern Art, 1981.

McCauley, Elizabeth Ann., A.A.E. *Disderi and the Carte de Visite Portrait Photograph.* New Haven: Yale University Press, 1985.

Newhall, Beaumont. *The History of Photography.* New York: Museum of Modern Art, 1964.

Rosenblum, Naomi. *The World History of Photography.* New York: Abbeville Press, 1984.

Scharf, Aaron. *Art and Photography.* New York: Museum of Modern Art, 1964.

Sontag, Susan. *On Photography.* New York: Dell, 1973.

Advertising and the Television Commercial

Arlen, Michael. *Thirty-Second Spot.* New York: Penguin Books, 1980.

Hall, Jim. *Mighty Minutes: An Illustrated History of Television's Best Commercials.* New York: Harmony Books, 1984.

Kurtz, Bruce. *Spots: The Popular Art of American Television Commercials.* New York: Arts Communications, 1977.

McLuhan, Marshall. *The Mechanical Bride.* New York: Vanguard. 1951.

Presbrey, Frank. *The History and Development of Advertising.* Westport, Conn.: Greenwood Press, 1961.

Schwartz, Tony. *The Resonant Chord.* New York: Doubleday Anchor, 1973.

———. *Media: The Second God.* Garden City, N.Y.: Doubleday, 1983.

Schudson, Michael. *Advertising, the Uneasy Persuasion.* New York: Basic Books, 1984.

Stern, Jane, and Michael Stern. *Auto Ads.* New York: David Obst Books, Random House, 1978.

Williamson, Judith. *Decoding Advertisements: Ideology and Meaning in Advertising.* London: Marion Boyars, 1979.

Television

Arlen, Michael. *The Living Room War.* New York: Viking Press, 1969.

Esslin, Martin. *The Television Age.* San Francisco: W. F. Freeman, 1982.

Gerbner, George. "The Dynamics of Cultural Resistance." In *Women in the Mass Media,* edited by Gaye Tuchman, Arlene Keplan-Daniels, and James Benet. New York: Oxford University Press, 1978.

Goethals, Gregor T. *The TV Ritual: Worship at the Video Altar.* Boston: Beacon Press, 1981.

Mander, Gerry. *Four Arguments for the Elimination of Television.* New York: Quill Publishers, 1978.

McGinniss, Joe. *The Selling of the President 1968.* New York: Pocket Books, 1969.

McNeil, Alex. *Total Television (A Comprehensive Guide to Programming From 1948 to the Present).* New York: Penguin Books, 1984.

Newcomb, Horace. *TV: The Most Popular Art.* Garden City, N.Y.: Anchor Books, 1974.

Postman, Neil. *The Disappearance of Childhood.* New York: Delacorte Press, 1982.

Youngblood, Gene. *Expanded Cinema.* New York: E. P. Dutton, 1981.

Film

Eidsvik, Charles. *Cineliteracy.* Boston: Random House, 1978.

Fell, John. *Film and the Narrative Tradition.* Norman, Okla.: University of Oklahoma Press, 1974.

Schickel, Richard. *Movies: The History of an Art and an Institution.* New York: Basic Books, 1964.

———. *The Disney Version.* New York: Avon Books, 1968.

Sklar, Robert. *Movie-Made America: A Cultural History of American Movies.* New York: Random House, 1975.

Wenden, D. J. *The Birth of the Movies.* New York: E. P. Dutton, 1974.

Computer and Art

Bolter, J. David. *Turing's Man: Western Culture in the Computer Age.* Chapel Hill, N.C.: University of North Carolina Press, 1984.

Daken, Joseph. *Computer Images: State of the Art.* New York: Stewart, Tabori, & Chang, 1983.

Wilson, Stephen. *Using Computers to Create Art.* Englewood Cliffs, N.J.: Prentice-Hall, 1986.

GLOSSARY

Abstract Expressionism A style of non-objective painting and sculpture that originated among New York artists in the late 1940s. It stressed intuition and spontaneity during the creative process as well as a strong emphasis on the artist's response to the materials used in the work. Also called Action Painting.

Abstraction Art based on forms that are not copied from nature as they appear to the eye. Abstraction is thus a quality that can vary in degree from slight distortion of natural shapes to a degree of abstraction that produces forms unrelated to those seen in nature. *See* non-objective.

Academy In art, an institution for setting standards of artistic practice, display, and education. In French art, the Academy (Académie des Beaux-Arts), founded during the reign of Louis XIV, was the dominant form of nineteenth-century French painting and vigorously opposed the avant-garde. In 1890 the official Salon sponsored by the Academy split in two. The Salon des Artistes Francaise continued the conservative tradition of the older salon; the Salon de la Nationale reflected the more liberal public mood. By 1905, government Salon sponsorship had negligible impact on the art world.

Action Painting *See* Abstract Expressionism.

aerial perspective A technique for representing spatial depth by using lighter colors and less distinct outlining of shapes to suggest distance.

aesthetic Pertaining to artistic form or beauty; artistic, in contrast to pragmatic or functional.

aesthetic protractor A device developed by Charles Henry to measure and calculate angles for lines in works of art that would produce the appropriate responses in the viewer. Influenced Seurat.

agit-prop Agitation-propaganda. Term for Marxist use of art to motivate the public to serve the ideals of the state. *See* Constructivism.

agora In the Greek city-state, an open space for public activities (business, law, politics).

airbrush A small hand-held spray gun used for producing an even, continuous flow of value or color.

alienation A feeling or condition of being a stranger, uncomfortable in the world. Alienation has been a major theme of avant-garde art. It reflects the freedom from tradition that has characterized Western culture since the late eighteenth and early nineteenth centuries.

allegorical Using figure or emblem to stand for a theme or idea.

analogous colors Hues that are next to each other on the color wheel.

Analytic Cubism The style of Cubism developed by Picasso and Braque between about 1907 and 1912. *Analytic Cubism* featured a limited range of colors, faceted abstract shapes, and a flattened sense of space.

art Definitions of art have varied from Kurt Schwitter's "Anything the artist spits is art" to a saying attributed to the Balinese people: "We have no art. We do everything as well as we can." *Art* thus has as wide a variety of meanings as it does specific contexts. In this text, *art* is defined as the expression of human feelings and ideas in material form. Art is also considered as the expression of basic cultural values. *See* icon.

art industry The network of museums and galleries, mass media publicity, and corporate sponsorship that helped produce and now accompanies the widespread acceptance of avant-garde art in postwar America. The term implies the current tendency of avant-garde art to take on the priorities of business and/or other dominant social institutions.

avant-garde   A French term meaning "out front." In general, it refers to innovative art. Specifically, avant-garde refers to the tradition of innovation, beginning with Courbet, that created the modern art that opposed Academic painting in the nineteenth century and has become established as a major cultural force in the twentieth century. *See* Modernism and Post-Modernism.

background   In this text, background refers to the information projected in the television image that is not totally subject to editing, as were earlier forms of Western perspective images. Background is a product of television's electronic base as well as the quantity of television's production.

Baroque   A style that characterized European art during the seventeenth century, with a sense of spatial openness and a high degree of emotional involvement of the spectator. Baroque art tended to combine the arts in an ensemble. Baroque painters made perspective more mobile and active in representational uses ranging from monumental church ceilings in Catholic countries to small oil paintings in Protestant Holland.

Bauhaus   A school of industrial design founded in Germany in 1919 by the architect Walter Gropius. Known for its attempts to integrate art and technology.

bohemian   A synonym for "outsider" or "uprooted" that came into use as a result of the large numbers of people from the country of Bohemia who settled in Paris during the eighteenth century. Later used to describe all "outsiders." The bohemian section of Paris was Montmartre, a hill in the north of the city.

bourgeoisie   French term for middle class. In this text it refers to the nineteenth-century middle class. *See* proletariat.

calligraphy   The art of beautiful writing.

camera   A lightproof box with a lens for imposing the image of a subject or scene on light-sensitive film.

camera obscura   A lightproof box with a lens for projecting an image of an object or scene onto a surface from which the image can be viewed or traced.

capitalism   An economic system based on private ownership of property and free enterprise. Capitalism stresses individualism as a cultural value. *See* industrial capitalism and consumer capitalism.

caricature   A drawing of a person that uses exaggerated features in order to produce a comical or satirical effect.

cartoon   A humorous drawing. The same word is used for a full-scale drawing for a mural or tapestry.

cathedral   The offical church of a bishop, containing his *cathedra,* or throne.

chiaroscuro   Shading or values that produce strong effects of light and dark.

cinematography   The art and techniques of making films.

classical   In general, the art of Greece and Rome. More specifically, the art of Greece in its full development (fifth century). *Classical* can refer to any style of art at its moment or period of perfection. *Classical* can also refer to any art that is based on principles of order and proportion in contrast to art based on expressiveness and emotional priorities.

collage   A two-dimensional work of art composed of differing kinds of materials—photographs, paper, cardboard, and so on. Traditional coloring and drawing media may also be applied.

commercial   In general, pertaining to business or profit. In particular, an advertisement on radio or television that dramatizes the product, service, or person featured.

complementary colors   Two contrasting hues that are found opposite each other on the color wheel. *See* the color wheel in the color section.

composition   The organization of parts within the whole. Rules of composition vary with each cultural period.

Concept Art   Art based on the primacy of the idea (or concept). Concept Art usually involved a strategy for dramatizing the importance of aspects of the art process other than the art object itself—artist as person, natural environment, political structure, etc.

Constructivism   The avant-garde movement identified with the pre-Stalinist phase of the Soviet state (1917–1927). Constructivists, basing their styles on Cubist and Futurist precedents, applied art to all areas of Soviet life, ranging from advertising to architecture to painting.

consumer capitalism Capitalism, especially in America, that arose during the twentieth century and was based on the commitment to including the working class as consumers (through higher wages and the increased motivation supplied by advertising).

content The comprehensive meaning of a work of art, including its theme, symbolism, structure, etc. Content can be defined as all the things the artist wishes to communicate by his or her choice of material and form in producing the work of art.

cool color A color generally in the blue, violet, or green section of the spectrum.

cosmos Greek term for universe. The term stresses the idea of an organized whole.

Counter-Reformation A late sixteenth- and seventeenth-century movement within the Roman Catholic church to counteract the challenge of the Protestant Reformation.

crisis of realism In the theory of Betty Edwards, the point in artistic development when preadolescents want to draw with a strong degree of realism (perspective). In Greek art, the confrontation between parallel perspective and linear perspective. In the nineteenth century, the conflict between perspective and new forms of nonperspective art. The nineteenth-century crisis of realism also reflected the split between the bourgeoisie and the proletariat.

Cubism A style of art developed by Picasso and Braque between c. 1907 and World War I that stressed the two-dimensionality of the painting surface and "broke down" the subject of the painting into a series of fragmented views and themes. *See* Analytic Cubism and Synthetic Cubism.

culture A system of ideas, customs, language, and beliefs that unite a group. Culture embodies a model of what it means to be a human being, an "enlarged humanity."

Dada A movement begun in Zurich during World War I that stressed absurdity and chance in producing an art aimed at debunking conventional art and institutions.

daguerreotype The form of photography developed by Niepce and Daguerre (patented by Daguerre in 1839).

design Arrangement of elements that make up a work of art. Synonym for composition.

diorama An illusionistic scene made up of projected imagery sometimes coupled with three-dimensional props, music, lighting effects, and so on. Dioramas were highly popular forms of entertainment in the nineteenth century.

Divisionism Seurat's term for his technique of "dividing" the painted surface into "atomic units" of color and geometric patterns of design. *See* Pointillism.

drama The presentation of a narrative action. In this text, drama is a "filter" that is part of normal network television broadcasting. *See* filter.

Earthworks (Earth Art) Sculptural projects involving landscape and natural processes.

edit To alter. In film, the process of recombining footage already shot and developed into a sequence reflecting the filmmaker's ideas, not the chronology of shooting.

ego In Freudian psychology, the center of the conscious personality that must balance the forces of the superego and the id. *See* Surrealism.

engraving An intaglio print made by the physical action of a hand-guided instrument producing lines in a metal plate or piece of wood. *See* Basic Printing Processes in the color section.

environments Natural surroundings. In art, the use of rooms or other architectural spaces to move beyond the traditional restrictions of painting, sculpture, etc.

erotic Pertaining to sexual appeal or desire.

etching An intaglio print made by producing lines by allowing acid to "bite" through a protective covering on a metal plate. The "bit" or lined plate can then be inked and printed. *See* Basic Printing Processes in the color section.

event In this text, any originating object or behavior or art form placed in front of a television camera for broadcast on network television. An event becomes modified before the viewer perceives it on the television screen by a certain number or combination of filters.

Expressionism Any form of art stressing emotional communication in the art object and the art process, specifically German Expressionism during the period between the wars.

fade   In film, a gradual darkening of the picture that indicates a change of scene.

Fauvism   Form of expressionist art in the early twentieth century led by Matisse (based on van Gogh).

feedback   In this text, the deliberate manipulation of the television background by groups and in ways other than those intended by the sponsor and broadcasting agents. *See* background.

Feminist Art   Art based on a specifically feminist agenda of values: female psychology, female cultural concerns, female social goals, and so on.

Film Age   The period from c. 1905 until the end of World War II. This period includes the art history periods of Cubism, Futurism, Dada, Constructivism, Expressionism, and Surrealism (among others).

filter   In the text, filter refers to any of three elements that alter the perception of events seen on network television: home, personality, drama.

form   Overall composition or design of a work of art. Also, a particular area or shape within a work of art, or a three-dimensional solid.

formal   Having to do with the design structure of a work of art without consideration of the content or subject matter.

Formalism   The theory of art that defines it exclusively in terms of its inner elements of design—color, line, shape, etc., with little emphasis on subject matter or content. Formalism is related to the "art for art's sake" concept that originated in the nineteenth century.

fresco   A mixture of pigment in lime water for application to a freshly plastered damp wall. The pigment dries as part of the plaster wall. The resultant mural is also called a fresco.

frieze   A horizontal band of relief sculpture or painted decoration.

Futurism   An Italian art movement of the early twentieth century that attempted to create an art based on the machine, science, technology, etc. Led by Marinetti, the Futurists borrowed heavily from Cubism for their general artistic style.

genre   In art, the presentation of a scene from everyday life as the subject. *Genre* is also used to mean a particular type of art—e.g., commercials or Hollywood musicals as "genres."

gouache   Opaque rather than transparent watercolor (opacity achieved by more pigment and an inert pigment such as precipitated chalk added to the medium).

halftone   A process for adapting photographs to mechanical printing presses by breaking down the photographic image into a series of dots that carry an amount of ink in proportion to the darkness (value) of the particular area of the photograph.

happenings   Art events developed in the 1960s, growing out of environments, in order to extend art beyond the traditional limitations of paintings, sculpture, etc.

hierarchy   An order based on authority or importance. In any hierarchy (social structure, system of ideas, etc.) the higher in the structure, the more important.

hologram, holography   A hologram is an image produced by the simultaneous intersection of three laser beams. It is recorded on film and, when properly viewed, has all of the spatial qualities of the visible third dimension.

hue   The quality that gives a color its name—red, blue, etc.

id   In Freudian psychology, the unconscious center of psychic energy. *See* ego and superego.

icon   Literally, Greek for "image." Usually refers to sacred paintings in the Greek Orthodox church. In this text, *icon* refers to any art considered as the expression of basic values of its culture. The term implies the element of belief that is part of all viable cultural expressions of art.

idealization   The representation of objects, events, people, etc., in art in a highly stylized and perfected way.

images d'epinal   Popular woodcuts mass-produced in the town of Epinal in eastern France for their propaganda use during the Napoleanic era.

Imagination   Baudelaire's term for the source of artistic creativity within the artist.

Impressionism   An art movement dating from the 1870s based on capturing the passing effects of light on everyday scenes. The work of Monet shows the most complete development of the Impressionist approach. For many artists, Impressionism marked the beginning phase of radically different personal styles of art. *See* Post-Impressionism.

industrial capitalism In this text, nineteenth-century capitalism, with its emphasis on industrial expansion over social and human concerns.

industrial revolution The transformation of Western culture by the revolutionary application of technology to industrial processes that began in the late eighteenth century with the replacement of human and animal sources of power by machines powered by coal and steam.

instantaneity Monet's term for his desire to capture the immediacy of his visual sensations as they appear to the eye.

intaglio A design sunk into a surface. In printing, lines below the surface carrying ink that, during the printing process, creates the black lines of the image (etching, engraving, wood engraving). *See* Basic Printing Processes in the color section.

intuitive perspective Perspective before Brunelleschi formalized linear perspective in specific mathematical terms. "Intuitive" perspective (e.g. that of Giotto) achieves a sense of three-dimensionality but lacks the organizing effectiveness achieved with Brunelleschi's discovery of the vanishing point.

iris The round opening behind the lens of the camera that controls light. An "iris shot" in film uses the round, dark frame of the iris shape as either a focusing device or a gradually closing element that produces a fade.

Judeo-Christian Having roots in both Judaism and Christianity.

jump cut In film, a sudden transition from one shot to the next.

kinetoscope Edison's first movie-viewing machine. It required the viewers to look, one at a time, through a peephole.

linear perspective Technique discovered by Brunelleschi for creating the illusion of three-dimensional space on a two-dimensional surface. It involved the use of the *vanishing point* to simulate how space appears in human sight.

lithograph Printing technique patented in 1799 by Aloys Senefelder that enabled an artist to draw an image directly on a stone for printing purposes. *See* Basic Printing Processes in the color section.

Marxist Refering to the ideas of Karl Marx, who criticized the excesses of nineteenth-century capitalism and prophesied the downfall of capitalism through workers' revolts. Marxist governments today range from communist regimes to socialist governments that apply Marxist ideas in varying degrees. Marx also criticized the individualism of Western culture, which is a major element of Western avant-garde art.

medieval Referring to the Middle Ages. *Medieval* can refer to the entire period from about A.D. 600 to almost 1400. In this text, *medieval* is restricted to the Gothic period, from about A.D. 1150 to 1400.

melodrama A form of drama popular in the nineteenth century that used stereotyped characters, intense emotion, simple plots, and a high degree of realism in presentation—whether drama, literature, or painting. Melodrama became a major element in the early history of the movies.

messianic Referring to the Messiah, or Savior. In Christianity, Jesus Christ.

Modernism A term used to describe the movement of Western art, beginning with Courbet and Manet, away from traditional themes, perspective, and sponsorship. In painting, it also included a departure from perspective. Modernism also refers to the sequence of styles that have evolved from this point of view. *See* Post-Modernism.

montage A picture composed of more than one original photograph that has itself become a unified composition. In film, it is Eisenstein's term for editing that combines images that are collectively more powerful than the individual shots or frames that make up the montage sequence.

Montmartre The bohemian section of nineteenth-century Paris, literally, "mount of martyrs," the hill in Paris where Saint Denis, the patron saint of France, is believed to have been martyred in the early Middle Ages.

mosaic A medium using small pieces of colored glass or stone (tesserae) fixed or imbedded in a background material, such as plaster or cement.

mural A painting on a wall.

myth A story about the origin of persons or things or customs. Cumulatively, myths express a cultural worldview. Art is a prime means for experiencing the myth of a given culture. *See* icon.

narrative art Art that pertains in some way to a story or literary theme. Narrative art can range in style from abstract (e.g. some Constructivist propaganda images) to realistic (e.g. Academic painting).

nickelodeon Term that describes the first theaters exclusively devoted to showing films ("nickle" plus "odeon," French for "theater").

non-objective Having no resemblance to natural forms or objects.

objective sensations Monet's term for the visual sensations that he claimed to translate directly from nature to his painting. He contrasted his *objective sensations* to the projection of feeling in Romantic and Academic paintings.

objectivity Referring to the object "as it is," in contrast to distortions or alterations resulting from personal impressions or feelings (subjectivity). *Objective* implies that any observer would see the same image or scene in the same way; an objective image is therefore verifiable. *See* linear perspective, subjectivity.

oil paint Paint in which oil, usually linseed oil, carries the pigment. Oil painting became popular in Europe in the fifteenth century because of its capacity for luminous color and exquisite detail. Its discovery is attributed to the van Eyck brothers, Jan and Hubert.

Op Art A post-World War II style of art based on imagery that creates perceptual responses based on the eye's own reflex actions to complementary colors, value changes, optical illusions, etc.

optical realism Imagery based on how things appear to the eye.

pan In film, a camera movement horizontally across the entire dimension of a scene.

Panathenaic procession In ancient Athens, the procession from the agora to the Parthenon undertaken each year to honor the goddess Athena on her birthday, the subject of a sculptural frieze that encompasses the entire outer dimension of the Parthenon.

parallel perspective A technique for projecting the illusion of three-dimensional space on a two-dimensional surface by using a system in which all lines that would be parallel in nature remain parallel in the image.

perspective The depiction of the illusion of three-dimensional space on a two-dimensional surface.

See aerial perspective, parallel perspective, linear perspective, intuitive perspective.

Perspective Age The period from 1425 to 1839, during which Western painting was dominated by perspective as its basic image structure. This period includes the art history categories of Renaissance, Baroque, and Romanticism (among others).

Photographic Age The period from the introduction of photography (c. 1839) until the arrival of film as a popular medium of public entertainment (c. 1905). This period includes the art history periods of Realism, Impressionism, and Post-Impressionism (among others).

photographic realism The style of nineteenth-century Academic painting after the discovery of photography, which attempted to rival the natural detail of the photographic image.

photography Creation of a perspective image by the use of a lens and light-sensitive film. *See* camera.

Photo-Realism A contemporary style in painting that derives its imagery from an exacting attention and duplication of photographic imagery. A major interest in a Photo-Realist work stems from the resultant differences (color, scale, detail, etc) between the completed work and the photographic source(s).

popular realism The combination of photographic realism and melodrama that developed during the nineteenth century—typified by a large sector of Academic painting. *Popular realism* implies easy accessibility in its visual and narrative elements. The mass media of the twentieth century in many ways took over the popular realism of the nineteenth-century Academic tradition.

Pop Art A style of painting that uses mass media imagery as a starting point for subject matter. Pop art became an important movement in American art during the early 1960s.

Post-Impressionism A term that loosely describes the artists and groups of artists in the 1880s and 1890s who kept the Impressionist emphasis on color but moved into more radically structural (e.g. Cézanne and Seurat) or emotionally expressive (e.g. van Gogh and Gauguin) forms of art.

Post-Modernism A term used to describe contemporary avant-garde, which is marked by an interest in retrieving and reinterpreting styles and themes of past periods of art in terms of present artistic needs. Post-Modernism is specifically different from the Modernist attitude, which sought (from the time of Manet until the late 1960s) for continually new styles of art different from those of the past. Post-Modernism is also characterized by an exploration of art beyond the traditional Modernist priority on painting and on museums as art spaces. *See* Modernism.

primary colors   Those hues that cannot be mixed from other hues. Pigment primaries are red, yellow, and blue.

proletariat   The nineteenth-century working class and poor, especially the working class before social legislation limited exploitation of their labor and improved their living conditions.

propaganda   Originally, part of the name of the Roman Catholic office charged with the propagation (or spread) of the faith. In general, any form of communication calculated to persuade a given public toward some idea or belief. Today, the word propaganda implies the use of manipulation and/or brainwashing.

Realism   Art based on reality, specifically, the art of Courbet, Manet, and other nineteenth-century artists, who used the term to contrast their efforts to depict the "heroism of modern life" with the works of Academic painters, which they considered "unreal" or out of touch.

Reformation   The period, beginning with Luther's revolt in 1520, during which Christianity in Europe divided into Protestant and Catholic denominations. The Reformation period lasted throughout the sixteenth century.

Renaissance   The period of "rebirth," beginning in the fifteenth century in Italy, that looked back to the Greek and Roman world for inspiration in the arts and other cultural areas. The Renaissance is generally considered to have lasted from about 1400 to about 1600.

representational art   Art which attempts to "make present" or re-present an object, person, scene, or experience for the viewer.

Romanticism   The art of the early nineteenth century characterized by a strong emphasis on subjective feeling and individualism.

Salon   The exhibitions juried (judged) and sponsored by the French Academy. *See* Salon d'Automne, Salon des Independents, Academy.

Salon d'Automne   A nongovernment salon founded in 1903. It was organized more completely than the somewhat anarchistic Salon des Independents.

Salon des Independents   The salon founded by George Seurat and Odilon Redon in 1884 as an alternative to the official government-sponsored salon; no jurying (judging) was required.

Salon des Refuses   The 1863 salon, supported by the government, that displayed works rejected from the official salon of that year, among them, Manet's *Luncheon on the Grass*.

simultaneous contrast   The visual phenomenon of seeing a flash of the complementary color within the main color in the visual field; the tendency of complementary colors to intensify each other when placed side by side.

stereotype   The rigid, fixed image or idea, usually used to refer to images of social and ethnic groups.

style   A characteristic handling of media, techniques, and elements of form that gives a work its identity as the product of a particular person, group, art movement, period, or society.

subjectivity   Pertaining to the personal point of view of the artist or viewer. Subjectivity stresses the inner qualities unique to individual perception, thought, and feeling in contrast to the external and verifiable qualities of "objectivity."

successive contrast   The visual phenomenon of seeing residual impressions of the complementary colors of those seen immediately previously in the viewer's visual field.

superego   In Freudian psychology, the outer layer of the personality given by parents and culture. The most superficial layer of personality. *See* Surrealism.

Surrealism   The post-World War I movement that drew inspiration from Freudian psychology and Dada. Under André Breton, Surrealism achieved a cohesive theoretical formulation.

symbol   A form of image implying or representing something other than itself.

Synthetic Cubism   The term used to describe the phase in the Cubism of Picasso and Braque after

1912 in which subject matter—including bits of paper and other materials—became an important part of the art object. Synthetic Cubist works also included a radically new openness to color in contrast to the almost monochrome color of earlier Cubist painting. *See* Analytic Cubism.

technology   According to Marshall McLuhan, any machine or instrument or organization that extends a human function.

Television Age   The period from the end of World War II (1945) until the present. This period encompasses art movements and styles ranging from Abstract Expressionism to Concept Art and the various expressions of art grouped under the term Post-Modernism.

vanishing point   In images based on linear perspective, the point at which receding parallel lines are made to converge. The vanishing point in such images resembles the way parallel lines in ordinary human vision appear to recede to a single point.

value   Lightness or darkness of a color.

video   In general, an artistic statement made in the medium of video tape. The term video also specifically refers to the new artform of "music videos" which have become popular since the advent of MTV in 1981.

INDEX

PHOTO CREDITS

Accademia, Venice, 2.20
Achenbach Foundation, San Francisco, 4.38
Acropolis Museum, Athens, 2.17
Albuquerque, Lita, 13.10, plate 33
Alf, Martha, 1.2
Alford, Jim, 2.8, Four-Color Process Printing in color section
Alinari/Art Resource, 2.2, 2.7, 2.19, 2.21, 2.26, 3.3, 3.10, 3.23, 3.24, 3.31, 4.5, 6.5, a.1
Ally and Gargano, Inc., 12.5
American School of Classical Studies, Athens, 2.5
Art Institute of Chicago, 3.18, 3.19, 6.1, 7.13 (plate 16), 7.18, 7.20, 7.22 (plate 18), 9.2, 13.8, 13.12
Askin, Walter, Silkscreen Color Processes ("Rainbow Score") in color section
Batten, Barton, Durstine, and Osborn, Inc. 12.16, 12.17
Bettman Archives, New York, 2.29, 4.23
Biblioteca Nazionale, Florence, 4.1
Bibliotheque Nationale, Paris, 2.3, 2.37, 2.38, 2.39, 2.40, 4.29, 4.30, 5.7, 6.15, 6.16
Mary Boone Gallery, New York, 13.16
British Library, London, 2.30 (plate 4)
Susan Caldwell, Inc., New York, plate 36
Cambridge University Press, 2.18, 2.24
Leo Castelli Gallery, New York, 11.13, 11.15, 11.17, 11.18, 11.19, 11.20
Chiat/Day Advertising, Los Angeles, 12.11, 12.12, 12.13, 12.14
Sterling and Francine Clark Art Institute, Williamstown, Mass., 5.18, 6.18 (plate 12)
Cleveland Museum of Art, 3.15, 3.16, 3.37, 3.44, 4.7, 4.35, 5.12, 6.8, 6.13, 7.5, 7.7, 7.12, 7.30, 8.5 (plate 21), 8.28, 9.2, 9.25, 11.11, 11.14, 13.8
James Corcoran Gallery, Los Angeles, 11.35 (plate 30)
Cordier and Eckstrom Gallery, New York, 13.12
Courtauld Institute Galleries, London, 6.21 (plate 13)
Walt Disney Productions, Inc., 8.19, 8.20 (plate 22), a.5 (plate 40)
Doolin, James, 11.13 (plate 29), 11.34
Edgarton, Samuel Y., Jr., 3.1
Electronic Arts Intermix, New York, 13.18, 13.19, 13.20 (plate 37), 13.21, 13.22 (plate 38), 13.23
Evan-Thomas, Mrs. James, 4.40 (plate 9)
Foote, Cone, and Belding, 12.6, 12.7
Ford Motor Company, 3.11
Frick Collection, New York, 3.22, 4.21, 4.31, 5.4
Giraudon/Art Resource, 2.31, 3.30, 5.14, 7.16, 9.6
Hitachi America, Ltd., 12.10
Hood Museum, Dartmouth College, 11.3
Humanities Research Center, Austin, Texas, 4.42
Iveagh Bequest, London, 4.13 (plate 6)
Janus Gallery, Los Angeles, 13.14 (plate 35), 13.15
Jefferson Medical College, Philadelphia, 8.8

Kunsthistorisches Museum, Vienna, 4.11, 4.27
Library of Congress, Washington, D.C., 8.3, 8.6, 8.25, 8.26, 10.16
Lord, Geller, Federico, Einstein, Inc., 12.1
Louvre, Paris, 2.4, 2.13, 3.21, 3.29, 4.22, 4.28, 4.39, 5.5, 5.16, 5.17, 5.23, 5.25, 6.2, 6.3 (plate 11), 6.4, 6.6, 6.17, 10.8
Lucasfilm, Ltd., 1.1 (plate 1), 1.24
McDonald's Corporation, 12.15
Mauritshuis, The Hague, 4.9
Mayfield Publishing Company, 1.3, 1.4
Louis K. Meisel Gallery, New York, 11.32 (plate 28)
Metropolitan Museum of Art, New York, 2.12, 2.14, 3.6, 3.36, 3.38, 3.39, 3.40, 3.41, 3.42, 3.43, 4.6, 4.24, 4.25, 5.20, 6.20, 7.4, 7.27, 8.7
Minolta Corporation, 12.4
M.I.T. Press, 7.14
Moderna Museet, Stockholm, 9.17
Musée de l'Homme, Paris, 1.9, 1.11, 1.16, 1.17, 1.18, 1.19
Musée Granet, Aix-en-Provence, 5.2
Musée Marmottan, Paris, 7.3
Musées Royaux des Beaux-Arts de Bilgique, Brussels, 4.26
Museo del Prado, Madrid, 4.32, 4.33, 4.34, 4.36
Museum of Fine Arts, Boston, 5.19, 7.6, 7.10, 7.29
Museum of Modern Art, New York, 3.4, 7.24, 7.31, 7.32, 8.13, 8.18, 9.5 (plate 23), 9.8, 9.10, 9.11, 9.13, 9.14, 9.15, 9.16, 9.20, 9.22, 9.24, 9.26, 11.4, 11.8, 11.9, a.8
Museum of Modern Art Film Stills Archives, New York, 1.22, 1.33, 8.1, 8.10, 8.12, 8.14, 8.15, 8.16, 8.17, 8.21, 8.22, 9.18, 9.19, 9.21, 9.27, 10.17, 12.2
National Aeronautics and Space Administration, 10.14, 10.15, 12.3, a.2, a.3, a.7
National Broadcasting Company, New York, 10.1, 10.2, 10.3, 10.4, 10.9, 10.10, 10.11, 10.12, 10.13, 10.18, 10.20, 10.23
National Gallery, London, 3.2, 3.17 (plate 5)
National Gallery of Art, Washington, D.C., i.8 (plate 1), 4.10, 4.12, 5.3 (plate 7), (plate 8), 6.7 (plate 10), 6.19, 7.8 (plate 14), 7.9 (plate 15), 7.17 (plate 18), 7.25 (plate 19), 7.28 (plate 20), 9.3, 9.4, 9.9, 9.28 (plate 24), 11.6 (plate 25), 11.27 (plate 26)
National Gallery of Scotland, Edinburgh, 7.26
National Museum, Athens, 2.11, 2.15, 2.22
Newsweek magazine, i.8, 10.21, 11.2
Philadelphia Museum of Art, 8.9
Philip Morris Incorporated, i.9
Phillips Collection, Washington, D.C., 1.8, 6.14, 12.9
Playboy magazine, 10.24
Polaroid Corporation, 1.20
Rijksmuseum, Amsterdam, i.6, 4.8
Rijksmuseum Kroller-Muller, Otterlo, Netherlands, 7.15
Rijksmuseum Vincent van Gogh, Amsterdam, 7.21
Rizzoli Publishers, Inc., 1.13, 1.14
Roger-Viollet, Paris, 7.1

CREDITS

After completing his bachelor's degree in painting at UCLA, ROBERT PELFREY received his master's degree in printmaking from California State University at Los Angeles. He has taught at Webster College in St. Louis, Merrimac Community College in St. Louis, and currently teaches at Cuesta Community College in San Luis Obispo, California.

MARY HALL-PELFREY studied art at Immaculate Heart College in Los Angeles and at Webster College in St. Louis before receiving her bachelor's degree in psychology and art therapy at Antioch University in Santa Barbara. Besides teaching art, Mary pursues her own work in painting, drawing, and photography. Mary and Robert have collaborated on videotapes of the artists Jim Doolin, Walter Askin, and Joyce Treiman and of Christo's *Running Fence* project.

They live on the central California coast and have three children.